Adapting Educational and Psychological Tests for Cross-Cultural Assessment

Edited by

Ronald K. Hambleton
University of Massachusetts at Amherst

Peter F. Merenda
University of Rhode Island

Charles D. Spielberger
University of South Florida

LEA
2005

LAWRENCE ERLBAUM ASSOCIATES, PUBLISHERS
Mahwah, New Jersey London

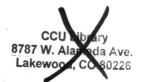

Lawrence Erlbaum Associates, Inc., Publishers
10 Industrial Avenue
Mahwah, New Jersey 07430

Cover design by Sean Sciarrone

Library of Congress Cataloging-in-Publication Data

Adapting educational and psychological tests for cross-cultural assessment / edited by Ronald K. Hambleton, Peter F. Merenda, Charles D. Spielberger

p. cm.
Includes bibliographical references and index.
ISBN 0-8058-3025-1 (cloth : alk. paper)
1. Educational tests and measurements—Designs and construction—Cross-cultural studies. 2. Psychological tests—Design and construction—Cross-cultural studies. I. Hambleton, Ronald K. II. Merenda, Peter Francis, 1922- III. Spielberger, Charles Donald, 1927-

LB3060.65.A33 2005
371.26'1—dc22

2003060545
CIP

Books published by Lawrence Erlbaum Associates are printed on acid-free paper, and their bindings are chosen for strength and durability.

Printed in the United States of America
10 9 8 7 6 5 4 3 2

Adapting Educational and Psychological Tests for Cross-Cultural Assessment

Contents

Preface

In 1989 I happened to read a report on the comparative levels of mathematics achievement of school children in five countries. The results surprised me, and so I began to wonder about the impact of a variety of methodological factors that might have influenced the results: the quality of sampling of students in each participating country, the particular choices of content and format for the test, but mostly, I wondered about the way that the test had been translated from English to the other languages in which the test was used in the study. International studies of educational achievement can be invaluable to policy makers and educators but not if methodological factors undermine the validity of the results. It struck me that possibly the surprising results were due to the fact that the test may have been made unintentionally easier or harder by the translators. What were their qualifications? How much time were they given to do the work? What empirical evidence was compiled to support the equivalence of the test in multiple languages? I called the testing agency responsible for conducting the study to discuss test translation methods. Unfortunately, I was not overly impressed with the details they provided for how the test had actually been translated and how they checked the linguistic, psychological, and statistical equivalence of the test in multiple language and cultural groups.

In my own subsequent checking for good test translation practices I was disappointed by the relatively low level of methodological sophistication that I found compared to the sophistication in the testing field for addressing other important topics such as test development, test score equating, and test score norming. This was my first serious exposure to the world of cross-cultural testing. I could see that there was important work to be done.

In 1991 I brought my concern about test translation methodology to the council of the International Test Commission (ITC). Today, the ITC is an organization of national psychological societies, testing agencies, and individual members, and is committed to improving testing practices around the world. The ITC council decided to form an international committee of scholars and practitioners to develop guidelines for test translation and adaptation, and we were fortunate to secure some financial assistance for the work of the committee from the National Center for Educational Statistics and the College Board in the United States. We were able to interest a number of international organizations in the work of the committee and they provided members. These organizations were the European Association of Psychological Assessment, European Test Publishers Group, International Association for Cross-Cultural Psychology, International Association of Applied Psychology, International Association for the Evaluation of Educational Achievement, International Language Testing Association, and the International Union of Psychological Science.

The committee members worked hard over 3 years and several meetings to organize the technical advances that had been made over the years on the topic of test translation and adaptation, and eventually the committee produced a final report that offered 22 guidelines (called the "International Test Commission Guidelines for Test Adaptation"). The guidelines themselves and the rationale for including each one in the collection is presented in chapter 1.

At about the time the Guidelines in draft form were being circulated around for comment, Tom Oakland from the University of Florida, in the United States, and an ITC council member, and I, decided to organize a conference that would introduce the Guidelines. This conference, sponsored by the ITC, was held at Georgetown University in the United States in the spring of 1999. Attendance at the Conference was high, and highlighted what the ITC knew, which was that a set of guidelines for test translation and adaptation would be well received by the testing field, and would be an important addition to the emerging literature.

At about the same time as the Conference, Professors Charles Spielberger and Peter Merenda came forward (Professor Spielberger had been a member of the committee that developed the Guidelines) and agreed to assist in the preparation of a book that would highlight important technical advances in the test translation and adaptation field. Professor Spielberger, himself, had been involved in more than 50 translations of his own instrument, State-Trait Anxiety Inventory, and Peter Merenda had been active in translations research for most of his career. The three of us teamed up to produce this book, which is a collection of many of the invited addresses from the ITC Conference at Georgetown University and invited chapters that were added to provide comprehensive coverage of the topic.

Chapter 1, written by myself, was prepared to introduce the ITC Guidelines for Test Adaptation. In addition, many of the issues that arise in test translation and adaptation work are described. Chapter 2 was prepared by Professors Fons van de Vijver and Ype Poortinga from the University of Tilburg in the Netherlands on the topic of conceptual and methodological issues in test adaptation. Had it not been for the goal of introducing the Guidelines in the first chapter, this chapter would have been the first one in the book because the authors present a framework for understanding the process of translation and adaptation that is relevant for all of the chapters. Chapter 3 was prepared by Professor Tom Oakland and he tackles the all important question of ethics and test adaptation. At the core of his work is a concern for validity of test scores in cross-cultural contexts.

Chapters 4 to 7 provide a wonderful array of advances in test translation and adaptation methodology. Chapter 4 by Steve Sireci, Liane Patsula (now at the Educational Testing Service in the United States), and myself from the University of Massachusetts in the United States, provides a comprehensive review of approaches for statistically identifying flawed test items that occur during the test translation and adaptation process. Chapter 5 by Professor Sireci was prepared to address the issues, strengths, and weaknesses associated with the uses of bilingual participants in establishing equivalence of different language versions of a test. Chapters 6 and 7 by Dr. Linda Cook, Dr. Alicia Schmitt-Cascallar, and Catharine Brown (chapter 7 only) from the Educational Testing Service provide descriptions of important methodology for statistically comparing tests in multiple languages, and a review of important issues that arise in translating and adapting tests. We regret to announce the untimely passing of Alicia Schmitt-Cascallar in 2003. She was an invited speaker at the ITC Conference at Georgetown University and was an important contributor to the research on testing methodology, including test translation and adaptation methodology.

Chapters 8 to 14 in the book were intended to shift the focus from primarily presentations of issues and methodology to the complicated world of test translation and adaptation applications. The applications of test translation and adaptation methodology include credentialing exams, intelligence tests, cognitive tests, tests used in industrial and organizational settings, admissions tests, and personality tests. Dr. Cyndy Fitzgerald, formerly of Microsoft and now a consultant to Caveon, describes in chapter 8 the process Microsoft uses to translate and adapt their credentialing exams. The use of on-line systems to expedite the work of test translators appears exemplary in the profession. In chapter 9, Dr. Carlos Maldonado (from the Putnam/Northern Westchester BOCES in the United States) and Professor Kurt Geisinger (from The University of St. Thomas, in the United States) describe problems with the English to Spanish translation and adaptation of one of the most popular intelligence instruments in the world: Wechsler Adult Intelligence Scale. In chapter 10, Professor Norbert Tanzer, (from Alliant International University in the United States and the University of Graz in Austria) makes a strong argument for simultaneous development of some psychological tests, rather than translating and adapting tests across languages and cultures. Professor Fritz Drasgow and Tahira Probst from the University of Illinois in the United States describe in chapter 11 their important work in establishing test equivalence across language groups and cultures with tests that are primarily used in industrial/organizational settings. In chapter 12, Drs. Michal Beller (from the Educational Testing Service), and Naomi Gafni and Pnina Hanani (from the National Institute for Testing and Evaluation in Israel) describe their ambitious efforts to produce college admissions tests for use in Israel in six languages. Chapter 13 by Peter Merenda (from the University of Rhode Island in the United States) presents many of his observations and findings in the test translation and adaptation field over his career. Few researchers have worked longer and more successfully in the field. Finally, in chapter 14, Professor Spielberger from the University of South Florida, and two of his colleagues, Manolete Moscoso and Thomas Brunner, from the same university, provide a wealth of information on the issues and methods associated with translating and adapting personality tests.

On behalf of myself and my co-editors, Peter Merenda and Charles Spielberger, we hope that this collection of 14 chapters furthers the mission of the International Test Commission by providing direction and stimulating research on the ever-increasingly important topic of test translation and adaptation. The growth of this field has been tremendous since my first queries in 1989. Today, the field is better developed, guidelines for good practice are in place, methodology has been organized and extended, and there are a growing number of exemplary examples for practitioners to follow. At the same time, there is considerably more research that needs to be done, and so we hope this collection of chapters stimulates others to advance this work.

—Ronald K. Hambleton

I

Cross-Cultural Adaptation of Educational and Psychological Tests: Theoretical and Methodological Issues

1

Issues, Designs, and Technical Guidelines for Adapting Tests Into Multiple Languages and Cultures

Ronald K. Hambleton
University of Massachusetts at Amherst

Considerable evidence exists today to suggest that the need for multilanguage versions of achievement, aptitude, and personality tests, and surveys, is growing (see, e.g., Ercikan, 2002; Hambleton, 2002; Hambleton & de Jong, 2003; Harkness, 1998). For example, the International Association for the Evaluation of Educational Achievement (IEA) conducted the Third International Mathematics and Science Study (TIMSS) in over 45 countries, which involved preparing mathematics and science tests in over 30 languages. Prominent examples of new test adaptation projects in the United States include studies to prepare Spanish versions of College Board's *Scholastic Assessment Test* (SAT), American Council on Education's *General Educational Development* (GED) test, the U.S. Department of Education's *National Assessment of Educational Progress* (NAEP), and achievement tests of several state departments of education. Substantially more test adaptations can be expected in the future as (a) international exchanges of tests become more common, (b) more exams are used to provide international credentials, and (c) interest in cross-cultural research grows.

Although the many reasons for adapting tests from one language and culture to another are clear—for example, facilitating comparative studies of school achievement across cultural and language groups, saving money and time associated with preparing new tests, and achieving fairness in assessment—methods and guidelines for preparing test adaptations and establishing the equivalence of scores are not well known (Hambleton, 1993, 1994; Hui & Triandis, 1985; van de Vijver & Hambleton, 1996). Some cross-cultural researchers have even suggested that a high percentage of the research in their field is flawed to the point of being invalid because of poorly adapted tests.

The purposes of this chapter are (a) to review several sources of error or invalidity associated with adapting tests and to suggest ways to reduce those errors, and (b) to describe a set of practical guidelines for adapting tests prepared by the International Test Commission (ITC) with the assistance of seven other large international agencies (see Hambleton, 1994; van de Vijver & Hambleton, 1996).

Before proceeding, a distinction needs to be made between test adaptation and test translation. The term *test adaptation* is preferred to the more popular and frequently used term *test translation* in this chapter because the former term is broader and more reflective of what should happen in practice when preparing a test that is constructed in one language and culture for use in a second language and culture. Test adaptation includes all the activities from deciding whether or not a test could measure the same construct in a different language and culture, to selecting translators, to deciding on appropriate accommodations to be made in preparing a test for use in a second language, to adapting the test and checking its equivalence in the adapted form. Test translation is only one of the steps in the process of test adaptation and even at this step, adaptation is often a more suitable term than translation to describe the actual process that takes place. This is because translators are trying to find concepts, words, and expressions that are culturally, psychologically, and linguistically equivalent in a second language and culture, and so clearly the task goes well beyond simply preparing a literal translation of the test content.

For our purposes too we use the term "test" throughout the chapter to include all types of educational and psychological instruments, and even surveys and questionnaires.

SOURCES OF ERROR OR INVALIDITY IN TEST ADAPTATION

The American Educational Research Association (AERA), American Psychological Association (APA), and National Council on Measurement in Education (NCME) *Standards for Educational and Psychological Testing* (1985) provides careful directions for educational measurement specialists and psychologists who select, develop, administer, and use educational and psychological tests. Three of the standards in this publication are especially relevant in the context of test adaptation:

> *Standard 6.2.* When a test user makes a substantial change in test format, mode of administration, instructions, language, or content, the user should revalidate the use of the test for the changed conditions or have a rationale supporting the claim that additional validation is not necessary or possible.

> *Standard 13.4.* When a test is translated from one language or dialect to another, its reliability and validity for the uses intended in the linguistic groups to be tested should be established.

> *Standard 13.6.* When it is intended that the two versions of dual-language tests be comparable, evidence of test comparability should be reported.

These standards provide a framework for considering sources of error or invalidity that might arise in efforts to adapt a test from one language and culture to another. For our purposes, sources of error or invalidity that arise in test adaptation can be organized into three broad categories: (a) cultural/language differences, (b) technical issues, designs, and methods, and (c) interpretation of results. Failure to attend to the sources of error in each of these categories can result in an adapted test that is not equivalent in the two language and cultural groups for which it is intended. Nonequivalent tests, when they are assumed to be equivalent, can only lead to errors in interpretation and faulty conclusions about the groups involved.

A good example of the misinterpretation that can follow from poor test adaptation is the following (the example was passed on by Richard Wolf of Columbia Teachers College, a leader during his career in the field of international assessment). In an international comparative study of reading (around 1990), American students were asked to consider pairs of words and identify them as similar or different in meaning: "Sanguine - pessimistic" was one of the pairs of words where American student performance was only slightly above chance (or about 54% of the American students answered the question correctly). In the non-English-speaking country ranked first in performance, about 98% of the students answered the question correctly. In the process of attempting to better understand the reason for the huge difference in performance, it was discovered that the word *sanguine* had no equivalent word in the language of this top-performing country and so the equivalent of the English word *optimistic* was used. This substitution made the question considerably easier and would have been answered correctly by a high percentage of the American students as well had they been presented with the pair of words "optimistic - pessimistic." The point of this example is to highlight the danger in drawing conclusions from international comparative studies of achievement without strong evidence that the test adaptation process resulted in two equivalent tests. Prior to 1990 many of the test adaptation initiatives for international studies involved little more than using a couple of good translators. This must be contrasted with the high level of test adaptation sophistication that is seen today in both TIMSS and Organization for Economic Cooperation and Development's Programme for International Student Assessment (OECD/PISA; see, e.g., Grisay, 2003; Hambleton, 2002).

What follows is a discussion of several common errors and how they might be addressed in practice.

Cultural/Language Differences Affecting Scores

The assessment and interpretation of cross-cultural results should not be viewed in the narrow context of just the translation or adaptation of tests (van de Vijver & Leung, 1997, 2000). Rather, this process should be considered for *all* parts of the assessment process, including construct equivalence, test administration, item formats used, and the influence of speed on examinee performance. These four factors are briefly considered next. They have received more attention in subsequent chapters.

Construct Equivalence. Construct equivalence encompasses both conceptual/functional equivalence as well as equivalence in the way the construct measured by the test is operationalized in each language/cultural group (Harkness, 1998). Determining that construct equivalence exists between different cultures under study is a prerequisite for doing any cross-national, cross-cultural, or cross-language comparisons. The use of nonequivalent constructs is one of the most serious errors in cross-language research. For example, it is of limited value to compare two countries in terms of their mathematics achievement when the content measured by the test is highly reflective of the mathematic curriculum in one country but not the other. Another example might be the construct of "quality of life." In one country the construct might include having many material items such as cars, homes, and television sets, whereas in another it could be the construct would include little more than food for survival and a doctor nearby. A comparison of scores from a quality-of-life test produced in one country and adapted for use in the other would have little value.

Determining whether construct equivalence exists between two cultures involves primarily judgmental strategies. A researcher must begin by using his or her common sense to answer such questions as, Is it sensible to compare these two cultures on this construct? Does the construct that is being measured have similar meaning in all cultures being compared? Is the construct operationalized in the same way in all cultures being studied?

To be able to answer yes to these questions and thus ensure conceptual/functional equivalence and equivalence of construct operationalization, several approaches might be taken. This may be done by interviewing or observing people from the cultures of interest, researching the cultures of interest, and asking others who know about the cultures. These ways are very subjective, and therefore, the use of multiple sources of evidence is highly recommended. Van de Vijver and Poortinga (see chap. 2, this volume) and Sireci, Patsula, and Hambleton (see chap. 4, this volume) have much more to say in their chapters about judging construct equivalence.

Test Administration. Communication problems between a test administrator and examinees can be a serious threat to the validity of test results. Perhaps the test directions are not clearly communicated because of adaptation problems. One way to circumvent problems, but always feasible, is to ensure that the instructions on the test itself are clear and self-explanatory, with minimal reliance on verbal communication (van de Vijver & Poortinga, 1991). Special problems can be expected with directions for rating scales used in attitude measurement too because they are not common in many countries (see Harkness, 1998).

The proper selection of test administrators can be helpful too. They should (a) be drawn from the target communities, (b) be familiar with the culture, language, and dialects, (c) have adequate test administration skills and experience, and (d) know the importance of following any standardized procedures associated with the test. Additionally, consistency in test administration across different groups can be improved by providing (basic) training to all test administrators. Training sessions should be preplanned as part of the test development process, stressing clear, unambiguous communication, the importance of following instructions, strictly following time limits, the influence of test administrators on reliability and validity, and so on.

Test Format. Differential familiarity with particular item formats presents another source of invalidity of test results in cross-cultural studies. In the United States, selected response items such as multiple-choice items have been used extensively in assessment (though that practice has been changing in the last 10 years, and today, we see more use of performance assessments). In cross-cultural studies, it cannot be assumed that everyone is as familiar with multiple-choice items as American students. Nationalities that follow the British system of education, historically at least, have placed much greater emphasis on essays and short-answer questions, compared to multiple-choice items. Thus, students from these countries are placed at a possible disadvantage when compared to their American counterparts. When constructed response formats such as essay questions are emphasized or serve as the dominant mode of assessment, persons with more experience with selected response formats such as multiple-choice items will be placed at a disadvantage. Sometimes a balance of item formats may be the best solution to ensure fairness and reduce sources of invalidity in the assessment process. This strategy has been adopted in recent international studies of achievement (e.g., TIMSS and OECD/PISA).

Another solution to the potential biasing effect associated with a particular item format is to include only those formats with which all groups being assessed are experienced. Whenever it can be demonstrated that examinees are not placed at a disadvantage, and when all variables of interest can still be measured, it would seem that multiple-choice items or simple rating scales should be preferred. The major advantage is that multiple-choice items or simple rating scales can be objectively scored. Thus, complications in scoring associated with open-ended responses are avoided. This is especially relevant in cross-cultural studies where it may be *more difficult* to translate the scoring rubrics than the test items! In addition, extensive, unambiguous instructions including examples and exercises help to reduce differential familiarity (van de Vijver & Poortinga, 1992). At the same time, adopting a single item format for a test runs the danger of having to narrow the intended construct of interest to those parts that can be measured with the single item format, and this too can distort the findings from comparative studies across national boundaries.

Speededness. It is often assumed that examinees will work fast on "speeded" tests (van de Vijver & Poortinga, 1991). But to know to work quickly is a test-taking skill that may not be known or understood by examinees in different cultures. In a study comparing Dutch and other ethnic students in the Netherlands, van Leest and Bleichrodt (1990) found that the speed factor increased score bias. Not all cultural groups have had the same experiences with speeded tests, and those that had not were placed at a serious disadvantage. There are numerous other studies highlighting item and test bias due to the role of test speededness (see, e.g., studies on ethnic bias on the *SATs* in the United States). For example, it is common to find items appearing late in a test to show more bias than items appearing earlier in a test. The bias is against poor readers, and often the problem is due to the role of speed in test performance. The best solution would seem to be to minimize test speededness as a factor in cognitive test performance unless it is a relevant part of the construct being measured. The last point is important because sometimes speed of performance is an integral part of the construct being measured such as it is with the ability to solve analytic reasoning problems. Then, speed is an important part of the construct, so examinees need to understand the need to work quickly.

Technical Issues, Designs, and Methods

There are five technical factors that can influence the validity of tests adapted for use in other languages and cultures: the test itself, selection and training of translators, the process of translation, judgmental designs for adapting tests, and data collection designs and data analysis for establishing equivalence. Each of these factors is considered briefly next. More extensive discussions of these factors appear in subsequent chapters.

The Test Itself. If a researcher knows that he or she will be using a test in a different language or culture, it is advantageous to take this into account at the outset of the test development process. Failure to do so can introduce problems later in the adaptation process that will reduce the validity of the adapted test (Hambleton & Patsula, 1999). Choice of item formats, stimulus material for the test, vocabulary, sentence structure, and other aspects that might be difficult to translate well can all be taken into account in preparing the test specifications. Such preventive actions can minimize later problems. For example, questions about money might be eliminated because currencies are different around the world and equivalent adaptations may be difficult to produce. Also, reading passages about country-specific topics such as "ice hockey" that would be unfamiliar in many cultures could be rejected in favor of passages about walking through a park or other activities that would have meaning across many language and cultural groups. Another problem that arises in adaptation of passages from English to other languages is the presence of the "passive tense" in the text. Whereas this tense is common in English writing, it does not exist in some other languages (e.g., Spanish).

With personality scales, for example, care must be taken to choose situations, vocabulary, and expressions that will adapt easily across language groups and cultures. For example, behaviors that may be common in the Western world may have a very different meaning or not be meaningful at all in some other cultures. A statement such as "I like to start conversations at a party" has little meaning in a culture where parties are unknown, or where women do not go to parties, or where approaching others may be perceived as inappropriate behavior. This is simply one of many examples that could be offered.

Selection and Training of Translators. The importance of obtaining the services of competent translators is obvious. Too often though, researchers have tried to go through the translation process with a single translator selected because he or she happened to be available—a friend, a wife of a colleague, someone who could be hired cheaply, and so on. Competent translation work cannot be assumed. Also, the use of a single translator, competent or not, does not permit valuable interactions among independent translators to take place to resolve different points that arise in preparing a test adaptation. A single translator brings, for instance, a perspective, a preference for certain words and expressions, which may not be the most suitable for producing a good adaptation of a test. Multiple translators can protect against the dangers of a single translator and his or her preferences and peculiarities.

At the same time, translators should be more than persons familiar and competent with the languages involved in the translation.

They should know the cultures very well, especially the target culture (i.e., the culture associated with the language of the adapted test). This knowledge is often essential for an effective adaptation. Also, subject matter knowledge in the adaptation of achievement tests is highly desirable. The nuances and subtleties of a subject area will be lost on a translator unfamiliar with the subject matter. Too often, translators without technical knowledge will resort to literal translations that are often problematic to target-language examinees and threaten test validity. For example, the sentence, "Je ne suis pas une valise," has an easy literal translation in English (I am not a suitcase) but the actual meaning of the sentence in French is "I am not that stupid." A literal translation from French to English would totally distort the meaning.

Finally, test translators would benefit from some training in test construction. For example, test translators need to know that when doing adaptations of achievement or aptitude tests they should not create clang associations that might lead test-wise examinees to the correct answers, or translate distractors in multiple-choice items unknowingly so that they have the same meaning. A test translator without knowledge of the principles of test and scale construction could easily make test material more or less difficult unknowingly, and correspondingly, lower the validity of the test in the target population.

Process of Translation. The problem of dialects within a language can become a threat to the validity of adapted tests. Which dialect is of interest, or is the goal to produce an adaptation that would apply across dialects within a language? This problem should be settled before the test adaption begins, and should be used in the selection and training of translators.

Frequency counts of words can be valuable in producing valid test adaptations. In general, it is best to translate words and expressions with words and expressions with approximately the same frequencies in the two languages in an effort to control for the difficulty of words across languages. A problem is that these frequency lists of words and expressions are not always available. This again is a reason for preferring translators who are familiar with both the source and target cultures and not just the languages.

"De-centering" is sometimes used in adapting tests. It may be that some words and expressions do not have equivalent words and expressions in the target language. It is even possible that the words and expressions do not exist in the target language. De-centering involves making revisions to the source-language test so that equivalent material can be used in both the source- and target-language versions. De-centering is possible when the source-language test is under development at the same time as the target-language version. This is the situation with tests intended for use in international assessments, and some credential tests (e.g., those produced by Microsoft) intended for worldwide use.

Judgmental Designs for Adapting Tests. The two most popular designs are *forward translation* and *backward translation*. With a forward-translation design, a single translator, or preferably, a group of translators adapt the test from the source language to the target language. Then, the equivalence of the two versions of the test is judged by another group of translators. Revisions can be made to the target-language version of the test to correct problems identified by the translators. Sometimes as a final step, yet another person, though not necessarily a translator, will take the target-language version of the test and edit the test to "smooth out" the language. Choppiness can result when translations from different individuals or groups are merged into a single version.

The main advantage of the forward-translation design is that judgments are made directly about the equivalence of the source- and target-language versions of the test. The validity of the judgments about the equivalence of the two versions can be enhanced by having a small group of examinees provide translators with their interpretations of the test or questionnaire directions, content, and formats. This can be done in what are called "think-aloud" studies.

The main weakness of the forward-translation design is associated with the high level of inference that must be made by the translators about the equivalence of the two versions of the test. Other weaknesses include (a) translators may be more proficient in one language than the other, (b) ratings of test equivalence involve judgments by persons who are bilingual, and so they may use insightful guesses based on their knowledge of both languages, (c) translators may be better educated than the monolingual examinees for whom the test is intended and so they miss some problems that would be confronted by the examinees, and (d) (the monolingual) test developers are not in a position to judge test equivalence themselves.

The back-translation design is the best known and most popular of the judgmental designs. In its most popular version, one or more translators adapts a test from the source language to the target language. Different translators take the adapted test (in the target language) and adapt it back to the source language. Then, the original and the back-translated versions of the test are compared and judgments are made about their equivalence. To the extent that the two versions of the test in the source language look similar, support is provided for the equivalence of the source and target versions of the test. The back-translation design can be used to provide a general check both on the quality of the translation and to detect at least some of the problems associated with poor translations or adaptations. Researchers especially like this design because it provides them with an opportunity to judge the original and back-translated versions of the test so that they can form their own opinions about the adaptation process. This is not a possibility for them with the forward-translations design unless they are proficient in the languages.

Although the back-translation design has merit and often can identify problems in an adaptation process, it would rarely provide a sufficient amount of evidence to support the valid use of an adapted test. Evidence of test equivalence provided by a back-translation design is only one of many types of evidence that should be compiled in a test adaptation study. One of the main shortcomings is that the comparison of two or more language versions of a test is carried out only in the source language. It is possible that the test adaptation could be poor although the evidence on the comparability of the original test and the back-translated test would suggest otherwise. This could happen if the translators used a shared set of adaptation rules that ensured that the back-translated test looked like the original test. A second shortcoming is that the adaptation could be poor because it retained inappropriate aspects of the source-language test such as the same grammatical structure and spelling. Such errors would facilitate back-translations but this design would hide serious shortcomings in the target version of the test. For example, the game "ice hockey" may be retained when adapting a test into Spanish and the words then would be easy to back-translate. Unfortunately, the game may have little meaning to many persons who speak only the Spanish language, and so the validity of the Spanish version of the test would be lowered.

Finally, this and other judgmental designs have drawbacks because samples of the intended populations for the tests never actually take the tests under testlike conditions (or, for that matter, any other conditions). There is ample evidence to suggest that reviewers are not able to identify all the flaws in test items and this is why test items are routinely field-tested prior to their use. Adapted tests need to be field-tested too to uncover problems that go unidentified by the translators even when a combination of optimal translation designs and excellent translators are used (see, e.g., Hambleton & Patsula, 1999).

Data Collection Designs and Data Analysis for Establishing Test and Item Equivalence. Three data collection designs are commonly used to evaluate the equivalence of factor structure of the test and of the test items (or rating scales) in different languages. Evaluation of these designs follows (substantially more details about the designs and appropriate statistical methods can be found in subsequent chapters of the book):

1. *Bilingual examinees take source and target versions of the test*. In this design, the same examinees take both the source and target versions of the test. The advantage of this design is that differences in examinee characteristics on the test (e.g., demographic characteristics) can be controlled (see Sireci, chap. 5, this volume; Sireci, 1997). Various item and test statistics can be compiled from the administration of each version of the test and compared to determine equivalence. However, the design is based on the assumption that bilingual examinees are equally proficient in each of the languages. This is highly unlikely to occur for a substantial number of examinees (Cziko, 1987; Rosansky, 1979) and so the assumption should be checked whenever possible. For a bilingual data collection design to be effective, it is often best that it be implemented with another data collection design so that convergent validity of results can be investigated.

A second major problem with this data collection design is that statistical results obtained from data collection may not be generalizable to the intended populations of monolinguals as bilingual examinees tend to be, on the average, different in important ways from their monolingual counterparts (Hambleton, 1993). In one study by Hulin, Drasgow, and Komocar (1982) with the *Job Descriptive Index,* these researchers learned that only 4% of the items in their attitude scale were identified as poorly translated with a bilingual sample of examinees. Over 30% of the items were identified as poorly translated when monolingual samples of examinees from the source- and target-language populations were used.

A variation of this bilingual design, which has the same limitations but is easier to implement, involves randomly assigning bilingual examinees to take one of the language versions of the test. In this case, a randomly equivalent populations design is in effect.

2. *Source-language monolinguals take the original and back-translated versions*. This design involves the administration of the original and back-adapted versions of the test to a sample of monolingual examinees in the source language. Item equivalence is identified by comparing participant performance on the original and

back-translated version of each item. Factor analysis might be applied to the data collected from each version of the test, and factor structures compared. The advantage of this design is that by using one sample of participants, the resulting scores are not confounded by differences in examinee characteristics (Hambleton & Bollwark, 1991).

Two major shortcomings, however, weaken the usefulness of this data collection design. First, no empirical data are collected from the target-language version of the test. That is, no target-language monolinguals are used, although the aim of the research is to apply the findings to the target-language version of the test and the target-language monolinguals. Second, the results that are obtained may not be independent because it cannot be ruled out that learning results from administering the first original-source language version of the test and that the learning affects examinee performance on the back-translated version of the test. Counterbalancing can reduce the significance of practice effects but it does complicate the analyses.

3. *Source-language monolinguals take source language and target-language monolinguals take target language*. A more suitable data collection design would involve monolinguals taking the source-language version of the test and a second sample of monolinguals taking the target-language version of the test. An assumption of equal ability distributions across the two groups is not usually tenable and, fortunately, such an assumption does not need to be made if the analyses are carried out within an item response theory (IRT) framework (Ellis, 1989, 1991; Ellis & Kimmel, 1992; Hambleton, Swaminathan, & Rogers, 1991; van de Vijver & Leung, 1997, 2000) and/or item equivalence studies are carried out using conditioning procedures (Holland & Wainer, 1993). The advantage of this design is that samples of the source and target populations are used in the analyses and therefore findings about the equivalence of the two language versions of the test are generalizable to the populations of interest.

One of the major investigations for establishing item equivalence proceeds like item bias studies (Hambleton et al., 1991; Sireci & Allalouf, 2003). Comparisons of the item statistics in the two language versions of the test (or more, if available) are made controlling for any ability differences in the two groups (see Hambleton & Kanjee, 1995a). Items showing differences are identified and carefully studied to determine possible explanations for the differences (see, e.g., Ercikan, 2002). A poor adaptation is one explanation. Unfortunately, these studies are unable to disconfound cultural differences and adaptation problems but they are often revealing, generally, of potential problems with the adapted version of the test. Item bias analyses come from both classical and modern test theory and can be applied to both binary and polytomous response data (Sireci & Allalouf, 2003).

Factors Affecting Interpretation of Results

In large-scale cross-cultural studies, the purpose of the test is to provide a basis for making comparisons between various cultural/language groups, so as to understand the differences and similarities that exist (Hambleton, 1993, 2002). Sometimes cognitive variables are of interest and other times the focus may be on the assessment of personality variables or general information (e.g., quality of life, health). It is hoped that results will be used for seeking ways of comparing groups and understanding the differences. Cross-cultural studies should not be used to support arguments about the superiority or exceptionality of nations as if the international comparative study is the equivalent of a horse race with winners and losers (Westbury, 1992). At best these studies provide only a "snapshot" of differences that exist, and provide only a limited basis for interpreting the results. In this context, to gain a better understanding when interpreting scores, other relevant factors external to the tests or assessment measures and specific to a nationality should be considered. Curricula, educational policies and standards, wealth, standard of living, cultural values, and so on, may all be essential factors for properly interpreting scores across cultural/language and/or national groups. A sampling of the factors that should normally be considered in interpreting test results across language and cultural groups is presented next.

Similarity of Curricula. To the extent that differences in curricula exist, achievement comparisons between different cultures will be tenuous if these curricula differences are not taken into account. Westbury (1992) noted that the results of the *Second International Mathematics Study* (SIMS) indicated that American students performed poorly in every grade and in every aspect of mathematics that was covered on the test. When comparing performance of Japanese and American students, major curricular differences between the two countries were noted. However, in areas of the curricula of the two countries that were similar, Westbury found no essential differences between student performance in the two countries. Analyses of curricula differences are obviously important in these international comparative studies of achievement, and this is why, despite some opposition (because of extra burden and cost), extensive questionnaire data are compiled along with the test data in each participating country.

Student Motivation. Wainer (1993) questioned whether demonstrated proficiency as measured by tests can be separated from motivation. He noted that in the *International Assessment of Educational Progress Study* (Lapointe, Mead, & Askew, 1992), all the (randomly) selected students from one participating country were made aware of the great honor of being chosen to represent their school and country, and thus had a responsibility to perform at their best. For students in some other countries, on the other hand, participation on this international comparative study was just another activity and not especially important to students because individual scores were not made available. For these students, the tests were "low-stakes." To interpret performance differences between countries with motivated students and those countries without motivated students without considering differential motivation to perform on the test could lead to a major misinterpretation of the findings.

Also, van de Vijver and Poortinga (1991) noted that it cannot be assumed that examinees will always try to achieve a high score. For example, it has been reported that for many Black South African students, the aim in tests was to achieve the minimum score needed to pass. This is because the imposed state education system at the time was perceived by many examinees to be detrimental to Blacks, and thus, students aspired only to the minimum required of them. In this context, it would not be unusual to expect levels of performance that may have little to do with true ability.

Sociopolitical Factors. The meaning and interpretation of test scores can also differ even when the scores are the same. Consider comparing test scores between students from developed and developing nations, or industrialized and mainly rural societies. In this context, performance of students may not be related to ability at all. Rather, performance may be a reflection of the lack of access to adequate resources, or the different quality of educational services available.

The point is that, for any meaningful interpretations of the results, the different social, political, and economic realities facing nationalities, as well as the relevance of educational opportunities in the light of these realities, must be considered (Olmeda, 1981). Thus, it is important for test developers and policymakers to be aware of those specific cultural issues that might impact on test performance.

PRACTICAL GUIDELINES FOR ADAPTING TESTS

The technical literature for guiding the test adaptation process is definitely incomplete (from a measurement perspective), and scattered through a plethora of international journals, reports, and books. There has been no single complete source that practitioners could turn to for advice, nor was a set of guidelines for adapting tests ever formalized until recently (Hambleton, 1994; van de Vijver & Hambleton, 1996). Also, until recently, the more complex measurement methods (e.g., item response models and structural equation models), which are very useful in formally establishing the equivalence of scores obtained from tests adapted for use in multiple languages and cultures, have not been well known to researchers who do test adaptations (e.g., Hulin, 1987). But, as is clear from the chapters in this book (see also Hambleton & de Jong, 2003), the situation has improved substantially since the early 1990s. In fact, two of the purposes of the ITC conference held at Georgetown University in the United States in 1999, were to bring researchers from around the world together to share their knowledge and experience about test adaptation, and to unveil the final version of the ITC Guidelines for Test Adaptation. The purposes of this section of the chapter are to describe the motivation for the ITC to prepare the Guidelines, to provide some of the background for preparing the Guidelines, and then to describe the 22 Guidelines and the rationale for including each of them.

In view of the fact that "high-stakes" are often associated with the results from cross-cultural or international comparative studies of educational achievement (see, e.g., the high level of interest there is today in financially supporting international comparative studies of achievement), the need for professionally developed and validated practical guidelines for adapting tests and establishing score equivalence seemed clear to the ITC as early as 1992. Technical standards or guidelines for assessment practices concerning test development, reliability assessment, validity assessment, and reporting were available in many countries (see, e.g., AERA, APA, & NCME, 1985, 1999), but rarely had much attention been given to the preparation of guidelines for adapting tests and establishing score equivalence. For example, in the widely used AERA, APA, and NCME Test Standards published in 1985 (which were the most influential test standards in the United States until the 1999 Test Standards were published), only three standards directly address the topic of test adaptations. And in Canada, a bilingual country, only three standards that addressed test adaptation appeared in the Canadian Psychological Association's test standards (which were available in 1993).

The ITC addressed this shortcoming by preparing a set of practical guidelines for adapting tests (see Hambleton, 1994; van de Vijver & Hambleton, 1996), referred to as the ITC Guidelines for Test Adaptation. Table 1.1 identifies the eight organizations who came together to develop the Guidelines. Table 1.2 identifies the committee members, who worked for 3 years to produce them. The ITC Guidelines for Test Adaptation are organized into four sections: context, test development and adaptation, administration, and documentation/score interpretations. The thinking of the ITC committee who produced the Guidelines was that the Guidelines would be more convenient to use if they were organized into meaningful categories. Guidelines in the context category address concerns about construct equivalence in the language groups of interest. The test development and adaptation category includes guidelines that arise in the process of adapting a test, everything from choosing translators to statistical methods for analyzing empirical data to investigating score equivalence. The third category, administration, addresses guidelines having to do with the ways that tests are administered in multiple language groups, and this includes everything from selecting administrators, to the choice of item formats, to establishing time limits. The fourth category of guidelines concerns documentation and score interpretations. Typically, researchers have provided very

TABLE 1.1
Participating Organizations in the Development of the International Test Commission Guidelines for Test Adaptation

International Test Commission (ITC)
European Association of Psychological Assessment (EAPA)
European Test Publishers Group (ETPG)
International Association for Cross-Cultural Psychology (IACCP)
International Association of Applied Psychology (IAAP)
International Association for the Evaluation of Educational Achievement (IEA)
International Language Testing Association (ILTA)
International Union of Psychological Science (IUPsyS)

TABLE 1.2
Committee Members and the Organizations They Represented

Chairperson
Ronald K. Hambleton (ITC) University of Massachusetts at Amherst, USA
Committee Members
Glen Budgell (ITC) Canadian Nurses Association, Canada
Rob Feltham (ETPG) NFER-Nelson, England
Rocio Fernandez-Ballesteros (EAPA) Universidad de Autonoma, Spain
John H. A. L. de Jong (ILTA) Cito, The Netherlands
Ingrid Munck (IEA) Statistics Sweden, Sweden
José Muñiz (ITC) Universidad de Oviedo, Spain
Ype Poortinga (IACCP) Tilburg University, The Netherlands
Isik Savasir (IUPsyS) Hacettepe University, Turkey
Charles Spielberger (IAAP) University of South Florida, USA
Fons van de Vijver (ITC) Tilburg University, The Netherlands
Jac N. Zaal (ITC) GITP International, The Netherlands
Research Associate
Anil Kanjee (ITC) University of Massachusetts at Amherst, USA

little documentation of the adaptation process to establish the validity of an adapted test, and misinterpretations of scores from tests in multiple languages have been common. The ITC Guidelines for Test Adaptation addressed concerns in this area.

The following was adopted by the ITC committee as a definition of a guideline for test adaptation: "A test adaptation guideline is a practice that is judged as important for conducting and evaluating the adaptation or parallel development of psychological and educational tests for use in different populations." The 22 Guidelines advanced by the ITC committee are summarized in the following discussion and in Table 1.3 (and were published in draft form earlier in Hambleton, 1994, and van de Vijver & Hambleton, 1996). They appear in this chapter with only minor modifications. In the committee's final report (ITC, 2001), each guideline was described by (a) a rationale for including the guideline, (b) steps for addressing the guideline in practice, (c) a list of common errors, and (d) a set of references. A complete example of one of the guidelines is provided in Table 1.4. What follows is a brief description of each guideline and the rationale for including the guideline on the list.

Context

1. C.1 Effects of cultural differences that are not important to the main purposes of the study should be minimized to the extent possible.

Rationale/Explanation. There are many factors affecting cross-cultural/language comparisons that need to be considered whenever two or more groups from different language/cultural backgrounds are compared, especially when a test is being developed or adapted, or scores are being interpreted. However, often it is necessary that some of these factors are not merely taken into account, but that practical steps be taken to either minimize or eliminate the unwanted effects of these factors on any cross-cultural/ language comparisons that are made. For example, the different levels of test motivation of participants in a recent International Assessment of Educational Progress study is one of the likely reasons for the very different performances of participants from these countries (Wainer, 1993).

2. C.2 The amount of overlap in the construct measured by the test in the populations of interest should be assessed.

Rationale/Explanation. Differences that exist between various cultural and language groups depend not only on different traditions, norms, and values, but also on different worldviews and interpretations. Thus, it is possible for the same construct to be in-

TABLE 1.3
ITC Guidelines for Test Adaptation

Context

C.1 (1) Effects of cultural differences that are not important to the main purposes of the study should be minimized to the extent possible.

C.2 (2) The amount of overlap in the construct measured by the test in the populations of interest should be assessed.

Test Development and Adaptation

D.1 (3) Test developers/publishers should ensure that the adaptation process takes full account of linguistic and cultural differences in the intended populations.

D.2 (4) Test developers/publishers should provide evidence that the language used in the test directions, scoring rubrics, and the items themselves are appropriate for all cultural and language populations for whom the test is intended.

D.3 (5) Test developers/publishers should provide evidence that the choice of testing techniques, item formats, test conventions, and other procedures are familiar to all intended populations.

D.4 (6) Test developers/publishers should provide evidence that item content and stimulus materials are familiar to all intended populations.

D.5 (7) Test developers/publishers should compile judgmental evidence, both linguistic and psychological, to improve the accuracy of the adaptation process and compile evidence on the equivalence of all language versions.

D.6 (8) Test developers/publishers should ensure that the data collection design permits the use of appropriate statistical techniques to establish construct and item equivalence among the language versions of the test.

D.7 (9) Test developers/publishers should apply appropriate statistical techniques to (a) establish the equivalence of the language versions of the test, and (b) identify problematic components or aspects of the test that may be inadequate in one or more of the intended populations.

D.8 (10) Test developers/publishers should provide information on the validity of the adapted versions of the test in the intended populations.

D.9 (11) Test developers/publishers should provide statistical evidence about the equivalence of items in all intended populations.

D.10 (12) Non-equivalent items across the intended populations should not be used in "linking" adapted versions of the test to a common score reporting scale. However, these same items may be useful for reporting scores in each population, separately.

Administration

A.1 (13) Those aspects of the environment that influence the administration of a test should be made as similar as possible across populations for whom the test is intended.

A.2 (14) Test developers and administrators should try to anticipate the types of problems that can be expected, and take appropriate actions to remedy these problems through the preparation of appropriate materials and instructions.

A.3 (15) Test administrators should be sensitive to a number of factors related to the stimulus materials, administration procedures, and response modes that can moderate the validity of the inferences drawn from the scores.

A.4 (16) Test administration instructions should be in the source and target languages to minimize the influence of unwanted sources of variation across populations.

A.5 (17) The test manual should specify all aspects of the test and its administration that require scrutiny in the application of the test in a new cultural context.

A.6 (18) The administrator should be unobtrusive and the administrator-examinee interaction should be minimized. Explicit rules that are described in the test administration manual should be followed.

Documentation/Score Interpretations

I.1 (19) When a test is adapted for use in another population, documentation of the changes should be provided, along with evidence to support the equivalence of the adapted version of the test.

I.2 (20) Score differences among samples of populations administered the test should not be taken at face value. The researcher has the responsibility to substantiate the meaningfulness of the differences with other empirical evidence.

I.3 (21) Comparisons across populations can only be made at the level of invariance that has been established for the scale on which scores are reported.

I.4 (22) The test developer should provide specific information on the ways in which the socio-cultural and ecological contexts of the populations might affect performance on the test, and should suggest procedures to account for these effects in the interpretation of results.

TABLE 1.4

An Example of Guideline D.1 in Its Complete Form

Guideline D.1: General and Professional Requirements

Test developers/publishers should ensure that the adaptation process takes full account of linguistic and cultural differences in the intended populations.

Rationale/Explanation

The expertise and experience of translators are perhaps the most crucial aspects of the entire process of adapting tests as they can significantly affect the reliability and validity of the test (Bracken & Barona, 1991). For example, translators without domain specific or technical knowledge often resort to literal translations that may cause misunderstanding in the target population and threaten the validity of the test (Hambleton & Kanjee, 1995b). Consequently, the selection of appropriately qualified translators is an important aspect of the test adaptation process. Though expertise in both languages is a basic requirement, familiarity and experience with (a) both cultures, (b) the contents of the test, and (c) the principles of developing tests, especially item writing, should also be included as part of the essential requirements for the selection and/or training of translators. Because a single translator cannot be expected to have all of the required qualities and brings a single perspective to the task of translation, in general, it seems clear that a team of specialists is needed to accomplish an accurate adaptation.

Steps to Meet the Guideline

1. As a basic minimum, ensure that translators are qualified and experienced in the source and target languages as well as in both cultures (Butcher & Garcia, 1978). Certification and/or prior experience is an important requirement. For instance, it cannot be assumed that bilinguals have equal command of both languages in all relevant domains or are equally familiar with both cultures.

2. Knowledge of the subject matter is an important requirement for any translator involved in adapting a test. Without at least some content knowledge, the subtleties and nuances of the subject matter can be lost. Prior familiarization with the subject matter for translators lacking domain-specific knowledge should be included as part of the test adaptation process.

Where is a bird with webbed feet most likely to live?

a. in the mountains
b. in the woods
c. in the sea
d. in the desert

When this question was translated from English into Swedish, "webbed feet" became "swimming feet," that then provided an obvious clue to Swedish children about the location of the correct answer. A translator with some knowledge of the principles of item writing would have noticed the flaw in the translation of the item stem and revised the translation.

4. A test adaptation project is best carried out by a team of specialists (see, for example, Grisay, 2003). Translators should participate in such a project team and be involved in the decision making process, and their opinions and views should be actively sought and acknowledged. According to Brislin (1986), this approach can greatly improve the quality of an adaptation. The teamwork approach can help to (1) enable the use of the back-translation methods (see step 5, below); (2) allow translators to compare and discuss their work and thus improve on the relevance and quality of translations; and (3) can help to ensure that specialist knowledge in all required fields is accessible.

5. One possible design is to use a team of translators working independently or in small groups to adapt the test. Later, independent evaluations of the test can be compared, and differences resolved to produce a single best translation. Another procedure is the use of monolingual test developers and translators simultaneously, where tests are first translated/adapted by a translator, edited by a monolingual test developer in the target language and then re-assessed by a bilingual (Brislin, 1986). Brislin (1986) noted that the advantage of this design is that monolingual test developers can rewrite tests so that they would be clear and technically acceptable for target language examinees, and this design minimizes situations where the target version is poor, but this problem might be missed because a highly skilled translator produced an excellent back-translated version of the flawed target version. In the case where only a single translator is available, the use of a member from the target language population to assist the translator is strongly recommended. In this situation, the translator can at least discuss the target language version with someone from the target language group who can indicate problem areas and may suggest revisions too.

Common Errors

1. Selection of translators or easily available individuals familiar to the test developer (i.e., friends or neighbors), simply because they are bilingual has been shown to be an unsuccessful practice (Brislin, 1986).

2. Failure to ensure that translators selected are familiar with the content area as well as experienced in test development. This problem has sometimes been reported by countries participating in TIMSS.

3. Translators are not given sufficient time to do their work. Again, this problem has sometimes been reported by countries participating in TIMSS.

References for Additional Study

Bracken, B. A, & Barona, A. (1991). State of the art procedures for translating, validating and using psycho-educational tests in cross-cultural assessment. School Psychology International, 12, 119–132.

Brislin, R. W. (1986). The wording and translation of research instruments. In W. J. Lonner & J. W. Berry (Eds), Field methods in cross-cultural psychology (pp. 137–164). Newbury Park, CA: Sage.

Grisay, A. (2003). Translation procedures in OECD/PISA 2000 international assessment. Language Testing, 20(2), 225–240.

Butcher, J. N., & Garcia, R. E. (1978). Cross-national application of psychological tests. The Personnel and Guidance Journal, 56(8), 472–475.

Hambleton, R. K., & Kanjee, A. (1995b). Translation of tests and attitude scales. In T. Husen & T. N. Postlewaite (Eds), International Encyclopedia of Education (2nd ed., pp. 6328-6334). Oxford, England: Pergamon.

Prieto, A. J. (1992). A method for translation of instruments to other languages. Adult Education Quarterly, 43, 1–14.

terpreted and understood in completely different ways by two cultures. For example, the concept of "intelligence" is known to exist in almost all cultures. However, in many Western cultures this concept is associated with producing answers quickly, whereas for many Eastern cultures, intelligence is often associated with thoughtfulness, reflection, and saying the right thing (Lonner, 1990). Cross-cultural researchers have to ensure that the construct measured by a test in the original source cultural/language group can be found in the same form and frequency in the other cultures that are being studied.

Test Development and Adaptation

1. D.1 Test developers/publishers should ensure that the adaptation process takes full account of linguistic and cultural differences in the intended populations.

Rationale/Explanation. The rationale for this guideline along with the other parts of this guideline description appear in Table 1.4. This one is used as an example of the information that is available for each guideline in the final report (see ITC, 2001).

2. D.2 Test developers/publishers should provide evidence that the language used in the test directions, scoring rubrics, and the items themselves are appropriate for all cultural and language populations for whom the test is intended.

Rationale/Explanation. One of the causes of poor test adaptation for cross-cultural research is that the source-language version of the test is often flawed, and therefore difficult to adapt. Another cause may be that concepts, expressions, and ideas used in the source-language version of the test do not have equivalents in the target language. One of many reasons for the success of recent TIMSS and OECD/PISA studies is the substantial effort that has gone into the source-language test development with clearly defined constructs and test specifications, careful item development and field-testing, and other activities associated with proper test development.

Also it is important to ensure that the vocabulary used for a test in two or more languages is comparable in terms of the level of difficulty of words, readability, grammar usage, writing style, and punctuation. In this context, the reasons for using the test, for example, assessment of adult literacy, and the reading level of participants (children vs. adults) should be carefully considered.

3. D.3 Test developers/publishers should provide evidence that the choice of testing techniques, item formats, test conventions, and other procedures are familiar to all intended populations.

Rationale/Explanation. Specific formats (e.g., multiple choice, essay, 5-point rating scales) and certain conventions and procedures in giving instructions and presenting test items may not be equally familiar to all populations. Conventions and procedures range from language use in test rubrics, layout and use of graphics, and presentation mode (e.g., paper and pencil, computer). To ensure fairness it is important that all formats, conventions, and procedures be familiar to all populations for whom adaptations of the test are intended and this may involve the development of extensive practice materials to reduce bias due to unfamiliarity of some aspects of the assessment process.

4. D.4 Test developers/publishers should provide evidence that item content and stimulus materials are familiar to all intended populations.

Rationale/Explanation. Any adapted test that proves easier or more difficult to read or understand because of the specific content will introduce an additional source of bias. In some parts of the world, different units are used to express quantity in, for example, weight, length, and money. An adaptation of a test can be more difficult for the target population if the units used are less familiar or if they require different mathematical operations (see, Hambleton, Yu, & Slater, 1999). Also, certain stimulus material (diagrams, tables, figures, famous landmarks) may not be equally familiar to all populations.

5. D.5 Test developers/publishers should compile judgmental evidence, both linguistic and psychological, to improve the accuracy of the adaptation process and compile evidence on the equivalence of all language versions.

Rationale/Explanation. The equivalence of meaning in questions/tasks/rating scales in different languages and cultures must be assessed. Judgmental methods of establishing translation equivalence are based on decisions by translators or groups of translators. The two most popular designs, forward translations and backward translations, were considered earlier in the chapter. But both designs have flaws, and so rarely would judgmental designs provide sufficient evidence to validate an adapted test.

6. D.6 Test developers/publishers should ensure that the data collection design permits the use of appropriate statistical techniques to establish construct and item equivalence among the language versions of the test.

Rationale/Explanation. The data collection design refers to the way that the data are collected to establish the equivalence among adapted versions of a test. A first requirement with respect to the data collection is that samples should be sufficiently large to allow for the availability of stable statistical information. Though this requirement holds for any type of research, it is particularly relevant in the context of test adaptation validation because the statistical techniques needed to establish test and item equivalence (e.g., confirmatory factor analysis, IRT approaches to the identification of potentially biased test items) can be most meaningfully applied with sufficiently large samples.

The design for the empirical study is a function of variations in (a) the nature of the participants (monolinguals or bilinguals), (b) the version of the test (original, adapted or back-adapted) used, and (c) the specific statistical technique applied (discussed in greater detail in Guideline D.7). Sireci (1997) provided a discussion of the problems and issues in linking multilanguage tests to a common scale. Woodcock and Munoz-Sandoval (1993) provided an example of test score linking of cross-language tests using IRT. See also subsequent chapters in the book.

7. D.7 Test developers/publishers should apply appropriate statistical techniques to (a) establish the equivalence of the language versions of the test, and (b) identify problematic components or aspects of the test that may be inadequate in one or more of the intended populations.

Rationale/Explanation. Statistical techniques provide useful information for assessing the equivalence of tests developed in more than one language (van de Vijver & Leung, 1997, 2000; van de Vijver & Tanzer, 1997; see also subsequent chapters in the book). These techniques should be used to supplement judgmental techniques as they are able to identify nonequivalent test items that may not be readily detected when using judgmental designs. Another advantage is that statistical techniques elicit information directly from the participants, within the context of an actual test administration, and are thus extremely useful for identifying items that might pose problems in practice.

8. D.8 Test developers/publishers should provide information on the validity of the adapted versions of the test in the intended populations.

Rationale/Explanation. Existing tests are often developed and standardized for use in one culture and adapted for use in another culture. Time and expense can be saved if existing tests are adapted (Brislin, 1986). However, many constructs may not be meaningful without major modifications in other cultures. Several examples have already been suggested in this chapter—intelligence, quality of life, and mathematics achievement. In some instances, it may even be possible to determine that a test is not worth translating, and thereby save considerable time, effort, and money. Even if the construct does exist in a second language or culture, behavioral manifestations and interpretations may vary considerably (Lonner, 1990). Construct validity evidence must be compiled in each population where the test will be used. As is well known, a construct validity investigation is time consuming to plan and carry out because it is typically extensive, and involves a variety of studies and methodologies including intertest, intratest, criterion-related, experimental, and multitrait multimethods (see van de Vijver & Tanzer, 1997).

9. D.9 Test developers/publishers should provide statistical evidence about the equivalence of items in all intended populations.

Rationale/Explanation. One of the most important statistical analyses in validating a test for use in two or more cultural or language populations is an item bias study or referred to currently as a "differential item functioning [DIF] study" (Holland & Wainer, 1993; Sireci & Allalouf, 2003; and several chapters in this volume). Basically, support for the equivalence of a test for two populations requires that there be evidence that when members of the two populations have equal ability, the two should perform in an equivalent fashion on each item. When performance is not equivalent, a sound reason must be available or the item should be deleted from the test. This does not mean that there cannot be overall performance differences on the test. In general, differences can often be expected. What it does mean is that when members of the two populations are matched on the construct measured by the test, if differences exist, then DIF is present and the properties of the item must be studied carefully prior to any use of the item in the test. Items flagged as "DIF" may be problematic because of a poor translation or because of the use of a term, situation, or expression that is unknown or unfamiliar to one of the populations. Many other possibilities exist, too. Perhaps the skill measured by the item is not part of the repertoire of the target-language population, or perhaps the item format is unfamiliar. Determining the reason for the difference is important because it influences the ultimate determination of what to do with the item.

This guideline can be meaningfully addressed once there is evidence that the construct is relevant in the populations of interest, and there is evidence that the translations or adaptations have been carefully checked (perhaps through a forward-translation design). Basically, there are three methodologies that can be used to conduct the types of analyses required by this guideline: (a) IRT procedures (see, e.g., Ellis, 1989, 1991; Ellis & Kimmel, 1992), (b) Mantel– Haenszel (MH) procedure and extensions (see, e.g., Hambleton, Clauser, Mazor, & Jones, 1993; Holland & Thayer, 1988; Holland & Wainer, 1993; Sireci & Allalouf, 2003), and (c) logistic regression (LR) procedures (Swaminathan & Rogers, 1990). All of these methodologies are "conditional" in the sense that comparisons are made between groups of persons (e.g., English and French) who are assumed to be "matched" on the ability or abilities measured by the test. With IRT procedures, examinees are matched using estimated ability scores (e.g., estimated using the item score patterns). With the other two procedures, the total test score (or a score adjusted by deleting questionable items) is used to match examinees. All three methodologies can produce reliable and valid results providing the sample sizes are of substantial size and they are implemented correctly and the results are interpreted carefully. Sample sizes of about 200 per population are needed for the MH and LR procedures. In general, substantially larger samples are needed with the IRT procedures (although the Rasch model requires sample sizes equivalent to the other two procedures).

10. D.10 Non-equivalent items across the intended populations should not be used in "linking" adapted versions of the test to a common score reporting scale. However, these same items may be useful for reporting scores in each population, separately.

Rationale/Explanation. Items on adapted tests, in some instances, may be identified as nonequivalent because they are poorly adapted or culturally inappropriate (Hulin, 1987). These items cannot be used in the "linking" of adapted versions of a test to a common score-reporting scale because they provide different information for the populations being compared. However, well-adapted items that are identified as nonequivalent (or culturally inappropriate) can still provide useful information about the specific populations themselves. Identifying the source of nonequivalence of these items can provide further insight about the respective cultural/language populations that can increase understanding of that population (Ellis, 1991).

Administration

1. A.1 Those aspects of the environment that influence the administration of a test should be made as similar as possible across populations for whom the test is intended.

Rationale/Explanation. In general, the number of administration problems to be expected will vary as a function of the cultural and linguistic distance between the population groups involved or between the culture in which the test was first applied and the culture in which the test will be applied. Knowledge of the culture and language of the target group is required to address this guideline. The developer is expected to address explicitly the problems most likely to affect comparability and to consider necessary actions. Empirical evidence should be presented to support a claim of comparability. If this is not possible, a judgmental argument can be put forward to justify the cross-cultural use of the adapted test.

2. A.2 Test developers and administrators should try to anticipate the types of problems that can be expected, and take appropriate actions to remedy these problems through the preparation of appropriate materials and instructions.

Rationale/Explanation. Test developers should have a strong background in intra-cultural test development. But additional experience is required to become sensitive to the intricacies and peculiarities of cross-cultural test administration. A practical approach is to provide a list of frequently occurring problems and other threats to test validity. For test administration, a thorough knowledge of the linguistic and cultural aspects of the target group is valuable. For example, 3 or 4 points on a rating scale in Turkey seems to be optimal (according to some psychologists in that country who reviewed a draft of the ITC Guidelines for Test Adaptation). With more points, semantics become problematic.

3. A.3 Test administrators should be sensitive to a number of factors related to the stimulus materials, administration procedures, and response modes that can moderate the validity of the inferences drawn from the scores.

Rationale/Explanation. Test administration conditions can be a source of unintended score variation. In order to maximize the validity and comparability of test scores across cultural groups, possible sources of score variation (e.g., meaningfulness of the directions and/or the test format) should be described.

4. A.4 Test administration instructions should be in the source and target languages to minimize the influence of unwanted sources of variation across populations.

Rationale/Explanation. Cross-cultural research will often address populations with very different backgrounds. When the participants begin to answer the actual test questions/tasks/ratings, the influence of unwanted sources of intergroup differences (e.g., the mode of participant response) should be minimized to the extent possible. Test directions are one way to address this concern.

5. A.5 The test manual should specify all aspects of the test and its administration that require scrutiny in the application of the test in a new cultural context.

Rationale/Explanation. Many aspects that are relevant to the administration of a test to other linguistic groups can be anticipated by the test developer. During the development and validation of the test in the source-language version, developers should collect information about the specific issues that could be relevant in an adapted version of the test. In some cases, the developer will even have data obtained from cultural minorities or cross-cultural applications available. Relevant information on the administration in these cultural groups should be provided in the test manual.

6. A.6 The administrator should be unobtrusive and the administrator–examinee interaction should be minimized. Explicit rules that are described in the test administration manual should be followed.

Rationale/Explanation. The influence of the administrator on test results can be substantial. The goal must be to minimize the effect by getting commitment from administrators to follow the standardized administration directions and related procedures. However, the administrator can also have a less obvious and undesirable influence. Administrator characteristics such as gender, age, race, even style of clothing, and the like, can influence test results, especially if the test is individually administered. If a newly adapted test is applied in a cultural group, it will be relatively easy, possibly with the help of local informants, to pinpoint administrator characteristics that might endanger the validity of the test score outcome. Appropriate actions (such as a small pilot study) can then be taken. Particularly in the case of a dissimilar cultural background between administrator and examinee, the potential negative impact of the administrator should be checked and steps taken to minimize any problems that are identified.

Documentation/Score Interpretations

1. I.1 When a test is adapted for use in another population, documentation of the changes should be provided, along with evidence to support the equivalence of the adapted version of the test.

Rationale/Explanation. Information regarding the specifics of the adaptation of a test can provide considerable insight about the suitability of using the test within a specific context. For example, knowing that certain cultural (economical, social, etc.) factors were taken into consideration in the adaptation of a test for Spanish speakers in a South American country can be extremely valuable in determining the suitability of the test for a similar use for Spanish speakers in, say, the United States. The entire procedure followed to adapt the test should be fully documented in the test manual so as to facilitate evaluation of the test by potential users. The documentation should include a detailed step-by-step account of the entire procedure, including the judgmental designs used, methods used to assess item and test equivalence of adapted versions of the test and the results, details about the selection and use of translators, the reasons and justifications for the use and inclusion of items as well as information about those items that were modified or not included, some of the major problems encountered in conducting the test adaptation process and how they were solved, all aspects relating to the administration of tests including the selection and training of administrators, and the interpretation of results.

2. I.2 Score differences among samples of populations administered the test should not be taken at face value. The researcher has the responsibility to substantiate the meaningfulness of the differences with other empirical evidence.

Rationale/Explanation. The common error in practice appears to be giving limited attention to the test adaptation process, and then interpreting any score differences among samples of populations as if they reflect true differences in the construct measured by the test. This disregard of test adaptation problems that routinely occur in practice and the need to validate tests in the cultures where they are used have seriously undermined the results from many cross-cultural studies. A technically sound test adaptation process is essential to establish the validity of the adapted test. At the same time and even with excellent adapted tests, researchers must still make every effort to interpret their findings with full knowledge of the cultures involved. This means, for example, that corroborating evidence should be compiled whenever possible, and when it cannot be, extreme caution should be shown in interpreting results obtained in different populations.

3. I.3 Comparisons across populations can be made only at the level of invariance that has been established for the scale on which scores are reported.

Rationale/Explanation. Sometimes it is possible to place the scores from different language versions of a test onto a common scale to facilitate score comparisons. With access to large samples, and powerful statistical models such as those from IRT (see, e.g., Hambleton et al., 1991), complex "equating" of scores from adapted versions of a test is possible when the construct is "reasonably equivalent" across the multiple versions of the test and the appropriate "equating" or "linking" data are available (e.g., see D.6). When this is possible, all types of comparisons of scores can be made including means, standard deviations, and distributions. But often scores from different language versions of a test have not been properly equated and then scores cannot be directly compared. Still, comparisons can be made about the role of the construct in each language group. For example, for an aptitude test adapted from English to Spanish, a researcher may be interested in comparing the predictive validity of the test in each language group. The main point of this guideline is to ensure that researchers do not make unwarranted comparisons of scores from multiple language versions of a test, and that they limit their interpretations to those for which validity evidence is available.

4. I.4 The test developer should provide specific information on the ways in which the socio-cultural and ecological contexts of the populations might affect performance on the test, and should suggest procedures to account for these effects in the interpretation of results.

Rationale/Explanation. In any cross-national/cultural study, the different factors that are relevant to the purpose for testing need to be considered to gain a complete understanding of the results (Bracken & Barona, 1991). The different socio-political factors that invariably affect performance on the test are all too often not considered (van de Vijver & Poortinga, 1991). For example, when comparing academic performance of students from developing and developed countries, differences in performance may not be related to lack of ability but rather to a lack of access to resources, or may be a reflection of the quality of educational services available.

CONCLUSIONS

To enhance the meaning and utility of cross-cultural research, it is important for researchers to carefully choose their test administrators, use appropriate item formats, and control for the speed effect. In addition, translators who are familiar with the target group and their culture, who know the content of the test, and who have received some training in test development, are the most capable persons for producing valid test adaptations. Appropriately chosen judgmental designs (such as forward translations) and data collection designs and statistical analyses (such as comparisons of results from monolingual examinees taking the test in their own language) can provide invaluable data bearing on the question of item and test equivalence across language and cultural groups. With regard to interpretation of scores, those specific background variables that impact on performance should be carefully considered. In this regard, differing curricula, levels of motivation, and socio-political factors may be especially important. Also, comparisons should not be undertaken only with emphasis on the differences. Similarities between language and cultural groups can also provide useful and relevant information.

The ITC Guidelines for Test Adaptation described in this chapter should provide a framework for researchers to design and carry out test adaptation studies. The ITC expectation is that the guidelines and associated descriptions will be useful to many organizations and improve the quality of test adaptations around the world and thereby contribute to the validity of cross-language and cross-cultural research (see ITC, 2001). There are a number of useful follow-up references for readers: Geisinger (1994) and Hambleton and Patsula (1999) provided detailed steps for conducting test adaptation projects (which are consistent with the ITC Guidelines); Hambleton et al. (1999) provided the findings from one of the first field tests of the ITC Guidelines; Harkness (1998) addressed the issues and methods associated with test adaptations with an emphasis on rating scales; van de Vijver and Poortinga (1997) offered a framework for investigating threats to the validity of cross-cultural score interpretations; and van de Vijver and Tanzer (1997) and Sireci and Allalouf (2003) provided comprehensive lists of statistical procedures.

ACKNOWLEDGMENTS

This chapter also appears as *Laboratory of Psychometric and Evaluative Research Report No. 353,* University of Massachusetts, School of Education, Amherst.

The author would like to thank the College Board for providing financial support for the study. However, the College Board is not responsible for any errors that may remain, nor should any endorsement by the College Board of the opinions expressed in this chapter be assumed.

The author thanks Fons van de Vijver and Ype Poortinga from Tilburg University in the Netherlands for their assistance in preparing this chapter, and to Liane Patsula and Anil Kanjee for their technical assistance.

REFERENCES

American Educational Research Association, American Psychological Association, & National Council on Measurement in Education. (1985). *Standards for educational and psychological testing.* Washington, DC: American Psychological Association.

American Educational Research Association, American Psychological Association, & National Council on Measurement in Education. (1999). *Standards for educational and psychological testing.* Washington, DC: American Educational Research Association.

Bracken, B. A., & Barona, A. (1991). State of the art procedures for translating, validating and using psychoeducational tests in cross-cultural assessment. *School Psychology International, 12,* 119–132.

Brislin, R. W. (1986). The wording and translation of research instruments. In W. J. Lonner & J. W. Berry (Eds.), *Field methods in cross-cultural psychology* (pp. 137–164). Newbury Park, CA: Sage.

Butcher, J. N., & Garcia, R. E. (1978). Cross-national application of psychological tests. *The Personnel and Guidance Journal, 56*(8), 472–475.

Cziko, G. (1987). Review of the Bilingual Syntax Measure I. In J. C. Alderson & K. J. Krahnke (Eds.), *Reviews of English language proficiency tests.* Washington, DC: Teachers of English to Speakers of Other Languages.

Ellis, B. B. (1989). Differential item functioning: Implications for test translation. *Journal of Applied Psychology, 74,* 912–921.

Ellis, B. B. (1991). Item response theory: A tool for assessing the equivalence of translated tests. *Bulletin of the International Test Commission, 18,* 33–51.

Ellis, B. B., & Kimmel, H. D. (1992). Identification of unique cultural response patterns by means of item response theory. *Journal of Applied Psychology, 77,* 177–184.

Ercikan, K. (2002). Disentangling sources of differential item functioning in multilanguage assessments. *International Journal of Testing, 2*(3), 199–215.

Geisinger, K. F. (1994). Cross-cultural normative assessment: Translation and adaptation issues influencing the normative interpretation of assessment instruments. *Psychological Assessment, 6,* 304–312.

Grisay, A. (2003). Translation procedures in OECD/PISA 2000 international assessment. *Language Testing, 20*(2), 225–240.

Hambleton, R. K. (1993). Translating achievement tests for use in cross-national studies. *European Journal of Psychological Assessment, 9,* 54–65.

Hambleton, R. K. (1994). Guidelines for adapting educational and psychological tests: A progress report. *European Journal of Psychological Assessment, 10,* 229–240.

Hambleton, R. K. (2002). Adapting achievement tests into multiple languages for international assessments. In A. C. Porter & A. Gamoran (Eds.), *Method-*

ological advances in cross-national surveys of educational achievement (pp. 58–79). Washington, DC: National Academy Press.

Hambleton, R. K., & Bollwark, J. (1991). Adapting tests for use in different cultures: Technical issues and methods. *Bulletin of the International Test Commission, 18,* 3–32.

Hambleton, R. K., Clauser, B. E., Mazor, K. M., & Jones, R. W. (1993). Advances in the detection of differentially functioning test items. *European Journal of Psychological Assessment, 9*(1), 1–18.

Hambleton, R. K., & de Jong, J. (Eds.). (2003). Advances in translating and adapting educational and psychological tests. *Language Testing, 20*(2), 127–240.

Hambleton, R. K., & Kanjee, A. (1995a). Increasing the validity of cross-cultural assessments: Use of improved methods for test adaptations. *European Journal of Psychological Assessment, 11,* 147–160.

Hambleton, R. K., & Kanjee, A. (1995b). Translation of tests and attitude scales. In T. Husen & T. N. Postlewaite (Eds), *International encyclopedia of education* (2nd ed., pp. 6328–6334). Oxford, England: Pergamon.

Hambleton, R. K., & Patsula, L. (1999). Increasing the validity of adapted tests: Myths to be avoided and guidelines for improving test adaptation practices. *Applied Testing Technology, 1*(1), 1–16.

Hambleton, R. K., Swaminathan, H., & Rogers, H. J. (1991). *Fundamentals of item response theory.* Newbury Park, CA: Sage.

Hambleton, R. K., Yu, J., & Slater, S. C. (1999). Field-test of the ITC guidelines for adapting educational and psychological tests. *European Journal of Psychological Assessment, 15*(3), 270–276.

Harkness, J. (Ed.). (1998). *Cross-cultural equivalence.* Mannheim, Germany: ZUMA.

Holland, P. W., & Thayer, D. T. (1988). Differential item performance and the Mantel–Haenszel procedure. In H. Wainer & H. I. Braun (Eds.), *Test validity* (pp. 129–145). Hillsdale, NJ: Lawrence Erlbaum Associates.

Holland, P. W., & Wainer, H. (Eds). (1993). *Differential item functioning.* Hillsdale, NJ: Lawrence Erlbaum Associates.

Hui, C. H., & Triandis, H. C. (1985). Measurement in cross cultural psychology. *Journal of Cross-Cultural Psychology, 16,* 131–152.

Hulin, C. L. (1987). A psychometric theory of evaluations of item and scale translations: Fidelity across languages. *Journal of Cross-Cultural Psychology, 18,* 115–142.

Hulin, C. L., Drasgow, F., & Komocar, J. (1982). Application of item response theory to analysis of attitude scale translation. *Journal of Applied Psychology, 67,* 818–825.

International Test Commission. (2001). *International Test Commission guidelines for test adaptation.* London: Author.

Lapointe, A. E., Mead, N. A., & Askew, J. M. (1992). *Learning mathematics* (Report No. 22-CAEP-01). Princeton, NJ: Educational Testing Service.

Lonner, W. J. (1990). An overview of cross-cultural testing and assessment. In R. W. Brislin (Ed.), *Applied cross-cultural psychology* (Vol. 14, pp. 56–76). Newbury Park, CA: Sage.

Olmedo, E. L. (1981). Testing linguistic minorities. *American Psychologist, 36,* 1078–1085.

Prieto, A. (1992). A method for translation of instruments to other languages. *Adult Education Quarterly, 43,* 1–14.

Rosansky, E. J. (1979). A review of the Bilingual Syntax Measure. In B. Spolsky (Ed.), *Some major tests: Advances in language testing (Series 1).* Arlington, VA: Center for Applied Linguistics.

Sireci, S. G. (1997). Problems and issues in linking tests across languages. *Educational Measurement: Issues and Practice, 16,* 12–19.

Sireci, S. G., & Allalouf, A. (2003). Appraising item equivalence across multiple languages and cultures. *Language Testing, 20*(2), 148–166.

Swaminathan, H., & Rogers, H. J. (1990). Detecting differential item functioning using logistic regression procedures. *Journal of Educational Measurement, 27,* 361–370.

van Leest, P. F., & Bleichrodt, N. (1990). Testing of college graduates from ethnic minority groups. In N. Bleichrodt & P. J. D. Drenth (Eds.), *Contemporary issues in cross-cultural psychology.* Amsterdam: Swets & Zeitlinger.

van de Vijver, F. J. R., & Hambleton, R. K. (1996). Translating tests: Some practical guidelines. *European Psychologist, 1,* 89–99.

van de Vijver, F. J. R., & Leung, K. (1997). *Methods and data analysis for cross-cultural research.* Thousand Oaks, CA: Sage.

van de Vijver, F. J. R., & Leung, K. (2000). Methodological issues in psychological research on culture. *Journal of Cross-Cultural Psychology, 31,* 33–51.

van de Vijver, F. J. R., & Poortinga, Y. H. (1991). Testing across cultures. In R. K. Hambleton & J. Zaal (Eds.), *Advances in educational and psychological testing* (pp. 277–308). Boston: Kluwer Academic.

van de Vijver, F. J. R., & Poortinga, Y. H. (1992). Testing in culturally heterogeneous populations: When are cultural loadings undesirable? *European Journal of Psychological Assessment, 8,* 17–24.

van de Vijver, F. J. R., & Poortinga, Y. H. (1997). Towards an integrated analysis of bias in cross-cultural assessment. *European Journal of Psychological Assessment, 13,* 29–37.

van de Vijver, F. J. R., & Tanzer, N. K. (1997). Bias and equivalence in cross-cultural assessment: An overview. *European Review of Applied Psychology, 47,* 263–279.

Wainer, H. (1993). Measurement problems. *Journal of Educational Measurement, 30,* 1–21.

Westbury, I. (1992). Comparing American and Japanese achievement: Is the United States really a low achiever? *Educational Researcher, 21,* 18–24.

Woodcock, R. W., & Munoz-Sandoval, A. F. (1993). An IRT approach to cross-language test equating and interpretation. *European Journal of Psychological Assessment, 9,* 233–241.

2

Conceptual and Methodological Issues in Adapting Tests

Fons J. R. van de Vijver and Ype H. Poortinga
Tilburg University, The Netherlands

Suppose that a Dutch psychologist decides to produce a Dutch-language version of an American intelligence test and that a subtest of general knowledge contains the item "Who is the president of the United States?" Such an item may well have good psychometric properties in an American sample. The Dutch psychologist may decide to use a verbatim translation, *"Wie is de president van de Verenigde Staten?"* The Dutch question is as clear as the English, and a back translation (Brislin, 1980, 1986; Werner & Campbell, 1970) will produce the English original. Moreover, the president of the United States may be better known to American citizens, but he is certainly not unknown in Europe. When using the test, the difficulty level of the item will presumably be lower in the United States than in The Netherlands. This difference is a reflection of the difference in knowledge of the populations: There are relatively more Americans than Dutch who know the president's name. Assuming that the subtest is unidimensional, it is quite likely that the item measures the underlying construct in an appropriate way in both countries. The conclusion may seem inescapable: The item is useful because the two language versions are similar and measures the same underlying construct in the two countries.

Still, the conclusion that the item is valid and useful because of the linguistic similarity is not straightforward. The problem is a possible lack of psychological similarity: Does the item have the same meaning in both countries? A psychologically more similar item in The Netherlands may ask for the name of the Dutch queen, the prime minister, or some other public figure. This "adaptation" of the original has lost in linguistic similarity, but it has gained in psychological similarity. Unfortunately, adaptation, maximizing psychological similarity, is not without problems either. First of all, such similarity has to be empirically established and cannot be merely assumed. In addition, by administering items in various language versions that differ in content, we strongly diminish the scope for comparisons of scores across populations. For example, what should we conclude from the (hypothetical) finding that in the United States 90% of a sample of adults know the name of the president, whereas 95% of the Dutch know the name of their queen. With sufficiently large samples such a difference may be statistically highly significant, but the interpretation of the difference is difficult, if not impossible, to give. It may reflect, for example, a difference of media exposure of the two persons in their countries instead of a difference in the construct of the test, general knowledge.

This short introduction may suffice to highlight major themes of the present chapter. First, linguistic and psychological perspectives on translations can converge, in which case translation is straightforward, but they also may yield different versions in the target language. In order to produce adequate instruments in another language, expertise in the source and the target language is necessary, but it is not sufficient (Behling & Law, 2000; Bracken & Barona, 1991; Brislin, 1980, 1986; Geisinger, 1994; Hambleton, 1994; J. Harkness, 1998; Merenda, 1994; Vallerand, 1989; van de Vijver, 2003). A psychological perspective is indispensable to producing high-quality instruments in the target language. Second, we need a theoretical framework in which we can define in a precise way what we mean by "psychological similarity."

In the first section of the chapter, we introduce two key terms in establishing such similarity: *bias* and *equivalence*. The second section extends this taxonomy to translations/adaptations. In the third section, methods are described to enhance the adequacy of translations/adaptations. Implications for test use are described in the final section.

The chapter can be seen as a theoretical background to the Guidelines for Adapting Educational and Psychological Instruments and Establishing Score Equivalence, presented in Table 1.3 in chapter 1. With this background in mind, it should be easier to appreciate the rationale of the Guidelines and to understand the positions adopted. References to the Guidelines are made where applicable.

BIAS AND EQUIVALENCE

The terms bias and equivalence have a slightly different meaning in the literature. Bias is often associated with the presence of nuisance factors. A measure is taken to be biased if scores of different language versions of an instrument are differentially affected by an unwanted and undesirable source of variance. For example, in a Swedish–English translation, the test item "Where is a bird with webbed feet most likely to live?" was used. The back translation of the Swedish translation of the English "bird with webbed feet" was "bird with swimming feet," which provides a much stronger clue to the solution than the English original item (Hambleton, 1994). Another example: In the European Values Survey, the Spanish scores on an item measuring loyalty deviated from the overall pattern of results for this country. Upon closer examination it appeared that, unlike in other languages, the Spanish word for loyalty that was used has the connotation of sexual faithfulness (Halman, personal communication, June 1998).

Equivalence has become associated with the measurement aspects of ethnic comparisons and, hence, with the consequences of bias. An item or instrument that is biased will yield inequivalent scores. Inequivalence or nonequivalence has become a generic term for lack of comparability of scores. In line with this tradition, we use inequivalence as a characteristic of test scores, which are affected by cultural bias.

From the perspective adopted in this chapter, bias (or lack thereof) is not an intrinsic property of an instrument, but a concomitant of the application of that instrument in a particular group for a particular purpose. It refers to all kinds of nuisance factors that challenge the interpretation of score differences between a group and some other group. Bias can best be understood from a generalizability perspective. Bias can be formally defined as *the unequal correspondence between the domain of observations and the universe of generalization.* As an example, suppose that a digit span test (measuring short-term memory span) is administered to American children and to rural children in Africa with poor school education, and that the Americans have a higher score. If the test scores are interpreted as the number of digits that children of the two groups can hold in short-term memory, the test may well be unbiased; the use of digits in domains such as arithmetic is likely to show similar differences. However, if the digit span scores are taken as referring to short-term memory capacity (which is the more common interpretation of these scores), the test is likely to be biased. There is evidence in cross-cultural psychology that short-term memory span hardly varies across cultures (e.g., Wagner, 1981). Yet, cross-cultural differences (the terms *cross-cultural* and *ethnic* are treated here as synonyms) in stimulus familiarity can have a pervasive influence on scores in many tests (Cole, 1996). The differences that are observed for the digit span test may not be replicated with instruments that utilize stimuli with more ecological validity for rural African children. In the study of bias we address the question of which changes (e.g., in the test instruction, stimuli, response procedures, sampling, administration, or scoring) will affect observed ethnic differences (Guideline 1).

Three Types of Bias

Although bias can result from a wide variety of sources, there is no need to distinguish between many categories. Different sources often give rise to similar kinds of bias. In our view, there are three categories of bias: construct bias, method bias, and item bias (van de Vijver & Leung, 1997a, 1997b, 2000; van de Vijver & Poortinga, 1997; van de Vijver & Tanzer, 1997) (see Table 2.1).

Construct Bias. This form of bias refers to differences in constructs across cultural groups. Table 2.2 presents an overview of important sources of construct bias. For example, the constituent elements of

TABLE 2.1
Types of Bias

Type of Bias	*Description*
Construct bias	Incomplete overlap of constructs in the cultural groups
Method bias	Generic term for all nuisance factors arising from aspects of method
Instrument bias	Instrument features, not related to the construct, that induce ethnic score differences
Administration bias	Communication failures between tester and testee
Item bias/differential item functioning	Anomalies of items (such as poor translations)

TABLE 2.2
Typical Sources for the Three Types of Bias in Cross-Cultural Assessment

Type of Bias	*Source of Bias*
Construct bias	• Dissimilarity in the definitions of the construct across cultures
	• Differential appropriateness of the behaviors associated with the construct (e.g., skills do not belong to the repertoire of one of the cultural groups)
Method bias	• Incomparability of samples (e.g., caused by differences in education, motivation)
	• Differential familiarity with stimulus material
	• Differential familiarity with response procedures
	• Differential response styles (e.g., social desirability, extremity scoring, acquiescence)
	• Differences in environmental administration conditions, physical (e.g., recording devices) or social (e.g., class size)
Item bias	• Poor item translation and/or ambiguous items
	• Item-related nuisance factors (e.g., item may invoke additional traits or abilities)

Note. See van de Vijver and Tanzer (1997).

a construct (e.g., behaviors, attitudes, or norms) are not exactly identical across groups. Advocates of culture-relativistic positions, such as found in indigenous psychologies (Sinha, 1997) and cultural psychology (Cole, 1996; Greenfield, 1997a, 1997b; Miller, 1997), tend to argue that (in the parlance of the present chapter) construct bias is the rule rather than the exception in cross-cultural psychology.

An example is the concept of intelligence. Most tests of intelligence tend to use an implicit definition of intelligence as made up of reasoning and logical thinking (such as the Raven tests), and to a lesser extent of acquired knowledge and memory (such as intelligence batteries like the Wechsler Intelligence Scale for Children and the Wechsler Adult Intelligence Scale). These elements are also found when individuals are asked to describe the characteristics of an intelligent person (Sternberg, Conway, Ketron, & Bernstein, 1981). But studies in non-Western settings have reported that everyday conceptions of intelligence are broader and also include social aspects. For example, Kokwet mothers (Kenya) said that an intelligent child knows its place in the family and its expected behaviors, like proper ways of addressing other people. An intelligent child is obedient and does not create problems (Mundy-Castle, 1974, quoted in Segall, Dasen, Berry, & Poortinga, 1990). Studies in Zambia (Serpell, 1993) and Japan (Azuma & Kashiwagi, 1987) similarly show that descriptions of an intelligent person go beyond the school-oriented domain with which intelligence is commonly associated in the United States and Europe. Another example of differential inclusiveness can be found in Ho's (1996) work on filial piety in China. He showed that, compared to the West, the Chinese tend to apply a broader definition. Obedience and paying respect to one's parents are elements that are also found in Western countries; but in addition, the Chinese concept refers to material care of parents when they grow older and need help.

The problem of poor sampling of the universe is compounded when we work with short instruments, as often is the case. Many years ago Triandis (1978) complained that our measures tend to be very small samples of the universes of interest. This leads to what Embretson (1983) called "construct underrepresentation." Small numbers of items, often chosen for their homogeneity, are interpreted as adequately covering broad constructs. Although this issue is not unique to cross-cultural psychology, it is particularly salient here. In particular when the cultural groups to be compared show a large cultural distance, narrow measures are likely to show bias due to restricted construct representation.

Method Bias. This is a generic term for a second type of bias, including all nuisance variables due to method-related factors. The term was coined because such factors usually are described in the method section of empirical papers. There are two forms of method bias.

The first is *instrument bias*. It involves all instrument properties that are not the target of study, but nevertheless induce differences in test scores. The best known source of instrument bias in mental testing is familiarity of subjects with stimuli and responses (or response formats). A good illustration can be found in work by Serpell (1979). He was interested in perceptual skills of Zambian and British children. They were asked to reproduce figures, using paper and pencil, plasticine, hand positions, and iron-wire modeling (which is popular in Zambia). As expected, the British children outperformed the Zambian children in paper-and-pencil drawings, whereas the Zambians scored significantly higher in the reproduction of iron-wire models. No differences were expected or found for the other media. Differential response familiarity provides a concise explanation of the findings.

Personality and attitude inventories can also show instrument bias. For example, Hui and Triandis (1989) found that, compared to Euro-Americans, Hispanics chose more often extremes on a 5-point rating scale. This tendency was not found when a 10-point scale was used.

The second category of method bias, *administration bias*, refers to score differences arising from difficulties with the instruction or other communication problems between tester and testee. Such problems are more likely to occur when tester or testee have to make use of a language other than their mother tongue. Loss of salient information may be due to the inability to express ideas in a second language (Gass & Varonis, 1991). Lack of knowledge of the culture of the testee may also lead to violations of local norms of courtesy. Both psychologists and survey researchers have addressed the potential influence of interviewer characteristics (such as gender, age, and ethnicity) on measurement outcome. In an overview of psychological studies of the race of tester on children's performance on intelligence tests, Jensen (1980) concluded that there is a paucity of methodologically adequate studies (e.g., almost no studies cross ethnicity of tester and testee). However, the available evidence does not point to large effects of tester's race. Survey researchers have examined the so-called deference theory. Cotter, Cohen, and Coulter (1982) found that subjects were more likely to display positive attitudes to a particular cultural group when they are interviewed by someone from that group (Reese, Danielson, Shoemaker, Chang, & Hsu, 1986). In general, however, the size of interviewer effects tends to be small and inconsistent across studies (Singer & Presser, 1989).

Instrument bias, especially, can have a pervasive effect on test scores. The influence of differences in education or previous test exposure may affect the score on some items with a school-related content. More likely, such a difference will affect most or all items. Thus, method bias is likely to have consequences for any psychometric comparison, if scores are generalized to a universe that goes beyond the school context. Then method bias will result in intergroup score differences that are not construct related, but due to measurement artifacts. The implications are serious. The researcher or practitioner, who compares scores across cultures (either explicitly by statistically testing these differences, or implicitly by applying a norm table to an individual from a different cultural group), will need to choose between two rival explanations: valid cross-cultural differences and method bias. The choice is often difficult to make, because of a lack of evidence to confirm or disconfirm either interpretation. Thus, it is important for test developers to acknowledge the importance of method bias and to attempt to reduce its influence to the extent possible (Hambleton, 1994; see also Sireci, Patsula, & Hambleton, chap. 4, this volume); all Administration Guidelines (13–18) serve this purpose.

Item Bias (or Differential Item Functioning). This type of bias refers to validity threats that affect separate items, whereas construct and method bias involve more general features of an instrument. The term item bias was used initially (e.g., Cleary & Hilton, 1968). After more than three decades of important psychometric developments in the detection of anomalous items (e.g., Ercikan, 2002; Holland & Wainer, 1993; Millsap & Everson, 1993; Sireci & Allalouf, 2003), this term was replaced by *differential item functioning*; it was felt that the term bias had too much the connotation of a deviation from a Euro-American standard, which was and still is the most frequently employed reference group in U.S. research. We adhere to the original term, because it stresses the close relationship with other types of bias and points to its essential feature: It is a validity threat and precludes a direct comparison of scores.

The most important sources of item bias are poor translations and different connotations of words. For example, according to (American) Webster's dictionary, aggressiveness is "marked by bold determination and readiness for conflict," whereas the (British) Oxford Collins dictionary gives as first meaning "the act or practice of attacking without provocation, especially beginning a quarrel or war." Here, the American meaning is only given as the third description. Interestingly, the words for "aggression" in, for example, German, French, Dutch, and presumably other languages are much closer in meaning to the British than to the American definition.

A bewildering collection of definitions and statistical techniques to identify item bias have been proposed. But there is more convergence in the field now than there was 10 or 20 years ago. One type of definition and a small set of statistical techniques have become accepted as most appropriate. It is essential in current definitions that item bias is defined as conditional on trait/ability level. What do we mean by this? Let us return to our example asking for the president of the United States. The higher score of American subjects on this question reflects a genuine difference of American and Dutch citizens and we would not want to dismiss this difference as bias (or as "adverse impact," to use another term introduced for invalid cross-cultural differences).

For an analysis of item bias, we split up each of the two samples in a number of score groups (this process is called conditioning). In the first American score group, we have all subjects with a total score of 1 on the test and, similarly, the first Dutch subgroup consists of all persons with a score of 1. The next score group contains all persons with test scores of 2; the same is done for the other scores. This procedure allows us to make a detailed analysis; instead of just comparing average scores, it is now possible to compare American and Dutch scores with the same score level (i.e., we compare conditional on score level). The item about the president of the United States shows item bias if American and Dutch subjects with the same total test score do not have the same average score on the item. More precisely, an item is taken to be biased if persons with the same standing on the test construct (operationalized as the same total test score) do not have the same expected score on the item (operationalized as the average score on the item) (Holland & Thayer, 1988; Shepard, Camilli, & Averill, 1981; van de Vijver & Leung, 1997a, 1997b, 2000).

Mellenbergh (1982; see also Clauser & Mazor, 1998) described a distinction between uniform and nonuniform bias. An item is uniformly biased if the difference in performance level is more or less constant across score levels (e.g., in each score group, the American testees outperform the Dutch by approximately the same amount). Bias is nonuniform if the size of the difference varies systematically across score levels. For example, in the low-scoring groups, there are relatively fewer Americans who know the name of their president than Dutch subjects knowing the name of their queen, but this difference gradually disappears for higher-scoring groups.

Levels of Equivalence

Bias challenges the comparability of scores obtained in different groups. More technically, bias threatens the equivalence of scores. In order to delineate the measurement consequences of bias for score comparability, four types of equivalence with hierarchically increasing opportunities of ethnic comparisons are distinguished here (Van de Vijver & Leung, 1997a, 1997b, 2000; van de Vijver & Poortinga, 1997) (see Table 2.3). The first is called *construct nonequivalence*. It is characterized by a complete lack of comparability; it amounts to "comparing apples and oranges." This type of equivalence is a consequence of construct bias. It is impossible to

TABLE 2.3
Types of Equivalence

Type of Equivalence	*Description*
Construct inequivalence	Instrument measures different constructs in two cultural groups (i.e., "comparing apples and oranges")
Structural equivalence/ functional equivalence	Instrument measures the same psychological construct across cultural groups
Measurement unit equivalence	Instrument has the same measurement unit and a different origin across cultural groups
Scalar equivalence/full score equivalence	Instrument has the same measurement unit and origin across cultural groups

carry out cross-cultural score comparisons that are based on inadequate or incomplete operationalizations.

The second type of equivalence is known under various names; the two most common are *structural equivalence* and *functional equivalence*. It is associated with a category of procedures that are used to establish the identity of constructs across groups, as operationalized in a specific measurement instrument. In general, this form of equivalence requires that patterns of correlations between variables are the same in each of the groups. It is addressed in many test adaptation projects (Guideline 2).

When a new language version of a test has been composed, the question of construct validity arises: Do the source and target language versions measure the same psychological construct? The question is relevant when an instrument has been literally translated. In such cases, confirmatory factor analyses or exploratory factor analyses, followed by target rotations, are often used to examine factorial similarity of the items across cultural populations (for details, see, e.g., Byrne, Shavelson, & Muthén, 1989; Little, 1997; van de Vijver & Leung, 1997a, 1997b, 2000; Watkins, 1989). Similarity of factor loadings for each item is often seen as a necessary condition for structural equivalence. This holds for literally translated instruments. When in the translation process changes have been in the target language version in order to ensure an adequate construct representation (i.e., when an adaptation has been made) the same factors should emerge, but a one-to-one correspondence between items in loading patterns cannot be expected. For example, there are over 40 translations of Spielberger, Gorsuch, and Lushene's (1970) State–Trait Anxiety Inventory (STAI). In most of these translations the primary aim was not to produce a verbatim reproduction of the English version, but to compose an instrument that would assess anxiety in the target culture as adequately as possible. With this goal in mind, the factor analytic techniques mentioned are less appropriate and an examination of the nomological network of the instrument (Cronbach & Meehl, 1955) is more important. The procedure examines the expected pattern of high correlations with other measures of anxiety that are already available in the target language, and low or zero correlations with measures of presumably unrelated constructs.

The next level of equivalence is called *measurement unit equivalence*. This level requires that scales in each group have the same metric (i.e., measurements are the same at interval level). Two measures show measurement unit equivalence when they have the same measurement unit, but a different origin. This is the lowest level of equivalence at which comparisons of score levels can be validly made, be it with restrictions. Individual differences found in group A can be compared with individual differences in group B. For example, if a test of extraversion meets this type of equivalence, the question can be answered whether gender differences in extraversion are identical across cultural groups. However, due to a possible difference in the origin of the scale, no direct comparisons between scores across groups can be made. Thus, it is not possible to decide whether the one group has a higher level of extraversion than the other, or that person X from group A is more extravert than person Y from group B when the scale shows measurement unit equivalence.

Absolute differences in score levels can be examined only when scores show the highest level of equivalence, called *scalar equivalence* or *full score equivalence*. Measures showing this type of equivalence have the same measurement unit and the same origin across groups. With this type of equivalence, scores can cross cultural borders without problems and can be validly compared for persons belonging to different cultural or ethnic groups.

Bias and Equivalence

Bias and equivalence are closely related; some authors indeed treat the terms as interchangeable. After having introduced the terminology, it is now possible to examine the relationships in some more detail. Bias may or may not lower the level of equivalence of comparisons, as illustrated in Table 2.4. The level of equivalence will deter-

TABLE 2.4
Influence of Bias on the Level of Equivalence

Type of Bias	*Level of Equivalence* *Structural*	*Measurement Unit*[a]	*Scalara,*[b]
Construct bias	yes	yes	yes
Method bias			
Uniform	no	no	yes
Nonuniform	no	yes	yes
Item bias			
Uniform	no	no	yes
Nonuniform	no	yes	yes

Note. See Van de Vijver and Leung (1997b). [a]The same measurement unit is assumed in each cultural group. [b]The same origin is assumed in each cultural group.

mine the type of comparison that is possible (Guideline 21). Direct score comparisons (e.g., members of group A are on average more extravert than are members of group B) require a higher level of equivalence (and hence less bias) than comparisons of constructs (e.g., can extraversion be taken as an identical construct in populations A and B?). Construct bias is the most serious challenge to score comparability, because it introduces a form of nonequivalence that precludes any cross-cultural comparison. For this reason nonequivalence may seem undesirable, yet such a position may be starting point of an exploration of important cross-cultural differences, that extend beyond method or item bias and even involve the conceptualization of a construct (Greenfield, 1997a; Poortinga & van der Flier, 1988).

If we are interested to know whether an instrument assesses the same trait or ability in different groups, it is sufficient to establish structural equivalence. Method bias in this case is unlikely to be a major concern. Statistical analyses of structural equivalence mainly consider correlations and method bias tends not to influence correlations; therefore, these statistics are not affected by method bias.

When item scores are analyzed, the picture is more complicated. Exploratory factor analyses, followed by target rotations, have been proposed to address structural equivalence. Differences in factor loadings across groups are taken as evidence of item bias (if just a few items are biased) or lack of structural equivalence (if several items are biased). If an item shows uniform bias, it is quite likely that correlations of the item with other items will remain invariant. Such an item will not be flagged as suspect in an exploratory factor analysis. However, exploratory factor analysis will be sensitive to nonuniform bias, because this type of bias is more likely to lead to different correlational patterns across cultural populations between the item and other items. It is well known from the item bias literature that uniform bias is much more common than nonuniform bias. So, it may well be that exploratory factor analysis, followed by target rotations, is an adequate procedure to identify item bias when only structural equivalence is sought.

In the discussion of the metrical types of equivalence (measurement unit and full score equivalence), the distinction between uniform and nonuniform bias should again be taken into account. Uniform bias does not challenge measurement unit equivalence, because at this level of equivalence scores still cannot be directly compared across cultures; adding a constant to all scores in a single group does not affect this type of equivalence. However, uniform bias will affect the comparability of scores that show scalar equivalence. On the other hand, nonuniform bias will lead to both measurement and full score inequivalence because this type of bias destroys the identity of the measurement unit across groups.

Sample Bias

So far all forms of bias in this section are concerned with inequalities in the generalization of test scores to a universe or domain of behavior in different cultural populations. One form of bias has not been mentioned, namely sample bias, or incomparability of samples. This concerns inequalities in the representativeness of samples for the cultural populations from which they are drawn. For example, in many studies university students serve as subjects, but in some countries entry to the university depends primarily on school performance, whereas in other countries the socioeconomic status of the parents is the primary selection criterion. Thus, there are systematic differences between samples in relevant background characteristics that provide an alternative explanation for any observed test score difference, in addition to the cultural characteristics of the populations concerned. One instance that is well documented in the cross-cultural literature concerns the cognitive consequences of literacy. In many older studies of this kind, the comparison of literates and illiterates also amounted to a comparison of schooled and unschooled persons, because schooling and literacy are confounded (one learns reading and writing at school). Thus, the difference in schooling provides an alternative explanation to literacy in the explanation of differences. Scribner and Cole (1981) studied literacy among the Vai in Liberia and Berry and Bennett among the Cree in Canada (1991). In these groups literacy is transmitted through informal (i.e., nonschool) education. Interestingly, both studies found small cognitive consequences of literacy.

OPTIONS IN TRANSLATING/ADAPTING TESTS

It was argued before that linguistic and psychological criteria for good translations do not always converge. A word, sentence, or generally, any text in an assessment instrument is well translatable if a transformation of the source language text into a target language retains all features of the source text. In other words, a text is translatable if linguistic and psychological considerations agree on what the best translation is. Linguistic considerations will focus on equality of aspects such as semantic meaning (does a back translation yield the original?), comprehensibility, readability, and style. Psychological considerations will refer to the absence of various types of bias, described in the previous section, and hence, will involve the pragmatics of language. Whereas linguistic considerations focus on textual aspects, psychological considerations place the instrument in a broader cultural context. Depending on the translatability of an instrument, three options are available in translations (various chapters in Harkness, van de Vijver, & Mohler, 2003, deal with issues of translations and multilingual questionnaire design).

Application Option

The translation process is simple when a linguistically appropriate translation also turns out to be psychologically adequate. Such a translation will often be literal and will not entail major changes in wording. Van de Vijver and Leung (1997b) called this option *application,* because the source language version can be simply applied in another cultural context. It is highly likely that a study of translation methods reported in cross-cultural journals, such as the *Journal of Cross-Cultural Psychology,* would show that the majority of all comparisons reported are based on literal translations. This option is the most frequently chosen in empirical research for two reasons. Such a translation is simple to make, which makes it a cost-effective choice. Moreover, all possibilities of comparisons associated with scalar equivalence are fully retained. The application option has an important limitation: It can be used only when bias (in particular construct and method bias) is unlikely. It is regrettable that many cross-cultural studies use the "quick-and-dirty" method of literal translation, without any serious concern for the pitfalls of cross-cultural comparison.

Adaptation Option

The second option is labeled *adaptation*. In our terminology, adaptation amounts to the literal translation of some stimuli and to a change of others so as to maximize their cultural appropriateness in the target culture. Adaptation has become the generic term in the present book as well as in many other publications in psychology to refer to the translation of instruments. This is a deliberate choice, which emphasizes the possible shortcomings of literal translations and the need to at least examine the psychological appropriateness of these translations, if not change salient aspects of the instrument. Adaptations are needed for tests that show a moderate translatability: Some instrument features, such as instruction, examples, and exercises, may well be directly translatable in the target language, whereas, in particular the wording of items, may have to be changed. Such modifications will be required in order to deal with various forms of bias as already discussed. Examples can be found in the literature on the STAI (Laux, Glanzmann, Schaffner, & Spielberger, 1981; Spielberger et al., 1970). The Minnesota Multiphasic Personality Inventory (MMPI) has been adapted to many cultural settings (Butcher, 1996); for example, Lucio, Reyes-Lagunes, and Scott (1994) adapted this inventory for Mexico, and Cheung (1989; Cheung & Leung, 1998) for China. As another example, Liu et al. (1994) adapted the Cognitive Abilities Screening Instrument, an instrument developed in the United States, to diagnose dementia in a Chinese population with a low level of formal education. Authors of adapted instruments do not always aim at cross-cultural comparisons; they rather aim at an adequate coverage of a particular construct in a cultural group. The limited scope for cross-cultural comparison is then taken for granted (Guideline 12).

Assembly Option

The third and last option is called *assembly*. It applies when instruments are poorly translatable. If a literal translation of an instrument is seriously challenged for reasons of construct and/or method bias and an adaptation of the instrument would not provide an adequate coverage of the construct, a test author may decide to develop (assemble) an entirely new instrument in the target language. Serpell's (1993) study of the local conceptualization of intelligence of individuals in Zambia and the development of a test on the basis of this conceptualization is an example. Another example is Church's (1987) study of Filipino personality, which led him to formulate directions for the construction of a culturally more appropriate personality instrument. Also Cheung et al. (1996) can be mentioned; they developed the Chinese Personality Assessment Inventory, an instrument that contains several indigenous personality dimensions such as "face" and "harmony." In all these examples, researchers attempted to get an adequate representation of the psychological construct by deriving the instrument from local conceptualizations, which they had studied prior to the development of the instrument. From an equivalence perspective, the assembly option does not offer any scope for direct score comparisons. Yet, these studies are relevant to cross-cultural psychology by demonstrating that a Western conceptualization or instrument does not apply to some other cultural context. Such studies are effective in achieving one of the first aims of cross-cultural and cultural psychology: the identification of Western bias in current theories and instruments in mainstream psychology (Berry, Poortinga, Segall, & Dasen, 1992).

The appropriate choice for either application, adaptation, or assembly is important in any project, because of its implications. If the aim is to achieve metric equivalence (measurement unit or full score), application is the most obvious choice, though some statistical models also allow for such comparisons with adapted instruments. The application option assumes the absence of construct and method bias (item bias can be remedied post hoc by item elimination). At a time when there is much pressure on scientists to publish, the application option can too easily become the default choice, because it combines a low investment to produce a translation with the (implicit) promise of metric equivalence. From a cross-cultural perspective, this is regrettable, because such a practice can easily lead to the administration of culturally inappropriate instruments and false assessment of psychological differences between cultural populations (Poortinga, 1975). We fully agree with the underlying principle of various Guidelines (e.g., 2, 4–11, and 20) (Hambleton, 1994; van de Vijver & Hambleton, 1996; see also Hambleton, chap. 1, this volume), that it is the task of researchers to show the adequacy of their instruments. This recommendation deviates from current practice, in which the burden of proof is actually placed on the shoulders of the test users.

Instead of maximizing the suitability of an instrument for cross-cultural comparisons, it is also possible to maximize the ecological validity of an instrument. This is achieved by means of the assembly option, and to a lesser extent, by means of the adaptation option. It appears, in sum, that maximizing suitability either for cross-cultural comparisons or for ecological validity in a specific cultural context may well lead to a different approach in the translation/adaptation process.

VALIDITY ENHANCEMENT

To deal effectively with bias a proactive approach is needed. A plea for such an approach, as expressed in the previous sections, is incomplete without an overview of methods and procedures to identify and control, or even eliminate bias. The present section attempts to present such an overview. However, a caveat is needed; it is impossible to provide an exhaustive listing. Each new test adaptation project will run into bias issues that, at least to some extent, will be unique to that project. On the other hand, there are many recurrent topics. This discussion of methods and procedures is based on what we see as important, recurring themes.

When there is a suspicion of construct bias and behaviors associated with the construct are not identical across ethnic groups, it is impossible to devise any instrument that will yield comparable scores across cultural populations. It is important to establish the extent to which there is lack of overlap (Guideline 2). The statement that filial piety is higher (or lower) in China than, say, the United Kingdom, is misleading without reference to the incomplete coverage of the Chinese construct, if based on a Western instrument that leaves aside material aspects of filial piety. If the conclusion is based on the Chinese definition, the instrument is overinclusive in the UK.

There are least two ways to deal with the problem. First, the construct that is measured can be redefined in such a way that reference is made to over- or underinclusiveness. Instead of referring to a comparison of filial piety in general, we may describe our results in terms of material and nonmaterial aspects of filial piety. Second, special statistical techniques can be applied that can deal with dissimilar stimulus sets, such as item response theory (Fischer & Molenaar, 1995; Hambleton & Swaminathan, 1985; Hambleton, Swaminathan, & Rogers, 1991; van der Linden & Hambleton, 1997) or structural equation modeling (Bollen, 1989; Byrne, 1998; Marcoulides & Schumacker, 1996) (Guideline 11). The underlying principle is a dissection of a large universe in one or more cross-culturally common subdomains, while retaining within each cultural group the relationships with the culturally unique subdomains.

A method to avoid construct bias is decentering (Werner & Campbell, 1970). The concept is nowadays used in different ways. In the original meaning, decentering refers to the simultaneous development of an instrument in various languages. Unlike in most translation/adaptation projects in which an existing instrument is translated in a target language, a group of test developers with representatives of the various target cultures is formed. Construct definitions or instrument features, such as the instruction and items that are biased in favor of a particular cultural group, are likely to be signaled by test developers from other cultures. Words or sentences that refer to culture-specific knowledge or customs and threaten the translatability of the instrument, can be removed and replaced by more universally applicable references. Alternatively, researchers may decide that translation equivalence is not feasible and that an instrument allowing for more precise quantitative comparison is out of reach. Examples of this kind of approach are rare, presumably because of its laboriousness, and because researchers who have worked with an instrument before have an interest in the extension of their database. The recent introduction of e-mail and the Internet may provide a new impetus.

More recently, the concept of decentering has also been used in the translation of existing instruments. It amounts then to the removal of culture-specific items and replacement with culturally more appropriate stimulus materials. In the terminology of the present chapter, this would be the adaptation option. For example, Cortese and Smyth (1979) used this approach to produce a Spanish version of an English acculturation questionnaire.

Related to decentering is the so-called convergence approach (Campbell, 1986). Suppose that an American and a Zimbabwean psychologist are interested in skills that are considered relevant by parents to be developed in children and the age at which these skills are mastered (called parental ethnotheories; S. Harkness & Super, 1992). Both psychologists develop a scale, attuned to their own cultural context, and both instruments are administered in both countries. Both similarities and differences in the data are then of interest. We are not aware of any empirical example of this procedure.

After data have been collected in various groups, there are (retroactive) procedures to analyze equivalence. Some of these procedures address construct and method equivalence simultaneously. These are attractive because of their power and easy implementation. For example, local informants can be asked to judge the adequacy of the conceptualization and the appropriateness of instruments (Guideline 2). In particular, groups of bilinguals may generate useful information about the adequacy of an instrument (see Sireci, chap. 5, this volume). Similarly, local surveys in the target population can be held, in which free-response questions are asked (Guidelines 3–6). Also, the instrument can be administered in a target language in a nonstandard way, asking for explanations of answers. These explanations will show whether questions are interpreted in the way intended by the test author.

When an instrument has been substantially modified in the translation/adaptation process, it becomes important to demonstrate its construct validity in the target group. It is good practice to provide evidence that supports the construct validity of an instrument after its adaptation (Guideline 10 and 20). For example, Cheung (1989), who adapted the MMPI to China, examined the scale's ability to discriminate between normals and patients and computed profiles for different diagnostic groups. Both lines of evidence supported the construct validity. Applications of multitrait–multimethod matrices (Campbell & Fiske, 1959), a methodologically sophisticated means of addressing method bias in test adaptations, are hard to find.

More common is the application of confirmatory factor analysis (e.g., Taylor & Boeyens, 1991; Watkins, 1989; Windle, Iwawaki, & Lerner, 1988) and exploratory factor analysis, followed by target rotations (McCrae & Costa, 1997; Piedmont & Chae, 1997; Schmidt & Yeh, 1992; Vandenberg & Hakstian, 1978). A recent innovation in exploratory factor analysis is simultaneous components analysis (e.g., Kiers, 1990; Kiers & ten Berge, 1989). Unlike in exploratory factor analysis, all data are treated together. A single set of principal components are estimated for all groups. These principal components are by definition identical across groups; so, there is no need to evaluate the agreement as in exploratory factor analysis. The proportion of variance accounted for by the joint principal components is compared to principal component analysis of the separate data sets. An example can be found in Zuckerman, Kuhlman, Thornquist, and Kiers (1991).

All Administration Guidelines (13–18) and two of the Documentation Guidelines (19 and 22) can be seen as recommendations on how to minimize method bias. Effective ways to address method bias are the extensive training of test administrators (including some training in intercultural communication if tester and testee have a different ethnic background), and a detailed test manual with precise instructions. Even when these recommendations are carefully observed, method bias may still threaten the validity of cross-cultural comparisons. In particular when the cultural distance between source and target group is large, samples will differ so much in outcome-relevant characteristics, such as education, motivation, or response style, that the assessment of these characteristics becomes the only means of control. Statistical procedures, such as covariance analysis, can then be applied to examine to what extent observed cross-cultural score differences are due to sample background characteristics (Guideline 11).

One more class of procedures for the analysis of equivalence in data are test–retest or training studies that allow for the cross-cultural comparison of gain patterns. Differential gain patterns provide strong evidence for poor equivalence of scores. An example can be found in Nkaya, Huteau, and Bonnet (1994). These authors administered Raven's Standard Matrices three times to sixth graders in France and Congo. There was a moderate improvement from the first to the second and no further gain from the second to the third administration in both groups when no time limit was applied. However, under timed conditions, both groups showed a clear increase in scores from the first to the second, but only the Congolese pupils had a further increase from the second to the third session. Such a finding obviously challenges the comparability of the scores obtained in first test administration.

The final set of validity-enhancing techniques are those that address item bias (Guidelines 7, 8, and 9). Both judgmental and psychometric procedures are dealt with elsewhere in this book (see chaps. 1 and 4) and are not discussed here.

CONCLUSION

A suspicion of cultural bias, or empirical evidence to this effect, means that the instrument concerned cannot be taken as equally representative of the universe or construct of interest in the populations under study. The most conservative strategy is to argue that the presence of bias precludes all comparisons. In our opinion this is the (only) correct strategy when constructs are defined in a culture-specific manner. However, alternative strategies are possible when constructs show overlap across cultures and when bias is not due to the construct per se, but to the way in which it is operationalized in a specific instrument. In this chapter we have made various distinctions that can help to identify bias and the (negative) consequences for the cross-cultural equivalence of test scores, as well as approaches that help avoid these consequences. Cross-cultural test adaptation has a conceptual side as well a psychometric side. In this chapter we have emphasized the former. In the use of tests cross-culturally and the interpretation of differences in patterns of scores and score levels, there are serious pitfalls, but many of them can be avoided if test authors and test users are aware of them.

REFERENCES

Azuma, H., & Kashiwagi, K. (1987). Descriptors for an intelligent person: A Japanese study. *Japanese Psychological Research, 29,* 17–26.

Behling, O., & Law, K. S. (2000). *Translating questionnaires and other research instruments.* Thousand Oaks, CA: Sage.

Berry, J. W., & Bennett, J. A. (1991). Cree literacy. Cultural context and psychological consequences. *Cross-Cultural Psychology Monographs, no. 1.* Tilburg, Netherlands: Tilburg University Press.

Berry, J. W., Poortinga, Y. H., Segall, M. H., & Dasen, P. R. (1992). *Cross-cultural psychology. Research and applications.* Cambridge, England: Cambridge University Press.

Bollen, K. A. (1989). *Structural equations with latent variables.* New York: Wiley.

Bracken, B. A., & Barona, A. (1991). State of the art procedures for translating, validating and using psychoeducational tests in cross-cultural assessment. *School Psychology International, 12,* 119–132.

Brislin, R. W. (1980). Translation and content analysis of oral and written material. In H. C. Triandis & J. W. Berry (Eds.), *Handbook of cross-cultural psychology* (Vol. 1, pp. 389–444). Boston: Allyn & Bacon.

Brislin, R. W. (1986). The wording and translation of research instruments. In W. J. Lonner & J. W. Berry (Eds.), *Field methods in cross-cultural research* (pp. 137–164). Newbury Park, CA: Sage.

Butcher, J. N. (Ed.). (1996). *International adaptations of the MMPI–2: Research and clinical applications.* Minneapolis: University of Minnesota.

Byrne, B. M. (1998). *Structural equation modeling with LISREL, PRELIS, and SIMPLIS.* Mahwah, NJ: Lawrence Erlbaum Associates.

Byrne, B. M., Shavelson, R. J., & Muthén, B. (1989). Testing for the equivalence of factor covariance and mean structures: The issue of partial measurement invariance. *Psychological Bulletin, 105,* 456–466.

Campbell, D. T. (1986). Science's social system of validity-enhancing collective believe change and the problems of the social sciences. In D. W. Fiske & R. A. Shweder (Eds.), *Metatheory in social science* (pp. 108–135). Chicago: University of Chicago Press.

Campbell, D. T., & Fiske, D. W. (1959). Convergent and discriminant validation by the multitrait-multimethod matrix. *Psychological Bulletin, 56,* 81–105.

Cheung, F. M. (1989). A review on the clinical applications of the Chinese MMPI. *Psychological Assessment, 3,* 230–237.

Cheung, F. M., & Leung, K. (1998). Indigenous personality measures: Chinese examples. *Journal of Cross-Cultural Psychology, 29,* 233–248.
Cheung, F. M., Leung, K., Fan, R. M., Song, W. Z., Zhang, J. X., & Chang, J. P. (1996). Development of the Chinese Personality Assessment Inventory. *Journal of Cross-Cultural Psychology, 27,* 181–199.
Church, T. A. (1987). Personality research in a non-Western setting: The Philippines. *Psychological Bulletin, 102,* 272–292.
Clauser, B. E., & Mazor, K. M. (1998). Using statistical procedures to identify differentially functioning test items. *Educational Measurement: Issues and Practice, 17,* 31–44.
Cleary, T. A., & Hilton, T. L. (1968). An investigation of item bias. *Educational and Psychological Measurement, 28,* 61–75.
Cole, M. (1996). *Cultural psychology. A once and future discipline.* Cambridge, MA: Harvard University Press.
Cortese, M., & Smyth, P. (1979). A note on the translation to Spanish of a measure of acculturation. *Hispanic Journal of Behavioral Sciences, 1,* 65–68.
Cotter, P. R., Cohen, J., & Coulter, P. (1982). Race-of-interviewer effects in telephone interviews. *Public Opinion Quarterly, 46,* 278–284.
Cronbach, L. J., & Meehl, P. E. (1955). Construct validity in psychological tests. *Psychological Bulletin, 52,* 281–302.
Embretson, S. E. (1983). Construct validity: Construct representation versus nomothetic span. *Psychological Bulletin, 93,* 179–197.
Erickan, K. (2002). Disentangling sources of differential item functioning in multilanguage assessments. *International Journal of Testing, 2,* 199–215.
Fischer, G. H., & Molenaar, I. W. (Eds.). (1995). *Rasch models. Foundations, recent developments, and applications.* New York: Springer-Verlag.
Gass, S. M., & Varonis, E. M. (1991). Miscommunication in nonnative speaker discourse. In N. Coupland, H. Giles, & J. M. Wiemann (Eds.), *Miscommunication and problematic talk* (pp. 121–145). Newbury Park, CA: Sage.
Geisinger, K. F. (1994). Cross-cultural normative assessment: Translation and adaptation issues influencing the normative interpretation of assessment instruments. *Psychological Assessment, 6,* 304–312.
Greenfield, P. M. (1997a). Culture as process: Empirical methods for cultural psychology. In J. W. Berry, Y. H. Poortinga, & J. Pandey (Eds.), *Handbook of cross-cultural psychology* (2nd ed., Vol. 1, pp. 301–346). Boston: Allyn & Bacon.
Greenfield, P. M. (1997b). You can't take it with you: Why ability assessments don't cross cultures. *American Psychologist, 52,* 1115–1124.
Hambleton, R. K. (1994). Guidelines for adapting educational and psychological tests: A progress report. *European Journal of Psychological Assessment, 10,* 229–244.
Hambleton, R. K., & Swaminathan H. (1985). *Item response theory: Principles and applications.* Dordrecht, Netherlands: Kluwer.
Hambleton, R. K., Swaminathan, H., & Rogers, H. J. (1991). *Fundamentals of item response theory.* Newbury Park, CA: Sage.
Harkness, J. (1998). Cross-cultural survey equivalence [Special issue]. *ZUMA Nachrichten* (no. 3). Mannheim, Germany: Zentrum für Umfragen, Methoden und Analysen.

Harkness, J. A., van de Vijver, F. J. R., & Mohler, P. Ph. (Eds.). (2003). *Cross-cultural survey methods.* New York: Wiley.

Harkness, S., & Super, C. (1992). Parental ethnotheories in action. In I. E. Sigel, A. V. McGillicuddy-DeLisi, & J. J. Goodnow (Eds.), *Parental belief systems: The psychological consequences for children* (2nd ed., pp. 373–392). Hillsdale, NJ: Lawrence Erlbaum Associates.

Ho, D. Y. F. (1996). Filial piety and its psychological consequences. In M. H. Bond (Ed.), *Handbook of Chinese psychology* (pp. 155–165). Hong Kong: Oxford University Press.

Holland, P. W., & Thayer, D. T. (1988). Differential item performance and the Mantel–Haenszel procedure. In H. Wainer & H. I. Braun (Eds.), *Test validity* (pp. 129–145). Hillsdale, NJ: Lawrence Erlbaum Associates.

Holland, P. W., & Wainer, H. (Eds.). (1993). *Differential item functioning.* Hillsdale, NJ: Lawrence Erlbaum Associates.

Hui, C. H., & Triandis, H. C. (1989). Effects of culture and response format on extreme response style. *Journal of Cross-Cultural Psychology, 20,* 296–309.

Jensen, A. R. (1980). *Bias in mental testing.* New York: Free Press.

Kiers, H. A. L. (1990). *SCA: A program for simultaneous components analysis.* Groningen, Netherlands: IEC ProGamma.

Kiers, H. A. L., & ten Berge, J. M. F. (1989). Alternating least squares algorithms for simultaneous components analysis with equal component weight matrices for all populations. *Psychometrika, 54,* 467–473.

Laux, L., Glanzmann, P., Schaffner, P., & Spielberger, C. D. (1981). *Das State–Trait Angstinventar. Theoretische Grundlagen und Handanweisung* [The State–Trait Anxiety Inventory. Theoretical background and manual]. Weinheim, Germany: Beltz Test.

Little, T. D. (1997). Mean and covariance structures (MACS) analyses of cross-cultural data: Practical and theoretical issues. *Multivariate Behavioral Research, 32,* 53–76.

Liu, H. C., Chou, P., Lin, K. N., Wang, S. J., Fuh, J. L., Lin, H. C., Liu, C. Y., Wu, G. S., Larson, E. B., White, L. R., Graves, A. B., & Teng, E. L. (1994). Assessing cognitive abilities and dementia in a predominantly illiterate population of older individuals in Kinmen. *Psychological Medicine, 24,* 763–770.

Lucio, E., Reyes-Lagunes, I., & Scott, R. L. (1994). MMPI–2 for Mexico: Translation and adaptation. *Journal of Personality Assessment, 63,* 105–116.

Marcoulides, G. A., & Schumacker, R. E. (1996). *Advanced structural equation modeling: Issues and techniques.* Mahwah, NJ: Lawrence Erlbaum Associates.

McCrae, R. R., & Costa, P. T. (1997). Personality trait structure as a human universal. *American Psychologist, 52,* 509–516.

Mellenbergh, G. J. (1982). Contingency table models for assessing item bias. *Journal of Educational Statistics, 7,* 105–118.

Merenda, P. F. (1994). Cross-cultural testing: Borrowing from one culture and applying it to another. In L. L. Adler & U. P. Gielen (Eds.), *Cross-cultural topics in psychology* (pp. 53–58). Westport, CT: Praeger/Greenwood.

Miller, J. G. (1997). Theoretical issues in cultural psychology. In J. W. Berry, Y. H. Poortinga, & J. Pandey (Eds.), *Handbook of cross-cultural psychology* (2nd ed., Vol. 1, pp. 85–128). Boston: Allyn & Bacon.

Millsap, R. J., & Everson, H. T. (1993). Methodological review: Statistical approaches for assessing measurement bias. *Applied Psychological Measurement, 17,* 297–334.

Nkaya, H. N., Huteau, M, & Bonnet, J. (1994). Retest effect on cognitive performance on the Raven-38 Matrices in France and in the Congo. *Perceptual and Motor Skills, 78,* 503–510.

Piedmont, R. L., & Chae, J-H. (1997). Cross-cultural generalizability of the five-factor model of personality: Development and validation of the NEO PI-R for Koreans. *Journal of Cross-Cultural Psychology, 28,* 131–155.

Poortinga, Y. H. (1975). Limitations on intercultural comparison of psychological data. *Nederlands Tijdschrift voor de Psychologie, 30,* 23–39.

Poortinga, Y. H., & van der Flier, H. (1988). The meaning of item bias in ability tests. In S. H. Irvine & J. W. Berry (Eds.), *Human abilities in cultural context* (pp. 166–183). Cambridge, England: Cambridge University Press.

Reese, S. D., Danielson, W. A., Shoemaker, P. J., Chang, T., & Hsu, H.-L. (1986). Ethnicity-of-interviewer effects among Mexican-Americans and Anglos. *Public Opinion Quarterly, 50,* 563–572.

Schmidt, S. M., & Yeh, R. (1992). The structure of leader influence: A cross-national comparison. *Journal of Cross-Cultural Psychology, 23,* 251–264.

Scribner, S., & Cole, M. (1981). *The psychology of literacy.* Cambridge, MA: Harvard University Press.

Segall, M. H., Dasen, P. R., Berry, J. W., & Poortinga, Y. H. (1990). *Human behavior in global perspective. An introduction to cross-cultural psychology.* New York: Pergamon.

Serpell, R. (1979). How specific are perceptual skills? *British Journal of Psychology, 70,* 365–380.

Serpell, R. (1993). *The significance of schooling. Life-journeys in an African society.* Cambridge, England: Cambridge University Press.

Shepard, L., Camilli, G., & Averill, M. (1981). Comparison of six procedures for detecting test item bias using both internal and external ability criteria. *Journal of Educational Statistics, 6,* 317–375.

Singer, E., & Presser, S. (1989). The interviewer. In E. Singer & S. Presser (Eds.), *Survey research methods* (pp. 245–246). Chicago: University of Chicago Press.

Sinha, D. (1997). Indigenizing psychology. In J. W. Berry, Y. H. Poortinga, & J. Pandey (Eds.), *Handbook of cross-cultural psychology* (2nd ed., Vol. 1, pp. 131–169). Boston: Allyn & Bacon.

Sireci, S. G., & Allalouf, A. (2003). Appraising item equivalence across multiple languages and cultures. *Language Testing, 20*(2), 148–166.

Spielberger, C. D., Gorsuch, R. L., & Lushene, R. E. (1970). *Manual for the State–Trait Anxiety Inventory ("Self-Evaluation Questionnaire").* Palo Alto, CA: Consulting Psychologists Press.

Sternberg, R. J., Conway, B. E., Ketron, J. L., & Bernstein, M. (1981). People's conceptions of intelligence. *Journal of Personality and Social Psychology, 41,* 37–55.

Taylor, T. R., & Boeyens, J. C. (1991). The comparability of the scores of Blacks and Whites on the South African Personality Questionnaire: An exploratory study. *South African Journal of Psychology, 21,* 1–11.

Triandis, H. C. (1978). Some universals of social behavior. *Personality and Social Psychology Bulletin, 4,* 1–16.

Vallerand, R. J. (1989). Vers une methodologie de validation trans-culturelle de questionnaires psychologiques: Implications pour la recherche en langue française [Toward a methodology for the transcultural validation of psychological questionnaires: Implications for research in the French language]. *Canadian Psychology, 30,* 662–680.

van de Vijver, F. J. R. (2003). Test adaptation/translation methods. In R. Fernández-Ballesteros (Ed.), *Encyclopedia of psychological assessment* (pp. 960–964). Thousand Oaks, CA: Sage.

van de Vijver, F. J. R. & Hambleton, R. K. (1996). Translating tests: Some practical guidelines. *European Psychologist, 1,* 89–99.

van de Vijver, F. J. R., & Leung, K. (1997a). Methods and data analysis of comparative research. In J. W. Berry, Y. H. Poortinga, & J. Pandey (Eds.), *Handbook of cross-cultural psychology* (2nd ed., Vol. 1, pp. 257–300). Boston: Allyn & Bacon.

van de Vijver, F. J. R., & Leung, K. (1997b). *Methods and data analysis for cross-cultural research.* Newbury Park, CA: Sage.

van de Vijver, F. J. R., & Leung, K. (2000). Methodological issues in psychological research on culture. *Journal of Cross-Cultural Psychology, 31,* 33–51.

van de Vijver, F. J. R., & Poortinga, Y. H. (1997). Towards an integrated analysis of bias in cross-cultural assessment. *European Journal of Psychological Assessment, 13,* 29–37.

van de Vijver, F. J. R., & Tanzer, N. K. (1997). Bias and equivalence in cross-cultural assessment: An overview. *European Review of Applied Psychology, 47,* 263–280.

van der Linden, W. J., &. Hambleton, R. K. (Eds.). (1997). *Handbook of modern item response theory.* New York: Springer-Verlag.

Vandenberg, S. G., & Hakstian, A. R. (1978). Cultural influences on cognition: A reanalysis of Vernon's data. *International Journal of Psychology, 13,* 251–279.

Wagner, D. A. (1981). Culture and memory development. In H. C. Triandis & A. Heron (Eds.), *Handbook of cross-cultural psychology* (Vol. 4, pp. 187–232). Boston: Allyn & Bacon.

Watkins, D. (1989). The role of confirmatory factor analysis in cross-cultural research. *International Journal of Psychology, 24,* 685–701.

Werner, O., & Campbell, D. T. (1970). Translating, working through interpreters, and the problem of decentering. In R. Naroll & R. Cohen (Eds.), *A handbook of cultural anthropology* (pp. 398–419). New York: American Museum of Natural History.

Windle, M., Iwawaki, S., & Lerner, R. M. (1988). Cross-cultural comparability of temperament among Japanese and American preschool children. *International Journal of Psychology, 23,* 547–567.

Zuckerman, M., Kuhlman, D. M., Thornquist, M., & Kiers, H. A. L. (1991). Five (or three) robust questionnaire scale factors of personality without culture. *Personality and Individual Differences, 12,* 929–941.

3

Selected Ethical Issues Relevant to Test Adaptations

Thomas Oakland
University of Florida

Psychology is acquiring global dimensions (Mays, Rubin, Saboruin, & Walker, 1996; Rosenzweig, 1999). Its scholarship, once dependent mainly on contributions from persons in Western Europe and North America, is broadening to include research and other forms of scholarship from psychologists in many countries in Africa, Asia-Pacific, Eastern Europe, and South America. Furthermore, its practices and technology are growing in popularity in many countries that recognize psychology's potential contributions to important social goals (e.g., higher educational attainment, more effective and efficient industrial and managerial practices) and to resolving vexing social issues (e.g., mental illness, violence prevention, racial-ethnic understanding, population control).

The globalization of psychology may be seen most readily in the international use of tests and other forms of data collection instruments. Their use helps address various needs: to facilitate research, describe behavior, identify talent, certify attainment of knowledge and other abilities and skills, improve educational and vocational selection, diagnose disorders, and monitor change. These needs are universal and prompt decisions by many countries to develop or in other ways acquire testing technology to help address these needs.

EARLY TEST DEVELOPMENT

China was the first country to use tests in a broad fashion, having developed standardized methods to assess competencies relevant to the work of civil servants more than 3,000 years ago (Zhang, 1988). Test development and use in Europe and North America occurred following the birth of psychology in the latter part of the 19th century within Western Europe.

CURRENT STATUS OF TEST USE

Information on the degree to which tests are used in the more than 200 countries in the world is incomplete. Research on tests used with adults generally remains unpublished (e.g., Bartram & Coyne, 1998a) or discusses regional patterns (e.g., Bartram & Coyne, 1998b; Muniz, Prieto, Almeida, & Bartram, 1999). Research on tests used with children and youth internationally is more substantial, broad-based, and accessible (Hu & Oakland, 1991; Oakland & Hambleton, 1995; Oakland & Hu, 1991, 1992, 1993).

To date, some 455 test titles used to assess children and youth in one or more of the 44 countries surveyed have been identified. Tests used in many of these countries typically were developed in and acquired from the United States, England, or France. Some tests were translated into the target country's language; others were not. The availability of national norms together with estimates of reliability and validity were found less frequently in adapted tests than in those developed locally (Oakland & Hu, 1991).

Attempts to develop tests in each county often are thwarted by various conditions. These include the unavailability of specialists in test development, political and social orientations that diminish the relevance of individual difference and highlight egalitarian attitudes, and psychology's reliance on theory rather than empirical approaches. In addition, small populations in many countries together with a failure to honor copyright protection of tests reduce a legitimate financial return on investment associated with developing tests.

Adapted tests generally are used under one of the following three conditions: for use in countries other than those in which they are developed; for use in countries in which they have been developed yet adapted for use with persons who differ in language, culture, or other important qualities; and for use in two or more countries in which cross-national practices occur.

The first condition (i.e., adapting tests for use countries other than those in which they are developed) has been common. For example, Oakland and Hu (1993) found that many tests developed originally in the United States, England, and France were adapted for use in other countries (e.g., adapting a measure of intelligence developed in the United States for use in Kuwait).

The second condition is becoming more common (i.e., adapting tests for use within their country of origin to improve their validity) as immigrants flee their war-ravaged native lands, migration increases due to political and economic changes, traditional border divisions become erased by new political alliances (e.g., the European Union), and other conditions that facilitate the flow of persons within new political and geographic sectors. For example, the number of first languages spoken by students in some public school districts within the United States exceeds 150. Within the United States, schools are required by law to assess children in their dominant language when being considered for special classes. Thus, the availability of tests adapted for use with persons who rely on foreign languages may help school districts comply with laws as well as facilitate assessment.

Recognition that we live in a global and international society has sparked considerable interest in cross-national test-related activities, especially in industry and education. For example, multinational corporations have develop personnel employment practices that rely on adapted tests. In addition, given a desire to develop world-class educational programs, many countries are participating in international studies on mathematics, science, and reading achievement; these studies rely heavily on adapted tests. As noted later, various governmental, nongovernmantal, and multinational corporations rely on information from cross-national studies when forming policy and instituting practices. The quality of adapted tests used to gather data will impact the validity and thus the usefulness of this information.

ELEVEN IMPORTANT STAKE-HOLDERS

Eleven or more groups of persons are likely to be involved in or are impacted by the use of adapted tests (see Table 3.1). They include the following.

1. Test authors develop a test that later is adapted with their authorization. The test adaptation may be completed either with or without the authors' involvement and assistance. For example, the State-Trait Anxiety Inventory has been adapted into more than 60 languages and dialects. Its author, Dr. Charles Spielberger, has assisted in approximately 25% to 30% of these adaptations. He re-

TABLE 3.1
Eleven Categories of Persons Involved in Translating Tests or Using Them

1.	Test authors who develop a test that later is adapted with their authorization
2.	Test companies that publish and distribute tests that later are adapted with their authorization
3.	Test authors who develop a test that later is adapted without their or the publisher's authorization
4.	Professionals employed to develop tests for use in multiple languages and countries
5.	Professionals who assist in adapting tests
6.	Professionals who educate others on the use of test adaptation methods
7.	Persons or organizations that need test information to make decisions
8.	Professionals who select and use adapted tests to acquire information
9.	Third parties (e.g., managers) who make use of data from adapted tests
10.	Persons who are tested with adapted tests and decisions are made about them
11.	Consumers of information obtained from cross-national studies that utilize adapted tests.

ported (Spielberger, personal communication, September 15, 1999) that most adaptations were unauthorized.

2. Test companies publish and distribute tests that later are adapted with their authorization. The test translation may be completed either with or without the company's involvement and assistance. Two examples are provided.

Dr. Richard Woodcock, the principal author of the Woodcock-Johnson Psycho-educational Battery-Revised (WJ-R), and its publisher, Riverside Press, have authorized the adaptation of the WJ-R for use in the Czech and Slovak Republics, Hungary, and Latvia. They also are assisting in these adaptations. Harcourt Assessment, Inc.[1] has authorized 26

[1]Given the test author's demise, Harcourt Assessment, Inc., the publisher and distributor of the WISC, is responsible for authorizing this test's adaptations.

official adaptations of the three versions of the Wechsler Intelligence Scale for Children (WISC), the WISC, the WISC-R, and the WISC-III, and has granted permission to translate and use the WISC in additional languages on a case-by-case basis for use in specific studies only. Remaining copies are to be destroyed when the study is complete. Harcourt Assessment, Inc. typically does not assist in these adaptations (L. Murphy, personal communication, August, 1999).

3. Test authors develop a test that later is adapted without their authorization or those of the publisher. For example, the various editions of the WISC constitute the most frequently used individually administered measure of children's intelligence in the world (Oakland & Hu, 1992). Although Harcourt Assessment, Inc. has authorized 26 official WISC adaptations, its use has been documented in at least 34 countries. Thus, many unauthorized editions exist.

4. Professionals trained in test development are employed to develop tests for use in multiple languages and countries. For example, Microsoft's Certified Professional Program staff produces 45 or more tests yearly in 16 languages for use in 75 countries to help certify the competencies of millions of persons who use its produces (Fitzgerald & Ward, 1998).

5. Professionals assist in adapting tests. Their work may include translating a test's language, developing and revising items, and collecting data resulting in establishing new national norms, as well as the test's other psychometric features (e.g., reliability and validity estimates). This work may be self-initiated or occur at the request of another party (e.g., a test distributor in need of an adapted test).

6. Those who educate others on test adaptations methods also constitute an important component. They must ensure that the nature of students' academic and professional preparation is current and thorough.

7. Five consumer groups are impacted by the use of adapted tests. The first consists of persons or organizations that need test information to make decisions. Some examples follow. A Norwegian psychologist needs to assess the mental abilities of an adolescent from Central Africa. An Australian multinational corporations needs to hire additional middle managers in its Asia office. A university admissions committee in Canada needs to make a decision on an application from an aspiring graduate student from Central America. The European Union seeks to assure comparable professional standards for physicians throughout Europe by using a common measure of medical practice competence. These and other needs by persons or organizations may stimulate a need for an adapted test.

8. The second consumer group consists of professionals who select and use adapted tests to acquire information. Teachers, counselors, nurses, physicians, managers, psychologists, and various other professionals (Oakland & Hu, 1991) routinely administer and score tests as well as interpret and report their results to assist in decision-making.

9. Professional specialists in test use (i.e., 2nd Parties) often test persons (e.g., 1st Parties) to help others (i.e., 3rd Parties) make informed and valid decisions about the persons tested. For example, the ultimate recipients of test information may include various 3rd Party professionals (e.g., human resource personnel, managers, educators, physicians, and judges) who may request that one or more persons be tested. They constitute the third consumer group.

10. The fourth consumer group consists of persons tested with adapted tests after which decisions are made about them. The degree to which professionals display suitable ethical behaviors strongly impacts the validity of test-related decisions made about those who are tested.

11. Various governmental and nongovernmental agencies, multinational corporations, and other consumers of information obtained from cross-cultural or cross-national studies comprise the fifth consumer group. They rely on this information when forming policy and promoting practices. In addition, numerous behavioral scientists conduct cross-national research. The quality of adapted tests used to gather data will impact the validity and thus the usefulness of information they receive.

TEST GUIDELINES AND STANDARDS

General Guidelines and Standards

Efforts to promote suitable practices governing the development and use of adapted tests can be guided by guidelines and standards at two levels. The first tier includes documents that address broad and important issues that impact test development and use in three areas: those that address conceptual and technical dimensions of test development and use (e.g., *Standards for educational and psychological testing,* prepared by the American Educational Research Association, American Psychological Associations [APA], & National Council on Measurement in Education, 1999), those that identify the professional skills and abilities needed by those who use tests (e.g., British Psychological Society, 1998a, 1999: Eyde, Moreland, Robertson, Primoff, & Most, 1988; International Test Commission,

2000; Joint Committee on Testing Practices, 1988) and those that address ethical issues.

In reference to ethical issues associated with test development and use, some professional associations have well-defined ethics statements that address a broad range of issues (APA, 2002; British Psychological Society, 1998b). Only some of these issues focus on test development and use. Other codes and documents address testing issues more directly (e.g., Canadian Psychological Association, 1987; Joint Committee on Testing Practices, 1988; Kendall, Jenkinson, DeLemos, & Clancy, 1997; National Council on Measurement in Education, 1995; Koene, 1997; Lindsay, 1996). Efforts to promote sound testing practices with adapted measures will benefit from scholarship in these three areas.

Guidelines and Standards More Focused on Adapted Tests

In addition, a second tier of documents is needed, those that address issues more focused on test adaptations and their use. Again, documents are needed to address technical standards, professional skills and abilities, and ethics.

Technical Standards. Progress is being made in developing conceptual and technical recommendations to help guide test adaptations that have universal application (Hambleton, 1994; 2001; also see chap. 1, this volume). These guidelines are critical to establishing sound practices for adapting tests and determining the equivalency of scores on them. These and other technical recommendations are subject to continued revisions.

Professional Skills and Abilities. Guidelines or standards that discuss professional qualities of those who use adapted tests are not available. However, a number of features of the International Guidelines for Test Use (International Test Commission, 2000) and other sources (e.g., Joint Committee on Testing Practices, 1988; Eyde, et al., 1988) are applicable to test adaptations.

Ethics. Scholarly literature on ethical issues associated with the development and use of adapted tests could not be located. International standards or guidelines that address these issues do not exist. Thus, one currently must rely on other documents that address ethical issues more broadly.

For example, the International Guidelines for Test Use (Bartram, 2001; International Test Commission, 2000) discusses five broad and important ethical issues: (a) the need to act in a professional and ethical manner, (b) to ensure that those who use tests have desired competencies, (c) to be responsible for test use, (d) to ensure that test materials are secure, and (e) to ensure test results are confidential. Ethical statements from other associations (e.g., APA, 2002; British Psychological Society, 1998b; Joint Committee on Testing Practices, 1988; Kendall et al., 1997; National Council on Measurement in Education, 1995) also include provisions relevant to adapted tests and should be consulted.

PURPOSE OF THIS CHAPTER

Discussion of ethical issues more specific to translate tests may promote sound technical and professional practice in this emerging area. Thus, the main purpose of this chapter is to review selected ethical principles and standards from one well-established ethics code (i.e., the American Psychological Association's Ethical Principles of Psychologists and Code of Conduct, hereafter referred to as the Ethics Code; 2002) in light of various practices that may be associated with adapting tests and their use. The behaviors of the 11 previously described groups involved in adapting tests and using information from them are referenced in light of 25 ethical standards. Reference to the previously identified 11 groups is made in an effort to suggest those groups that may be most vulnerable to each of the 25 standards.

GENERAL ETHICAL PRINCIPLES

Codes that address ethical behaviors typically are based on general principles. For example, the general principle *to do no harm* may constitute the bedrock ethical principle that permeates all professional ethics codes (Koocher & Keith-Spiegel, 1998). The Ethics Code rests on five critical principles. They are paraphrased below and serve as a basis for understanding the 25 ethical standards that follow.

Beneficence and Nonmaleficence. Psychologists strive to benefit those with whom they work and whom they serve. They seek to safeguard the welfare and rights of those with whom they interact. They are alert to and guard against personal, financial, social, organizational, or political factors that may lead to misuse of their influence.

Fidelity and Responsibility. Psychologists establish and maintain relationships of trust with whom they work. They are aware of their professional and scientific responsibilities to society and to the specific communities in which they work. They uphold professional standards of conduct, clarify their professional roles and obligations, accept appropriate responsibility for their behavior, and seek to manage conflicts of interest that could lead to exploitation or harm.

Integrity. Psychologists seek to promote accuracy, honesty, and truthfulness in the science, teaching, and practice of psychology. They do not steal, cheat, or engage in fraud or subterfuge, or intentionally misrepresent facts. They strive to keep their promises and to avoid unwise or unclear commitments.

Justice. Psychologists recognize that fairness and justice entitle all persons to have access to and benefit from the contributions of psychology and to equal quality in the processes, procedures, and services being conducted by psychologists. Psychologists take precautions to ensure that their potential biases, boundaries of competence, and limitations of their expertise do not lead to or condone unjust practices.

Respect for People's Rights and Dignity. Psychologists respect the dignity and worth of all people, and the rights of individuals to privacy, confidentiality, and self-determination. Psychologists are aware of and, through their work, respect cultural, individual, and role differences, including those based on age, gender, gender identify, race, ethnicity, culture, national origin, religion, sexual orientation, disability, language, and socioeconomic status.

TWENTY-FIVE ETHICS STANDARDS

The following 25 standards are among the 89 standards that comprise the APA Ethics Code. In contrast to the five previously described principles that are unenforceable, standards describe behaviors members are expected to display and are enforceable; violations may lead to sanctions. Examples used herein are intended to identify possible areas of applications to practices associated with adapting tests and their use. Examples are not derived of incidence surveys and are not intended to be exhaustive of all potential issues and problems that may be associated with this work.

2.01 Boundaries of Competence

(a) Psychologists provide services, teach, and conduct research with populations and in areas only within the boundaries of their competence, based on their education, training, supervised experience, consultation, study, or professional experience.

Example. Persons assist in adapting tests, use them in applied work, and design tests often work in uncharted waters. Technical guidelines governing test translation are new and developing. Literature on this topic is sparse. Few university programs exist internationally to help prepare professionals in this important and specialized area. Thus, most knowledge specific to test adaptations and their use is self-acquired.

Self-acquired knowledge should be supported by formal education, training, and supervised experiences, when possible. Furthermore, work performed as a team, in which members nurture, advise, and supervise one another, may result in higher standards than when work is performed alone.

Knowledge of literature on methods to use when adapting tests, including guidelines for their adaptations (Hambleton, 1994, 2001; see also chap. 1, this volume), is indispensable to this work. Nevertheless, this literature is not widely known and thus not widely applied. Moreover, these guidelines are subject to revision as professionals develop both theory and technology to improve test adaptations (e.g., Hambleton, 2001).

Those who use adapted tests should be especially cautious given the recent and emerging nature of this field. Practitioner should not assume an adapted test is comparable to the parent test. Groups 1-9 (Table 3.1) may be most affected by this standard.

2.03 Maintaining Competence

Psychologists undertake ongoing efforts to develop and maintain their competence.

Example. Persons engaged in adapting tests and using them should devote a major part of their professional life to this work in order to become competent in its many complex features. Competence is likely to require facility with languages, developmental and cognitive psychology, individual differences, cultural and social anthropology, sociology, psychometrics and statistics, and knowledge of the settings in which the tests will be used. In addition, the maintenance and growth of knowledge and applications in any emerging field require an affiliation with area leaders and scholars, attendance at national and international conferences, and other fast-track methods to acquire state-of-the-art knowledge. Information provided through journals and books, although helpful, may be outdated by the time it is published. Groups 1-8 (Table 3.1) may be most affected by this standard.

2.04 Bases for Scientific and Professional Judgments

Psychologists' work is based upon established scientific and professional knowledge of the discipline.

Example. Many components important to the development of quality adapted tests and their use are well established, strong, and long-standing. For example, quantitative methods associated with test development, including those to establish norms and estimate reliability and validity, have a long tradition in Western psychology and constitute some of the strongest pillars of psychology (e.g., Anastasi & Urbina, 1997; Embretson & Hershberger, 1999; Haladyna, 1999; McDonald, 1999). Conceptual and theoretical advances in test development during the last two decades also contribute to our institutional strength (e.g., Byrne, 1998: Loehlin, 1998; Schumacker & Marcoulides, 1998). Thus, the basis for scientific judgments rests on a firm foundation.

In addition, professional judgment in using tests also finds support in a 100 year tradition of using tests to make practical decisions about individuals and groups, in the various graduate professional programs that prepare applied professionals to use tests, and in a rich scientific literature on test use (e.g., Sattler, 1988).

This knowledge provides a rich legacy. This knowledge base is vital to professionals involved in adapting tests. This knowledge is especially critical to the work of those who design and develop adapted tests and in other ways assist in their adaptation. This knowledge is less critical yet still helpful to those who use adapted tests as well as consumers of results from studies that rely on adapted tests. If asked, professionals should be able to refer to scientific and professional literature as a basis for their work. All groups (Table 3.1) may be affected by this standard.

2.01 Boundaries of Competence

(a) Where scientific or professional knowledge in the discipline of psychology establishes that an understanding of factors associated with age, gender, gender identity, race, ethnicity, culture, national origin, religion, sexual orientation, disability, language, or socioeconomic status is essential for effective implementation of their services or research, psychologists have or obtain the training, experience, consultation, or supervision necessary to ensure the competence of their services, or they make appropriate referrals....

Example. The study of individual differences in cognitive and other personal qualities gave rise to the discipline of psychology. Psychology remains committed to the study of individual differences. The study of individual differences often extends to the study of group differences. Research and practice in psychology have revealed that reliable and important differences in cognitive and other personal qualities exist as a function of age, gender, race, ethnicity, socioeconomic status, and other demographic qualities. These differences often are revealed through test data (Herrnstein & Murray, 1994; Jensen, 1980).

However, some do not accept these research findings and instead believe group differences are due to biased and invalid tests (e. g., Mercer, 1973; Oakland, 1977; Reynolds & Brown, 1984). The work of those engaged in adapting tests and using them occurs in social and cultural contexts. The views and attitudes of the general public often are strongly voiced, express important points, and should not be ignored.

Those engaged in adapting tests and using them should be sensitive to views and attitudes that tests are likely to be inherently invalid when used with different groups within one country and especially when used cross-nationally. Efforts to ensure that tests used with different groups have comparable validity and equilibrated scores are needed to overcome these negative expectations (Hambleton, 1994, 2001; see also chap. 1, this volume).

Adapted tests should be used only after demonstrating suitable psychometric qualities based on data acquired from the target populations. In addition, professionals who hold biased attitudes toward one or more groups (e.g., age, gender, race, ethnicity, socioeconomic status) that may affect their work take steps to overcome their biases or refer work to others who lack these biases. Groups 1–5 and 7–11 (Table 3.1) may be most affected by this standard.

1.01 Misuse of Psychologists' Work

If psychologists learn of misuse or misrepresentation of their work, they take reasonable steps to correct or minimize the misuse or misrepresentation.

Example. On occasion, professionals may be asked to engage in adapting tests or using them when the work seemingly has dubious merit. For example, although possessing knowledge that a sample is unrepresentative of the target population, professionals may be told to utilize an existing data set, perhaps even to duplicate subsamples, in an effort to acquire larger or more representative norms or to establish other psychometric qualities. Applied psychologists may be told to use an adapted test that lacks empirical validity and to describe it as comparable to one of the standard tests used in the industry. These conditions should be avoided.

An adapted test that appears to be valid, based on face validity standards, should not be used if technical evidence that supports its validity for use with the target group and for specific purposes is lacking. Psychologists do not engage in activities in which their abilities and skills are likely to be misused. Professionals are obligated to speak out when abuses and misuses occur and take reasonable steps to correct or minimize them. Groups 6, 8, and 9 (Table 3.1) may be most affected by this standard.

3.05 Multiple Relationships

(a) A multiple relationship occurs when a psychologist is in a professional role with a person and (1) at the same time is in another role with the same person, (2) at the same time is in a relationship with a person closely associated with or related to the person with whom the psychologist has the professional relationship, or (3) promises to enter into another relationship in the future with the person or a person closely associated with or related to the person.

A psychologist refrains from entering into a multiple relationship if the multiple relationship could reasonably be expected to impair the psychologist's objectivity, competence, or effectiveness in performing his or her functions as a psychologist, or otherwise risks exploitation or harm to the person with whom the professional relationship exists.

Multiple relationships that would not reasonably be expected to cause impairment or risk exploitation or harm are not unethical.

(b) If a psychologist finds that, due to unforeseen factors, a potentially harmful multiple relationship has arisen, the psychologist takes reasonable steps to resolve it with due regard for the best interests of the affected person and maximal compliance with the Ethics Code.

(c) When psychologists are required by law, institutional policy, or extraordinary circumstances to serve in more than one role in judicial or administrative proceedings, at the outset they clarify role expectations and the extent of confidentiality and thereafter as changes occur.

4.06 Consultations

When consulting with colleagues, (1) psychologists do not disclose confidential information that reasonably could lead to the identification of a client/patient, research participant, or other person or organization with whom they have a confidential relationship unless they have obtained the prior consent of the person or organization or the disclosure cannot be avoided, and (2) they disclose information only to the extent necessary to achieve the purposes of the consultation. (See also Standard 4.01, Maintaining Confidentiality.)

Example. Issues important to 3.05 and 4.06 are similar and thus are considered together. Those engaged in developing and adapting tests may acquire knowledge about a client-company that, if utilized outside of that setting, may be harmful. For example, a client-company (A) contracted with a test developer to adapt a test that is likely to negatively impact sales of a comparable test by its competitor (B). The test developer later is asked by company B to work on improving its test so as to maintain its market leadership. The test developer's proprietary knowledge, gained from working in company A, would greatly assist her or his work in company B. The aforementioned standard is designed to address this and other events that arise from consultation activities that may contribute to multiple relationships. Groups 1–5 (Table 3.1) may be most affected by these standards.

3.07 Third-Party Requests for Services

When psychologists agree to provide services to a person or entity at the request of a third party, psychologists attempt to clarify at the outset of the service the nature of the relationship with all individuals or organizations involved. This clarification includes the role of the psychologist (e.g., therapist, consultant, diagnostician, or expert witness), an identification of who is the client, the probable uses of the services provided or the information obtained, and the fact that there may be limits to confidentiality.

Example. A company (i.e., Party 3) may need information on an applicant or current employee (Party 1) and thus ask a psychologist and other assessment specialist (Party 2) to conduct the needed assessment. Party 2 should clarify the nature and priorities of their responsibilities and should know prior to initiating their assessment services the extent to which their findings can be communicated to party 1. Furthermore, Party 2 should communicate to Party 1 the manner in which the test findings may be used by Party 3 and whether Party 1 will receive the results of the tests, be able to challenge the findings, and be permitted to present additional evidence. Groups 7–10 (Table 3.1) may be most affected by this standard.

2.05 Delegation of Work to Others

Psychologists who delegate work to employees, supervisees, or research or teaching assistants or who use the services of others, such as interpreters, take reasonable steps to (1) avoid delegating such work to persons who have a multiple relationship with those being served that would likely lead to exploitation or loss of objectivity; (2) authorize only those responsibilities that such persons can be expected to perform competently on the basis of their education, training, or experience, either independently or with the level of supervision being provided; and (3) see that such persons perform these services competently.

Example. Persons responsible for adapting tests or providing assessment services that use such tests often delegate various technical tasks to subordinates. The tasks performed by subordinates may be technical, routine, and time-consuming yet nevertheless have an impact on the eventual quality of services rendered. Tasks are delegated to subordinates only when the subordinates are properly prepared to perform them and receive proper supervision. Groups 1–6 (Table 3.1) may be most affected by this standard.

6.01 Documentation of Professional and Scientific Work and Maintenance of Records

Psychologists create, and to the extent the records are under their control, maintain, disseminate, store, retain, and dispose of records and data relating to their professional and scientific work in order to (1) facilitate provision of services later by them or by other professionals, (2) allow for replication of research design and analyses, (3) meet institutional requirements, (4) ensure accuracy of billing and payments, and (5) ensure compliance with law. (See also Standard 4.01, Maintaining Confidentiality.)

6.02 Maintenance, Dissemination, and Disposal of Confidential Records of Professional and Scientific Work

(a) Psychologists maintain confidentiality in creating, storing, accessing, transferring, and disposing of records under their control, whether these are written, automated, or in any other medium.

(b) If confidential information concerning recipients of psychological services is entered into databases or systems of records available to persons whose access has not been consented to by the recipient, psychologists use coding or other techniques to avoid the inclusion of personal identifiers.

(c) Psychologists make plans in advance to facilitate the appropriate transfer and to protect the confidentiality of records and data in the event of psychologists' withdrawal from positions or practice.

Example. Issues described under 6.01 and 6.02 discuss somewhat similar issues and thus are considered together. The importance of providing documentation for one's work became very clear to the author while serving on panels that reviewed allegations of ethical misconduct of psychologists and attorneys. The inability to provide evidence supporting one's work often is seen as an absence of one's work. Failure to provide sufficient documentation is a leading cause of findings of ethical misconduct, even when such charges may be unwarranted.

Those involved in adapting tests are responsible for fully documenting their work so as to facilitate others' understanding and evaluation of this work. This documentation includes the conceptual and theoretical nature of the adaptation process, the project design, nature of the data acquired during this process, the data used to estimate a test's reliability and validity, names and credentials of the persons employed (including the translators), the amount of time devoted to one's work, and similar issues. Those who use adapted tests must be equally diligent in maintaining a record of their work.

Care is needed in the creation, maintenance, dissemination, storage, retention, and disposal of these records. One may be asked to display these data years later on issues currently unimaginable. The reputations of some eminent psychologists (e.g., Sir Cyrl Burt) have been tarnished after their demise and the credentials of many living professionals have been denigrated due to their failures in this important record-keeping area.

Adapted tests should be considered important professional resources and intellectual property that warrant security and thus proper maintenance of records ("Test Security", 1999). Such records include the results of those tested with adapted tests together with data that provide evidence of the adapted test's norms and other psychometric qualities. Groups 1–5 and 7–9 (Table 3.1) may be most affected by these standards.

9.05 Test Construction

Psychologists who develop tests and other assessment techniques use appropriate psychometric procedures and current scientific or professional knowledge for test design, standardization, validation, reduction or elimination of bias, and recommendations for use.

Example. Tests constitute technology that, prior to use, must meet minimum standards (e.g. American Educational Research Association, 1999). Adapted test also can be expected to meet these minimum standards. However, adapted tests may have psychometric characteristics that do not meet these standards. For example, normative data may be absent or unrepresentative. Estimates of reliability and validity acquired on the adapted test may be absent or meager.

Psychologists refrain from personally misusing assessment techniques and discourage others from doing so. The absence of needed data or evidence that an adapted test's psychometric qualities may be inadequate calls into question the usefulness and proper application of the test and thus its use. A test of this standard is met, in part, by the proper application of methods for adapting tests consistent with those advanced by Hambleton (1994, 2001; see also chap. 1, this volume). Current professional knowledge for designing, standardizing, validating, as well as identifying and minimizing bias always is subject to ongoing changes in light of new research and theory. Groups 1–5 (Table 3.1) may be most affected by this standard.

9.06 Interpreting Assessment Results

When interpreting assessment results, including automated interpretations, psychologists take into account the purpose of the assessment as well as the various test factors, test-taking abilities, and other characteristics of the person being assessed, such as situational, personal, linguistic, and cultural differences, that might affect psychologists' judgments or reduce the accuracy of their interpretations. They indicate any significant limitations of their interpretations.

Example. The saying, "A workman is only as good as his tools" is applicable to the work of those who provide assessment services through the use of adapted tests. Assessment specialists who use an adapted test are familiar with its psychometric qualities. Knowledge of a test's validity in light of the intended purpose for which a test is being used is particularly critical in forming judgments as to the degree to which a test user may have confidence in making decisions based on a test's scores. In addition, the use of a test with a subgroups (e.g., those of a particular age, gender, or race) on whom psychometric data are absent may be inappropriate. Those who use adapted tests are expected to know the quality of their tools, to communicate this information accurately to others when requested, and to form judgments as to the applicability of these tools in light of research evidence. Groups 7 and 8 (Table 3.1) may be most affected by this standard.

9.07 Assessment by Unqualified Persons

Psychologists do not promote the use of psychological assessment techniques by unqualified persons, except when such use is conducted for training purposes with appropriate supervision.

Examples. Professional competencies of psychologists to use tests vary considerably both within and between countries (Oakland & Hu, 1991). One cannot expect all persons who use tests to be qualified to do so. Some examples follow.

Within the United States, many psychologists seek to strengthen their professional practice and thus their income by offering assessment services despite having little preparation in test use. Within Europe, professional and academic standards differ considerably from country to country. Psychologists in many European countries also may have little to no training in test use. The preparation of psychologists in many South American countries favors theoretical and qualitative aspects of psychology and provides little preparation in qualitative aspects, including assessment methods.

These and other conditions often result in psychologists being unqualified to use tests. Furthermore, a lack of knowledge of specific features of an adapted test they intend to use (e.g., its validity with a specific group) also diminishes their competence to make wise and informed judgments. Groups 7–9 (Table 3.1) may be most affected by this standard.

9.08 Obsolete Tests and Outdated Test Results

(a) Psychologists do not base their assessment or intervention decisions or recommendations on data or test results that are outdated for the current purpose.

(b) Psychologists do not base such decisions or recommendations on tests and measures that are obsolete and not useful for the current purpose.

Example. Measures of cognitive abilities (i.e., intelligence, academic aptitudes, achievement) often are renormed every decade to ensure their currency, given the belief that significant differences occur in these abilities during this period of time. Measures of temperament, personality, and self-concept generally are renormed less frequently, given the belief that significant time-related differences in these qualities do not occur as frequently. Adapted tests also are subject to revision so as to prevent their obsolescence and ensure their currency. Groups 1–5 and 6–8 (Table 3.1) may be most affected by this standard.

3.11 Psychological Services Delivered To or Through Organizations

(a) Psychologists delivering services to or through organizations provide information beforehand to clients and when appropriate those directly affected by the services about (1) the nature and objectives of the services, (2) the intended recipients, (3) which of the individuals are clients, (4) the relationship the psychologist will have with each person and the organization, (5) the probable uses of services provided and information obtained, (6) who will have access to the information, and (7) limits of confidentiality. As soon as feasible, they provide information about the results and conclusions of such services to appropriate persons.

(b) If psychologists will be precluded by law or by organizational roles from providing such information to particular individuals or groups, they so inform those individuals or groups at the outset of the service.

9.10 Explaining Assessment Results

Regardless of whether the scoring and interpretation are done by psychologists, by employees or assistants, or by automated or other outside services, psychologists take reasonable steps to ensure that explanations of results are given to the individual or designated representative unless the nature of the relationship precludes provision of an explanation of results (such as in some organizational consulting, preemployment or security screenings, and forensic evaluations), and this fact has been clearly explained to the person being assessed in advance.

Example. The preceding two standards address the need to be sensitive to communicating information to clients and others, and thus underscore the importance of language-related issues when testing and conveying test results. As noted later, failure to attend to language-related issues may attenuate a valid assessment of target qualities.

Language abilities rarely are assessed directly. Language typically is used as a vehicle of communication in order to test other personal qualities. One or more of the four language functions (e.g., reading, writing, listening, and speaking) typically are used to assess target qualities (e.g., vocational interests, intelligence, personality). Assurance that a person's language skills are sufficiently developed and do not attenuate the assessment of the target qualities should be provided (Cummins, 1984; Oakland, Bernal, Holley, Natalicio, Leas, & Richard, 1980).

Knowledge of two important language qualities often is needed when using adapted tests: language competence and, among those who use two or more languages, language dominance.

Language competence refers a person's abilities to understand what others say, to speak, to read, and to write. A person may display deficient, average, or above average abilities in one or more of these four language functions. Those who are deficient in one or more functions should not be tested using methods that assume adequate skills in deficit functions. Also, methods used to deliver services, including explanations of test results, should be consistent with the recipient's language competence.

Knowledge of language dominance is important when assessing persons who are able to use one or more of the four language functions in two or more languages. Dominance refers to whether a person's language skills are less developed, about the same, or more developed in one than other languages. One typically tests using the more dominant language. Those who display comparable dominance in two languages may need to be tested in both languages.

Persons facile in two or more languages generally code information in the language in which it was acquired. For example, personal and social qualities may have been acquired in one's native language whereas academic skills may be been acquired in one's second language. When this occurs, measures of personal and social qualities should be assessed using one's native language whereas measures of academic qualities should utilize the second language.

Test results should be communicated to clients through their most dominant language and in light of their competence in using their dominant language. Groups 7–10 (Table 3.1) may be most affected by these standards.

9.11. Maintaining Test Security

The term *test materials* refers to manuals, instruments, protocols, and test questions or stimuli and does not include *test data* as defined in Standard 9.04, Release of Test Data. Psychologists make reasonable efforts to maintain the integrity and security of test materials and other assessment techniques consistent with law and contractual obligations, and in a manner that permits adherence to this Ethics Code.

Example. Adapted tests should be considered important professional resources and intellectual property that warrant security. Their use is jeopardized by not restricting their sale and use to properly prepared professionals, allowing unqualified persons to review the test, photocopying test protocols and manuals, and in other ways allowing nonprofessionals access to the adapted test. Groups 1–5 and 7–10 (Table 3.1) may be most affected by this standard.

5.02 Statements by Others

(a) Psychologists who engage others to create or place public statements that promote their professional practice, products, or activities retain professional responsibility for such statements.

(b) Psychologists do not compensate employees of press, radio, television, or other communication media in return for publicity in a news item.

(c) A paid advertisement relating to psychologists' activities must be identified or clearly recognizable as such.

Example. Psychologists engaged in adapting tests are responsible for supervising the manner in which such tests are communicated to others. Statements that suggest an adapted test is equivalent to the parent scale, provides equivalent scores, and in other ways suggest their equality or validity must be supportable by credible scientific data. Testimonial evidence is insufficient. Psychologists take reasonable steps to correct misleading statements. Groups 1–5 and 7–9 (Table 3.1) may be most affected by this standard.

7.01 Design of Education and Training Programs

Psychologists responsible for education and training programs take reasonable steps to ensure that the programs are designed to provide the appropriate knowledge and proper experiences, and to meet the requirements for licensure, certification, or other goals for which claims are made by the program.

Example. Programs that prepare persons to translate tests need suitable resources. These resources include but are not limited to students and faculty with strong backgrounds in psychometric theory and practice (including test development), faculty knowledgeable in the theory and practice of test adaptations, needed hardware and software, together with practicum and internship experiences in which students learn to translate tests under close and able supervision. Program directors should work to ensure that needed resources are obtained. Furthermore, given anticipated changes in test translation theory and methods, efforts are needed to ensure the currency of the program's academic, professional, and practical dimensions. Group 6 (Table 3.1) is most affected by these standards.

8.02 Informed Consent to Research

(a) When obtaining informed consent is required, psychologists inform participants about (1) the purpose of the research, expected duration, and procedures; (2) their right to decline to participate and to withdraw from the research once participation has begun; (3) the foreseeable consequences of declining or withdrawing; (4) reasonably foreseeable factors that may be expected to influence their willingness to participate such as potential risks, discomfort, or adverse effects; (5) any prospective research benefits; (6) limits of confidentiality; (7) incentives for participation; and (8) whom to contact for questions about the research and research participants' rights. They provide opportunity for the prospective participants to ask questions and receive answers.

Example. A subtle and important change occurred when the APA Publication Manual: Fourth Edition (1994) required publications to refer to those with whom psychologists conduct research as *participants,* not *subjects*. The term *participants* acknowledges greater respect for the rights of those from whom test data are acquired. When participating in data collection for adapted tests, participants should be informed of the purposes of the tests, that participation is voluntary, and that they will experience no adverse consequences if they choose not to participate. They also should be informed of possible benefits, risks, and limits of confidentiality together with the name and address of persons to contact should they have questions or comments. Groups 1–5 and 7–11 (Table 3.1) may be most affected by this standard.

8.11 Plagiarism

Psychologists do not present portions of another's work or data as their own, even if the other work or data source is cited occasionally.

Example. Plagiarism occurs commonly in test adaptation work (Oakland & Hu, 1991), especially when a test is adapted without the approval of its authors and publisher. Those who adapt a test by utilizing items from other tests without the approval of authors and publishers are likely to be violating ethical standards. This practice should not be condoned. Furthermore, this practice may violate laws in those countries that provide copyright protection to intellectual property. As noted in the next section, professionals should acquire additional information about suspected practices and, if needed, take steps to discontinue them. Groups 4–8 (Table 3.1) may be most affected by this standard.

1.03 Conflicts Between Ethics and Organizational Demands

If the demands of an organization with which psychologists are affiliated or for whom they are working conflict with this Ethics Code, psychologists clarify the nature of the conflict, make known their commitment to the Ethics Code, and to the extent feasible, resolve the conflict in a way that permits adherence to the Ethics Code.

Example. Psychologists frequently work in settings that do not adhere to formally adopted ethics codes. For example, they may be employed by an organization that believes it must have a particular test adapted for an intended use by a near-by date. However, the data from the adapted test may not warrant its intended use. Nevertheless, directors within the organization may believe some test is better than no test and decide to use the adapted test. This decision poses an ethical dilemma for psychologists. They are encouraged to seek to resolve this dilemma in ways that permit the adherence of an ethics code. All groups (Table 3.1) may be affected by this standard.

1.04 Informal Resolution of Ethical Violations

When psychologists believe that there may have been an ethical violation by another psychologist, they attempt to resolve the issue by bringing it to the attention of that individual, if an informal resolution appears appropriate and the intervention does not violate any confidentiality rights that may be involved.

Example. A professional who suspects that test translation practices may violate ethical or legal standards first should consult with those involved in test adaptation work to ascertain whether violations are occurring. If they are, the professional should take steps to discontinue the use of the translated test personally and by the profession. As noted later in Standard 1.05, efforts to educate and, if warranted, sanction those who violate ethical standards should be considered. Groups 1–5 and 7–9 (Table 3.1) may be most affected by this standard.

1.05 Reporting Ethical Violations

If an apparent ethical violation has substantially harmed or is likely to substantially harm a person or organization and is not appropriate for informal resolution ... or is not resolved properly in that fashion, psychologists take further action appropriate to the situation. Such action might include referral to state or national committees on professional ethics, to state licensing boards, or to the appropriate institutional authorities. This standard does not apply when an intervention would violate confidentiality rights or when psychologists have been retained to review the work of another psychologist whose professional conduct is in question.

Example. The adjudication of alleged ethical violations requires the accused person to belong to a professional association that (a) has an established code of ethics that details standards relevant to the alleged violation and (b) provides an operational system of review and enforcement. Upon finding an unethical behavior, possible outcomes may range from letters of warning to removal of one's license to practice and expulsion from membership in the association. Civil legal action also may be initiated. All groups (Table 3.1) may be affected by this standard.

A FINAL NOTE

This volume discusses various issues important to adapting tests and their use. This chapter reviewed six ethical principles and 25 standards from APA'S Ethical Principles of Psychology and Code of Conduct (2002) in light of various practices that may be associated with adapting tests and their use.

Ethical issues form one of the important cornerstones of professional practice, including that associated with adapting tests and using them. Thus, further discussion of ethical issues associated with the important work in this area seems warranted.

Further discussions at conferences, in journals, and in other forums may shed light on a need to further promote knowledge and application of ethical issues that impact test development and use, including that associated with adapted tests. In addition, discussions should consider a need to develop an ethics code that transcends national boundaries and addresses broad and prevailing issues important to testing practices. Research that identifies important and prevailing behaviors that either may pose ethical dilemmas or clearly violate ethical behavior is warranted before developing a behavior-based ethics code.

The profession is fortunate to have various forms of scholarship that discuss ethics. These include the following: American Psychological Association. (2002), British Psychological Society (1998a, 1998b), British Psychological Society Steering Committee on Test Standards (1999), Canadian Psychological Association (1987), Eyde et al. (1988), International Test Commission (2000), Joint Committee on Testing Practices (1988), Kendall et al. (1997), Koene, (1997), Koocher and Keith-Spiegel (1998), Lindsay (1996), and the National Council on Measurement in Education (1995). Further efforts to examine ethics issues can use these and other existing resources as a springboard for this work.

AUTHOR'S NOTES

Thomas Oakland is University of Florida Research Foundation Professor, past president of the International Test Commission, past president of the International School Psychology Associations, and President of the International Foundation for Children's Education.

Appreciation is expressed to Drs. Ronald Hambleton and Fons van de Vijver for their constructive comments on an earlier draft of this manuscript.

REFERENCES

American Educational Research Association, American Psychological Association, & National Council on Measurement in Education. (1999). *Standards for educational and psychological testing.* Washington DC: American Educational Research Association.

American Psychological Association. (1994). *Publication manual of the American Psychological Association: Fourth Edition.* Washington, DC: Author

American Psychological Association. (2002). Ethical principles of psychology and code of conduct. *American psychologist, 57,* 1060–1073.

Anastasi, N., & Urbina, S. (1997). *Psychological Testing: Seventh Edition.* Upper Saddle River, NJ: Prentice Hall.

Bartram, D., & Coyne, I. (1998a). *The ITC/EFPPA survey of testing and test use in countries world-wide.* Technical report for the ITC Council.

Bartram, D., & Coyne, I. (1998b). *The ITC/EFPPA survey of testing and test use in countries within Europe.* Technical report for the EFPPA Task Force.

British Psychological Society. (1998a). *Certificate and register of competence in occupational testing general information pack (Level A).* Leicester, England: Author.

British Psychological Society (1998b). *Code of conduct, ethical principles and guidelines.* Leicester, England: Author.

British Psychological Society. (1999). *Certificate and register of competence in occupational testing general information pack (Level B).* Leicester, England: Author.

British Psychological Society Steering Committee on Test Standards. (1999). *Checklist of competencies in educational testing: Foundation level.* Leicester, England: Author

Byrne, B. (1998). *Structural equation modeling with Lisrel, Prelis, and Simplis.* Mahwah, NJ: Lawrence Erlbaum Associates.

Canadian Psychological Association. (1987). *Guidelines for educational and psychological testing.* Ottawa: Author.

Cummins, J. (1984). *Bilingualism and special education: Issues in assessment and pedagogy.* Clevedon, Avon, England: Multilingual Matters Ltd.

Embretson, S., & Hershberger, S. (1999). *The new rules of measurement.* Mahwah, NJ: Lawrence Erlbaum Associates.

Eyde, L. D., Moreland, K. L., Robertson, G. J., Primoff, E. S., & Most, R. B. (1988). *Test user qualifications: A data-based approach to promoting good test use. Issues in Scientific Psychology.* Washington, DC: American Psychological Association.

Fitzgerald, C., & Ward, P. (1998). *Computer-based testing: A Global perspective.* An address to the meeting of the International Congress of Applied Psychology, San Francisco, CA.

Haladyna, T. (1999). *Developing and validating multiple-choice test items.* Mahwah, NJ: Lawrence Erlbaum Associates.

Hambleton, R. K. (1994). Guidelines for adapting educational and psychological tests: A progress report. *European Journal of Psychological Assessment, 10,* 229–244.

Hambleton, R. (2001). The next generation of ITC test translation and adaptation guidelines. *European Journal of Psychological Assessment, 17*(3), 164–172.

Herrnstein, D. J., & Murray, C. (1994). *The Bell curve.* New York: The Free Press.

Hu, S., & Oakland, T. (1991). Global and regional perspectives on testing children and youth: An international survey. *International Journal of Psychology, 26*(3), 329–344.

International Test Commission (2000). *International guidelines for test-use.* Punta Gorda, Florida: Author

Jensen, A. (1980). *Bias in mental testing.* New York: The Free Press.

Joint Committee on Testing Practices. (1988). *Code of fair testing practices in education.* Washington DC: American Psychological Association.

Kendall, I., Jenkinson, J., De Lemos, M., & Clancy, D. (1997). *Supplement to guidelines for the use of psychological tests.* Melbourne: Australian Psychological Society.

Koene, C. J. (1997). Tests and professional ethics and values in European psychologists. *European Journal of Psychological Assessment, 13,* 219–228.

Koocher, G. P., & Keith-Spiegel, P. (1998). *Ethics in psychology* (2nd ed.). New York: Oxford University Press.

Lindsay, G. (1996). Psychology as an ethical discipline and profession. *European Psychologist, 1,* 79–88.

Loehlin, J. (1998). *Latent variable models.* Mahwah, NJ: Lawrence Erlbaum Associates.

Mays, V., Rubin, J., Saboruin, M., & Walker, L. (1996). Moving toward a global psychology. *American Psychologist, 51,* 485–487.

McDonald, R. (1999). *Test theory.* Mahwah, NJ: Lawrence Erlbaum Associates.

Mercer, J. (1973). *Labeling the mentally retarded.* Los Angeles: University of California Press.

Muniz, J., Prieto, G., Almeida, L., & Bartram, D. (1999). Test use in Spain, Portugal, and Latin American countries. *European Journal of Psychological Assessment, 15,* 151–157.

National Council on Measurement in Education. (1995). *Code of professional responsibilities in educational measurement.* Washington, DC: Author.

Oakland, T. (Ed.). (1977). *Psychological and educational assessment of minority children.* Larchmont, NY: Brunner-Mazel.

Oakland, T., Bernal, E., Holley, F., Natalicio, D., Leas, R., & Richard, L. (1980). Assessing students with limited English speaking abilities. *Texas Outlook, 64,* 32–33.

Oakland, T., & Hambleton, R. (Eds.). (1995). *International perspectives on assessment of academic achievement.* Norwell, MA: Kluwer Academic.

Oakland, T., & Hu, S. (1991). Professionals who administer tests with children and youth: An international survey. *Journal of Psychoeducational Assessment, 9*(2), 108–120.

Oakland, T., & Hu, S. (1992). The top ten tests used with children and youth worldwide. *Bulletin of the International Test Commission,* 99–120.

Oakland, T., & Hu, S. (1993). International perspectives on tests used with children and youth. *Journal of School Psychology, 31,* 501–517.

Reynolds, C., & Brown, R. T. (1984). *Perspectives on bias in mental testing.* New York: Plenum.

Rosenzweig, M. (1999). Continuity and change in the development of psychology around the world. *American Psychologist, 54,* 252–259.

Sattler, J. (1988). *Assessment of children: Cognitive applications.* San Diego: Author.

Schumacker, R., & Marcoulides, G. (1998). *Interaction and nonlinear effects in structural equation modeling.* Mahwah, NJ: Lawrence Erlbaum Associates.

Standards for educational and psychological testing. (1999). Washington DC: American Educational Research Association.

Test security: Protecting the integrity of tests. [Editorial]. (1999). *American Psychologist, 54,* 1078.

Zhang, H. (1988). Psychological measurement in China. *International Journal of Psychology, 23,* 101–117.

4

Statistical Methods for Identifying Flaws in the Test Adaptation Process

Stephen G. Sireci
University of Massachusetts at Amherst

Liane Patsula
Educational Testing Service

Ronald K. Hambleton
University of Massachusetts at Amherst

In conducting cross-cultural research, it is imperative that researchers examine the assessment instruments they are using for any problematic translations/adaptations.[1] In particular, when there is interest in comparing test results obtained from different cultures, researchers should investigate the assessment instruments they are using for construct, method, and item bias (see, e.g., van de Vijver &

[1]In cross-lingual assessment, the term *adaptation* is considered preferable to *translation* because the former term does not imply a literal word-to-word translation. The test adaptation process is typically more flexible, allowing for more complex word substitutions so that the intended meaning is retained across languages, even though the translation is not completely literal (Geisinger, 1994). In this chapter, we use the two terms interchangeably, because many readers new to this area may be unfamiliar with what we mean by *adaptation*.

Leung, 1997; van de Vijver & Tanzer, 1997). For if such biases exist and are not identified, comparative inferences across cultures will not be valid. For this reason, the *Standards for Educational and Psychological Testing* (American Educational Research Association, American Psychological Association, & National Council on Measurement in Education, 1999) and the *Guidelines for Adapting Educational and Psychological Tests* (see chap. 1, this volume) require cross-cultural researchers to provide evidence of the comparability of different language versions of an assessment when scores from the different versions are intended to be comparable.

Although there are both judgmental and statistical strategies to identify and address bias, this chapter focuses on statistical techniques for addressing construct, method, and item biases that may be present in cross-lingual assessments. This chapter, which expands on many of the ideas presented in chapter 2 by van de Vijver and Poortinga, is divided into three sections. The first section includes descriptions of statistical techniques to assess construct equivalence. The second section presents strategies to assess and address method bias. In the third section, classical and modern methods for identifying item bias are listed and discussed. Table 4.1 presents an overview of the methods and examples described in the chapter. This table follows the classification scheme provided in van de Vijver and Tanzer (1997), who partitioned common sources of bias in cross-cultural assessment into these three categories.

STATISTICAL TECHNIQUES TO ASSESS CONSTRUCT EQUIVALENCE

Cross-cultural researchers can use statistical techniques both before and after field-testing to evaluate the construct equivalence of their assessment instruments. Given that there are no test or item score data before field-testing, researchers are limited in the amount of information they can gather. Therefore, the majority of research on the construct equivalence of translated assessment instruments has been conducted on field-test or operational data.

Before Field-Testing

In the absence of item response data, the construct equivalence of different language versions of an assessment can be examined by gathering data from subject matter experts representing the different languages and cultures of interest. Similar to content validity studies conducted on educational tests, items on an assessment can be rated

TABLE 4.1
Source of Bias in Test Adaptations and Some Seminal References

Source of Bias	*Description*	*References*
Construct Bias	Construct not relevant in all cultures (conceptual equivalence); construct is not operationally defined consistently across cultures; measurement of the construct is not consistent across cultures	Hambleton (1993, 1994) Hui & Triandis (1985) Geisinger (1994) Reise, Widaman, & Pugh (1993) Sireci, Bastari, & Allalouf (1998) van de Vijver & Tanzer (1997)
Method Bias	Biases in test administration conditions; unfamiliarity of item formats in one or more cultures; differential response styles (e.g., social desirability); incomparability of samples (selection bias); interviewer effects (e.g. halo effects)	van de Vijver & Tanzer (1997)
Item Bias	Faulty translation; differential relevance of items across cultures; nuisance factors	Allalouf, Hambleton, & Sireci (1999) Angoff & Cook (1988) Budgell, Raju, & Quartetti (1995) Ellis (1995) Gierl, Rogers, & Klinger (1999) Hulin, Drasgow, & Komocar (1982) Sireci & Berberoglu (2000) Swaminathan & Rogers (1990)

according to one or more criteria to shed light on the construct measured. An innovative example of the use of subject matter experts to evaluate construct equivalence is the study conducted by Hui and Triandis (1985). In this study, small samples of judges from different cultures evaluated the "similarity in meaning of pairs of items to be used in an assessment" (p. 141). The authors used individual differences multidimensional scaling to discover the characteristics the judges used in making their similarity ratings. If the characteristics used to rate item similarity are consistent across judges, preliminary evidence of construct equivalence is provided. If judges from different cultures use different characteristics, this information can be used to modify one or both versions of the assessment.

The Hui and Triandis (1985) study illustrates one means of gathering cross-cultural data on an assessment before it is administered. Although there is little research in this area, other designs using content experts from different language backgrounds, or bilingual content experts, are also possible. For example, bilingual experts could be asked to rate the similarity in difficulty of items from an achievement test. This procedure may identify items that would later be flagged for bias if studies of differential item functioning (DIF) were conducted after the test was administered.

After Field-Testing

After field-testing, when examinee response data are available, there exist at least four statistical approaches for assessing construct equivalence across assessment instruments: exploratory factor analysis, confirmatory factor analysis, multidimensional scaling, and comparison of nomological networks. In this section, we briefly describe each approach.

Exploratory Factor Analysis. Exploratory factor analysis is one of the oldest and most popular methods for evaluating whether different language versions of a test measure the same construct. In fact, van de Vijver and Poortinga (1991) and Poortinga (1991) described factor analysis as the most frequently used statistical technique to assess whether a construct in one culture is found in the same form and frequency in another culture (e.g., Butcher & Garcia, 1978). The exploratory factor analysis approach involves factor analyzing item or test score data separately for each cultural group. The resulting factor loading matrices are then inspected visually for consistency across groups. Although this approach is intuitively appealing, comparing separate factor structures is difficult, and there are no commonly agreed upon rules for deciding when the structures can be considered equivalent. Therefore, statistical approaches, especially those that can simultaneously accommodate multiple groups, are preferable. Confirmatory factor analysis and weighted multidimensional scaling are two such approaches.

Confirmatory Factor Analysis. In confirmatory factor analysis (CFA) the structure of an assessment is hypothesized a priori and examinee data are used to evaluate the viability of the hypothesized structure (see, e.g., Byrne, 1998, 2001, 2003). The hypothesized structure is incorporated into a structural equation model and is constrained to be equal across all groups. A typical construct equivalence hypothesis tested using CFA is whether the factor loading matrix is equivalent across all groups. The structure of the factor loading matrix is usually an "independent clusters structure" (McDonald, 1985), which specifies that: (a) each measured variable has a nonzero loading on only the factor it was designated to measure, (b) correlations among the factors (i.e., lower diagonal of the phi matrix) are freely estimated, and (c) the errors associated with the factor loadings (i.e., theta delta matrix) are uncorrelated (Marsh, 1994).

In the cross-lingual assessment arena, researchers have used CFA to evaluate whether the factor structure of an original version of an assessment is consistent across subsequent versions translated into another language (e.g., Brown & Marcoulides, 1996; Reise, Widaman, & Pugh, 1993; Robie & Ryan, 1996; Sireci, Bastari, & Allalouf, 1998). CFA is an attractive option for evaluating construct equivalence across adapted instruments because it can handle multiple groups simultaneously, statistical tests of model fit are available, and descriptive indices of model fit are provided. When an assessment comprises items that are scored dichotomously, CFA may be problematic because the underlying models are linear and the relationships among dichotomous items are often nonlinear (McDonald, 1982). However, this limitation may be overcome by grouping items together into parcels before the analysis. An example of using CFA to evaluate the construct equivalence of different language versions of a test is provided in a subsequent section.

Multidimensional Scaling. Multidimensional scaling (MDS) is another attractive approach for evaluating construct equivalence across different language versions of an assessment. Like exploratory factor analysis, MDS analysis does not require specifying test structure a priori. However, like CFA, the data from multiple groups can be analyzed simultaneously. Using an individual differences MDS analysis, such as the INDSCAL model (Carroll & Chang, 1970), a common structure can be fit simultaneously to all groups, and then structural differences across groups can be assessed by looking at the "group (subject) weights," which are used to modify the common structure to best fit the data for each group. MDS provides a means for discovering the dimensionality underlying examinees' response data, and for evaluating whether this dimensionality is consistent across all groups (or versions of the test) of interest. Another attractive feature of MDS is that it does not require a linear model to derive the structure underlying the data.

Example of CFA and MDS Analysis of Construct Equivalence. Sireci, Bastari, and Allalouf (1998) used CFA and MDS to evaluate the construct equivalence of items from the verbal reasoning section of the *Psychometric Entrance Test* (PET), which is a test used by colleges and universities in Israel for making admissions decisions (Beller, 1994; see also chap. 12, this volume). Figure 4.1 presents a two-dimensional representation of the items derived using MDS. The items tended to be grouped together in the MDS space according to their content specifications (analogies, logic, reading comprehension, sentence completion). Of more interest is Fig. 4.2, which presents the group weights on these same dimensions. Data from two groups of examinees who took the Hebrew versions of the test and two groups who took the Russian version (sample sizes were about 1,300 for each group) were used in the analysis. As can be seen in Fig. 4.2, the group weights were very similar, which suggests similarity of structure (construct equivalence) across groups.

Sireci, Bastari, and Allalouf (1998) also used CFA to evaluate the construct equivalence of these two different versions of this test. Following the content specifications, they fit a four-factor model to the data for both groups. Four different CFA models were fit to the data. The first model constrained the four underlying factors to be com-

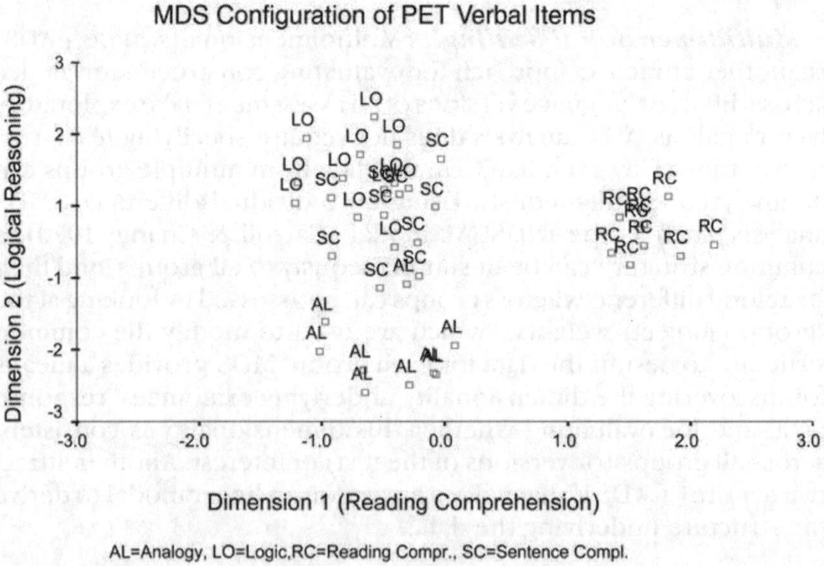

FIG. 4.1. MDS configuraton of PET verbal items. AL = analogy, LO = logic, RC = reading comprehension, SC = sentence completion.

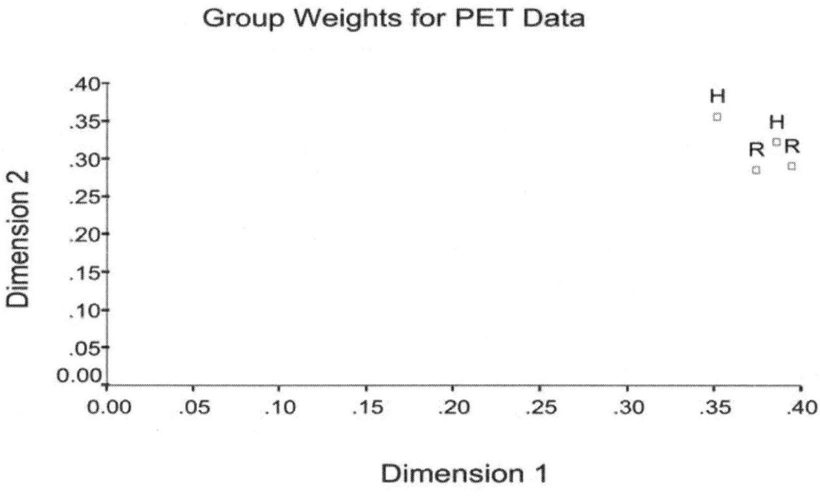

FIG. 4.2. Group weights for PET data. Note: H = Hebrew, R = Russian.

mon across the Hebrew and Russian groups, the second model constrained the factor loading matrix to be the same across groups, the third model constrained the errors associated with these factor loadings to be the same, and the fourth specified the correlations among the factors to be equivalent. The results of their analysis are summarized in Table 4.2. In all four models, the goodness of fit indices were high (.96 or above) and the root mean square residuals were low (.076 or below). Although these findings were consistent with the MDS analyses, using data from another assessment, they illustrated this is not always the case. They recommended using both MDS and CFA to evaluate the construct equivalence of different language versions of an assessment.

Comparison of Nomological Networks. Construct equivalence is a very general term that states the same psychological construct is measured across all studied groups, and it is measured with equal fidelity in all groups. Exploratory factor analysis, CFA, and MDS can provide important evidence regarding the consistency of test structure across different language versions of an assessment. However, equivalent structure does not necessarily imply equivalent constructs. Structural equivalence is a necessary, but insufficient condition for construct equivalence. Therefore, many researchers

TABLE 4.2
Summary of CFA Results for PET Data

Model	*GFI*[a]	*RMSR*[b]
Four-factor model common for all groups	.97	.057
Equivalent factor loadings for all groups	.96	.060
Equivalent errors of factor loadings for all groups	.96	.066
Equivalent correlations among factors	.96	.076

[a]GFI = goodness of fit index.
[b]RMSR = root mean square residual

have suggested going beyond studies of structural equivalence when evaluating the constructs measured by different language versions of an assessment (e.g., van de Vijver & Tanzer, 1997). These researchers suggest taking a more global approach that involves investigating the relationships among test scores and other variables hypothesized to be related to the construct measured.

In the same article where they introduced the term "construct validity," Cronbach and Meehl (1955) introduced the term "nomological network." They used this term to underscore the fact that a test cannot be validated using a single criterion. Rather, they argued test scores should be evaluated within a multivariate framework that considers all manifestations of the construct measured. With respect to cross-cultural assessment, the comparability of the interrelationships of test scores with other variables should be consistent across cultures, as well as across different language versions of an assessment, for construct equivalence to hold. Thus, comparison of nomological networks across test versions is a theoretically strict assessment of construct equivalence.

Comparing the relationships among test scores and multiple external criteria is a difficult task to do in a single language, and is further complicated when multiple cultural groups and test versions are involved. The identification and measurement of valid external variables are just two major problems to be overcome. Therefore, it is not surprising that comprehensive studies comparing nomological networks across cultures are difficult to find. However, cross-cultural researchers should examine the reliability of each cultural version of their assessment instruments and search for both convergent and discriminant validity evidence in each cultural group.

Summary

Exploratory factor analysis is still a common approach for assessing cross-cultural construct equivalence. However, contemporary test specialists are realizing the advantages of CFA and MDS for this purpose. The use of MDS to assess cross-cultural construct equivalence is growing in popularity as it can be used before and after field-testing, it makes no assumptions about the relationship among test items, does not require the structure to be specified a priori, and allows one to evaluate the dimensionality structure of a number of tests *simultaneously*. CFA is attractive in that it can be used to confirm a hypothesized structure and provides a framework for statistical testing of rival hypotheses regarding test structure. MDS and CFA provide important information regarding the consistency of test structure across different cultural groups and different language versions of a test. However, the relationships of test scores to other variables should be studied in all cultural groups of interest to more fully evaluate cross-cultural construct equivalence.

STATISTICAL STRATEGIES TO ADDRESS AND ASSESS METHOD BIAS

In addition to assessing construct bias, researchers must also assess method bias in cross-cultural assessment. Van de Vijver and Tanzer (1997) described method bias as coming from sources found in the method section of empirical studies. According to van de Vijver and Tanzer there are three types of method bias: sample, instrument, and administration bias. *Sample bias* refers to substantive differences across cultural or linguistic groups that are irrelevant to the construct measured (e.g., differences in motivation to do well, or socioeconomic status). *Instrument bias* refers to inconsistencies in the functioning of the measurement instrument across groups (e.g., differential familiarity with testing formats). *Administration bias* refers to administration problems, such as nonstandardized administration procedures (e.g., administrators in one group misunderstand testing instructions). In this section, we describe some procedures that can be used to assess method bias.

Addressing Sample Bias

If cultural groups are thought to differ on important variables irrelevant to the construct measured, comprehensive research designs and statistical analyses can be used to control for these "nuisance" variables. Analysis of covariance, randomized-block designs, and other statistical techniques (regression analysis, partial correlation, etc.) can be used to partial out the effects of unwanted sources of variation among the groups. However, such analyses require gathering data on these external variables and making sure the assumptions of the statistical procedures are met (e.g., homogeneity of regression).

Assessing Instrument and Administration Bias

There are at least three statistical strategies for assessing whether instrument and/or administration bias exists between the cultures under study: monotrait-multimethod studies, use of collateral information, and examination of change. In a monotrait-multimethod study (van de Vijver & Tanzer, 1997), multiple assessment procedures are used to measure the same trait across groups. If the group differences are not consistent across the different assessment methods, one or more of the assessments may be biased.

Collateral information can also be used to evaluate instrument or administration bias. This strategy involves analysis of a variable *related* to the construct of interest. If the differences noted across groups with respect to the collateral information are inconsistent with the differences noted with respect to test scores, instrument or administration bias may be present. One example of the use of collateral information to detect instrument and/or administration bias is the use of response time information, where the amount of time it takes examinees from different groups to answer an item is compared (Sireci, Foster, Olsen, & Robin, 1997). Contemporary assessments delivered by a computer make such comparisons easier to do than ever before. Using standard statistical tests or more complex structural equation modeling (Byrne, 2001), one can determine whether the response times are significantly different across cultures. If cross-cultural differences in response times are present, extending the time limits for some or all groups may be warranted.

A third strategy for detecting instrument and/or administration bias is to retest examinees within each culture (van de Vijver & Tanzer, 1997). Unexpected differences in test–retest change across cultures could reflect instrument or administration bias (e.g., Foorman, Yoshida, Swank, & Garson, 1989; van de Vijver, Daal, & van Zonneveld, 1986). For example, if there are greater gains in Culture A than Culture B, it could be an indication that Culture A was not as familiar with the testing format as was Culture B and thus did not perform as well on the pretest and received lower pretest scores. Such studies should be conducted if differential familiarity with the testing format is suspected. If such differential familiarity exists, each culture should have sufficient exposure to the test administration conditions and item formats before their scores are compared.

Summary

Assessing whether any method bias exists between different cultures is a step that is often overlooked in cross-cultural studies. Nevertheless, it is an important step. If method bias were present and it is not addressed, results from the study will be misleading. On the other hand, if method bias can be detected and addressed using statistical analyses or by familiarizing examinees with the assessment situation, one can move to the next step in evaluating the comparability of measurement instruments across cultures—assessing item equivalence.

STATISTICAL TECHNIQUES TO ASSESS ITEM BIAS

Before discussing techniques for assessing item bias, we first differentiate between three important, but distinct terms: *item impact, differential item functioning (DIF),* and *item bias*. Item impact refers to a significant group difference on an item, for example when one group has a higher proportion of examinees answering an item correctly than another group. Item impact may be due to true group differences in proficiency or due to item bias. Analyses of DIF attempt to sort out whether item impact is due to overall group differences in proficiency or due to item bias. To do this, examinees in two groups of interest are matched on the proficiency being measured. Examinees of equal proficiency who belong to different groups should respond similarly to a given test item. If they do not, the item is said to function differently across groups. Analyses of item impact and DIF are statistical in nature. Analyses of item bias, on the other hand, are essentially qualitative. An item is said to be biased against a certain group when examinees from that group perform more poorly on the item relative to examinees in the reference group who are of similar proficiency, *and the reason for the lower performance is irrelevant to the construct the test is intended to measure*. Therefore, for item bias to exist, a characteristic of the item that is unfair to one or more groups must be identified (e.g., a concept that is more familiar to examinees in one group than the other when the concept itself it not central to the skill being assessed). Thus, statistical techniques for identifying item bias seek to identify items that function differentially across examinees who belong to different groups, but are of equal proficiency. Once these items are identified, they are subjected to qualitative review to explain the observed differences.

When the explanation for the difference appears to be unrelated to the purpose of the testing, the item is labeled as "biased."

In this section, we describe several of the most popular methods that have been used for detecting bias in test items that are binary scored. More comprehensive discussions of DIF methods for analyzing binary data can be found in Camilli and Shepard (1994), Clauser and Mazor (1998), Holland and Wainer (1993), Millsap and Everson (1993), Potenza and Dorans (1995), and Sireci and Allalouf (2003). A list of DIF methods for analyzing test data is presented in Table 4.3. This table provides citations for each method and indicates the types

TABLE 4.3
Selected Methods for Detecting Differential Item Functioning

Method	*Sources*	*Appropriate for*	*Applications to Cross-Lingual Assessment*
Delta Plot	Angoff (1972, 1993)	Dichotomous data	Angoff & Modu (1973) Cook (1996) Muniz et al. (2001) Robin, Sireci, & Hambleton (2003)
Standardization	Dorans & Kulick (1986); Dorans & Holland (1993)	Dichotomous data	Sireci, Fitzgerald, & Xing (1998)
Mantel–Haenszel	Holland & Thayer (1988); Dorans & Holland (1993)	Dichotomous data	Allalouf et al. (1999) Budgell et al. (1995) Muniz et al. (2001)
Logistic Regression	Swaminathan & Rogers (1990)	Dichotomous data Polytomous data Multivariate matching	Allalouf et al. (1999) Gierl et al. (1999)
Lord's Chi-Square	Lord (1980)	Dichotomous data	Angoff & Cook (1988)
IRT Area	Raju (1988,1990)	Dichotomous data Polytomous data	Budgell et al. (1995)
IRT Likelihood Ratio	Thissen et al. (1988) Thissen et al. (1993)	Dichotomous data Polytomous data	Sireci & Berberoglu (2000)
SIBTEST	Shealy & Stout (1993)	Dichotomous data	

of data for which each method is appropriate. Readers are referred to Penfield and Lam (2000) for an extensive review of methods for conducting DIF studies of polytomous response data.

There are several applications of DIF methodology to the problem of evaluating translated/adapted items (e.g., Allalouf, Hambleton, & Sireci, 1999; Angoff & Cook, 1988; Budgell, Raju, & Quartetti, 1995; Sireci & Berberoglu, 2000). The methods selected for discussion in this chapter represent methods that have seen the most application in the test adaptations literature. The methods discussed are: delta plot, standardization, Mantel–Haenszel, and methods based on item response theory (IRT).

The Delta Plot Method

For test items that are binary scored (e.g., right/wrong), a simple scatter plot of the proportion correct statistics (*p* values) for each item is often informative as a preliminary check on the functioning of the items across languages or cultures. (In the case of binary responses to psychological items, *p* values become the proportion of persons agreeing with the item.) To create such a plot, the *p* values from one cultural group are portrayed on one axis, and the *p* values from another cultural group are portrayed on the other axis. Using these two axes, each item is represented as a point in this two-dimensional space. If the difficulties of the items are consistent across cultures, they will fall along a straight line with a 45-degree angle. Even with item difficulty consistency over cultural groups, some scatter about the straight line is expected because of sampling errors. If an item is much more difficult (or fewer persons agree with the statement, if the item is from a psychological test) in one culture than the other, the item will fall away from this straight line, and this item, and others like it, are studied further for potential bias. One criticism of producing a scatter plot of *p* values to evaluate DIF is lack of control of impact. Because *p* values are group dependent, it is difficult to make meaningful comparisons of *p* values across groups. For instance, *p* values obtained from a group of very capable persons would differ from *p* values obtained from a group of less capable persons. This difference may have nothing to do with bias. In a case like this, differences in *p* values would not necessarily be indicative of item nonequivalence across cultures. Most likely, they would be due the difference in proficiency between the groups, or to an interaction of item nonequivalence and group differences in proficiency. To address this problem, Angoff (1972, 1993) suggested plotting "item delta values" for each group, rather than item *p* values.

Because item *p* values are ordinal measurements, it is customary to assume that the item *p* values were obtained by respondents from normal ability distributions, and report the *p* values as normal deviates on a scale with mean = 13 and standard deviation of 4 (referred to as "ETS delta values" after the organization that pioneered their use in test development work). Thus, for a *p* value of (say) .50 the corresponding delta value would be 13. If the *p* value for an item were .84, the delta value would be 9.0, and for an item *p* value of .16, the delta value would be 17.0. Clearly, delta values for hard items have high values, and are low for easy items. It has become customary for a delta difference of 1.5 between two groups to be worthy of serious review, after any overall group difference has been taken into account (Holland & Wainer, 1993). When producing a scatter plot of delta values, the intercept of the (linear equating) line running through the scatter plot reflects the overall ability difference between the groups. Points on the delta plot that fall within a narrow ellipse reflect items that have approximately equal relative difficulty in both cultures. An example of a delta plot is presented in Fig. 4.3. This figure presents the delta values computed from respondents who took either the French (vertical axis) or English (horizontal axis) version of an international certification exam (from Muniz, Hambleton, & Xing, 2001). The fact that the linear equating line does not pass through the origin reflects the overall difference in proficiency between the two groups, which is .77 (in favor of the English examinees—that is, the respondents taking the exam in English performed a bit better) in this case. A confidence band is drawn around this linear equating line and items that fall outside this band are identified as DIF items. Those items that were identified for DIF using more sophisticated statistical procedures are also highlighted in the figure (for more details, see Muniz et al., 2001). In this case, the delta plot procedure flagged the same items.

The delta plot method for evaluating cross-cultural DIF is relatively easy to apply and the results are easy to interpret. However, it has been shown that delta plots overlook items that are potentially biased when they vary in their discriminating power (Dorans & Holland, 1993). For these reasons, the delta plot method is suggested as a preliminary check only, or in those situations where sample sizes prohibit more sophisticated statistical analyses. Muniz et al. (2001) demonstrated that the delta plot method was an effective method for identifying items that were functioning very differently across language groups, even when the sample sizes were as small as 50 persons per group. Delta plots have also been used effectively with large sample sizes (Angoff & Modu, 1973; Cook, 1996).

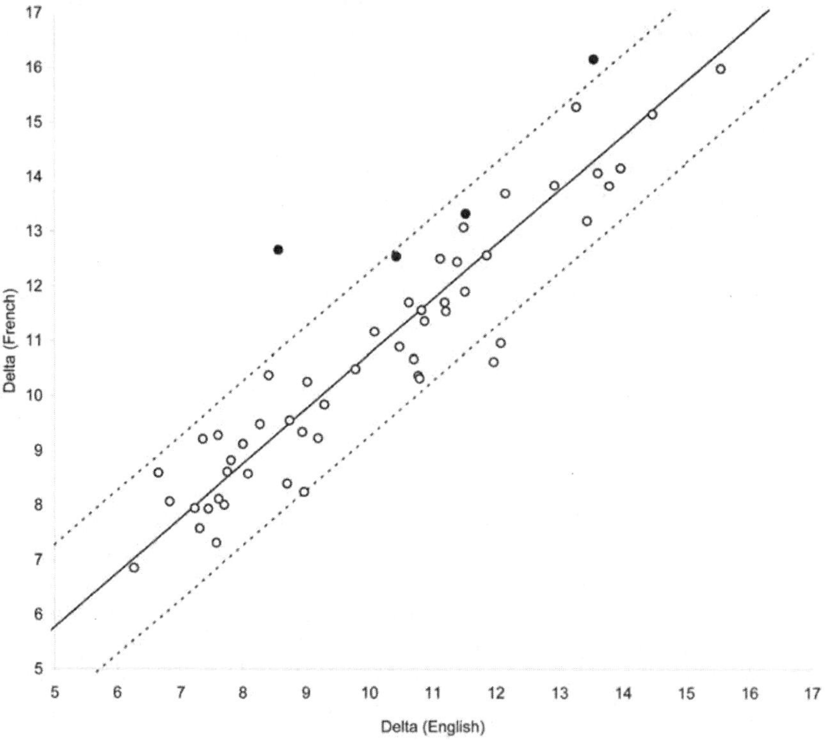

FIG. 4.3. Plot of English (N=2000) and French (N=1333) group delta values. (With mean difference .77 adjusted)

The Standardization Index

The standardization index for detecting DIF was proposed by Dorans and Kulick (1986). This method can be described as a "conditional *p* value" method, where separate *p* values are computed for each item conditional on total test score. For example, examinees who took different language versions of an item could be matched on total test score. The idea here is that there may be a few problematic items, but overall, matching examinees from the two language groups is a reasonable way to find equivalent groups of examinees. Then, for examinees with a given test score, the proportion of examinees who answered the item correctly is computed for each group and compared. If the item is without problem, the two groups of equivalent or near equivalent overall performance should perform about the same on the item. This process is repeated for all other levels of test score. In practice, test score intervals are typically computed to match examinees so that the sample sizes per test score interval are not too small (i.e., thick matching). To make the task of flagging DIF items easier, Dorans and Kulick proposed the standardization index, which describes the average over scores or intervals on the test score scale of the conditional *p* values for the two groups. With small samples, sometimes as few as five or six test score intervals are chosen. This index (STD-P) is computed as:

$$STD - P = \frac{\sum_m w_m \left(E_{fm} - E_{rm}\right)}{\sum_m w_m}$$

where w_m = the relative frequency of the focal group at score level m (or the proportion of the reference and focal groups at the score level, the researcher's choice), and E_{rm} and E_{fm} are the proportion of examinees at score level m who answered the item correctly in the reference and focal groups, respectively. The reference group could represent examinees who responded to the original version of an item, and the focal group could represent examinees who responded to the adapted version of the item. Sometimes too the weights might be chosen to correspond to the focal group, and other times, they might be chosen to represent the proportion of both reference and focal group at a score level. The choice of weights depends on the researcher's primary concern.

The standardization index ranges from -1.0 to 1.0. Although there is no statistical test associated with the statistic, an effect size can be computed. For example, a STD-P of .10 indicates that, on average, examinees in the reference group who are matched to examinees in the focal group exceed the performance of the focal group at each score interval by .10 on the proportion-correct scale. An STD-P value of .10 has been used as a criterion for flagging items for DIF (e.g., Sireci, Fitzgerald, & Xing, 1998). Using this criterion, if 10 items on a test were flagged for DIF, and they were all in favor of one of the two groups, the aggregate level of DIF on the test would be about 1 point on the total raw test score scale in favor of the reference group. Using real and simulated data, Muniz et al. (2001) also concluded the standardization index was effective for flagging adapted versions of items for DIF when sample sizes were small.

Mantel–Haenszel Method

The Mantel–Haenszel (MH) method for identifying DIF is similar to the standardization index in that examinees from two different groups are matched on the proficiency of interest and the likelihood of success on the item is compared across groups. The MH procedure is an extension of the chi-square test of independence (Mantel & Haenszel, 1959) to the situation where there are three levels of stratification. In the context of DIF, these levels are: examinee group (e.g., two language/cultural groups), matching variable interval (scores upon which examinees in different groups are matched), and item response (correct or incorrect). For each level of the matching variable (typically, total test score), a two-by-two table is formed that cross-tabulates examinee group by item performance. An attractive feature of MH is that a statistical test for DIF is provided In addition to providing a test for statistical significance, an effect size can also be computed and rules of thumb exist for classifying these effect sizes into small, medium, and large DIF (Dorans & Holland, 1993). Details regarding computation and interpretation of the MH statistic can be found in Holland and Thayer (1988) or Dorans and Holland (1993).

The delta plot, standardization, and MH methods are popular because they require only modest sample sizes and they do not require specialized statistical software for conducting the analysis. In addition, the MH method has been shown to be particularly powerful in detecting DIF. For this reason, it is often used as the standard for comparison in studies that compare DIF detection methods. One shortcoming of these methods is that they are not effective in identifying "nonuniform" DIF. Nonuniform DIF describes the situation where the probability of success on an item changes across groups at different points along the proficiency continuum. Methods based on IRT and logistic regression do not have these limitations. A second shortcoming is that these and other methods considering in this chapter are limited to binary data. Fortunately most of the methods have now been generalized to handle polytomous response data but those methods will not be discussed here (see, e.g., Penfield & Lam, 2000).

IRT Methods

There are several methods for detecting DIF with binary data that are based on IRT (see Hambleton, Swaminathan, & Rogers, 1991). Essentially, all of these methods evaluate whether a common set of item parameters can be used to describe the functioning of an item in each language/cultural group. If different parameters are needed to describe the functioning of the item in each group, then the item is flagged for DIF. One IRT DIF method is Lord's chi-square method, which tests for the equality of item discrimination and item difficulty parameters across groups (Lord, 1980). Angoff and Cook (1988) used this method to identify common items to be used to equate the Scholastic Aptitude Test (SAT) and the Prueba de Aptitud Academica (Spanish version of the SAT).

Another IRT-based DIF method is Raju's test of the area between two item characteristic curves (Raju, 1988, 1990). In this analysis, the characteristic curve (ICC) for an item is computed separately for each group. Next, the area between the two ICCs is tested for statistical significance. For data scored dichotomously, this method improved upon Lord's chi-square method in that differences in item performance due to guessing (i.e., the *c* parameter) could also be evaluated. Although this procedure has been used predominantly with dichotomously scored items, it could also be extended to the polytomous case.

Budgell et al. (1995) compared the DIF detection results for Lord's chi-square, Raju's signed and unsigned areas, and the MH procedures across numerical and reasoning tests that were originally developed in English and then adapted into French. They found a high degree of consistency across these methods in identifying items with significant DIF.

A third popular IRT-based method for detecting DIF is the likelihood ratio procedure (Thissen, Steinberg, & Wainer, 1988, 1993). Using this procedure, two IRT models are fit to examinee response data and the difference between the fit of these models to the data is evaluated for statistical significance. The first model fit to the data is a "no-DIF" model where the same item parameters are used to calibrate the item in each group. The second model fit to the data is a DIF model where separate parameters are used to calibrate the item in each group. That is, the no-DIF model treats the item as equivalent across groups, and the DIF model treats the item as a separate item in each group. Obviously, the DIF model is less parsimonious because it involves estimating more parameters to fit the data. To determine whether these extra parameters are necessary (i.e., are separate parameters needed to calibrate this item in each group?), the likelihoods associated with each model (i.e., likelihood of obtaining the data if the model were true) are compared. The difference between the likelihoods of each model is distributed as chi-square[2], and the degrees of

[2]Actually, it is the log of the likelihood that is distributed as chi-square and in practice –2 times the log of the likelihood is used to compare fit across the models.

freedom associated with this chi-square test are simply the difference in the number of parameters estimated by each model.

The IRT likelihood ratio test has been widely applied to the investigation of DIF across subgroups who take a test in a single language using both dichotomous and polytomous IRT models (Thissen, Steinberg, & Gerrard, 1986; Thissen et al., 1988; Wainer, 1995; Wainer, Sireci, & Thissen, 1991). Recently, there have been some applications of this technique to the problem of detecting flaws in item adaptations (Sireci & Berberoglu, 2000). Advantages of this method are its statistical power, flexibility in handling both dichotomous and polytomous data, and ability to simultaneously evaluate items in more than two groups. However, the procedure has one major drawback. It is extremely time consuming to apply. For each item, multiple IRT models must be fit to the data. When the assessment comprises a large number of items, and the no-DIF model is rejected, isolating the specific DIF items is an arduous process (Sireci & Berberoglu, 2000).

Summary

Statistical methods for investigating problematic items due to flawed language/cultural adaptation range from simple methods based on visual analysis, to complex methods based on modern measurement theory. The choice of a particular method depends on several factors including sample sizes, number of items composing the assessment, scoring of the items, and availability of statistical software. In those situations involving relatively small sample sizes and items that are scored dichotomously, the delta plot and standardization methods are recommended. As sample sizes increase, the MH and IRT methods may be preferable. In any case, it must be remembered that before conducting investigations of flaws at the item level, construct and method biases must be ruled out. All DIF detection methods assume the stratifying variable used to match examinees, be it total test score, a latent variable score (i.e, IRT score), or a variable external to the assessment, is valid for the purpose of matching. Any systematic bias in this variable will not be detected at the item level and will reduce the validity of DIF results. To avoid being in this situation, we recommend following careful adaptation procedures (e.g., the International Test Commission Test Adaptation Guidelines, see chap. 1, this volume, or Hambleton & Patsula, 1999) and performing statistical checks on construct and method bias.

CONCLUSIONS

Assessing and comparing individuals who function in different languages and cultures is challenging. Critiques of the literature in this area have pointed out many threats to the internal validity of cross-cultural studies such as construct bias, method bias, and item bias. In this chapter, we have outlined and described statistical methods researchers can use to evaluate these threats to the validity of their cross-cultural assessment instruments. In our experience, the results of such analyses can be used to modify subsequent instrument development, resulting in more valid assessment, and more valid comparisons across individuals who differ with respect to language and culture.

REFERENCES

Allalouf, A., Hambleton, R. K., & Sireci, S. G. (1999). Detecting the causes of differential item functioning in translated verbal items. *Journal of Educational Measurement, 36*(3), 185–198.

American Educational Research Association, American Psychological Association, & National Council on Measurement in Education. (1999). *Standards for educational and psychological testing.* Washington, DC: American Educational Research Association.

Angoff, W. H. (1972). Use of difficulty and discrimination indices for detecting item bias. In R. A. Berk (Ed.), *Handbook of methods for detecting test bias* (pp. 96–116). Baltimore: Johns Hopkins University Press.

Angoff, W. H. (1993). Perspectives on differential item functioning methodology. In P. W. Holland & H. Wainer (Eds.), *Differential item functioning* (pp. 96–116). Baltimore: Johns Hopkins University Press.

Angoff, W. H., & Cook, L. L. (1988). *Equating the scores of the Prueba de Aptitud Academica and the Scholastic Aptitude Test* (Rep. No. 88-2). New York: College Entrance Examination Board.

Angoff, W. H., & Modu, C. C. (1973). *Equating the scores of the Prueba de Aptitud Academica and the Scholastic Aptitude Test* (Research Rep. No. 3). New York: College Entrance Examination Board.

Beller, M. (1994). Psychometric and social issues in admissions to Israeli universities. *Educational Measurement: Issues and Practice, 13,* 12–21.

Brown, R., & Marcoulides, G. A. (1996). A cross-cultural comparison of the Brown Locus of Control Scale. *Educational and Psychological Measurement, 56,* 858–863.

Budgell, G., Raju, N., & Quartetti, D. (1995). Analysis of differential item functioning in translated assessment instruments. *Applied Psychological Measurement, 19,* 309–321.

Butcher, J. N., & Garcia, R. E. (1978). Cross-national application of psychological tests. *The Personnel and Guidance Journal, 56*(8), 472–475.

Byrne, B. (1998). *Structural equation modeling with LISREL, PRELIS, and SIMPLIS.* Mahwah, NJ: Lawrence Erlbaum Associates.

Byrne, B. (2001). Structural equation modeling with AMOS, EQS, and LISREL: Comparative approaches to testing for the factorial validity of a measuring instrument. *International Journal of Testing, 1,* 55–86.

Byrne, B. (2003). Confirmatory factor analysis. In R. Fernandez-Ballesteros (Ed.), *Encyclopedia of psychological assessment* (Vol. 1). Thousand Oaks, CA: Sage.

Camilli, G., & Shepard, L. A. (1994). *Methods for identifying biased test items.* Thousand Oaks, CA: Sage.

Carroll, J. D., & Chang, J. J. (1970). Analysis of individual differences in multidimensional scaling via an N-way generalization of Eckart–Young decomposition. *Psychometrika, 35,* 283–319.

Clauser, B. E., & Mazor, K. M. (1998). Using statistical procedures to identify differentially functioning test items. *Educational Measurement: Issues and Practice, 17,* 31–44.

Cook, L. L. (1996, August). *Establishing score comparability for tests given in different languages.* Paper presented at the meeting of the American Psychological Association, Toronto, Canada.

Cronbach, L. J., & Meehl, P. E. (1955). Construct validity in psychological tests. *Psychological Bulletin, 52,* 281–302.

Dorans, N. J., & Holland. P. W. (1993). DIF detection and description: Mantel–Haenszel and standardization. In P. W. Holland & H. Wainer (Eds.) *Differential item functioning* (pp. 35–66). Hillsdale, NJ: Lawrence Erlbaum Associates.

Dorans, N. J., & Kulick E. (1986). Demonstrating the utility of the standardization approach to assessing unexpected differential item performance on the scholastic aptitude test. *Journal of Educational Measurement, 23,* 355–368.

Ellis, B. B. (1995). A partial test of Hulin's psychometric theory of measurement equivalence in translated tests. *European Journal of Psychological Assessment, 11,* 184–193.

Foorman, B., Yoshida, H., Swank, P., & Garson, J. (1989). Japanese and American children's styles of processing figural matrices. *Journal of Cross-Cultural Psychology, 20,* 263–295.

Geisinger, K. F. (1994). Cross-cultural normative assessment: Translation and adaptation issues influencing the normative interpretation of assessment instruments. *Psychological Assessment, 6,* 304–312.

Gierl, M. J., Rogers, W. T., & Klinger, D. (1999, April). *Using statistical and judgmental reviews to identify and interpret translation DIF.* Paper presented at the meeting of the National Council on Measurement in Education, Montreal, Quebec, Canada.

Hambleton, R. K. (1993). Translating achievement tests for use in cross-national studies. *European Journal of Psychological Assessment, 9,* 57–68.

Hambleton, R. K. (1994). Guidelines for adapting educational and psychological tests: A progress report. *European Journal of Psychological Assessment, 10,* 229–244.

Hambleton, R. K., & Patsula, L. (1999). Increasing the validity of adapted tests: Myths to be avoided and guidelines for improving test adaptation practices. *Journal of Applied Testing Technology, 1,* 1–16.

Hambleton, R. K., Swaminathan, H., & Rogers, H. J. (1991). *Fundamentals of item response theory.* Newbury Park, CA: Sage.

Holland, P. W., & Thayer, D. T. (1988). Differential item functioning and the Mantel–Haenszel procedure. In H. Wainer & H. I. Braun (Eds.), *Test validity* (pp. 129–145). Hillsdale, NJ: Lawrence Erlbaum Associates.

Holland, P. W., & Wainer, H. (Eds.). (1993). *Differential item functioning.* Hillsdale, NJ: Lawrence Erlbaum Associates.

Hui, C. H., & Triandis, H. C. (1985). Measurement in cross-cultural psychology. *Journal of Cross-Cultural Psychology, 16,* 131–152.

Hulin, C. L., Drasgow, F., & Komocar, J. (1982). Application of item response theory to analysis of attitude scale translations. *Journal of Applied Psychology, 67,* 818–825.

Lord, F. M. (1980). *Applications of item response theory to practical testing problems.* Hillsdale NJ: Lawrence Erlbaum Associates.

Mantel, N., & Haenszel, W. (1959). Statistical aspects of the analysis of data from retrospective studies of disease. *Journal of the National Cancer Institute, 22,* 19–48.

Marsh, H. W. (1994). Confirmatory factor analysis models of factorial invariance: A multifaceted approach. *Structural Equation Modeling, 1,* 5–34.

McDonald, R. P. (1982). Linear versus non-linear models in item response theory. *Applied Psychological Measurement, 6,* 379–396.

McDonald, R. P. (1985). *Factor analysis and related methods.* Hillsdale, NJ: Lawrence Erlbaum Associates.

Millsap, R. J., & Everson, H. T. (1993). Methodology review: Statistical approaches for assessing measurement bias. *Applied Psychological Measurement, 17,* 297–334.

Muniz, J., Hambleton, R. K., & Xing, D. (2001). Small sample studies to detect flaws in test translation. *International Journal of Testing, 1,* 115–135.

Penfield, R. D., & Lam, T. C. M. (2000). Assessing differential item functioning in performance assessment: Review and recommendations. *Educational Measurement: Issues and Practice, 19*(3), 5–15.

Poortinga, Y. H. (1991). Conceptual implications of item bias. In P. L. Dann, S. H. Irvine, & J. M. Collis (Eds.), *Advances in computer-based human assessment* (pp. 279–290). Dordrecht, Netherlands: Kluwer Academic.

Potenza, M. T., & Dorans, N. J. (1995). DIF assessment for polytomously scored items: A framework for classification and evaluation. *Applied Psychological Measurement, 19,* 23–37.

Raju, N. S. (1988). The area between two item characteristic curves. *Psychometrika, 53,* 495–502.

Raju, N. S. (1990). Determining the significance of estimated signed and unsigned areas between two item response functions. *Applied Psychological Measurement, 14,* 197–207.

Reise, S. P., Widaman, K. F., & Pugh, R. H. (1993). Confirmatory factor analysis and item response theory: Two approaches for exploring measurement invariance. *Psychological Bulletin, 114,* U552–U566.

Robie, C., & Ryan, A. M. (1996). Structural equivalence of a measure of cross-cultural adjustment. *Educational and Psychological Measurement, 56,* 514–521.

Robin, F., Sireci, S. G., & Hambleton, R. K. (2003). Evaluating the equivalence of different language versions of a credentialing exam. *International Journal of Testing, 3*(1), 1–20.

Shealy, R. & Stout, W. (1993). A model-based standardization differences and detects test bias/DTF as well as item bias/DIF. *Psychometrika, 58,* 159–194.

Sireci, S. G., & Allalouf, A. (2003). Appraising item equivalence across multiple languages and cultures. *Language Testing, 20*(2), 148–167.

Sireci, S.G., Bastari, B., & Allalouf, A. (1998, August). *Evaluating construct equivalence across adapted tests.* Invited paper presented at the meeting of the American Psychological Association, San Francisco.

Sireci, S. G., & Berberoglu, G. (2000). Evaluating translation DIF using bilinguals. *Applied Measurement in Education, 13*(3), 229–248.

Sireci, S. G., Fitzgerald, C., & Xing, D. (1998). *Adapting credentialing examinations for international uses* (Laboratory of Psychometric and Evaluative Research Rep. No. 329). Amherst: University of Massachusetts, School of Education.

Sireci, S. G., Foster, D., Olsen, J. B., & Robin, F. (1997, March). *Comparing dual-language versions of international computerized certification exams.* Paper presented at the meeting of the National Council on Measurement in Education, Chicago.

Swaminathan, H., & Rogers, H. J. (1990). Detecting differential item functioning using logistic regression procedures. *Journal of Educational Measurement, 27,* 361–370.

Thissen, D., Steinberg, L., & Gerrard, M. (1986). Beyond group mean differences: The concept of item bias. *Psychological Bulletin, 99,* 118–128.

Thissen, D, Steinberg, L., & Wainer, H. (1988). Use of item response theory in the study of group differences in trace lines. In H. Wainer & H. I. Braun (Eds.), *Test validity* (pp. 147–169). Hillsdale, NJ: Lawrence Erlbaum Associates.

Thissen, D., Steinberg, L., & Wainer, H. (1993). Detection of differential item functioning using the parameters of item response models. In P. W. Holland & H. Wainer (Eds.), *Differential item functioning* (pp. 67–114). Hillsdale, NJ: Lawrence Erlbaum Associates.

van de Vijver, F. J., Daal, M., & van Zonneveld, R. (1986). The trainability of abstract reasoning: A cross-cultural comparison. *International Journal of Psychology, 21,* 589–615.

van de Vijver, F. J. R., & Leung, K. (1997). *Methods and data analysis for cross-cultural research.* Thousand Oaks, CA: Sage.

van de Vijver, F. J., & Poortinga, Y. H. (1991). Testing across cultures. In R. K. Hambleton & J. Zaal (Eds.), *Advances in educational and psychological testing* (pp. 277–308). Dordrecht, Netherlands: Kluwer Academic.

van de Vijver, F. J., & Tanzer, N. K. (1997). Bias and equivalence in cross-cultural assessment: an overview. *European Review of Applied Psychology, 47,* 263–279.

Wainer, H. (1995). Precision and differential item functioning on a testlet-based test: The 1991 Law School Admissions Test as an example. *Applied Measurement in Education, 8,* 157–186.

Wainer, H., Sireci, S. G., & Thissen, D. (1991). Differential testlet functioning: Definitions and detection. *Journal of Educational Measurement, 28,* 197–219.

5

Using Bilinguals to Evaluate the Comparability of Different Language Versions of a Test

Stephen G. Sireci
University of Massachusetts at Amherst

Psychometricians, educational researchers, and clinicians have long been confronted with the problem of assessing individuals who operate in different languages. In these contexts, the reality of a multilingual world precludes the use of a single assessment instrument. For this reason, tests are typically adapted for use in more than one language. Unfortunately, the adaptation process does not guarantee that the multiple-language forms of a test are equivalent (see, e.g., van de Vijver & Leung, 2000). Thus, the fundamental problem in cross-lingual assessment is disentangling test effects from group effects when comparing groups and individuals who took different language versions of a test (for a full discussion, see Hambleton & de Jong, 2003).

It has long been argued that when a test is translated (or adapted) from one language to another, the two different language versions cannot be considered equivalent. Due to the recent increase in cross-lingual assessment (e.g., Beller, 1994; Foster, Olsen, Ford, & Sireci, 1997; International Association for the Evaluation of Educational Achievement, 1994; Sireci, Xing, & Fitzgerald, 1999), this point has been reemphasized by many contemporary test specialists (e.g., Angoff & Cook, 1988; Geisinger, 1994; Hambleton,

1993, 2002; Olmedo, 1981; Prieto, 1992; Sireci, 1997; van de Vijver & Tanzer, 1997). However, this caution is almost as old as the practice of testing itself. Terman (1916) recognized the inability to directly compare scores from the English version of the Stanford-Binet with the original French-language Binet assessment. Similarly, in his seminal article on summated rating scales, Likert (1932) cautioned against using attitude scales across different "cultural" groups. Nevertheless, today, the world is becoming a smaller place and cross-lingual assessment activities are increasing. Therefore, methods are needed to evaluate the comparability of tests used across different languages.

The cross-cultural research and cross-lingual assessment literature contains several innovative examples of research designs and statistical methods useful for evaluating the comparability of tests that are translated or adapted across one or more language groups (e.g., Allalouf, Hambleton, & Sireci, 1999; Budgell, Raju, & Quartetti, 1995; Ellis & Kimmel, 1992; Hulin, Drasgow, & Komocar, 1982; Sireci, Fitzgerald, & Xing, 1998). Van de Vijver and Poortinga (1997) and van de Vijver and Tanzer (1997) drew on this literature to develop a taxonomy of measurement bias and equivalence relevant to cross-lingual assessment. In this taxonomy, bias comprises construct bias, method bias, and item bias; and equivalence comprises structural equivalence, measurement unit equivalence, and full scale equivalence. These categories determine the types of comparative inferences that can be made across different language assessments. Essentially, for comparative inferences across individuals who have taken different language versions of a test to be valid, it must be demonstrated that the different language tests are measuring the same construct, they are measuring this construct adequately, and the test scores from the different versions are on a common scale.

Although a great deal of work has been done on evaluating the sources of bias in cross-lingual assessment (see, e.g., recent studies by Allalouf, 2003; Allalouf et al., 1999; Ercikan, 2002), much less has been done to evaluate scale equivalence. Research designs and statistical analyses have been used to promote score comparability across language groups, but their strengths and limitations have not been fully evaluated. The goal of this chapter is to critique some of the methodology in this area, focusing on those designs that employ test takers who are proficient in two languages (bilinguals) and are able to respond to both "original" and "translated/adapted" test items. Drawing on research in this area, the strengths and limitations of these different research design options are discussed.

THE PROBLEM OF ACHIEVING FULL SCALE EQUIVALENCE IN CROSS-LINGUAL ASSESSMENT

The formidable problems in cross-lingual assessment are best illustrated by example. Suppose we wanted to compare the mathematics achievement of a group of French-speaking and a group of English-speaking students in the same grade and province in Canada. Suppose further that the same curriculum framework is in place for all students in this hypothetical study. Two versions of the achievement test are constructed. The first is the original test, which was developed in French; the second is the adapted version in English. For the purpose of this example, we assume construct equivalence (see Gierl, 2000, for an example of how to check construct equivalence). After the tests are administered, we observe a difference in performance across the French and English groups. Does this observed difference represent a true group difference in math achievement, a difference in difficulty between the test forms, or both?

To better understand this problem, we pretend we have a "true" achievement scale on which both groups are calibrated and that, on average, the French group truly outperforms the English group by .25 standard deviation (*SD*) units. To keep things as simple as possible, this true score scale has a mean of zero and standard deviation of one, and the fictitious math test comprises only five items. We approach the problem using both classical test theory and item response theory (IRT) (see, e.g., Hambleton, Swaminathan, & Rogers, 1991). An advantage in using IRT is that the groups' scores and item difficulty statistics can be expressed on the same score scale.

Scenario 1. First, we consider the situation where the *items are equivalent across the French and English languages*. That is, when the items were translated from French to English, the translation/adaptation process did not alter the fundamental "essence"of the items (i.e., they are linguistically and statistically equivalent in both languages). Given this assumption, if we calculated classical and IRT item statistics, the results may look like those in Table 5.1. Two conclusions are evident from Table 5.1. First, in looking at the *p* values (proportion of students who answered the item correctly) and mean test scores, we see that the French group outperformed the English group. This is a correct conclusion; remember, we simulated the French group to be .25 *SD* units above the English group. Second, we see that the *b* parameters (IRT item difficulty estimates) are the same in both groups. This result illustrates the well-known item parameter "sample invariance" feature of IRT calibration

TABLE 5.1
Illustrative Classical and IRT Statistics When Item Equivalence Holds Across Languages (French Group Is "Truly" .25s Units Above English Group)

	Classical p *Values*		*IRT* b *Parameters*	
Item	*English*	*French*	*English*	*French*
1	.50	.52	1.25	1.25
2	.60	.62	0.00	0.00
3	.55	.57	.63	.63
4	.65	.67	–0.63	–0.63
5	.70	.72	–1.25	–1.25
Mean Score[a]:	3.0	3.1	0.0	0.25

Note. **Conclusion 1:** The French group outperforms the English group. **Conclusion 2:** IRT item parameter estimates are invariant across the two groups.
[a]The mean scores are on the raw score scale for the classical statistics and on a standardized theta scale (0,1) for the IRT statistics.

(Hambleton et al., 1991). That is, IRT item parameter estimates are not dependent on the sample used to calibrate them. This feature of IRT is why IRT scaling methods are most often used to calibrate tests administered to different language groups (e.g., Angoff & Cook, 1988; Ellis, 1989; Hulin & Mayer, 1986; Woodcock & Muñoz-Sandoval, 1993).

Scenario 1 illustrates that when the items are equivalent across languages, no problems in interpreting group differences occur. There are no test differences and so observed differences can be attributed to differences between the two language groups. Unfortunately, in practice we do not know whether the items are equivalent across languages. Let us see what these results might look like if the items were more difficult in one of the two language versions of the test.

Scenario 2. Here we simulate a situation where, on average, *the items are easier in English by* .5 SD *units*. Our group effect (French group outperforms the English group by .25 *SD* units) remains. This scenario represents the situation where the adaptation of the test into English made the English version of the test easier than the French version. This situation could happen if, for example, the translators inadvertently introduced clues to the correct answers when adapting the items, or used simpler language throughout the test. Table 5.2 presents the fictitious results for this scenario.

The most striking observation in Table 5.2 is that the first conclusion is incorrect. The French group was defined as superior to the English group, yet the item *p* values and group means indicate the English group is superior. This finding is a consequence of the fact that the items are more difficult in French than in English. In this scenario, the magnitude of the difference between the average item difficulties across the two languages is greater than the magnitude of the difference between the true achievement of the two groups (.50 vs. .25, respectively). Our incorrect conclusion results because the classical and IRT models did not account for the fact that the English versions of the items are easier.

The second conclusion is also incorrect. The simulation conditions for this scenario specified the English items as being easier, yet

TABLE 5.2

Illustrative Classical and IRT Statistics When French Items Are More Difficult (French Group is "Truly" .25σ Units Above English Group)

	Classical p *Values*		*IRT* b *Parameters*	
Item	*English-French*		*English-French*	
1	.50	.48	1.25	1.25
2	.60	.58	0.00	0.00
3	.55	.53	.63	.63
4	.65	.63	−0.63	−0.63
5	.70	.68	−1.25	−1.25
Mean Score[a]:	3.0	2.9	0.0	−0.25

Note. **Conclusion 1:** The English group outperforms the French group. **Conclusion 2:** The items are equivalent across the two languages (i.e., no DIF).

[a]The mean scores are on the raw score scale for the classical statistics and on a standardized scale (0,1) for the IRT statistics.

the IRT difficulty parameter estimates (b-parameters) are the same for both language groups. How can this be?

The IRT difficulty parameters (estimates) of the English and French versions of the items appear to be equivalent because they appear to be on a common scale; however, they are not on a common scale. None of the English students answered the French items, and none of the French students answered the English items. Therefore, the parameter estimates for the French items are calculated using data from only the French students, and the parameter estimates for the English items are calculated using data from only the English students. For example, the English version of Item 1 represents an item that is about 1.25 *SD*s above the mean of the item difficulties of all the English items. There is no way of knowing the deviation of this item from the mean of the French item difficulties. Similarly, the French version of Item 1 represents an item that is about 1.25 *SD*s above the mean of the item difficulties of all the French items. Although both items have a deviation value of 1.25, they represent deviations from the mean of different scales (i.e., the English scale and the French scale). These language-specific deviation values are not comparable across languages. Now consider that only 48% of the French students answered Item 1 correctly, whereas 50% of the English students answered the item correctly. Because the *b* parameters were the same for the English and French versions of this item, the result is that the mean score for the French group on the score scale is lowered in comparison to the English group. A similar adjustment occurs for the other items. The results of this analysis provide conclusions opposite to what we know to be true. The items appear equivalent across languages (when they aren't) and the English students appear to perform better than the French students (when the reverse is true).

In Scenario 2, we specified both group and item differences across languages. The reason our analyses yielded incorrect conclusions is the scaling model did not account for these two factors. In reality, when the differences between items and groups are unknown, some assumptions must be made. We must either assume the items are equivalent across the languages, and then look for group differences; or assume the groups are equivalent and then look for item differences. Scenario 2 reflects the assumptions made when calibrating the items using the default options of a typical IRT program such as Bilog (Mislevy & Bock, 1990). This type of analysis will scale the *b* parameters concurrently (onto a common scale), without (correctly) accounting for differences between the groups, making results like those presented in Table 5.2 entirely possible. The use of a scale transformation procedure, such as Stocking and Lord (1983), which adjusts the parameters from one calibration to be on the same scale as items from a different calibration, cannot even be considered because there are no common (i.e., nontranslated) items available to make such an adjustment.

Is Scenario 2 realistic? Probably not. Given careful test translation and adaptation procedures (for developments in test adaptation procedures see Hambleton, chap. 1, this volume; Hambleton & Patsula, 1999; & Mullis, Kelly, & Haley, 1996), it is unlikely *all* items in one language version of a test would be more difficult than their counterparts in the other language version. A more likely scenario would have some of the items being more difficult in French, and others more difficult in English. In any event, the important point is that item nonequivalence and group nonequivalence can, and probably do, occur simultaneously in cross-lingual assessment. When these two factors are present, traditional scaling methods are insufficient for drawing inferences about differences between the tests and groups across languages. What is needed to make such inferences is either a way of accounting for the group differences within the calibration or scoring models, or a set of items that can be considered equivalent across the two languages. As we describe next, one way to identify items that can be considered equivalent across languages is to administer the tests to bilingual examinees.

USING BILINGUALS TO EVALUATE DIFFERENT LANGUAGE VERSIONS OF A TEST

One approach for evaluating the equivalence of two different language versions of a test is to administer the separate language versions to a group of test takers who are proficient in both languages (bilinguals). The logic underlying this approach is that by using a single group of test takers, "language group" effects are eliminated, and full scale equivalence can be achieved. Thus, observed differences in test or item performance across languages can be attributed to the linguistic differences between the tests or items.

Although the use of a single group usually eliminates group differences in most research designs, there are some deficiencies in this logic when applied to the cross-lingual assessment dilemma. The most conspicuous problem is the implicit assumption that bilinguals are equally proficient in both languages. For example, if a group of bilinguals performs differently on the "Language A" and "Language B" versions of an item, attributing this difference to a faulty adaptation assumes the bilinguals would perform the same on both language versions of the item if the adaptation was adequate. However, a bilingual examinee may be stronger in one language than the other. Therefore, a plausible rival hypothesis is that bilinguals perform better on items administered in their stronger language, even when the two versions of the item are truly equivalent.

A second flaw in this logic is that it describes bilinguals as a single, homogeneous group of test takers; when in reality, a group of bilingual test takers is likely to comprise individuals with very different backgrounds, proficiencies, and linguistic skills (Baker, 1988; Valdés & Figueroa, 1994). For example, in the United States, a group of English-Spanish bilinguals could include people whose first language is English and who learned Spanish in high school, Spanish-speaking immigrants (from a wide variety of countries) who recently learned to speak English, and second-generation immigrants who learned English as a second language in primary school. Therefore, the assumption that bilinguals represent a single "type" of test taker is unreasonable. As I discuss later, the linguistic diversity within a group of bilinguals should be incorporated into the research design when using bilinguals to evaluate tests administered in different languages.

A more subtle, but serious problem in using bilinguals to evaluate tests is the questionable comparability of bilinguals and monolinguals (Hambleton & Kanjee, 1995). This problem was previously termed the representation problem (Sireci, 1997). For example, in educational testing, bilinguals are likely to be very different from their monolingual cohorts. Bilinguals who are highly proficient in two languages may be representative of only the highest-achieving students in either monolingual group. Conversely, bilinguals who are marginally proficient in one or both languages may represent only the lowest-achieving students of one of the monolingual groups. In any event, the distribution of proficiency in a bilingual sample is likely to be very different from the corresponding distributions of their monolingual cohorts.

Although using bilinguals to evaluate tests administered in different languages is tricky, when appropriate research designs and state-of-the-art data analytic techniques are used, bilinguals may provide valuable information regarding test equivalence and score comparability. In the remainder of this chapter, research design options for using bilinguals to evaluate different language tests are presented, confounding variables that need to be controlled are noted, and suggestions for using bilinguals to conduct more comprehensive evaluations of tests administered in different languages are provided.

RESEARCH DESIGN ALTERNATIVES USING BILINGUALS

Single-Group Designs

The single-group bilingual design involves the administration of two different language versions of a test to a single group of bilingual test takers. In this design, no stratifications within the bilingual group are made to identify different "types" of bilinguals. However, the administration of the different language tests is usually counterbalanced. That is, about half of the examinees take the test in Language A first and the other half take the test in Language B first. This procedure is similar to the single-group design described in the test-equating literature (e.g., Kolen & Brennan, 1995).

The single-group bilingual design can be used to adjust total test scores on the different language versions. For example, Boldt (1969) evaluated the score comparability of the English-and Spanish-language versions of the SAT (Scholastic Aptitude Test). By testing a small (N = 140) group of Spanish-English bilingual high school students with both versions of the test, he concluded that subtracting 200 points from a student's Spanish-language test score provided an estimate of the student's expected score on the English-language test.

This design can also be used to evaluate the performance of individual items across the two languages. For example, the performance of the bilinguals on each item can be used to evaluate differential item functioning (DIF) across the languages. If items function differently in the two languages (in terms of item statistics such as item difficulty or item discrimination), the items are flagged as functioning differentially across languages, and are not used to anchor the tests onto a common scale. Instead, items that exhibit similar statistics across the two languages ("no DIF" items) could be used in an anchor-test equating design to calibrate or link the tests onto a common scale. Both classical test theory and IRT procedures can be used to equate the scales in this fashion.

There are at least three main drawbacks to the single-group bilingual design. Obviously, the design does not account for the presence of different kinds of bilingual test takers. If the study were done using predominantly Language A–dominant bilinguals, the results may not generalize to a situation where more Language B–dominant bilinguals are used. A second drawback is the presence of a practice effect. Because the examinees answer each question in both languages, familiarity with the item in the first test form may affect examinees' responses to the corresponding item in the second test form. Although the counterbalancing feature may adjust for this on average, the results may differ from what would have been observed if examinees responded to a single test form. The third drawback is that the procedure is relatively uneconomical. Testing a single group of test takers with two forms doubles the test administration time required to complete the study. A related disadvantage is that the examinees may be unmotivated or too tired to take a second form that is so similar to the first.

A notable example of the single group bilingual design was the study conducted to link the Spanish Assessment of Basic Education (SABE) to its English-language counterparts, the California Achievement Test (CAT) and the Comprehensive Test of Basic Skills (CTBS) (CTB/McGraw-Hill, 1988). Several features of this study are impressive. First, to ensure the bilingual students were proficient in both languages, teacher evaluations and language proficiency tests were used to screen out students who were not proficient in both English and Spanish. Second, rather than have the bilingual students take two separate tests, the students were administered shorter sets of English and Spanish anchor items. The performance of the bilinguals on these anchor items was used to derive conversion tables for comparing students' performance on the SABE with students' performance on the CAT and CTBS.

Although the specific research design employed in the SABE study addressed some of the shortcomings of the single-group design, by using more than one group of bilinguals, the internal and external validity of this type of study can be improved.

Multiple-Group Designs

Two-Group Design. The simplest multiple-group bilingual design employs two randomly equivalent groups of bilinguals. These groups can be created by spiraling two test forms or randomly assigning examinees to forms. In this design, each group takes only one of the two test forms, eliminating any potential practice effect. In addition, because the groups are randomly equivalent, no group effect should be present. This design is also more economical than the single-group design. Data on both test forms can be gathered in the amount of time it takes to administer a single test form.

Creating the Two Test Forms. The type of test each group takes can be more complicated when using bilinguals than when performing a two-group equating design. The most straightforward option is to have one group take the Language A form, and the other group take the Language B form. Although this option parallels the two-group equating situation (each group takes an intact test or anchor form), it is not optimal when testing bilinguals. Using this design, the performance of the first group in Language B cannot be evaluated, nor can the performance of the second group in Language A. A better alternative may be to have each group take a hybrid form that contains items in both Language A and Language B.

Sireci and Berberolu (2000) provided an example of this type of mixed-language administration design. They evaluated the translation fidelity of two sets of items from two versions of a teacher evaluation form. The original version of this test was in Turkish and the adapted version was in English. To control for the practice effect, examinees responded to only one language version of each item; however, both Turkish and English items appeared on each of the two test forms. This was accomplished by alternating between the two languages on each form. On the first form, all odd-numbered items were in English and all even-numbered items were in Turkish. The reverse pattern occurred on the second form. For example, item number one on the first form was presented in English and its Turkish counterpart appeared as item number one on the second form; item number two on the first form was in Turkish and its English counterpart appeared as item number two on the second form, and so on. In addition, two English items were included on each form. These items provided an anchor that was used within an IRT analysis to verify that the assumption of randomly equivalent groups was appropriate. The design of this study is presented in Fig. 5.1. The items administered in English in both forms (Anchors 1 and 2) were used to evaluate whether the bilingual examinees taking each test form were randomly equivalent. IRT-based DIF analyses were then conducted to test whether the English and Turkish versions of each item could be calibrated using the same parameters.

The effect of alternating between languages on examinees' performance is unknown. An alternative strategy is to have separate sec-

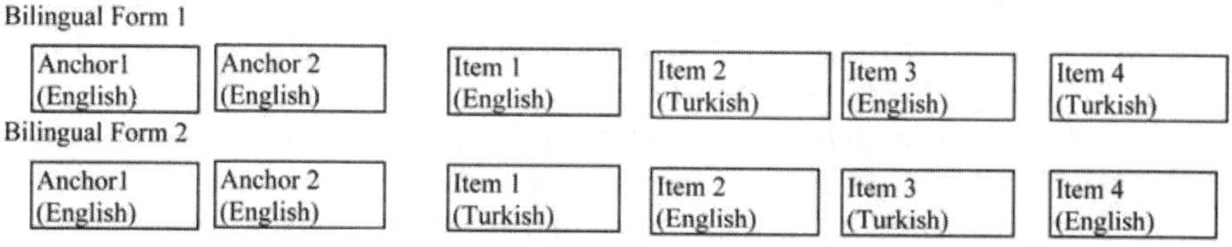

FIG. 5.1. Example of mixed-language administration design for bilingual test takers.

tions of the test for each language. Sireci and Berberolu (2000) recommended interviewing the bilingual examinees to discover if alternating the language of the items within an exam was confusing or impeded their performance in some way.

Sireci and Berberolu (2000) concluded that bilinguals were useful for identifying items that were not equivalent across languages. However, they acknowledged that the procedure could not "prove" items not flagged for DIF were equivalent across languages. Nevertheless, they suggested items that did not display DIF were better candidates for anchoring the separate language scales than were the flagged items, or items that had not been evaluated.

A limitation of the Sireci and Berberolu (2000) study was that only one type of bilingual test taker was used. The bilingual sample comprised students at a Turkish university where English was the primary language of instruction. Although they did screen out students who self-reported themselves as "poor" in reading or understanding English, their design did not include any bilinguals whose first language was English. A more thorough evaluation of translation fidelity would include both English-Turkish as well as Turkish-English bilinguals. Thus, where feasible, the two-group bilingual design can be improved by including more than one type of bilingual examinee.

Four-Group Design. An obvious addition to the two-group bilingual design is to have two groups of bilinguals, who differ with respect to native language, take each test form. The first group would comprise bilinguals who are dominant in the first language and the second group would comprise bilinguals who are dominant in the second language. Individuals in each group would be assigned to one of the two (possibly mixed-language) test forms. In addition to ensuring a more representative group of bilinguals, this design allows for the analysis of performance differences between the two types of bilinguals. DIF analyses could be conducted separately for each group. For example, if an item appears statistically equivalent for both Turkish-English and English-Turkish bilinguals, further evidence is gathered that the item is the "same" in both languages. If an item exhibits DIF in one bilingual group, but not in the other bilingual group, information is gathered pertaining to the different linguistic interpretations of the item.

If single-language test forms were used in a four-group design, traditional analysis of variance procedures could be useful for evaluating test (translation) effects and group effects. This situation is depicted in Fig. 5.2, which involves an analysis of hypothetical English and Spanish versions of an assessment. If an interaction effect

	Test Form	
	English	Spanish
Dominant Language		
English	?	?
Spanish	?	?

Possible Outcomes and Interpretations:

No effects: support for equivalence of test forms across languages

Main effect for test form: translation problem

Main effect for dominant language: group difference

Interaction effect: group and/or test form non-equivalence, no support for translation equivalence

FIG. 5.2. Hypothetical four-group design.

were present, it would indicate that the language in which one was tested does make a difference. If a main effect for language version of the test were present, it would indicate a translation problem. A main effect for language dominance group would indicate that the two types of bilinguals are not equal. Several analyses could be conducted using different dependent variables (e.g., item scores, total test scores, or subscores on specific content areas). Thus, extensions of the two-group design would provide increased information regarding the interaction between the native language orientation of bilinguals and language of the item.

Multiple-Group Designs. The four-group design could naturally be extended to more groups. For example, a design may include a group of examinees who are considered to be "equally proficient" in both languages. Designs could also be used that treat bilinguals of different backgrounds separately. For example, a study comparing English and Spanish versions of a test may want to look at differences between Caribbean, Central American, Mexican, and South American Spanish-English bilinguals. The specific choice of number of groups to be included in the analysis should be motivated by traditional research design concerns such as identification of extraneous variables, sample size, and control for plausible rival hypotheses.

As the number of potential groups increases, an obvious question is whether continuous measures of language dominance could be incorporated into the research design, rather than the use of multiple, discrete groups. For example, measures of Language A and Language B proficiency could be regressed across item and test performance data to discover if they are related to DIF indices or to total test score differences. For example, Pennock-Román (1995) used regression analyses to determine the effects of linguistic factors on Puerto Rican Spanish-English bilinguals' GRE (Graduate Record Examination) test performance. A central focus of her analysis was whether the language version of a test affects the inferences drawn about bilingual examinees. Using these designs, she found that English proficiency explained up to 34% of the variance in GRE Verbal test scores. Although her analyses did not investigate the comparability of tests administered in different languages, they are illustrative of the types of information that can be gathered using sophisticated bilingual group designs.

Designs Using Bilinguals and Monolinguals

The limitations of designs that use separate groups of monolingual examinees were discussed previously as were the limitations of bilingual designs. The monolingual designs are limited because these models are unable to achieve full scale equivalence. The bilingual designs are limited by the representation problem. This section proposes a more comprehensive design that uses both types of examinees.

Using Bilinguals to Identify Anchor Items for Monolingual Analyses. Monolingual group designs need some mechanism for accounting for differences in proficiency between the two language groups. If an external criterion strongly related to the proficiency being measured were available, it could be used to adjust for group differences on the tests. However, valid external criteria are rarely, if ever, available. A second option for accounting for language group differences is to use a set of items that are psychometrically equivalent in the two languages (anchor items). Given equivalent items, differences in group performance on these items can be used to adjust the scores on one of the two test forms (as is done in traditional equating analyses), or these items can be used to calibrate the other items onto a common scale, as described later (see Woodcock & Muñoz-Sandoval, 1993, for an illustration of this procedure).

It is in the identification of equivalent items that bilinguals may be particularly useful. If a set of items has been evaluated for DIF across languages using a comprehensive bilingual group design (such as the four-group bilingual design described earlier), items that do *not* display DIF could be used to develop a set of anchor items, which could be used to link different language versions of other items onto a common scale. For example, using IRT calibration procedures, two separate language versions of a test can be calibrated simultaneously (using monolingual test takers), and the parameters for the anchor items (identified as such using bilinguals) can be constrained to be equal across the two language groups. These constraints have the consequence of creating a common scale for all the other test items (assuming, of course, that the unidimensionality assumption of IRT holds for the data, and the set of anchor items adequately represents the construct measured). An alternative IRT-based procedure would be to calibrate the two language forms separately and then use the anchor items to adjust the parameters from one form onto the scale of the other form (e.g., see the Stocking & Lord, 1983, transformation procedure). Of course, the equivalence of these items would also need to be defended based on qualitative analyses conducted by bilingual test specialists. The set of anchor items would need to be representative of the entire test with respect to content and statistical characteristics.

Do the bilingual analyses certify that the items selected as anchors are truly equivalent across the two languages? Unfortunately, they do not. However, coupled with state-of the-art test development and test adaptation procedures (Hambleton, 1994; Mullis, Kelly, & Haley, 1996; see also Hambleton, chap. 1, this volume), a great deal of evidence can be provided to *support* use of these items as anchors. For example, a four-group bilingual design coupled with conscientious test development and adaptation procedures could provide the following types of evidence regarding the psychometric equivalence of the selected anchor items:

- The test developers consider the items to be measuring the same constructs in both languages.
- The items are deemed to be equivalent by bilingual subject matter experts (e.g., psychologists or curriculum experts).
- The items are deemed to be equivalent by linguistic experts.
- The items do not display DIF for bilinguals whose native language was the source language.
- The items do not display DIF for bilinguals whose native language was the target language.

Furthermore, if independent criterion data were available, statistical relationships among the items and external criteria could be studied to ascertain whether these relationships are similar across languages.

Although these divergent types of evidence do not certify the items are the same in both languages, they certainly provide a strong argument that items satisfying these requirements are suitable anchor items. Clearly, using such items as anchors improves upon previous designs that scale the different language items concurrently without using an anchor, or make scale transformations based on items that satisfy only a few of these criteria.

DATA ANALYSIS CONSIDERATIONS

In the previous section, the suggestion was made that items identified as psychometrically equivalent using bilinguals could be used to help form a common scale across two different language test forms. In this section, several options for accomplishing this scaling are described.

Consider the situation faced by a psychometrician who has completed a series of comprehensive DIF studies using bilinguals. Based on the statistical and judgmental criteria listed previously, the psychometrician identified a set of items to be used as anchor items. She or he also acquired data on both language versions of the test from the relevant monolingual groups. Two options are available. First, the psychometrician could simultaneously calibrate the different language items onto a common scale by constraining the parameters for the anchor items to be equal across the two language groups. The parameter estimates for the other items would be estimated separately for each language version of the item. The second option is to perform further DIF analyses by using the anchor items to form a common scale across the two language groups. After items that function differently across languages are identified, the test could be calibrated by constraining all other items (i.e., the non-DIF items) to be equal across the two languages. This iterative approach uses both bilingual and monolingual examinees to link the different language exams onto a common scale.

Given these two alternatives, and lack of a strong research base to choose between them, the second alternative, performing further DIF analyses, seems best. Using an IRT approach, this method would estimate the parameters separately for the different language groups for all items except the anchor items (whose parameters would be constrained to be equal). These items could then be evaluated for DIF using a likelihood ratio procedure (e.g., Sireci & Berberolu, 2000; Thissen, Steinberg, & Wainer, 1988, 1993). However, non-IRT DIF procedures could also be applied using the examinees' performance on the anchor items as the stratifying variable (e.g., Allalouf et al., 1999; Budgell et al., 1995; Sireci & Allalouf, 2003). The final calibration run would estimate the parameters for any items that displayed DIF in the previous analyses separately for each language group, and would constrain the parameters to be equal for those items that did not display DIF (Angoff & Cook, 1988). Although classical test theory approaches could be used for the final calibration, IRT calibration is preferred (assuming unidimensionality holds) given its statistical advantages (Hambleton et al., 1991).

Although this idea is appealing theoretically, applications of this procedure will help determine its utility. It is important to note that regardless of the data analytic strategy chosen, the validity of the set of anchor items is critical. The analyses outlined here assume that the set of items used to anchor the scale across languages is appropriate. The validity of this anchor should be supported using external criteria such as judgments by subject matter experts and analysis of construct equivalence (Sireci et al., 1999). The anchor items should be considered representative of the full-length test forms with respect to statistical and content characteristics.

One further option that has not yet been applied to the cross-lingual assessment area is the use of anchor items as one of several criteria for matching different language test takers. For example, examinees in different language groups could be matched on a multivariate matching criterion comprising performance on the anchor items, grades in relevant courses, socioeconomic status, and other variables deemed relevant to the construct. Sireci (1997) suggested that propensity scores could be used for matching examinees in this context. In addition, DIF studies have been conducted across groups operating in the same language (e.g., females and males) using logistic regression to condition the analysis using multiple variables (Clauser, Nungester, Mazor, & Ripkey, 1996; Mazor, Kanjee, & Clauser, 1995). This strategy also holds promise for linking score scales across different language versions of a test.

CONCLUSIONS

In this chapter, the use of research designs involving bilingual test takers to evaluate tests administered in different languages were reviewed. Psychometric techniques in this area are just developing and so further empirical research is needed. Of course, bilingual examinees may not be available in all cross-lingual assessment situations. However, in those situations where bilinguals can be incorporated into the research design, greater evidence regarding test and item comparability can be gathered. Given the lessons learned in this review, some suggestions for using bilinguals to optimize analyses of test equivalence across languages are offered.

First, studies of test equivalence across languages should include analyses of both bilingual and monolingual examinees. Designs using bilinguals are uniquely beneficial for evaluating item equivalence across a common group of test takers. The results of these analyses should provide valuable evidence for selecting anchor items to be used in subsequent analyses. However, test development, selection, and administration decisions should not be made solely on the basis of analyses using bilinguals. Rather, these analyses should be part of a larger study that also evaluates the performance of monolingual groups on each language version of the test, and explores relationships among test scores, item scores, and other variables within the nomological network related to the construct measured.

Second, when bilinguals are used to evaluate test and item equivalence across languages, the bilinguals should not be treated as a single group. Minimally, the performance of two groups of bilinguals representing dominance in each of the two languages should be investigated. Therefore, a key feature of bilingual research designs is a mechanism for classifying bilinguals into two or more groups, as well as certifying they are proficient in the two languages (Baker, 1988). Single-group bilingual designs, where the bilinguals take both language versions of tests or items, are not recommended due to the problems of fatigue, motivation, and practice effect.

Third, the advantages of using mixed-language test versions, rather than single-language test versions, should be considered in bilingual designs. Mixed-language versions gather data on both languages from both groups of bilinguals. This procedure is advantageous because it allows all examinees the opportunity to demonstrate their proficiency in the subject area tested in both languages. However, if test language-by-native-language interaction effects are of primary interest, a design using separate language forms may be preferred. In either case, the groups taking the test forms should be randomly equivalent (via random assignment or spiraling test forms). Furthermore, the assumption of random equivalence can be evaluated using a few common items (preferably in both languages) in both forms.

Fourth, the effect of DIF across languages should be evaluated with respect to the different content areas involved in the assessment. If DIF items are predominantly associated with some content areas, comparisons across language groups with respect to these content areas may not be justified. By looking at the patterns of DIF within content areas, limitations on the types of cross-lingual inferences that can be made will emerge.

The *Standards for Educational and Psychological Testing* (American Educational Research Association [AERA], American Psychological Association [APA], & National Council on Measurement in Education [NCME], 1985) were clear in requiring evidence for the comparability of tests administered in different languages: "when it is intended that the two versions of dual-language tests be comparable, evidence of test comparability should be reported" (p. 75). This standard was especially emphasized in the recent revision of these standards: "When multiple language versions of a test are intended to be comparable, test developers should report evidence of test comparability" (AERA, APA, & NCME, 1999, p. 99). The change from "two versions" to "multiple" versions acknowledges the great increase in multilingual assessment over the past 15 years since the last publication of the Test Standards. The suggestions outlined in this chapter should help researchers and test developers do the best they can in evaluating different language versions of a test, and in providing evidence of score comparability.

Some tests, such as the athletic competitions featured in the World Olympics, transcend linguistic barriers. Unfortunately, cross-lingual comparisons of knowledge and other psychological skills are typically not measurable using "language-independent" assessments. There are probably too many factors involved in cross-lingual assessment to ever conclude that test differences can be completely separated from language group differences. Therefore, we must do all we can to account for linguistic effects when making comparisons of individuals who operate in different languages. Studying the test performance of bilinguals on dual-language tests provides a promising framework for evaluating these effects.

REFERENCES

Allalouf, A. (2003). Revising translated differential item functioning items as a tool for improving cross-lingual assessment. *Applied Measurement in Education, 16*(1), 55–73.

Allalouf, A., Hambleton, R K., & Sireci, S. G. (1999). Identifying the sources of differential item functioning in translated verbal items. *Journal of Educational Measurement, 36,* 185–198.

American Educational Research Association, American Psychological Association, & National Council on Measurement in Education. (1999). *Standards for educational and*

psychological testing. Washington, DC: American Educational Research Association.

Angoff, W. H., & Cook, L. L. (1988). *Equating the scores of the Prueba de Aptitud Academica and the Scholastic Aptitude Test* (Report No. 88-2). New York: College Entrance Examination Board.

Baker, C. (1988). Normative testing and bilingual populations. *Journal of Multilingual and Multicultural Development, 9,* 399–409.

Beller, M. (1994). Psychometric and social issues in admissions to Israeli Universities. *Educational Measurement: Issues and Practice, 13,* 12–20.

Boldt, R. (1969). *Concurrent validity of the PAA and SAT for bilingual Dade School County high school volunteers* (College Entrance Examination Board Research and Development Report 68-69, No. 3). Princeton, NJ: Educational Testing Service.

Budgell, G. R., Raju, N. S., & Quartetti, D. A. (1995). Analysis of differential item functioning in translated assessment instruments. *Applied Psychological Measurement, 19,* 309–321.

Clauser, B. E., Nungester, R. J., Mazor, K., & Ripkey, D. (1996). A comparison of alternative matching strategies for DIF detection in tests that are multidimensional. *Journal of Educational Measurement, 33,* 202–214.

CTB/McGraw-Hill. (1988). *Spanish assessment of basic education: Technical report.* Monterey, CA: McGraw-Hill.

Ellis, B. B. (1989). Differential item functioning: Implications for test translations. *Journal of Applied Psychology, 74,* 912–920.

Ellis, B. B., & Kimmel, H. D. (1992). Identification of unique cultural response patterns by means of item response theory. *Journal of Applied Psychology, 77,* 177–184.

Ercikan, K. (2002). Disentangling sources of differential item functioning in multilanguage assessments. *International Journal of Testing, 2*(3&4), 199–215.

Foster, D., Olsen, J. B., Ford, J., & Sireci, S. G. (1997, March). *Administering computerized certification exams in multiple languages: Lessons learned from the international marketplace.* Paper presented at the meeting of the American Educational Research Association, Chicago.

Geisinger, K. F. (1994). Cross-cultural normative assessment: Translation and adaptation issues influencing the normative interpretation of assessment instruments. *Psychological Assessment, 6.* 304–312.

Gierl, M. J. (2000). Construct equivalence on translated achievement tests. *Canadian Journal of Education, 25*(4), 280–296.

Hambleton, R. K. (1993). Translating achievement tests for use in cross-national studies. *European Journal of Psychological Assessment, 9,* 57–68.

Hambleton, R. K. (1994). Guidelines for adapting educational and psychological tests: a progress report. *European Journal of Psychological Assessment, 10,* 229–244.

Hambleton, R. K. (2002). Adapting achievement tests into multiple languages for international assessments. In A. C. Porter & A. Gamoran (Eds.), *Methodological advances in cross -national ssurveys of educational achievement* (pp. 58–79). Washington, DC: National Academy Press.

Hambleton, R. K., & de Jong, J. (Eds.). (2003). Advances in translating and adapting educational and psychological tests [Special Issue]. *Language Testing, 20*(2), 127–240.

Hambleton, R. K., & Kanjee, A. (1995). Increasing the validity of cross-cultural assessments: Use of improved methods for test adaptations. *European Journal of Psychological Assessment, 11,* 147–157.

Hambleton, R. K., & Patsula, L. (1999). Increasing the validity of adapted tests: Myths to be avoided and guideleines for improving test adaptation practices. *Applied Testing Technology, 1*(1), 1–16.

Hambleton, R. K., Swaminathan, H., & Rogers, H. J. (1991). *Fundamentals of item response theory.* Newbury Park, CA: Sage.

Hulin, C. L., Drasgow, F., & Komocar, J. (1982). Applications of item response theory to analysis of attitude scale translations. *Journal of Applied Psychology, 67,* 818–825.

Hulin, C. L., & Mayer, L. J. (1986). Psychometric equivalence of a translation of the Job Descriptive Index into Hebrew. *Journal of Applied Psychology, 71,* 83–94.

International Association for the Evaluation of Educational Achievement. (1994). *TIMSS main study manuals: Population 1 and 2.* Hamburg, Germany: Author.

Kolen, M. J., & Brennan, R. L. (1995). *Test equating: Methods and practices.* New York: Springer-Verlag.

Likert, R. (1932). A technique for the measurement of attitudes. *Archives of Psychology, 140,* 44–53.

Mazor, K. M., Kanjee, A., & Clauser, B. (1995). Using logistic regression and the Mantel–Haenszel with multiple ability estimates to detect differential item functioning. *Journal of Educational Measurement, 32,* 131–144.

Mislevy, R. J., & Bock, R. D. (1990). *PC-BILOG 3: Item analysis and test scoring with binary logistic items.* Mooresville, IN: Scientific Software.

Mullis, I. V. S., Kelly, D. L., & Haley, K. (1996). Translation verification procedures. In M. O. Martin & I. V. S. Mullis (Eds.), *Third international mathematics and science study: Quality assurance in data collection* (pp. 1–14). Chestnut Hill, MA: Boston College.

Olmedo, E. L. (1981). Testing linguistic minorities. *American Psychologist, 36,* 1078–1085.

Pennock-Román, M. (1995). *Measuring developed academic abilities using Spanish- versus English-language tests: PAEG/GRE relationships for Puerto Ricans who are more proficient in Spanish than in English* (GRE Report No. 89-01). Princeton, NJ: Educational Testing Service.

Prieto, A. (1992). A method for translation of instruments to other languages. *Adult Education Quarterly, 43,* 1–14.

Sireci, S. G. (1997). Problems and issues in linking assessments across languages. *Educational Measurement: Issues and Practice, 16*(1), 12–19, 29.

Sireci, S. G., & Allalouf, A. (2003). Appraising item equivalence across multiple languages and cultures. *Language Testing, 20*(2), 147–165.

Sireci, S. G., & Berberolu, G. (2000). Using bilinguals to evaluate translated assessment questions. *Applied Measurement in Education, 13*(3), 229–248.

Sireci, S. G., Fitzgerald, C., & Xing, D. (1998, April). *Adapting credentialing examinations for international uses.* Paper presented at the meeting of the American Educational Research Association, San Diego.

Sireci, S.G., Xing, D., & Fitzgerald, C. (1999, April). *Evaluating translation DIF across multiple groups: Lessons learned from the Information Technology industry.* Paper presented at the meeting of the National Council on Measurement in Education, Montreal, Quebec, Canada.

Stocking, M. L., & Lord, F. M. (1983). Developing a common metric in item response theory. *Applied Psychological Measurement, 7*, 201–210.

Terman, L. M. (1916). *The measurement of intelligence.* Boston: Houghton-Mifflin.

Thissen, D, Steinberg, L., & Wainer, H. (1988). Use of item response theory in the study of group differences in trace lines. In H. Wainer & H. I. Braun (Eds.), *Test validity* (pp. 147–169). Mahwah, NJ: Lawrence Erlbaum Associates.

Thissen, D., Steinberg, L., & Wainer, H. (1993). Detection of differential item functioning using the parameters of item response models. In P.W. Holland, & H. Wainer (Eds.), *Differential item functioning* (pp. 147–169). Mahwah, NJ: Lawrence Erlbaum Associates.

Valdés, G., & Figueroa, R. A. (1994). *Bilingualism and testing: A special case of bias.* Norwood, NJ: Ablex.

van de Vijver, F. J. R., & Leung, K. (2000). Methodological issues in psychological research on culture. *Journal of Cross-Cultural Psychology, 31*, 33–51.

van de Vijver, F. J. R., & Poortinga, Y. H. (1977). Towards an integrated analysis of bias in cross-cultural assessment. *European Journal of Psychological Assessment, 13*, 29–37.

van de Vijver, F., & Tanzer, N. K. (1997). Bias and equivalence in cross-cultural assessment. *European Review of Applied Psychology, 47*(4), 263–279.

Woodcock, R. W., & Muñoz-Sandoval, A. F. (1993). An IRT approach to cross-language test equating and interpretation. *European Journal of Psychological Assessment, 3*, 1–16.

6

Establishing Score Comparability for Tests Given in Different Languages

Linda L. Cook
Educational Testing Service

Alicia P. Schmitt-Cascallar
Assessment Group International, Brussels, Belgium

Adapting tests for administration to different language groups and administering the adapted tests to examinees of different cultures is a practice that has a long history in the field of psychological assessment. Work of Terman (1916) indicates how long ago researchers were aware of problems related to using instruments developed for one population to assess attributes of a second population that may differ in background and culture.

The practice of adapting tests that were developed for a specific population, and then administering the tests to the second population, which may differ in both language and culture, is one that has increased greatly over the past decade. Hambleton (1993) and Sirici (1997) listed a number of factors contributing to the increased interest in test adaptations. Among these factors are: enhancing the fairness of comparisons of individuals and groups from different language and cultural backgrounds; facilitating comparative studies across national, ethnic, and cultural groups; and facilitating the comparison of achievement of students in different countries. Added to this list is the increasing globalization of many businesses, leading to the need to develop and adapt tests used to certify employees in their native language. Each of the factors is dependent on the ability to compare scores obtained on tests that are administered to groups that differ in both language and culture.

Regardless of the reasons for adapting a test given in one language for administration in a second language or multiple languages, the issues that surround the appropriate methodology for adapting the test to support valid comparisons of scores are extremely complex.

Poortinga (1989) pointed out that comparisons of the abilities of individuals or groups may be misleading for two reasons. One reason is related to the attribute that is being measured, and he gave as an example the futility of comparing the height of one person to the weight of a second individual. The second is related to the scale units used for the comparison; for example, one cannot make a direct comparison of the length of two objects if one object is measured in inches and the other in centimeters. These seem like obvious points to make when one is referring to physical attributes such as height, weight, and length. However, the situation immediately becomes more complex when the comparisons are extended to scores obtained on psychological and educational assessments.

Consider, for example, a test of algebra that contains some word problems. Consider further that the test has been constructed in English and scaled using data from an English-speaking population. The test is then translated into Spanish and administered to a group of Spanish-speaking students. If the Spanish-speaking students do not score as well on the test as the English-speaking students, how do we know whether the differences in scores are because the groups differ in their ability in algebra, or due to the fact that the translation of the algebra word problems into Spanish made the problems inherently more difficult for the Spanish-speaking examinees?

Another possibility is that the test administered in Spanish requires more reading time than the test administered in English, thus rendering it more speeded for the Spanish-speaking population. Should speed be a factor in the assessment of algebra ability for the Spanish-speaking group and not for the English-speaking group?

In addition, it might be possible that the instructions for the test were not translated clearly and the Spanish-speaking examinees were confused regarding key test-taking strategies, such as whether or not they would be penalized for guessing responses to questions.

The list of reasons for differences between the scores obtained on the algebra test by the Spanish- and English-speaking groups just given is most certainly not exhaustive; it is only meant to illustrate how difficult it is to avoid construct irrelevant sources of variance in test scores when comparing scores on adapted tests.

Procedures for addressing issues of construct irrelevant variance in test scores and consequently promoting an increased level of comparability of scores on adapted tests have been extensively described by a number of researchers. (See Geisinger, 1994, Sireci, 1997, and Hambleton, 1993, for thorough discussions of these procedures.) The procedures include translation and back-translation of the instrument to be adapted, pilot testing and screening the test items for differential item functioning, field testing and scaling, development of administration procedures, and validation research. This latter point is extremely important because, in spite of the most meticulous level of attention paid to methodological issues, it simply may not be possible to obtain construct equivalence for a test given to multiple populations that differ in language and culture. Consequently, it is important for validation research to be carried out on any adapted test to ensure that valid score comparisons and interpretations are supported by the test scores.

The focus of this chapter is on only one factor affecting the comparability of scores obtained on adapted tests: Poortinga's (1989) second reason for misleading comparisons, unequivalent scale units. In the following sections of this chapter, we provide a basis for understanding statistical methods that are currently available for equating and scaling educational and psychological tests, describe and critique specific scale-linking procedures used in test adaptation studies, and illustrate selected linking procedures and issues by describing and critiquing three studies that have been carried out over the past 20 years to link scores from the Scholastic Assessment Test (SAT) to the Prueba de Aptitud Academica (PAA).

OVERVIEW OF LINKING METHODS

Linn (1993) discussed the fact that many different techniques are available for linking test results and that the terminology used to describe the techniques has not always been used clearly. Linn went on to describe five different ways of linking test scores and how the type of linking affects score comparisons and interpretations. He made the point that inferences that assume the interchangeability of scores require strong methods to link the scales of the tests. Other types of inferences may be satisfied with weaker forms of linking, but these weaker forms of linking are by nature context, group, and time dependent.

In his 1993 article, Linn described five methods of linking educational and psychological tests, only four of which are described here. These four methods are: equating, calibration, statistical moderation, and prediction.

Equating. Linn (1993) reserved the term *equating* for linkings that provide scores that can be used interchangeably. He made the point that the strongest form of scale linking is equating. Linn referred to Lord (1980) and his definition of equating, which requires that the term "equated scores" be used only when the choice of which version or form of a test to take is a matter of indifference to the examinee and score user. It is clear that if the comparisons of scores on two tests require the tests to be considered interchangeable (e.g., scores on a form of the SAT administered in October and scores on a form of the SAT administered in June) then equating procedures must be used. Linn pointed out that the requirements for equating are that the test forms must measure the same construct with equal degrees of reliability; that is, the forms must be interchangeable. Others have pointed out (van de Vijver & Poortinga, 1991) that not only must the test forms be interchangeable for an adequate equating study to take place, the physical conditions of the test administration must also be comparable.

Calibration. Linn (1993) described *calibration* as a means of comparing scores on tests that satisfy less stringent requirements than the requirements for equating tests. He provided the following as examples of calibration: linking tests that differ considerably in length and, consequently, reliability; and linking tests that may be used to compare students at different developmental levels (typically referred to in the literature as vertical scaling studies).

Linn (1993) listed the requirements for calibration as: "[the tests] must measure the same construct. But may differ in reliability. May also differ in the level at which the measures are most useful" (p. 90). Linn pointed out that calibration provides a means of comparing scores on tests that satisfy less stringent requirements than those for equated tests. However, there is a price to pay. There exists the possibility that several different types of calibration studies can be carried out and each calibration will provide the answer to a different question. Linn cited a personal communication from Mislevy and Stocking as pointing out that when tests X and Y are not equally reliable, a calibration that transforms Y scores to the X scale can answer the question: "For what X value is the person's Y score most likely?" The authors pointed out that the same calibration will most likely provide incorrect answers to questions about the characteristics of the distributions of scores for groups taking tests X and Y.

Statistical Moderation. The third linking procedure described by Linn (1993), *statistical moderation,* refers to procedures that usually involve the use of scores on an external examination to moderate scores that are obtained on the exams that are to be compared. Statistical moderation is a technique that can be used to compare scores on achievement tests measuring different subject areas. For example, colleges sometimes wish to compare scores earned by students who take different SAT II subject tests. A common metric for the SAT II subject test scores is developed using the SAT I Verbal and Math scores as the external examination in a statistical moderation study. Statistical moderation, unlike the two previously discussed linking methods, does not require the two assessments that will be linked to measure the same construct. However, this procedure, when used in linking work, requires a common external examination, and the success of the procedure depends very heavily on the strength of the relationship between the external examination and the measures that are to be linked.

One of the key disadvantages of statistical moderation techniques is that they are context, group, and time dependent. Consequently, a relationship established between scores on two assessments developed using statistical moderation techniques might vary according to the group of examinees selected to participate in the moderation study.

Prediction. The fourth linking procedure described by Linn (1993) is *prediction*. Linn commented that as long as there is some degree of relationship between the performance on one assessment with the performance on another, it is possible to link the two assessments through prediction. Of course, the strength of the linking of the two assessments will depend on the strength of the relationship between scores obtained on the two assessments. Some of the weaknesses of prediction, when used as a linking procedure, are that the prediction equations are group dependent. Also, prediction equations are unidirectional; that is, separate linkings must be used to predict scores on test Y from test X and scores on test X form test Y.

APPLICATION OF FOUR LINKING METHODS TO LINKING SCORES ON TESTS GIVEN IN DIFFERENT LANGUAGES

It is important to consider the establishment of comparable scores for tests that have been adapted to different languages and are administered to candidates in their native languages from the perspective of the linking framework provided by Linn (1993).

First, it is clear that it is nearly impossible to link tests adapted to different languages, and then give these tests to examinees in their native languages and consider the linked tests to be equated. The reason for this is that, given the problems associated with adapting tests for different language and cultural groups (Hambleton, 1993) it is unlikely that the assumption of parallel forms (forms very similar in content and statistical characteristics), which are required by equating procedures, can be met.

It should also be clear that it is very unlikely that one can say it is a matter of indifference to an examinee whether he or she takes a test in the original language or the translated target language (Lord, 1980, stated this result as an outcome of equated scores). Perhaps if it were possible to adapt the test perfectly, and the examinees were perfectly bilingual, such a statement could be considered. However, neither of these situations typically exists in cross-lingual/cross-cultural assessments.

The implications for attempting to link tests adapted to different languages and given to students in the original and target languages are quite clear. It is unlikely that any linking study, no matter how carefully executed, will provide comparable scores in the sense of "equated scores."

An important question to ask is whether or not it is possible to link scores on tests used for cross-lingual assessments and consider those scores to be "calibrated" using Linn's (1993) criteria. According to Linn, linking via calibration does not require that the tests be of equal reliability, but only that they measure the same construct. In order to answer the question of whether or not calibration is possible, the nature of the assessment must be taken into consideration. For example, it is much more likely that a mathematics test given in English to an English-speaking group and in Spanish to a Spanish-speaking group will measure the same construct for the two groups than it is that a test of verbal ability given under the same circumstances will measure the same construct for the two groups.

If either equating or calibration procedures are not viable because of the nature of the examinations that the practitioner wishes to link, moderation procedures are often turned to. Statistical moderation studies must be carefully designed to meet the unique needs of a cross-lingual linking study. The reason the studies must be carefully designed is the requirement that a common external test be taken by the original and target language groups. It is difficult to see how this is possible if the two groups are strictly monolingual. However, there are probably two ways that a "common" external test can be simulated and the results of a moderation study can be approximated. One way is to adapt the common test into the original and target language with sufficient care so that it would act as a "common" link between the two measures when given to the respective language groups. A second way is to give the common test in either the target or original language to a bilingual group and consequently the test may perform as a "common" external examination. Both these procedures have been used with some degree of success in cross-lingual linking studies.

The fourth procedure described by Linn (1993) is prediction. Typically prediction studies result in scores on test X predicted by scores on test Y. In order to develop the prediction equation, some group of examinees must take both tests. Linn cautioned that the results of prediction studies have a number of limitations. In addition, he cautioned that the relationship that is used to determine the prediction equations is group specific. This has particular implications for the application of this type of linking procedure to cross-lingual assessments. Given that a prerequisite for developing the prediction equations is that one group must take both tests, the implication for a prediction-based cross-lingual linking study is that the group used for the linking study must be bilingual. The disadvantage of using a bilingual group for this type of study is that the results of the study may not generalize to the situation of interest, that is, the situation in which tests in original and target languages are given to examinees who are monolingual in these languages.

One advantage of prediction studies as the basis for linking two tests given in different languages is that the procedures permit the use of language-moderating variables and consequently may provide a more accurate answer to the question of how well an individual student would perform if given the test in the target language.

LINKING TESTS GIVEN IN DIFFERENT LANGUAGES

Ideally, those interested in linking assessments that have been adapted to different languages and are given to monolingual examinees in their own languages, would like to be able to compare the skills and abilities of examinees taking the different assessments as though the scores obtained on the assessments were entirely interchangeable (equated). However, as pointed out previously in this chapter, this ideal situation is difficult (if not impossible) to obtain because data collected in cross-lingual linking studies is not well accommodated by typical equating models.

Sireci (1997) provided an excellent overview of the technical issues associated with linking tests used in cross-lingual assessments. He began his review by discussing the fact that some practitioners believe that simply translating a test from one language to another is a sufficient condition for cross-lingual assessment. Sireci pointed out the fallacy in this line of reasoning by noting that unintended effects of the translation may produce items that differ in difficulty and other characteristics across the different languages (see Geisinger, 1994; Hambleton, 1993, 1996; Olmedo, 1981; Prieto, 1992).

According to Sireci (1997), designs used to link assessments given in different languages fall into three categories: (a) separate monolingual group designs, (b) bilingual group designs, and (c) matched monolingual designs. Separate monolingual group designs will necessarily involve some procedure for developing "overlapping items," whereas the latter two designs have as their central requirement the development of approximations to overlapping groups of examinees.

Separate Monolingual Group Designs. These designs all involve the administration of tests in original and target languages to their respective language groups and linking the tests through a set of items that is somehow considered "common" to both language groups. Item response theory (IRT) applications to this type of design have been considered quite promising. IRT models have been used to link tests administered to monolingual groups in several studies (e.g., Angoff & Cook, 1988).

The major criticism of IRT-based monolingual linking studies is that these studies make an untestable assumption about the equivalence of item parameters in the two populations. In other words, the invariant item parameter property of IRT models likely does not hold up across the different language samples. Sireci (1997) expanded on the problems of using IRT to link different language tests. He pointed out that "to provide empirical evidence of item invariance across languages, a valid matching criterion is required. The IRT proficiency scale (theta scale) is a fallible matching criterion because there are no true common items" (p. 14). Sireci went on to point out that IRT scaling procedures such as concurrent calibration and the Stocking–Lord (1983) procedure do not resolve the problem because they require some measure of the differences in proficiency between the two language groups; this measure is theoretically impossible to obtain without a true set of common items.

Another way of stating the problems associated with the use of IRT procedures for monolingual designs is that these procedures assume construct equivalence across the common items, and ultimately across the different tests administered to the monolingual groups. Using Linn's (1993) discussion of the classification of linking studies, the results of most monolingual linking studies would be classified, at best, as statistical moderation studies (studies that involve linking tests of different constructs) and would be subject to all of the cautions that are typically applied when interpreting the results of moderation studies.

In spite of the criticisms of monolingual group designs raised earlier, it should be noted that application of this type of design occurs frequently and often provides very useful results. The issues associated with this type of design revolve around the interpretation of the results of the study. The results are sometimes interpreted as though they were the outcome of an equating study. It is important to note that simply because an equating design has been used, it does not mean that the study has produced equated scores. Equivalent scores, in the sense of those obtained from a typical equating study, will occur only if the underlying assumptions of the equating model are met by the data. However, applications of monolingual designs often result in scores that can be considered sufficiently comparable for the purposes they are used for.

Bilingual Group Designs. Sireci (1997) described three variants of a bilingual group design. The first is one in which a single group of bilingual examinees take both language versions of the test in counterbalanced order. Sireci pointed out that one drawback of this type of design may be practice effects. This is particularly true if the two examinations represent close adaptations of a single test. The second bilingual design is one in which randomly equivalent bilingual groups each take a different language version of the tests to be linked. Sireci made the point that a potential flaw in this design is the possibility that the random groups may end up not being equivalent. The third is one in which randomly equivalent bilingual groups respond to a mixture of original and target language items.

Sireci (1997) continued by saying that one of the major problems with bilingual designs is operationally defining *bilingual*. It is difficult to locate examinees that are equally proficient in both languages of interest, particularly when one considers language proficiency as it relates to the construct being assessed. Additional issues related to the use of bilingual groups in cross-lingual assessments are described in detail in Sireci (chap. 5, this volume).

A major drawback of bilingual linking designs is that the bilingual group may not represent either of the monolingual groups that are the groups of interest in a comparative study. This limitation has serious implications for the generalization of the results of the cross-lingual linking study performed using a bilingual group to monolingual groups.

Matched Monolingual Designs. Given the problems described previously with simple monolingual groups designs and bilingual groups, the possibility of using a design that matches separate monolingual groups on some of the variables that might affect linking results is quite attractive. However, such designs have rarely been used with success. Matched monolingual designs attempt to bypass the need for common items to assess differences in skills/abilities by using groups for the linking study that are matched on criteria that are relevant to whatever skills or abilities are assessed by the different language tests.

As Sireci (1997) pointed out, the effects of matching groups for conventional types of equating designs have been investigated fairly extensively (see Cook, Eignor, & Schmitt; 1989; Eignor, Stocking, & Cook, 1990; Kolen, 1990; Livingston, Dorans, & Wright, 1990; Skaggs, 1990). The results of these studies are mixed. Livingston et al. suggested that equating may be improved via matching on propensity scores (Rosenbaum & Rubin, 1983), whereas Cook et al. advised against such techniques. The same cautions mentioned when evaluating the use of bilingual groups for cross-lingual linking studies should be mentioned in the context of using matched groups for these types of linking studies.

A key point made by Linn (1993), when discussing the linking study classifications, was that all linking studies other than true equating studies suffer from the problem that the results are group dependent. Consequently, the results of a cross-lingual linking study performed using monolingual groups constructed so that they are matched on particular variables that are key to the ability measured may not generalize to the more heterogeneous monolingual groups that are ultimately the groups of interest.

In the next section of the chapter, three linking studies that have been carried out over the past 20 years for the purpose of linking scores on the SAT and the PAA are discussed. Each study is critiqued from the perspective of the previous discussion on linking designs.

DEVELOPING A RELATIONSHIP BETWEEN PAA AND SAT SCORES

The series of studies that were carried out to develop a relationship between scores on the SAT and scores on the PAA were designed to develop a common metric that would facilitate comparisons of scores obtained on the two tests. The researchers working on all of the studies were aware that the basic differences in language, customs, and values might possibly invalidate comparisons among groups taking the two tests. Nevertheless, these researchers were committed to developing the optimal methodology that could be used to construct as unbiased a metric as possible.

It is important at this point to emphasize that the PAA is not a direct translation and adaptation of the SAT. Although the PAA is designed to measure the same constructs as the SAT, the PAA contains different items and is developed quite independently of the SAT. A decision was made by the College Board, early in the history of the PAA testing program, that because of the complexities and difficulties involved in adapting a test from one language to the other, the "parallelism" between the two tests would be better preserved if each test was designed to measure the "same construct," but in a different language.[1]

A distinguishing feature of the PAA is that it is designed to be used in multiple Hispanic contexts. The various Hispanic populations, for example, Mexican and Puerto Rican, differ from one another in much the same way as, say, residents of the United States and residents of Great Britain. Both of these groups speak English, but the nuances of the language differ in the different countries. Differential item functioning (DIF) analyses are carried out on the PAA to ensure the validity of the construct the test measures across the different Hispanic populations (see, e.g., Sireci & Allalouf, 2003).

The first study conducted for the purpose of linking scores on the PAA to scores on the SAT was carried out by Angoff and Modu (1973) in the fall of 1971. The results of the Angoff/Modu study were used to compare scores on the PAA to scores on the SAT for about a 10-year period. Advances in technology, as well as the realization that it is good practice to repeat and revise the results of linking studies periodically, led to the repetition of the PAA/SAT linking in the study of Angoff and Cook (1988). The Angoff–Cook study followed the basic design of the earlier study, but replaced the classical test theory methodology with IRT techniques. The most recent linking study carried out for the PAA and the SAT I was conducted by Schmitt, Dorans, Magrina, and Cook (1998). The purpose of this study was to provide an updated linking of the two tests that reflected recent changes in the test specifications. The third study employed a very

---

[1]It should be noted that, in contrast to the decision not to directly translate the two tests, the procedure used in the past to link the PAA and SAT (described later) depends on the translation of a "common" set of linking items.

different methodology for linking the two tests than that used by the previous two studies. What follows is a brief discussion and critique of the three linking studies.

Angoff–Modu Study. Angoff and Modu (1973) developed a methodology to provide a conversion of the verbal and mathematical scores on the Spanish-language PAA to the respective verbal and mathematical scores on the SAT. Both tests were administered to secondary school students for college admissions purposes. As mentioned previously, although the PAA and SAT shared the same structure and format, the tests were each composed of independent original items; that is, the tests were not adapted versions of each other. The purpose of the study carried out by Angoff and Modu was to provide conversion tables between the PAA and SAT that would facilitate direct comparisons of subgroups of the two language groups who had taken the appropriate test in their respective languages. In addition, it was expected that the conversion tables would aid in the evaluation of the likelihood of the success in mainland colleges that might be obtained by students from Puerto Rico.

The Angoff and Modu (1973) study consisted of two phases. The first phase involved the selection of "common" items used as an anchor test in the "equating" study and the second phase consisted of the actual "equating." The method used in the first phase was to choose two sets of items, one originally in English and the second originally in Spanish, and to translate each set into the other language. After translation, the two item sets (one in Spanish and one in English) were administered to the appropriate monolingual students for pretest purposes. The pretest administrations for this study were carried out in the fall of 1970. On the basis of the analysis of the pretest data, two sets of items, one verbal and the second mathematical, were selected as "common" item sets to be used for the respective verbal and math "equatings."

In the "equating" phase of the study, the "common" items, appearing in both Spanish and English, were administered in the appropriate language along with the operational form of the PAA in November 1971, and with the operational form of the SAT in January 1972. The data from these administrations were used to conduct both linear and equipercentile "equatings" of the PAA and the SAT verbal and math tests.

Several aspects of this early study are worth describing in detail. Phase I of the study consisted of building the "common" item or linking test that would be used to evaluate differences in ability between the Spanish-speaking PAA group and the English-speaking SAT group. The initial pool of items that would be used to form the linking tests was drawn in approximately equal numbers from the PAA and SAT item pools. These items were translated into the second language by a small group of bilingual experts. An effort was made to produce a set of items, in English and in Spanish, that were, as nearly as possible, equal in meaning in the two languages. At a later time, all the items were back translated to their original language and the back translations (the versions that had undergone two translations) were compared with the original text.

The common item set was then pretested by administering to groups of students taking either the PAA or SAT in the appropriate language. Following pretesting, the items were screened statistically by plotting the item difficulty or delta values of the verbal and math items taken by the Spanish- and English-speaking groups. (See Angoff and Modu, 1973, for a description of "delta.") The purpose of the delta plots was to enable the identification of items that had a different meaning for the two groups, PAA and SAT. Items were considered as "equally appropriate" to the Spanish- and English-speaking groups on the basis of their proximity to the major axis of the ellipse of the delta plot. Figures 6.1 and 6.2, taken from Angoff and Modu (1973), illustrate the results of the delta plots for the verbal and math linking item sets.

An important point to note when comparing the plot of verbal items to the plot of math items is the greater degree of dispersion of the verbal items about the major axis of the ellipse of the delta plot. Angoff and Modu (1973) interpreted the greater scatter of the verbal items as indicating that the verbal items did not have quite the same psychological meaning for the two language groups. They went on to say that the scatter was sufficient to cast doubt on the quality of any equating carried out with these items. The situation was improved by discarding the most aberrant items; however, the authors continued to express concern that item-by-group interactions indicated by the data found in the delta plots made the equating "much less trustworthy than would be expected of an equating of two parallel tests intended for members of the same language-culture" (p. 14).

Phase II of the study consisted of the actual "equating" of the PAA and the SAT, using the linking item set constructed in Phase I. Forty verbal items and 25 math items were selected as "common" items for Phase II of the study. The items were administered, along with an operational version of the respective tests in the November 1971 administration of the PAA, and the January 1972 administration of the SAT. Three conventional equating procedures were used to link scores on the PAA with scores on the SAT. A Tucker linear, an

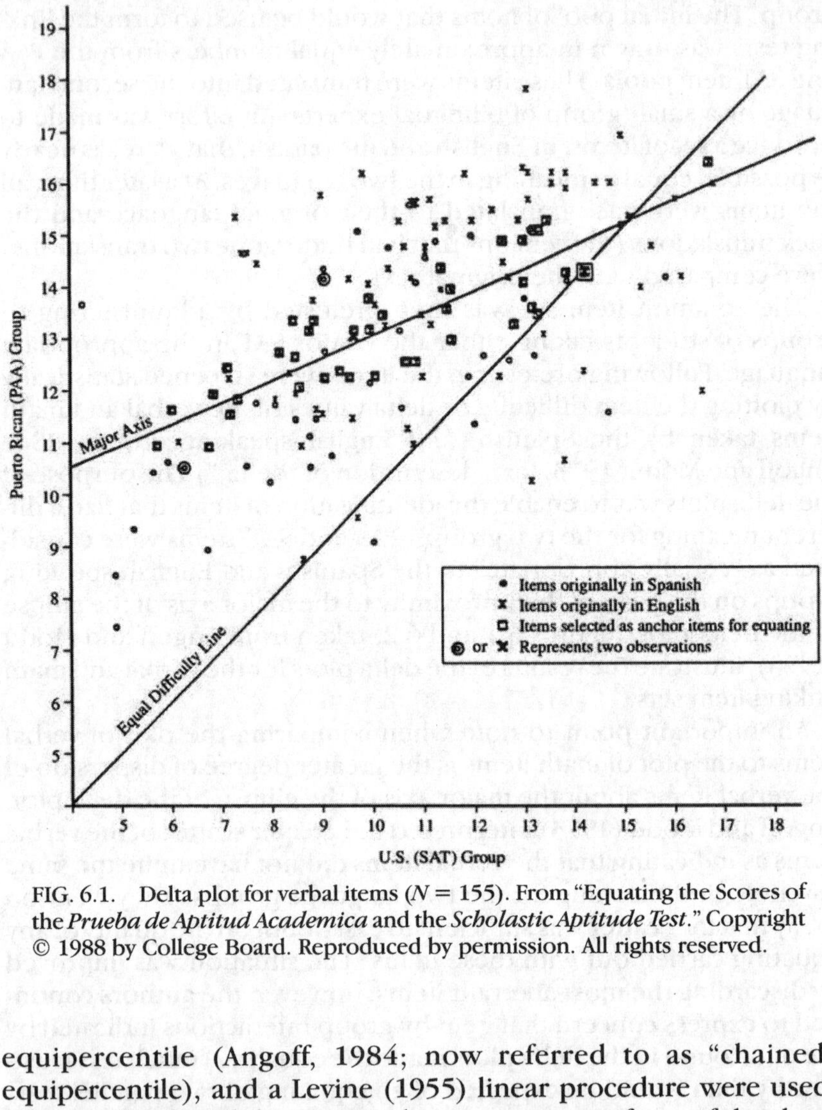

FIG. 6.1. Delta plot for verbal items ($N = 155$). From "Equating the Scores of the *Prueba de Aptitud Academica* and the *Scholastic Aptitude Test*." Copyright © 1988 by College Board. Reproduced by permission. All rights reserved.

equipercentile (Angoff, 1984; now referred to as "chained" equipercentile), and a Levine (1955) linear procedure were used. Because the data did not meet the assumptions of any of the three conventional equating models, it was decided to average the results of the three models, giving more weight to the equipercentile results. Figures 6.3 and 6.4 show conversion plots for the verbal and math "equatings."

The results of the verbal "equating" indicated that a PAA midscale value (500) was equivalent to an SAT Verbal score (350) substantially below midvalue. The results of the math "equating" indicated that a PAA score of 500 resulted in an even lower SAT Math score (319).

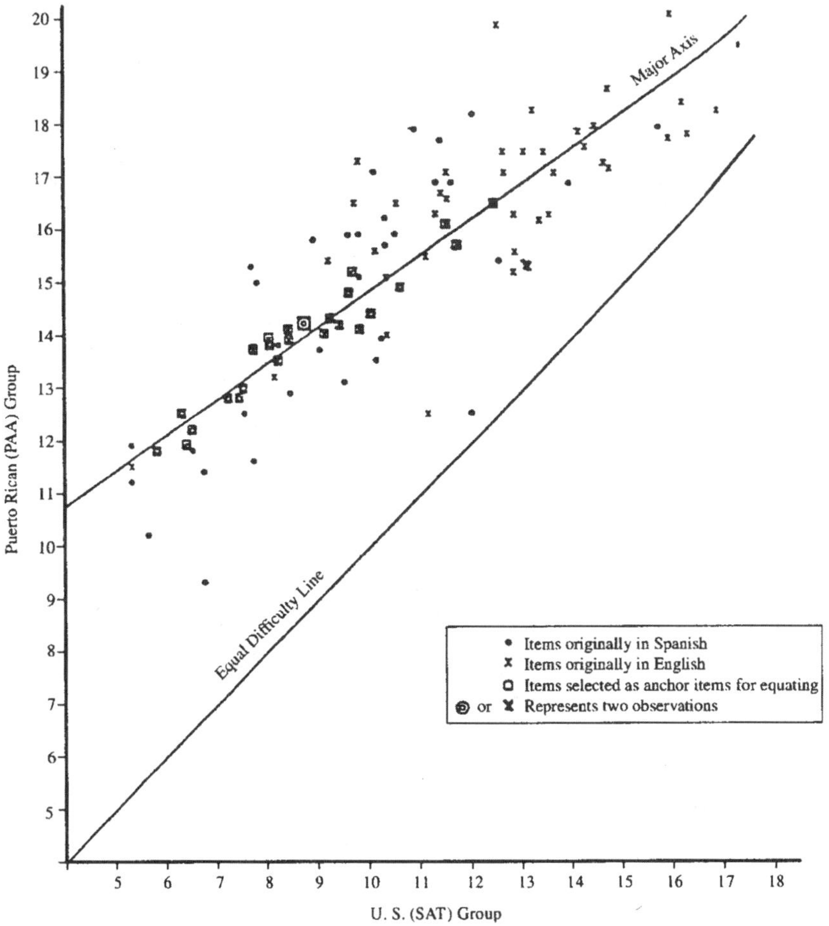

FIG. 6.2. Delta plot for math items ($N = 155$). From "Equating the Scores of the *Prueba de Aptitud Academica* and the *Scholastic Aptitude Test*." Copyright © 1988 by College Board. Reproduced by permission. All rights reserved.

Angoff and Modu (1973) cautioned that "the accuracy of these conversions is limited by the appropriateness of the method used to derive them and the data assembled during the course of the study. It is hoped that these conversions will be useful in a variety of contexts but ... in order to be useful they will need in each instance to be supported by additional data peculiar to the context" (p. 41).

Angoff–Cook Study. The study carried out by Angoff and Cook (1988) used the same basic design as that used by Angoff and Modu

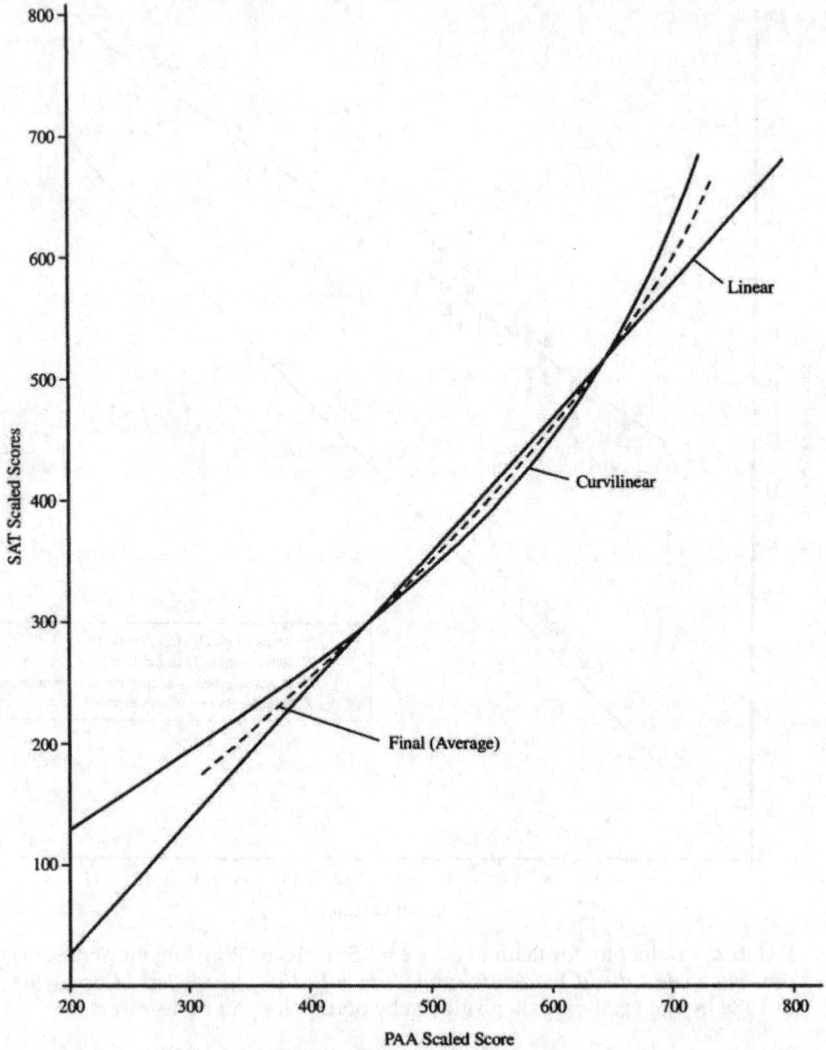

FIG. 6.3. Equating results for verbal tests. From "Equating the Scores of the *Prueba de Aptitud Academica* and the *Scholastic Aptitude Test*." Copyright © 1988 by College Board. Reproduced by permission. All rights reserved.

(1973) but employed IRT methodology to replace both the delta plot item screening used to select the "common" item test and the conventional equating methodology used in the earlier study.

Similar to the previous study, the Angoff and Cook (1988) study was carried out in two phases. Phase I consisted of the selection of

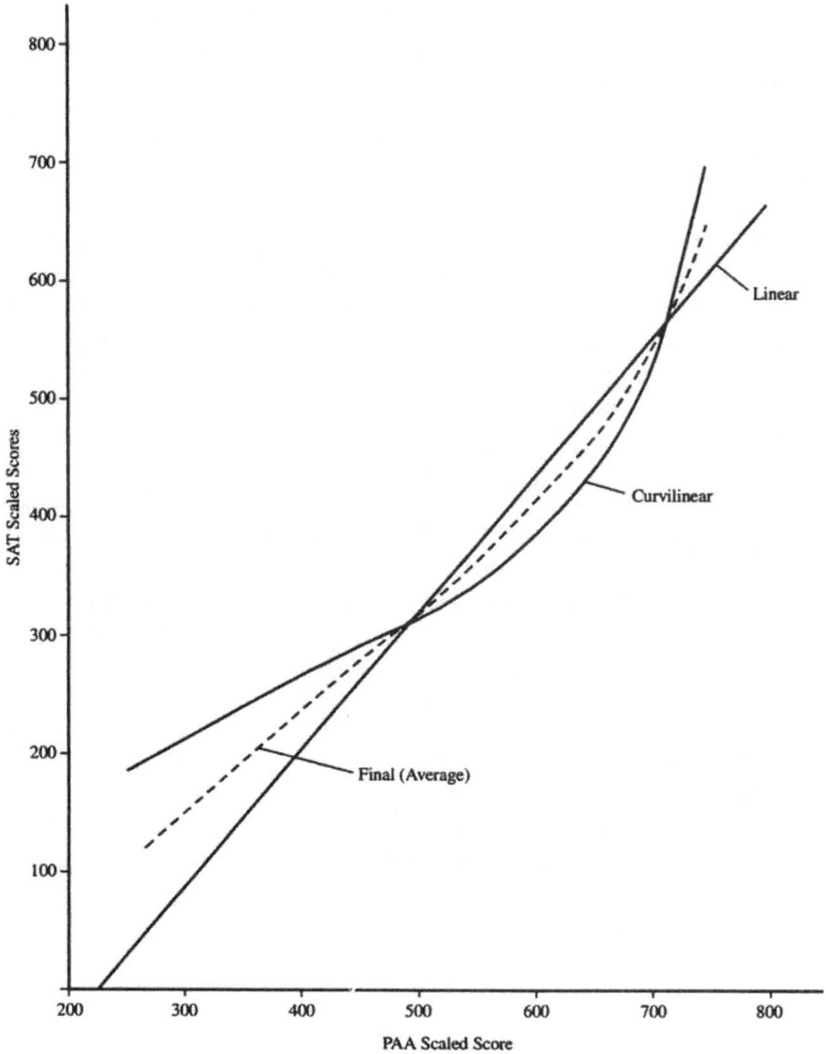

FIG. 6.4. Equating results for math tests. From "Equating the Scores of the *Prueba de Aptitud Academica* and the *Scholastic Aptitude Test*." Copyright © 1988 by College Board. Reproduced by permission. All rights reserved.

the linking items that would be used in Phase II, the "equating" phase of the study. The methodology established in the earlier study for adapting, back adapting, and pretesting the items was followed for the Angoff and Cook study. The difference between Phase I of the two studies was in the methodology used to screen the items for selection as "common" items. Angoff and Cook evaluated items by comparing, both visually and statistically, the differences between the IRT item characteristic curves (ICCs).

Figure 6.5 gives examples of plots of ICCs for verbal and math items estimated for the Spanish- and English-speaking groups. Panel A of Fig. 6.5 shows that for all levels of ability (theta) the PAA group has a higher probability of obtaining a correct answer to the item than the SAT group. Such an item obviously could not be considered as a "common" item for the two groups and was consequently dropped during the item-screening phase of the study. Panel B of Fig. 6.5 contains a comparison of ICCs obtained for a math item given to the PAA and SAT groups. In contrast to the curves shown in Panel A, the ICCs for the math item given to the two groups of examinees are almost identical; that is, individuals at all levels of ability in both groups have the same probability of obtaining a correct answer to the item. The item favors neither of the two groups. Items such as this one were considered ideal for inclusion in the set of "common" items used to link the two math tests.

The "equating" phase of the study paralleled that of the Angoff and Modu (1988) study with the exception of the use of IRT procedures. The verbal and math "common" item sets were administered along with their respective operational tests (PAA or SAT) to the appropriate monolingual groups. The SAT data were collected in December 1985 and the PAA data at the October 1986 administration. The IRT equating method used in this study was IRT concurrent equating (Cook & Eignor, 1983; Petersen, Cook, & Stocking, 1983). Only IRT curvilinear equating results were reported for the study. These results are presented for the verbal and math tests in Figs. 6.6 and 6.7.

It is clear from a review of the graphs shown in Figs. 6.6 and 6.7 that the relationship between the PAA and SAT scales is markedly curvilinear. This was also the case for the equating results obtained in the Angoff and Modu (1973) study; however, Angoff and Modu chose to average the curvilinear results with the linear results. The results of the Angoff and Cook (1988) study indicated that the differences between the PAA and SAT scales at a PAA score of 500 were about 180 to 185 points. Their results indicated similar differences for the math linking, that is, at a PAA score of 500, differences between the PAA and SAT scale were about 180 to 185 points.

The results of the Angoff and Cook (1988) study yielded substantially lower conversions of PAA verbal scores to the SAT verbal scale than the earlier study, especially in the midrange of the score scale. The conversions to the SAT mathematical scale showed better agreement with the earlier results. The authors speculated that differ-

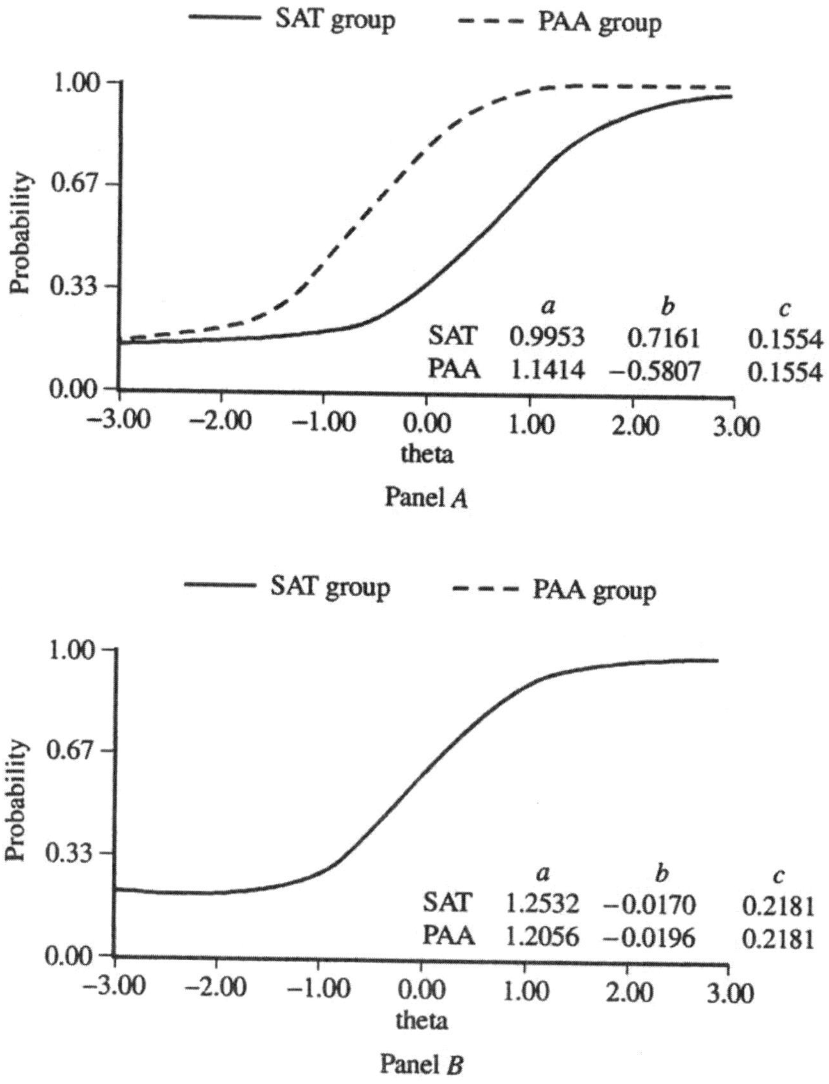

FIG. 6.5. Item response curves: Plots of item response functions for verbal (Panel A) and mathematical (Panel B) items given to PAA and SAT groups, illustrating poor and good agreement between groups. From "Equating the Scores of the *Prueba de Aptitud Academica* and the *Scholastic Aptitude Test*." Copyright © 1988 by College Board. Reproduced by permission. All rights reserved.

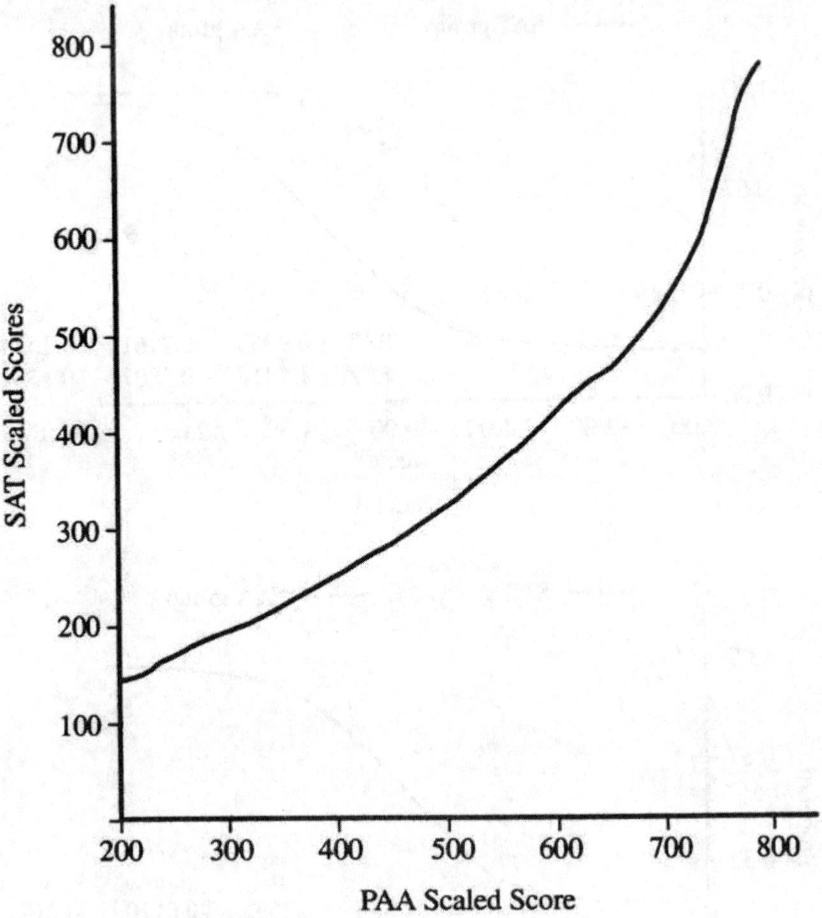

FIG. 6.6. Equating results for verbal tests. From "Equating the Scores of the *Prueba de Aptitud Academica* and the *Scholastic Aptitude Test*." Copyright © 1988 by College Board. Reproduced by permission. All rights reserved.

ences in results could be attributed to differences in methodology or to the inherent difficulties of "equating" verbally loaded tests for different language groups.

Critique of the Previous Two Studies. The score-linking methodologies employed in the two studies, IRT curvilinear equating procedures and the Tucker, Levine, and equipercentile procedures, are reasonable procedures to use if the question of interest is a comparison of distributions of scores for two groups of examinees

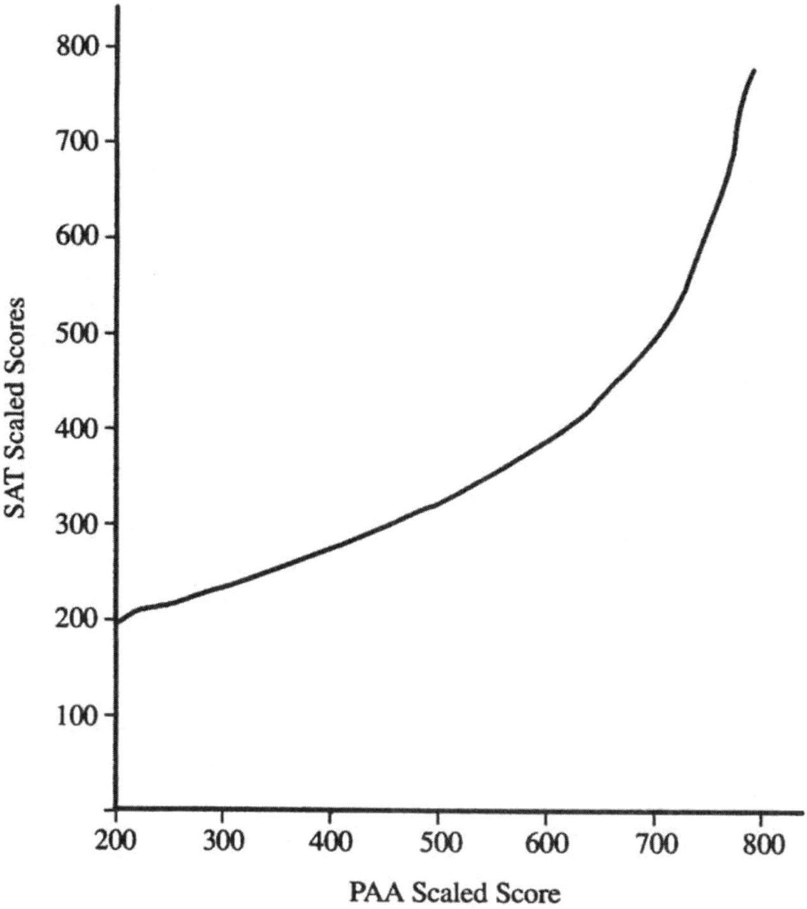

FIG. 6.7. Equating results for math tests. From "Equating the Scores of the *Prueba de Aptitud Academica* and the *Scholastic Aptitude Test*." Copyright © 1988 by College Board. Reproduced by permission. All rights reserved.

(or, in the case of the linear methods, the first two movements of the distribution). Recall that the original purposes of the PAA/SAT linking, as described by Angoff and Modu (1973), were: (a) to compare the distributions of scores of subgroups from the two populations, and (b) to evaluate the probable success of Puerto Rican students who were interested in eventually attending colleges on the mainland and were submitting PAA scores for admission purposes.

Depending on how well the data met the assumptions of the statistical models used for linking, and how well the linking was executed, it is possible that the methodology employed in the Angoff and Modu (1973) and the Angoff and Cook (1988) studies could provide a reasonable basis for comparisons of distributions of scores. The reason for this is that the purpose of the IRT, linear, and equipercentile procedures employed in these two studies is to transform the distribution of scores obtained on one test to match that of the second test, for a particular group of examinees.

Although it is theoretically possible for the statistical techniques used in these studies to provide end results that meet the goal of comparable scores, the goal is probably not met by the results of the two studies because of the nature of the data used for the linking. However, the procedure used would have provided a solution to the problem provided the assumptions underlying the methodology were met.

Consider the second reason for carrying out the PAA/SAT linking, that is, to evaluate the success of students from Puerto Rico in mainland colleges and universities. How is it possible to use the relationship established between the PAA and SAT in the two previous studies to predict how well a high school student in San Juan may do when he or she attends a college in, say, Miami? What does it mean to say that a student receiving a 500 on the PAA would receive a score of 320 on the SAT? If the high school student in San Juan speaks no English, he or she will surely not receive a score of 320 on the SAT and will have a very difficult time of study in a US college or university.

Pennock-Román (1995) investigated the relationship between scores on graduate-level admissions tests given in English and Spanish to a group of students who were more proficient in Spanish than English and concluded that proficiency in English contributed to the student's scores on the GRE (Graduate Record Examination) verbal, math, analytic, psychology, and biology tests. Pennock-Román found that English proficiency contributed differently depending on the level of proficiency of the student and depending on the content of the test. She discussed the fact that it is quite possible for a talented second-language student to receive a below-average score on the GRE verbal test simply because of slower reading comprehension.

The implications of the Pennock-Román (1995) study for the PAA/SAT linking studies are that if the major purpose of a study is to provide a means for evaluating how well a student in Puerto Rico will do in a mainland college or university, then some measure of ability in English must be taken into consideration. The methodology used for the PAA/SAT I linking study that is described next attempts to take these implications into account.

Schmitt, Dorans, Magrina, and Cook Study. In the spring of 1994, a new SAT I was introduced. The new test contains new item types and was built to revised content and statistical specifications. (See Cook, 1995, for a description of the revisions to the SAT.) In October 1996, the PAA was also revised to include new item types and revised content and statistical specifications. Changes to the PAA parallel the changes introduced to the SAT I. Specifically, the new PAA Verbal does not include antonyms and has a higher percentage of verbal items that relate to critical reading passages (56% vs. 31%). In addition to the traditional multiple-choice items, the new PAA Math includes items where the examinee produces his or her own response. (See The College Board, 1995, for an extensive description of the changes to the new PAA.) One difference between the SAT I and the new PAA is that the SAT I allows the use of calculators in the Math test.

The two prior PAA/SAT linking studies provided concordance tables between scores on former versions of the PAA and the SAT (Angoff & Cook, 1988; Angoff & Modu, 1973). These scaling studies used "common" items to adjust for any differences between the SAT and PAA groups. Because of the issues described earlier, the latest study approached the comparability of scores between the SAT I and the PAA from a different perspective. Concordance tables obtained though the "equating" methods used in the earlier two studies assume that the two tests are basically alternate forms representing the same construct. Inasmuch as the Spanish-language PAA and the English-language SAT I each contain items that are specifically developed for and pretested with their respective populations in mind, the PAA and SAT I cannot be considered to be alternate forms.

For the third PAA/SAT I study, by Schmitt et al. (1998), a predictive approach was used. It was assumed that development of a concordance table was not essential to the success of the study. Consequently, a prediction approach employing a measure of English-language ability, the English Second Language Achievement Test (ESLAT), as a moderator variable provided the basic design for the study.

Prior studies are relevant to this research. A regression method was used by Alderman (1981) and Boldt (1969) to study the relationship between tests given in English and Spanish to different cultural groups. In the Alderman study, students were tested on the SAT, PAA, TOEFL (Test of English as a Foreign Language), and ESLAT. Language proficiency (TOEFL or ESLAT) was considered as a moderator variable in predicting SAT test results from PAA test results. Higher language proficiency, as measured by these tests, resulted in a stronger relationship between the SAT and PAA scores. These results underline the importance of using a measure of language proficiency when creating a prediction equation between the SAT and PAA. Because all PAA examinees also take the ESLAT for admissions purposes, the ESLAT results can be used as such a language moderator variable.

The sample for the third PAA/SAT I study (Schmitt et al., 1998) was all available candidates who took the new PAA in Puerto Rico from October 1996 throughout June 1997 and who also took the SAT I from January 1996 to June 1997. Only the last score of the students that repeated the test within the defined period was considered in the analyses. Each student included in the study had the following test scores: (a) SAT I Verbal and Math, from the January 1996 to the June 1997 administration, (b) PAA Verbal and Math, from the October 1996 to the June 1997 administrations, and (c) ESLAT, from the October 1996 to the June 1997 administrations. Both linear and curvilinear multiple regression prediction models were considered for the prediction of SAT I scores from PAA scores and the ESLAT.

Schmitt et al. (1998) found the correlations between SAT I and PAA/ESLAT in the sample to be very noteworthy. The correlation between PAA Math and SAT I Math was .82, indicating that the tests are measuring similar, but not the same constructs. In addition, SAT I Math correlated .57 with ESLAT, a correlation indicating that ESLAT is acting as a language proficiency moderator variable for the math scores. Table 6.1 contains the correlations for these test scores.

The correlations between ESLAT and SAT I Verbal show an even stronger suggestion of a language proficiency moderator variable, with SAT I Verbal correlating .73 with ESLAT and considerably less, .62, with PAA Verbal. Note that PAA Math has only a slightly lower correlation with PAA Verbal (.60) than the correlation shown by SAT I Verbal and PAA Verbal. It is clear from these data that any concor-

TABLE 6.1
Correlations Between SAT and PAA Verbal and Math and the ESLAT

Test Score	*ESLAT*	*PAA-M*	*PAA-V*	*SAT-M*	*SAT-V*
ESLAT	1.00	.51	.45	.57	.74
PAA-MATH	.51	1.00	.61	.82	.60
PAA-VERBAL	.45	.61	1.00	.56	.62
SAT-MATH	.57	.82	.56	1.00	.69
SAT-VERBAL	.73	.60	.62	.69	1.00

dance table developed using tests with this configuration of correlation coefficients would be of questionable value, regardless of the chosen linking methodology. One question for this study was whether or not PAA Verbal could add much to the prediction of SAT I Verbal scores beyond what ESLAT could do on its own.

The equations for predicting SAT Verbal and SAT Math scores from PAA scores and ESLAT scores are approximated by the following formulae: For SAT Verbal,

$$\text{Estimated SAT Verbal} = .371*\text{PAA Verbal} + .779*\text{ESLAT}-284.$$

Note that the weight assigned to ESLAT is more than twice that assigned to PAA Verbal.

The approximate equation for predicting SAT Math from PAA Math and ESLAT makes it obvious that PAA Math is the more important predictor:

$$\text{Estimated SAT Math} = .688*\text{PAA Math} + .259*\text{ESLAT} -150.$$

It can be seen that PAA Math has a weight that is more than twice as large as that for ESLAT.

It should be noted that the equations for predicting SAT Verbal and Math appear to have limited applicability because they cannot be used for scores below 550 on ESLAT. Schmitt et al. (1998) found that scores for examinees with ESLAT scores below 550 in the sample have an erratic relationship with the variables of interest. This was interpreted as meaning that a certain level of English-language ability, as measured by ESLAT, is needed before scores become systematically related to the other test scores, and more important before the relationships between scores on similar constructs measured in Spanish and English stabilize. The prominent role of ESLAT in predicting SAT Verbal scores even in this group of high ESLAT scores (550 is almost a standard deviation [118] above the mean of 446 in the full PAA population) brings to the fore the problems of trying to link scores on tests such as the PAA and the SAT I that are given in different languages to groups of different cultural backgrounds. Linking scores using prediction methodology would appear to provide more interpretable results than attempting to establish a concordance table using the conventional anchor test equating methodology employed in the two earlier studies.

The design of the third study does have a number of drawbacks that should be pointed out. The study is a prediction study using a bilingual group design. Drawbacks of prediction studies and bilingual group designs were pointed out earlier in this chapter, but the bilingual group design used in this study is different from the designs discussed earlier in that ESLAT was used as a concomitant variable. An apparent drawback of this design is that the prediction equations obtained from the study are group specific and the bilingual sample used for the study is not representative of all examinees taking the PAA. The sample consisted of students primarily from private high schools in Puerto Rico with higher levels of English-language proficiency than typically found among Puerto Rico high school students. However, it is just this type of examinee that typically seeks postsecondary education in the United States. Consequently, although the results of the study may not describe the relationship between scores obtained on the PAA and the SAT I for all students in high schools in Puerto Rico, the results may be quite valid for the selected number of students who intend to continue their education in the United States.

Schmitt et al. (1998) pointed out that the generalization to other groups beyond those represented by the sample (including groups taking the PAA in Latin American countries, other than Puerto Rico) may not be appropriate because the relationship between SAT I and PAA and ESLAT may differ in these other countries.

An additional drawback of the methodology represented by this study is that it did not result in a single concordance table that permits direct comparisons of subgroups of students taking the PAA with subgroups of students taking the SAT I. As a result of this study, score users were provided with a table that required entering with both a PAA and ESLAT score and reading predicted SAT I scores from the body of the table. Consequently the gain in validity in the score predictions was counterbalanced by a loss of practicality or convenience to the score user.

Because application of the methodology used to develop the relationship between PAA and SAT I scores in the third study did not result in a concordance table, it is not possible to compare the results of this study with those obtained in the previous two studies carried out by Angoff and Modu (1973) and Angoff and Cook (1988). Although, it should be pointed out that because both the tests (PAA and SAT) have been modified considerably since the previous two studies were completed, comparisons of results across the three studies would be questionable, even if the methodology used to link the tests in study three supported the development of a concordance table.

DISCUSSION

A number of important lessons can be learned from an evaluation of the work that has been done over the past 20 years that has focused on linking scores obtained on the PAA to scores obtained on the SAT. Each of the three studies discussed here attempted to improve on the results of the past studies by applying the most current thinking in psychometric theory and the most recent technological developments. Still, even the most recent study, carried out by Schmitt et al. (1998), exhibited a number of serious drawbacks. Certainly the experiences gained from the three PAA/SAT linking studies strongly demonstrate how difficult it is to obtain comparable and valid scores on tests that are given to groups that differ in language and culture.

Probably the most significant advance in the Angoff–Modu study (Angoff & Modu, 1973) was the application of the delta plot technique for detecting items in the "common" item–equating set that did not behave similarly for the Spanish-speaking and English-speaking groups. Angoff and Modu used this new technique, which initially had been developed for screening items for racial bias (Angoff & Ford, 1973). The procedure involved plotting item difficulty values (deltas) for items administered to the two groups of interest, and deleting those items that fell away from the major axis of the elipse formed by the plot. Angoff and Modu realized early on that one serious pitfall in cross-lingual/cross-cultural studies was that in spite of the most meticulous translation and back translation, items that are expected to behave similarly (as "common" items in an anchor test design) must be screened statistically, particularly those items that have a heavy verbal/linguistic component. Recent research by Muniz, Hambleton, and Xing (2001) shows too that delta plots can still be useful in detecting problematic items even with small sample sizes.

The study carried out by Angoff and Cook (1988) built on the design of the earlier study with some methodological and technological improvements. The authors hoped that the use of IRT procedures, to replace the use of the classical test theory procedures that were used in the first study, would provide improved results. Indeed, the IRT procedures for detecting DIF (see Lord, 1980), proved to be very powerful procedures for screening common items. The authors were quite confident that by the time they had completed the item screening they were able to construct a "common" test that could be used for linking purposes without risk of advantaging either group of interest. However, the authors began to question the underlying assumptions of the work they were doing. Were the two tests (PAA and SAT) measuring constructs that were similar enough to support the development of a concordance table? What did it mean to use a score on the PAA for a student who spoke only Spanish to estimate a student's score on the Verbal section of the SAT?

As a result of the concerns raised by the authors of the second PAA/SAT linking study, the methodology used for the third study was completely revised. The authors of the third study (Schmitt et al., 1998) used regression procedures to develop the relationship between PAA and SAT I scores. In the course of the analysis of the data for the third study, they found that the correlations between scores obtained on the PAA Verbal and SAT I Verbal tests (for the bilingual sample used in the study) was only slightly higher than the correlation between scores obtained on the PAA Verbal and the PAA Math tests. Although, as pointed out earlier, there are statistical techniques that can be used to develop concordance tables when tests do not measure the same thing (and, indeed, the work done for study two is an excellent example of this type of work) the question remains, how does one interpret the results of the application of a concordance table developed under these circumstances?

Schmitt et al. (1998) chose to develop prediction equations for predicting SAT scores from PAA scores. The equations took into account not only the verbal or math ability of the examinee as measured by the PAA, but also considered the examinee's English-language ability, as measured by the ESLAT. Although the prediction equations are awkward to use and cannot be used readily in the comparison of groups of examinees, they do provide a more accurate answer to the question of how a student who scores at a specific level on the PAA will score on the SAT I.

Questions that remain to be explored when considering the linking of the PAA and the SAT I are: the description of the similarity or differences between the constructs measured by the PAA and the SAT I and how these similarities or differences are impacted by English-language ability. In addition, it is important to keep in mind that colleges are not so much interested in predicting SAT I scores from a PAA score as they are interested in making valid decisions about how successful students will be if they are admitted to the particular college. The relationship between the PAA and the SAT I scores that was developed in the third PAA/SAT I study requires validation by examining the relationship between the predicted SAT I scores and performance in college, as measured by freshman grade point average or some other criterion of importance.

It is important to keep the results and lessons learned from the three PAA/SAT studies in mind when reviewing the work of other test adaptation projects. Adapting tests is not a trivial process, but it is an extremely important process that impacts greatly on the validity of test scores. Depending on the ultimate use of the test scores, it can be extremely important for students, employees, and other populations to be given the opportunity to demonstrate their skills and abilities on tests that are given in their native tongue. Two important lessons learned from the three PAA/SAT studies indicate that:

1. It is important to take into account how the test scores will be used and interpreted. The design of the linking study and the models chosen for linking will depend greatly on the possible uses and interpretations of the test scores.
2. There is no simple way of doing a high-quality job of adapting tests to different languages and cultures. Adapting tests is a painstaking process that requires careful execution. Not only must careful attention be paid to the test developmental process, attention to the test administration and score interpretation process is equally as important.

Fortunately good work is being carried out in the test adaptation area and with the increasing interest in the field, solutions to what may appear to be intractable problems today will most likely be available to us in the future.

ACKNOWLEDGMENTS

The authors appreciate the technical contributions of Anthony Magrina, Neil Dorans, and Daniel Eignor to the preparation of this chapter.

REFERENCES

Alderman, D. L. (1981). *Language proficiency as a moderator variable in testing academic aptitude* (TOEFL Research Rep. No. 10, RR81-41). Princeton, NJ: Educational Testing Service.

Angoff, W. H. (1984). *Scales, norms, and equivalent scores.* Princeton, NJ: Educational Testing Service.

Angoff, W. H., & Cook, L. L. (1988). *Equating the scores of the Prueba de Aptitud Academica and the Scholastic Aptitude Test* (College Board Rep. No. 88-2). New York: College Entrance Examination Board.

Angoff, W. H., & Ford, S. F. (1973). Item-race interaction on a test of scholastic aptitude. *Journal of Educational Measurement, 10,* 95–106.

Angoff, W. H., & Modu, C. C. (1973). *Equating the scales of the Prueba de Aptitud Academica and the Scholastic Aptitude Test* (Research Rep. No. 3). New York: College Entrance Examination Board.

Boldt, R. (1969). *Concurrent validity of the PAA and SAT for bilingual Dade County high school volunteers* (Statistical Rep. No. 69-31). Princeton, NJ: Educational Testing Service.

The College Board. (1995). *Cambiod en el examen de admision del College Board: La nueva PAA* [Changes in the College Board admissions tests: The new PAA]. San Juan: Oficina de Puerto Rico y de Actividades Latinamericanas.

Cook, L. L. (1995, April). *Lessons learned: Implementing change in the SAT.* Paper presented at the meeting of the National Council on Educational Measurement, San Francisco.

Cook, L. L., & Eignor, D. R. (1983). Practical considerations regarding the use of item response theory to equate tests. In R. K. Hambleton (Ed.), *Applications of item response theory* (pp. 175–195). Vancouver: Educational Research Institute of British Columbia.

Cook, L. L., Eignor, D. R., & Schmitt, A. P. (1989, April). *Equating achievement tests using samples matched on ability.* Paper presented at the meeting of the American Educational Research Association, San Francisco.

Eignor, D. R., Stocking, M. L., & Cook, L. L. (1990). Simulation results of the effects on linear and curvilinear observed- and true-score equating procedures of matching on a fallible criterion. *Applied Measurement in Education, 3,* 37–55.

Geisinger, K. F. (1994). Cross-cultural normative assessment: Transition and adaption issues influencing the normative interpretation of assessment instruments. *Psychological Assessment, 6,* 304–312.

Hambleton, R. K. (1993). Adapting achievement tests for use in cross-national studies. *European Journal of Psychological Assessment, 9,* 57–68.

Hambleton, R. K. (1996, April). *Guidelines for adapting educational and psychological tests.* Paper presented at the meeting of the National Council on Educational Measurement, New York.

Kolen, M. J. (1990). Does matching in an equating work? A discussion. *Applied Measurement in Education, 3,* 97–104.

Levine, R. S. (1955). *Equating the score scales of alternate forms administered to samples of different ability* (Research Bulletin No. 23). Princeton, NJ: Educational Testing Service.

Linn, R. L. (1993). Linking results of distinct assessments. *Applied Measurement in Education, 6,* 83–102.

Livingston, S. A., Dorans, N. J., & Wright, N. K. (1990). What combination of sampling and equating methods works best? *Applied Measurement in Education, 3,* 73–95.

Lord, F. M. (1980). *Applications of item response theory to practical testing problems.* Hillsdale, NJ: Lawrence Erlbaum Associates.

Muniz, J., Hambleton, R. K., & Xing, D. (2001). Small sample studies to detect flaws in test translation. *International Journal of Testing, 1,* 115–135.

Olmedo, E. L. (1981). Testing linguistic minorities. *American Psychologist, 36,* 1078–1085.

Pennock-Román, M. (1995). *Measuring developed academic abilities using Spanish vs English-langauge tests: PAEG/GRE relationships for Puerto Ricans who are more proficient in Spanish than in English* (GRE Research Rep. No. 89-01). Princeton, NJ: Educational Testing Service.

Petersen, N. S., Cook, L. L., & Stocking, M. L. (1983). IRT versus conventional equating methods: A comparative study of scale stability. *Journal of Educational Statistics, 8,* 137–156.

Poortinga, Y. H. (1989). Equivalence of cross-cultural data: An overview of basic issues. *International Journal of Psychology, 24,* 737–756.

Prieto, A. (1992). A method for translation of instruments to other languages. *Adult Education Quarterly, 43,* 1–14.

Rosenbaum, P. R., & Rubin, D. B. (1983). The central role of the propensity score in observational studies for causal effects. *Biometrika, 70,* 41–55.

Schmitt, A. P., Dorans, N. J., Magrina, A. & Cook, L. L. (1998). *Predicting scores on the English Language SAT from the Spanish Language PAA and the Spanish Language English as a Second Language Achievement Test.* Paper presented at the meeting of the American Educational Research Association, San Diego.

Sireci, S. G. (1997). Technical issues in linking tests across languages. *Educational Measurement: Issues and Practice, 16,* 12–19.

Sireci, S. G., & Allalouf, A. (2003). Appraising item equivalence across multiple languages and cultures. *Language Testing, 20*(2), 147–165.

Skaggs, G. (1990). To match or not to match samples on ability for equating: A discussion of five articles. *Applied Measurement in Education, 3,* 105–113.

Stocking, M. L., & Lord, F. M. (1983). Developing a common metric in item response theory. *Applied Psychological Measurement, 7,* 201–210.

Terman, L. M. (1916). *The measurement of intelligence.* Boston: Houghton Mifflin.

van de Vijver, F. J. R. & Poortinga, Y. H. (1991). Testing across cultures. In R. K. Hambleton & J. Zaal (Eds.), *Advances in educational and psychological testing* (pp. 277–308). Dordrecht, Netherlands: Kluwer Academic.

7

Adapting Achievement and Aptitude Tests: A Review of Methodological Issues

Linda L. Cook
Educational Testing Service

Alicia P. Schmitt-Cascallar
Assessment Group International, Brussels, Belgium

Catherine Brown
Educational Testing Service

Interest in adapting tests that have been developed for a particular language and culture for use with a second language and cultural group has been prevalent among educational and psychological researchers and practitioners for most of the 20th century. As an example, Hambleton and Bollwark (1991) discussed early translations of the Binet–Simon intelligence test. They point out that the test was translated from French to English in 1911 and used to evaluate intelligence of residents of the New Jersey-based Vineland Training School. Hambleton and Bollwark went on to say that by 1916 the Binet–Simon had been translated into seven different languages (citing Stanley & Hopkins, 1972). They continued by pointing out other important intelligence tests and related scales that have been translated into the primary language of the examinees to be tested.

Van de Vijver (2002), van de Vijver and Lonner (1995), and van de Vijver and Leung (1997, 2000) pointed out that recently there has been a steady increase in publications that deal with cross-cultural differences and comparisons. They attributed the increase in these publications to such things as the globalization of the economy, tourism, migration streams, and related political changes.

The purpose of this chapter is to review the methodological issues that are associated with the adaptation of achievement and aptitude measures. The chapter consists of six sections. The first section provides an overview of the central issues of bias and equivalence as they relate to cross-cultural/cross-lingual comparisons of assessment results. The overview is followed by separate sections that focus on issues associated with: (a) construct equivalence, (b) equivalence of measurement units, (c) translating tests and test material, (d) score interpretation and test use, and (e) test administration.

OVERVIEW OF CENTRAL ISSUES

Van de Vijver and Leung (1997) pointed out that "a recurring theme in multicultural assessment is the question of the extent to which instruments developed in Western countries can be applied in different cultural contexts" (p. 61). They listed four questions that those interested in multicultural assessment might ask:

> Does a test provide an adequate coverage of the same psychological construct in all cultural groups at hand?
>
> Can a standard administration be applied or should the administration be adapted?
>
> How can we cope with the often immense variation in mastery of the native and host language in migrant groups?
>
> Are alternatives available when Western tests turn out to be inappropriate? (p. 61)

The four questions are all quite relevant to those situations in which achievement and aptitude tests are adapted for cross-cultural/cross-lingual application. Perhaps the most central of these issues is the issue of adequate coverage of the same construct in all cultural groups of interest. Much of the literature on cross-cultural assessment has been devoted to the examination and evaluation of comparability of constructs across different cultures and languages.

Questions of the impact of test administration procedures as well as language variation are particularly important to the adequate adaptation of achievement and aptitude tests and to the validity of cross-cultural score comparisons.

Van de Vijver and Tanzer (1997) articulated three types of bias that could possibly impact cross-cultural, cross-lingual assessments: construct bias, method bias, and, item bias.

They also discussed the impact of two types of equivalence on cross-cultural research and evaluations: construct equivalence and measurement unit equivalence. The point made by van de Vijver and Tanzer is that in every cross-cultural study, the key question is whether or not the scores obtained on the assessments given to the different populations can be interpreted in the same way. They emphasized that the issues of bias and equivalence are central to this question.

Van de Vijver and Tanzer (1997) defined *construct bias*[1] as occurring if the construct measured is not identical across cultural groups. They used, as an example, Western intelligence tests. These authors made the important point that construct bias is not a term that applies to a specific instrument, but rather to characteristics of a cross-cultural comparison. They pointed out that an instrument that reveals bias in a comparison of Japanese and German subjects may not show bias in a comparison of German and Danish subjects.

Van de Vijver and Tanzer (1997) also discussed *method bias,* which they further broke into sampling, instrument, and administration bias. They pointed out that the term method bias was so coined because it refers to biases arising from the methodology employed in empirical studies.

According to van de Vijver and Tanzer (1997), sampling bias arises from sampling differences related to variables (other than the variable of interest) that may impact study results. They gave as examples cultural groups that differ in educational background or motivation. If neither of these are variables of interest, they can surely confound comparisons of the particular variable that is the focus of the study.

In a discussion of instrument bias, van de Vijver and Tanzer (1997) used stimulus familiarity as a well-known example. They expanded on this example by citing the work of Hui and Triandis (1989), who found that Hispanics tended to choose extremes on a 5-point rating scale more often than did White Americans. Hui and Triandis discov-

[1]Construct bias has been discussed extensively by van de Vijver and Leung (1997), van de Vijver and Poortinga (1991), and Poortinga (1995).

ered that confounding due to choice preference was eliminated when a 10-point scale was introduced.

The third type of method bias discussed by van de Vijver and Tanzer (1997) is administration bias. Other authors, as well, have raised administration bias as a threat to the validity of interpretations of scores on adapted tests. For example, Geisinger (1994) discussed the fact that different cultural or national groups vary in their levels of sophistication with differing item formats and he suggested that a sufficient number of practice exercises be used to familiarize the examinees with a new format.

Finally, in addition to discussing construct and method bias, van de Vijver and Tanzer (1997) discussed *item bias* as an important type of bias confounding cross-cultural studies. They list the following sources of item bias in these types of studies: "poor item translation and/or ambiguous items; nuisance factors (e.g., item may invoke additional traits or abilities); cultural specifics (e.g., incidental differences in connotative meaning and/or appropriateness of the item content)" (p. 268).

Needless to say, item bias issues pose formidable challenges to the validity of any cross-cultural comparison of aptitude or achievement test scores. Issues related to item bias, such as test translation and procedures to detect differential item functioning (DIF), are discussed in chapter 4 of this volume and so are not be considered further here.

In a discussion of equivalence[2] in cross-cultural studies, van de Vijver and Tanzer (1997) made the distinction between construct equivalence and measurement unit equivalence. They defined *construct equivalence* as meaning that the same construct is measured across all cultural groups of interest regardless of whether the measurement instruments that are used are identical. They went on to say that it is quite possible for the same instrument to measure different constructs for different cultures; or, the construct measured by the same instrument may only partially overlap between two cultures.

Equally as important as construct equivalence, van de Vijver and Tanzer (1997) defined a second type of equivalence, *measurement unit equivalence,* as the situation that exists if two measures have the same measurement unit but different origins. They clarified this definition by stating: "In other words, the scale of one measure is shifted with a constant offset as compared to the other measure" (p. 266). They made the point that scores on scales with these properties can-

[2]See also van de Vijver and Leung (1997, 2000) and Poortinga (1989) for discussions of equivalence in cross-cultural studies.

not be directly compared, but if the offsetting factor is known, scores can be adjusted making them suitable for comparison.

Ultimately, if one is to make valid comparisons of scores on achievement or aptitude tests, one must achieve what van de Vijver and Tanzer (1997) referred to as scalar equivalence, which they defined as the highest level of measurement unit equivalence for two scales. They pointed out that this type of equivalence can be obtained when two scales have the same origin and unit of measurement. They continued by saying that the achievement of scalar equivalence is a prerequisite for the cross-cultural comparison of assessment results. They emphasized that any form of bias, method, construct, and so forth, will challenge and lower the measurement unit equivalence of the measures.

CONSTRUCT EQUIVALENCE

This section of the chapter provides a discussion of the importance of construct equivalence in cross-cultural studies as well as a review of selected procedures used to evaluate the equivalence of constructs across multiple populations.

The Importance of Construct Equivalence

A great deal of both theoretical and empirical work in the area of construct equivalence is prevalent in the literature of cross-cultural assessments. Authors such as Poortinga (1983, 1989), van de Vijver and Leung (1997), and van de Vijver and Tanzer (1997) have developed eloquent definitions and discussions of construct equivalence.

Along these lines, Poortinga (1989) discussed what he referred to as the "logic of comparison." He made the point that a comparison between individuals or groups can be misleading for two reasons. The first is that the attribute used for the comparison may not be the same across individuals or groups (construct equivalence). He gave as an example, the comparison of height and weight; that is, it does not make sense to say that one person is taller than another person is heavy. The second reason is that the units of measurement may not be the same (measurement unit equivalence); for example, length measured in inches cannot be directly compared to length measured in centimeters.

Poortinga (1989) expanded on the relationship between construct and measurement unit equivalence by pointing out that the probability that two test versions differing (significantly) in content will form comparable measurement scales is very low. In other words, construct equivalence would appear to be a necessary condition for measurement equivalence to exist.

In a second paper, Poortinga (1983) explored even further the relationship between construct equivalence and other forms of equivalence. He discussed the implications of an analysis that shows differences in the assessment results across populations. He made the point that the researcher is left with deciding whether or not the lack of comparable results arises from inequivalent constructs, inequivalent measurement units, or from true differences among the populations.

Poortinga (1983) continued by saying that analysis of the comparability of test results often leads one to the domain of construct validation. He acknowledged that the notions of construct equivalence and construct validation overlap considerably, but he made a very important distinction between the two concepts. The point he made is a key one. In an analysis of construct equivalence, the main question is whether the *same* construct is being measured; whereas, in an analysis of construct validity the key issue is *which* construct is being measured.

Poortinga (1983) stressed the importance of theory-oriented research. He emphasized that, "meaningful analysis of comparability requires a theoretical framework on the basis of which it can be stipulated explicitly which relationships between which variables have to be invariant over groups" (p. 246). As an example, Poortinga referred to the writings of Van der Flier and Drenth (1980). According to Van der Flier and Drenth, one can argue that measurements of height and weight provide comparable results across cultures, even though the correlation between these variables may differ across populations. They made the point, however, that if height and weight are to be used to infer the value of a third variable, say, waist circumference, then in order to be considered equivalent measures across the populations of interest, height and weight and waist circumference must have similar correlations across these populations. Consequently, without a well-developed theory about the relationship of height, weight, and waist circumference, it would be difficult to evaluate the equivalence or the validity of measures across the populations of interest.

Van de Vijver and Tanzer (1997) defined construct equivalence as "the same construct is measured across all cultural groups studied, regardless of whether or not the measurement of the construct is based on identical instruments across all cultures" (p. 265). They pointed out that construct inequivalence can occur when constructs only partially overlap across cultures or when constructs are associated with different behaviors or characteristics as a result of cultural differences. They provided the following summary of sources of construct bias (lack of equivalence): "only partial overlap in the definitions of the construct across cultures; differential appropriateness of the behaviors associated with the construct (e.g., skills do not belong to the repertoire of one of the cultural groups); poor sampling of all relevant behaviors (e.g., short instruments); incomplete coverage of all relevant aspects/facets of the construct (e.g., not all relevant domains are sampled)" (p. 268).

These authors continued by articulating the following valuable strategies for identifying and addressing issues of construct bias (or equivalence) in cross-cultural assessments:

- decentering (i.e., simultaneously developing the same instrument in several cultures)
- convergence approach (i.e., independent within-culture development of instruments and subsequent cross-cultural administration of all instruments)
- use of informants with expertise in local culture and language
- use of samples of bilingual subjects
- use of local surveys (e.g. content analyses of free-response questions)
- non-standard instrument administration (e.g., "thinking aloud")
- cross-cultural comparison of nomological networks (e.g., convergent/discriminant validity studies, monotrait-multimethod studies, connotation of key phrases) (p. 272).

Following is a discussion of some of the more common strategies for evaluating construct equivalence that were previously identified, with selected examples of successful applications.

Evaluation of Construct Equivalence

Hui and Triandis (1985) described various methods that are used to demonstrate construct equivalence and they made a very strong point for the use of multiple approaches to the problem. They began by describing regression methods as a way of demonstrating equivalence across populations. They made the point that it is straightforward to conclude that assessments that are equivalent across populations would be related in a similar manner to an external criterion. They continued by saying that this is a simple and economical approach to the question of equivalence. But, they pointed out that differences in variability of samples and reliability of instruments can cause fluctuations in regression coefficients that are "essentially false alarms."

Hui and Triandis (1985) also discuss item response theory (IRT) approaches to the establishment of equivalence (see Sireci & Allalouf, 2003). They stated that an instrument that "has similar ICCs (item characteristic curves) across cultures has, at least in part, demonstrated its item equivalence [and consequently construct equivalence] and scalar equivalence" (p. 139).

Angoff and Cook (1988) discussed the use of IRT methods to develop a set of construct equivalent items that are used for the purposes of linking tests of developed ability given to Spanish-speaking and English-speaking examinees. They concluded that IRT methods were quite effective when used for this purpose. The Angoff–Cook study is expanded upon in chapter 6 of this volume.

In addition to a discussion of regression methods and IRT methods, Hui and Triandis (1985) discussed structural congruence. They pointed out the fact that if a construct is to be considered equivalent across cultures, the internal structures and the relationship among these structures should be the same across the cultures of interest. They suggested factor analysis and multidimensional scaling as statistical techniques that could be usefully employed to understand how a construct operates across different cultures.

Sireci, Fitzgerald, and Xing (1998) used a combination of principal components analysis, confirmatory factor analysis, and multidimensional scaling to evaluate the construct equivalence of Microsoft's Networking Technology Server exam administered to English, French, German, and Japanese examinees in their native languages. The authors conducted a principal components analysis with both item-level and -parcel data. (Use of clusters of items, or parcels, in factor analytical work is advisable to avoid spurious difficulty factors that could be introduced if correlations are based on item-level data.) The multidimensional scaling analysis was performed only on item-parcel data.

A number of authors point to the applicability of confirmatory factor analysis procedures to the evaluation of construct equivalence across populations (see, e.g., Gierl, 2000). Everson, Guerrero, and Laitusis (1998) investigated the construct equivalence of the SAT I mathematics test (SAT-M) and the mathematics section of the Prueba de Aptitud Academica (PAA-M) administered to a group of bilingual high school students from Puerto Rico. The authors used both exploratory and confirmatory factor analysis techniques. Everson et.al. used a clustering technique to develop the input to the exploratory factor analysis.

EQUIVALENCE OF MEASUREMENT UNITS

Establishing a common metric for scores obtained on achievement or aptitude tests given in different languages to examinees with different cultural backgrounds is extremely difficult for many of the reasons pointed out earlier in this chapter, particularly those related to the possibility of an adapted test measuring a different construct once it has been translated into different languages and given to examinees with different cultural backgrounds. The reason this presents a serious problem is that one of the underlying assumptions of most methods that are used to establish a common metric (scale-linking methods) is that the assessments that will be linked measure the same, or very similar, constructs. Chapter 6 of this volume provides an overview and discussion of procedures and issues related to establishing equivalent measurement units.

TRANSLATING TESTS AND TEST MATERIALS

Cross-cultural studies involving comparisons of achievement or aptitude across cultures with different languages commonly use instruments that have been translated to a target language and adapted to the target culture. The process of developing equivalent instruments in more than one language involves not only translation of the test items and test materials, but other changes such as changes in item format and testing procedures (test adaptation). Multiple issues pertaining to test translation need to be considered in order to have instruments that are appropriate for cross-cultural comparisons. "A good translation must reflect not only the meaning of the original item, but should also try to maintain the same relevance, intrinsic interest and familiarity of the item content; otherwise what the item measures may be altered" (Ercikan, 1999, p. 2).

A panel of 13 members was formed in 1992 by the International Test Commission to develop technical standards for test adaptation. The committee produced a set of 22 guidelines for adapting educational and psychological tests (Hambleton, 1994, 1996; see also chap. 1, this volume). Seven of these guidelines specifically address issues related to the translation process as it impacts the validity of instruments developed for cross-cultural/cross-lingual comparisons of aptitude and achievement. As a way of organizing our review of issues related to test translation, each of these guidelines is presented with a brief explanation and pertinent references.

1. *Instrument developers/publishers should ensure that the adaptation process takes full account of linguistic and cultural differences among the populations for whom adapted versions of the instrument are intended.* Experienced and well-qualified translators are crucial to the process of test translation because their task has a major effect on reliability and validity of test scores. The guidelines stress that because, in addition to expertise in both (or more) languages, familiarity and experience with the cultures, the content of the test, and measurement principles are essential, a team of specialists needs to be involved. A common error has been to use easily available individuals that are not qualified. Even when translation companies are used and terms of contract specify that bilingual and content specialists are to translate the items, large translation differences can be found. Reckase and Kunce (1999) concluded that, especially for more technical items of certification tests, a solution to these differences would be to use "very knowledgeable translators and careful checks on the meaning of the items by bilingual content experts" (p. 16). In their study of translation accuracy in automotive technician credentialing examinations, Reckase and Kunce also requested that the translators be native speakers of the target language. The use of translators dominant in the target language has been recommended by Woodcock (1985) and Hambleton (1993) so that translations are natural and effective. Studies of bilingualism have demonstrated that it is easier for persons dominant in a target language to recognize a word in a source language and to effectively remember the corresponding meaning in the target language than vice-versa (Perez, 1975).

2. *Instrument developers/publishers should provide evidence that the language used in the directions, rubrics, and items themselves as well as in the handbook are appropriate for all cultural and language populations for whom the instrument is intended.* The test in the source language can be unnecessarily complicated making accurate translations difficult or it can have concepts, expressions, and ideas that do not have equivalents in the target language (Hambleton, 1993; Ercikan, 1998, 2000). The level of difficulty of words, readability, grammar usage, writing style and punctuation need to be comparable across languages. One way to minimize differences in difficulty of words is to use frequency lists of words (Hambleton & Kanjee, 1993). The problem is that not only are these language word lists not always available, but if they exist they may not be in the language of the specific target group. For technical translations, use of glossaries of technical terms has been recommended by Reckase and Kunce (1999). When certain words or ex-

pressions do not exist in the target language, "decentering" or adding cultural specific value items to the source instrument may be necessary. The flexibility of having the option of "decentering" or changing the source instrument in order to achieve equivalence across languages is more probable when the source and target language instruments are being developed simultaneously (Hambleton & Kanjee, 1995).

3. *Instrument developers/publishers should provide evidence that item content and stimulus materials are familiar to all intended populations.* When instruments are being developed in anticipation of translation to a different language and for use in a second culture, it is important to avoid different units of measurement, currency or other stimulus materials (e.g., diagrams, tables figures, or famous landmarks) that could differentially affect the performance of different populations. These possible sources lending to appropriate performance should be taken into consideration in the instrument development phase. Hambleton and Kanjee (1995) recommended that units of measurement, such as inches, feet, and so on, be avoided because they tend to vary from one nationality to another.

4. *Instrument developers/publishers should implement systematic judgmental evidence, both linguistic and psychological, to improve the accuracy of the adaptation process and compile evidence on the equivalence of all language versions.* Judgmental methods should be used before the instrument is administered or evaluated statistically. The most popular judgmental methods to establish translation equivalence are forward translations and backward translations. The forward-translation design involves the translation of the instrument from the source language into the target language by one group of translators while its equivalence to the source language is judged by another group of translators. The backward-translation design involves the re-translation of the instrument into the source language by a different group of translators and its evaluation as to its equivalence to the original instrument by a judge or set of judges. Although the backward-translation design has been used extensively (Brislin, 1970). Hambleton and Patsula (1998) contended that this method does not directly evaluate the similarity of the constructs measured by the two versions of the test. "The main disadvantage of this design is that the evaluation of test equivalence is carried out in the source language only" (Hambleton & Kanjee, 1995, p. 151). Although this method can provide an initial check on the equivalence of the translation, "there is little evidence to support the position that translators or other judges are capable of predicting the equiva-

lence of versions of an instrument from a review, however carefully it may be done" (Hambleton & Kanjee, 1993, p. 10).

5. *Instrument developers/publishers should ensure that the data collection design permits the use of appropriate statistical techniques to establish item equivalence between the different language versions of the instrument.* Sufficient sample sizes for both source and target language groups need to be met so that statistical techniques (e.g., multidimensional scaling, factor analysis, IRT, item bias) can be applied meaningfully. Three data collection designs were described by Hambleton (1993):

- Bilingual examinees take source and target versions.
- Source language monolingual examinees take the original and back-translated versions of the test.
- Source language monolinguals take source version and target language monolinguals take target version.

Hambleton (1993) made the point that designs using bilinguals are often difficult to carry out because it is hard to locate bilinguals that are equally proficient in both languages. He continued by saying that evidence gathered using a bilingual sample might not generalize to the monolingual population of interest. He was also critical of designs that involve monolinguals evaluating source and back-translated versions of an instrument. He pointed out that one of the main shortcomings of this type of comparison is that the source instrument and the back-translated instrument may appear comparable even though the translation was poor. This could occur if the translators used a shared set of translation rules or if the translation retained inappropriate aspects of the source language such as the same grammatical structure, and the like. Hambleton favored the design for which one group of monolinguals takes the source version of the instrument and a second group of monolinguals take the target version and the two versions are "linked" by a set of common items. The advantage of this design is that samples of the source and target populations are used in the analyses and the findings are more likely to generalize to the populations of interest.

6. *Instrument developers/publishers should apply appropriate statistical techniques to (a) establish the equivalence of the different versions of the instrument, and (b) identify problematic components or aspects of the instrument that may be inadequate to one or more of the intended populations.* As a supplement to the judgmental techniques, statistical methods can be used to ensure the appropriateness of test translations. Hambleton (1993) recommended a study of factorial structures of multiple language versions of a test as

a valuable way of assessing the adequacy of the translation of the test from source to target language.

7. *Instrument developers/publishers should provide statistical evidence of the equivalence of questions for all intended populations.* Differential item function or item bias analyses can be used to evaluate if item performance is comparable across populations after ability is taken into consideration. A review of these methods was presented in chapter 4 (this volume).

SCORE INTERPRETATION AND TEST USE

The process of achievement or aptitude testing could be considered, in and of itself, a means to an end. The test produces a score that is interpreted by various users for different purposes. In educational testing situations, a score is believed to hold some meaning about an examinee's ability or mastery of a particular domain of knowledge or information. In cross-cultural studies, testing provides a basis for comparisons to be made between different language and cultural groups so that differences and similarities between groups can be better understood (Hambleton & Bollwark, 1991). However, interpreting the results of achievement and aptitude tests given to groups speaking different languages is not a straightforward task for test developers and users because unintended differences in test difficulty and content alone may contribute to observed differences in scores between groups or individuals (Sireci, 1997).

In the past, test developers have behaved as if the only important factor in adapting a test to a different culture is the translation of the language originally used in the test to the new language. As mentioned in an earlier section of this chapter, simply translating a test from one language to another does not guarantee score comparability across the languages involved and, using this line of reasoning, the cultures also involved (Angoff & Cook, 1988; Geisinger, 1994; Hambleton, 1993; Prieto, 1992; Sireci, 1997). As Hambleton (1994) stated, a casual approach to test adaptation leads to a false belief that score differences between samples or populations can be interpreted as if they are real.

Language translation has been alluded to as one factor that, though an important aspect of test adaptation, by itself is not sufficient to make test results from different language versions of a test comparable. Particular differences in linguistic habits go together with specific differences in thought and behavior, making it impossible to separate language from culture. Hence, consideration of language alone will likely prove insufficient.

In addition to language, there are several other factors that must be taken into consideration if scores on tests that have been adapted for use in multiple languages and cultures are to be meaningfully interpreted. Factors impacting the ability of a test user to draw valid interpretations include: test administration conditions, curricula, educational policies, examinee motivation, economic status, standard of living, cultural values, unfamiliar test item formats, test anxiety, and test speededness (Hambleton & Kanjee, 1993; van de Vijver & Poortinga, 1991).

Hambleton and Kanjee (1993) described in detail some of the main factors to be taken into consideration when interpreting achievement test results in cross-cultural studies. Similarity of curricula is one of the factors that should be given serious attention. To the extent that curricula differ, any comparison of achievement levels between different cultures will be weak unless these curriculum differences are somehow also taken into account. Examples of the impact of differing curricula can be found throughout the literature. For example, on first inspection, the results of the Second International Mathematics Study (SIMS) seem to indicate that U.S. students performed at levels well below their Japanese counterparts in every grade and every aspect of mathematics. However, when differences in curricula were noted and controlled for, no significant differences were found between the performance of the U.S. and Japanese students (Westbury, 1992).

The impact of student motivation on test scores is a concern when interpreting the results of scores in all testing situations; however, the issue of cultural differences further complicates the impact of this factor. Hambleton and Kanjee (1993) highlighted the finding of Wainer (1993) in which he questioned whether demonstrated proficiency as measured by tests can be separated from motivation at all. Wainer pointed to the International Assessment of Educational Progress (IAEP) study (Lapointe, Mead, & Askew, 1992) as evidence. In this study, Korean students outperformed their American counterparts. However, Korean students were told that being chosen to participate in the study was a great honor for them, their schools, and their country and that they had a responsibility to perform their best. American students, on the other hand, were not given any motivating messages and approached participation in the study as if it were simply another activity.

Understanding the impact of sociopolitical factors is another important aspect of score interpretation. Comparing scores between developed and developing nations is not a straightforward and simple task. It requires an understanding of the available resources and the different quality of educational services that can be brought to bear on any decision about differences in true ability reflected in test scores (Hambleton & Kanjee, 1993; Olmedo, 1981).

Van de Vijver and Hambleton (1996), together with an international committee of psychologists and psychometricians, put together a set of guidelines for adapting educational and psychological tests. They include guidelines for documentation and score interpretation that are very useful for practitioners attempting to make use of scores. The guidelines for documentation and score interpretation are as follows:

1. *When an instrument is translated/adapted for use in another population, documentation of the changes should be provided, along with evidence of the equivalence.* Van de Vijver and Hambleton made the point that understanding any changes that have been made to enhance the validity of an adapted instrument is important to test users when determining whether or not a particular instrument is appropriate for their purposes in the new context. In addition to information about any changes made to the instrument, test users should also have access to information about the equivalence of the source and target language versions of the test, specifications about the translation procedure, and the results of item bias analyses or of a factor analysis. It is also important for test users to know if certain cultural factors (such as economic, curricula, political differences, etc.) were taken into account in the construction of the test.

2. *Score differences among samples of populations administered the instrument should not be taken at face value. The researcher has the responsibility to substantiate the differences with other empirical evidence.* It is very important to note that the meaning of intergroup differences can be interpreted in many ways. Van de Vijver and Hambleton urged that if a researcher does choose to embrace a particular interpretation of the scores, she or he has an obligation then to provide evidence in support of her or his choice. A collection of evidence often requires further measurement of alternative factors. A test that has been adapted through technically sound procedures may require less extra effort in support of score interpretation because validity of the instrument has already been established to some extent. Van de Vijver and Hambleton made the point that even in the best of circumstances, researchers should make every effort to display careful interpretations of results from multiple versions of a test.

3. *Comparisons across populations can only be made at the level of invariance that has been established for the scale on which*

scores are reported. Van de Vijver and Hambleton referred here to the concept of the comparison scale, an important concept when discussing score interpretation. Issues related to the establishment of measurement scale equivalence have been discussed earlier in this chapter. When large sample sizes are available, it is possible to place the scores from different language versions of a test on a common scale in order to make comparisons about the construct. The main point of this guideline is to once again encourage researchers not to make unwarranted comparisons of scores from multiple versions of a test unless validity evidence is available.

4. *The instrument developer should provide specific information on the ways in which the sociocultural and ecological contexts of the populations might affect performance on the instrument, and should suggest procedures to account for these effects in the interpretation of results.* Van de Vijver and Hambleton formalized in this guideline a practical way of dealing with the inevitable sociocultural and ecological factors that contribute to the interpretation of scores. The best way to convey relevant information to the test user is to provide a test manual that specifies all variables that were examined in the development of the instrument (i.e., cultural characteristics of the target groups, socioeconomic status, age, gender, education). With the results of analyses like these readily available to test users, they have better information about how to account for these factors when interpreting scores (Bracken & Barona, 1991; van de Vijver & Poortinga, 1991).

For score interpretation to be meaningful, it is also critical to establish that adapted measures assess the same construct in the new language or culture. Issues related to the evaluation of construct equivalence were also discussed in an earlier section of this chapter. Determining that an adapted measure covers the same dimensions in the same quantities for linguistically and culturally different populations is critical to the proper interpretation and use of test scores (Eysenck & Eysenck, 1983). As mentioned previously, one technique for establishing this is factor analysis. Normative information also can provide important information to a professional who is trying to derive meaning from a score by placing an individual within a distribution of test takers. However, it is very important to establish that the norms developed for the test given to one linguistic and cultural group are suitable for interpreting the scores of a second linguistic and cultural group. (See Geisinger, 1994, for a discussion of issues related to using normative information in cross-cultural and cross-lingual assessments.)

TEST ADMINISTRATION

As mentioned in an earlier section of this chapter, method bias is the generic term that refers to any validity threatening factors related to test administration conditions (van deVijver & Hambleton, 1996). Lack of experience with item structures, test formats, or the testing situation in general can all contribute to a bias of this nature. Other aspects of the administration, such as the physical conditions of the room, a subject's motivation, administrator effects, and communication problems between the administrator and the person taking the test can all create bias in the test results. Method bias may be present to some degree in all cross-cultural comparisons of achievement and aptitude test scores and can lead to interpretation of differences in scores between groups that are caused by the administration procedure as if they provided an interpretation of true differences in ability level (Hambleton & Kanjee, 1993; van de Vijver & Hambleton, 1996).

Examination of bias due to administrative procedures can be done in several ways. One way is to repeat the test administration. A study of the cross-cultural similarity of score changes from the first to the second test administration can give important clues about the validity of the score inferences to be made. When individuals from different groups with equal test scores on the first administration have, on average, dissimilar scores on the second occasion, one can question the validity of the score inferences made from the first administration. Another way to examine bias due to the way an instrument is administered is to administer the instrument in a nonstandard way. This can be done by soliciting all kinds of information and responses from examinees about the interpretation of instructions, items, response alternatives, and motivation for selecting certain answers (van de Vijver & Hambleton, 1996).

There are ways to avoid problems associated with administration bias. One highly recommended approach is to ensure that instructions on the test itself are clear and self-explanatory, with minimal reliance on verbal communication from the test administrator (van de Vijver & Poortinga, 1991). In all testing situations, it is important to understand the cultures that test takers come from, but at the very least, administrators should be able to communicate in the examinee's native language (Geisinger, 1994; Geisinger & Carlson, 1992). In sum, it is most appropriate to have test administrators who are drawn from the target population, are familiar with the culture as well as its language, have test administration experience and knowledge, and possess some measurement expertise (Hambleton & Kanjee, 1993).

It is also important to encourage consistency in test administration procedures across different groups that are being tested. The best way to achieve this is to provide consistent training to all test administrators. Training for test administrators should stress clear and unambiguous communication, the importance of carefully following test administration instructions, adhering to time limits consistently, and the potential influence of test administrators on the validity of inferences drawn from scores (Hambleton & Kanjee, 1993).

Van de Vijver and Hambleton (1996) also provided clear and concise guidelines for test administration of adapted tests:

1. *Instrument developers and administrators should try to anticipate the types of problems that can be expected, and take appropriate actions to remedy these problems through the preparation of appropriate materials and instructions.* As van de Vijver and Hambleton pointed out, anticipating administration problems is not extremely complex. The task is made simple when a pilot study is run that uses the test in a nonstandard way to solicit various responses from examinees. Careful observation along with feedback from respondents can help uncover potential administration influences.

2. *Instrument administrators should be sensitive to a number of factors related to the stimulus materials, administration procedures, and response modes that can moderate the validity of the inferences drawn from the scores.* Although literal translations of materials are often preferred, test administrators should be familiar with problems that this might create. For example, there may be some aspects of the instructions that are implicit but are not conveyed in the translation.

3. *Those aspects of the environment that influence the administration of an instrument should be made as similar as possible across populations for whom the instrument is intended.* It is well known that controlling environmental conditions in field research is virtually an impossibility. However, test administrators should be made aware of the various environmental factors that can influence score validity so that they can make every effort to be consistent.

4. *Instrument administration instructions should be in the source and target languages to minimize the influence of unwanted sources of variation across populations.* As has already been noted, providing test instructions in the native language is an important method for minimizing a source of unwanted group differences. In addition to this, lengthy test instructions that contain various exercises and examples can also help to decrease differences related to the administration itself.

5. *The instrument manual should specify all aspects of the instrument and its administration that require scrutiny in the application of the instrument in a new cultural context.* Van de Vijver and Hambleton pointed out that as test developers work to adapt the test for use in a different culture and language, they will uncover specific issues about the use of this test in the new cultural context. Test administrators benefit by knowing about the experience of the test developers and should be made aware of potential problems so that they can avoid repetition.

6. *The administration should be unobtrusive and the administrator–examinee interaction should be minimized. Explicit rules that are described in the manual for the instrument should be followed.* An important and common source of errors in cross cultural comparisons results from uncontrolled interactions between administrator and examinee. The manual for test administrator should specify problems that are often seen and offer solutions.

CONCLUSION

The purpose of this chapter has been to review the methodological issues that are associated with the adaptation of achievement and aptitude measures. In the chapter, we focused on six areas: (a) construct equivalence, (b) equivalence of measurement units, (c) translating tests and test material, (d) differential item functioning, (e) score interpretation, and (f) test administration.

We found the number of advances that have been made in these particular areas over the past decade to be quite reassuring. Researchers interested in cross-cultural/cross-lingual comparisons of aptitude and achievement measures have become much more aware of the complexity of issues that impact upon the ability to make valid comparisons of assessment results.

We attribute this growing sophistication to several factors. For one, a variety of economic and political forces leading to a global economy along with diverse migration streams have necessitated the administration of tests in multiple languages. Consequently, an increasing number of practitioners are becoming interested in this area of assessment and are bringing a wide variety of practical problems to the attention of researchers. In addition, new methodologies such as IRT and structural equation modeling have been brought to bear on the problem.

We predict that the next decade will show an even greater increase in the need for and use of adapted tests. With this expanded use of assessments designed for one culture and language administered to other cultural and linguistic groups will come increased knowledge of the abilities and aptitudes actually measured for these cross-cultural groups as well as improved ways of carrying out the necessary comparisons.

ACKNOWLEDGMENTS

The authors would like to acknowledge the contributions of Daniel Eignor to this chapter. His editorial assistance was greatly appreciated.

REFERENCES

Angoff, W.H., & Cook, L. L. (1988). *Equating the scores of the "Prueba de Aptitud Academica" and the "Scholastic Aptitude Test"* (Report No. 88-2). New York: College Entrance Examination Board.

Bracken, B. A., & Barona, A. (1991). State of the art procedures for translating, validating and using psychoeducational tests in cross-cultural assessment. *School Psychology International, 12,* 119–132.

Brislin, R. W. (1970). Back-translation for cross-cultural research. *Journal of Cross-Cultural Psychology, 1,* 185–216.

Ercikan, K. (1998). Translation effects in international assessments. *International Journal of Educational Research, 29,* 543–553.

Ercikan, K. (1999, April). *Translation DIF in TIMSS.* Paper presented at the meeting of the National Council of Measurement in Education, Montreal, Canada.

Ercikan, K. (2000). Disentangling sources of differential item functioning in multilingual assessments. *International Journal of Testing, 2,* 199–215.

Everson, H. T., Guerrero, A., & Laitusis, V. (1998, April). *Preliminary evidence of construct equivalence of mathematics tests administered across languages: An analysis of findings from the SAT I and the Prueba de Aptitud Academica tests.* Paper presented at the meeting of the American Educational Research Association, San Diego.

Eysenck, H. J., & Eysenck, S. B. G. (1983). Recent advances in the cross-cultural study of personality. In J. N. Butcher & C. D. Spielberger (Eds.), *Advances in personality assessment* (Vol. 2, pp. 41–69). Hillsdale, NJ: Lawrence Erlbaum Associates.

Geisinger, K. F. (1994). Cross-cultural normative assessment: translation and adaptation issues influencing the normative interpretation of assessment instruments. *Psychological Assessment, 6,* 304–312.

Geisinger, K. F., & Carlson, J. F. (1992). *Assessing language-minority students* (Report No. EDO-TM-92-4). Washington DC: ERIC Clearinghouse on Tests, Measurement, and Evaluation.

Gierl, M. (2000). Construct equivalence on translated achievement tests. *Canadian Journal of Education, 25*(4), 280–296.

Hambleton, R. K. (1993). Translating achievement tests for use in cross-national studies. *European Journal of Psychological Assessment, 9*(1), 57–58.

Hambleton, R. K. (1994). Guidelines for adapting educational and psychological tests: A progress report. *European Journal of Psychological Assessment, 10,* 229–244.

Hambleton, R. K. (1996, March). *Guidelines for adapting educational and psychological tests.* Paper presented at the meeting of the National Council of Measurement in Education, New York.

Hambleton, R. K., & Bollwark, J. (1991). Adapting tests for use in different cultures: Technical issues and methods. *Bulletin of the International Test Commission, 18,* 229–244.

Hambleton, R. K., & Kanjee, A. (1993, April). *Enhancing the validity of cross-cultural studies: Improvements in instrument translation methods.* Paper presented at the meeting of the American Educational Research Association, Atlanta, GA.

Hambleton, R. K., & Kanjee, A. (1995). Translating tests and attitude scales. In T. Husen & T. N. Postlewaite (Eds.), *International encyclopedia of education* (2nd ed., pp. 6328–6334). New York: Pergamon.

Hambleton, R. K., & Patsula, L. (1998). Adapting tests for use in multiple languages and cultures. *Social Indicators Research, 45,* 153–171.

Hui, C. H., & Triandis, H. C. (1985). Measurement in cross-cultural psychology: A review and comparison of strategies. *Journal of Cross-Cultural Psychology, 16,* 131–152.

Hui, C. H., & Triandis, H. C. (1989). Effects of culture and response format on extreme response style. *Journal of Cross-Cultural Psychology, 20,* 296–309.

Lapointe, A. E., Mead, N. A., & Askew, J. M. (1992). *Learning mathematics* (Report No. 22-CAEP-01). Princeton, NJ: Educational Testing Service.

Olmedo, E. E. (1981). Testing linguistic minorities. *American Psychologist, 36,* 1078–1085.

Perez, A. (1975). *Measurement of bilingual ability.* Unpublished master's thesis, University of Puerto Rico, San Juan.

Poortinga, Y.H. (1983). Psychometric approaches to intergroup comparison: The problem of equivalence. In S. H. Irvine & J. W Berry (Eds.), *Human assessment and cross-cultural factors?* (pp. 237–258). New York: Plenum.

Poortinga, Y. H. (1989). Equivalence of cross-cultural data: An overview of basic issues. *International Journal of Psychology, 24,* 737–756.

Poortinga, Y. H. (1995). Uses of tests across cultures. In T. Oakland & R. K. Hambleton (Eds.), *International perspectives on academic assessment* (pp. 187–206). Boston: Kluwer Academic.

Prieto, A. (1992). A method for translation of instruments to other languages. *Adult Education Quarterly, 43,* 1–14.

Reckase, M. D., & Kunce, C. (1999, April). *Translation accuracy of a technical credentialing examination.* Paper presented at the meeting of the National Council of Measurement in Education, Montreal, Canada.

Sireci, S. G. (1997). Problems and issues in linking assessment across languages. *Educational Measurement: Issues and Practice, 16,* 12–19.

Sireci, S. G., & Allalouf, A. (2003). Appraising item equivalence across multiple languages and cultures. *Language Testing, 20*(2), 147–165.

Sireci, S. G., Fitzgerald, C., & Xing, D. (1998, April). *Adapting credentialing examinations for international uses.* Paper presented at the meeting of the American Educational Research Association, San Diego.

Stanley, J. C., & Hopkins, K. D. (1972). *Educational and psychological measurement and evaluation.* Englewood Cliffs, NJ: Prentice-Hall.

van de Vijver, F. J. R. (2002). Cross-cultural assessment: Value for money? *Applied Psychology: An International Review, 51*(4), 545–566.

van de Vijver, F. J. R., & Hambleton, R. K. (1996). Translating test: Some practical guidelines. *European Psychologist, 1,* 89–99.

van de Vijver, F. J. R., & Leung, K. (1997). *Methods and data analysis for cross-cultural research.* Thousand Oaks, CA: Sage.

van de Vijver, F. J. R., & Leung, K. (2000). Methodological issues in psychological research on culture. *Journal of Cross-Cultural Psychology, 31,* 33–51.

van de Vijver, F. J. R., & Lonner, W. (1995). A bibliometric analysis of the *Journal of Cross-Cultural Psychology, 26,* 591–602.

van de Vijver, F. J. R., & Poortinga, Y. H. (1991). Testing across cultures. In R. K. Hambleton & J. Zaal (Eds.), *Advances in educational and psychological testing* (pp. 277–308). Dordrecht, Netherlands: Kluwer Academic.

van de Vijver, F. J. R., & Tanzer, N. K. (1997). Bias and equivalence in cross-cultural assessment: An overview. *European Review of Applied Psychology, 47,* 263–279.

Van der Flier, H., & Drenth, P. J. D. (1980). Fair selection and comparability of test scores. In L. J. T. van der Kamp, W. F. Langerak, & D. N. M. de Gruijter (Eds.), *Psychometrics for educational debates.* New York: Wiley.

Wainer, H. (1993). Measurement problems. *Journal of Educational Measurement, 30,* 1–21.

Westbury, I. (1992). Comparing American and Japanese achievement: Is the United States really a low achiever? *Educational Researcher, 21,* 18–24.

Woodcock, R. W. (1985). *Woodcock Language Proficiency Battery, Spanish Form: Technical summary* (Assessment Services Bulletin No. 9). Allen, TX: DLM.

II

Cross-Cultural Adaptation of Educational and Psychological Tests: Applications to Achievement, Aptitude, and Personality Tests

8

Test Adaptation in a Large-Scale Certification Program

Cyndy T. Fitzgerald
Caveon Test Security

Certification is an expanding, voluntary activity that bridges the gap between academic credentials and the demands of a rapidly evolving workplace. Professional certification programs have been growing at a rapid pace over the past several years. McKillip and Cox (1998) indicated that there are over 700 certification programs available in the United States, alone. With the availability of the computer to deliver exams, the capability of these programs to deliver examinations to a worldwide market is now possible (e.g., Mills, Potenza, Fremer, & Ward, 2002). In the information technology (IT) arena, many companies such as Microsoft and Novell deliver their computer-based exams to over 100 countries. Delivery of an exam in English, however, is not sufficient. In order to respond to the global demand for its certification programs, Microsoft and others in the certification business must adapt their exams into multiple languages and cultures.

Delivery, culture, terminology, and variability in the quality of the people doing the translations or reviews create major headaches for testing agencies. Japanese, for example, is very different than French or German. Creating certification exams in the IT arena are not like building an achievement or aptitude exam; the turnover is very fast, so not only does it have to be done properly, it has to be done quickly. The process of adapting exams into multiple languages is referred to by many of the IT companies as localization. Many of the same standards that are applied to localizing software products need to be applied to localization of certification exams.

There are many obstacles that must be overcome in the development of a computer-based test (see Mills et al., 2002). These obstacles increase 10-fold when the tests being developed are for an IT certification program testing one's skill with operating systems such as Windows 2000 or Windows NT Server 4.0 along with testing one's skill with software application development.

There are four major obstacles that must be overcome in developing an IT certification exam. First, tests need to be developed very quickly. Because computer software is constantly being updated, the courseware and certification exams must also be updated with the same speed. Second, because the software, courseware, and exam development are all being done in tandem, resources are severely constrained. Although Microsoft includes external technical contributors in its exam development process, exam developers still rely heavily on the internal subject matter experts (SMEs), who are also developing the software product itself. Third, the exams need to be localized into multiple languages. This substantially increases the standards that must be adhered to in the exam development process. The International Test Commission (ITC) developed 22 guidelines for adapting tests from one language to another (summarized by Hambleton, 1994; see also chap. 1, this volume). Adherence to the ITC Test Adaptation Guidelines and additional Microsoft standards makes item writing and adaptation complex and time consuming. Testing at a computer introduces additional complexity: Exams in all languages need to be reviewed in their computer-based form for quality assurance purposes. For example, this review includes comparisons of screen shots in an exam with the actual interface of the localized software product. Finally, due to the speed of exam development and the need for localization of the exams, there are many psychometric and validity issues that must be addressed.

The focus of this chapter is to describe the way in which credentialing exams at Microsoft are adapted and validated for use in multiple languages. The expectation is that the chapter will highlight the challenges, and ways in which these challenges could be addressed by other organizations. The remainder of this chapter has been organized around the major steps involved in adapting credentialing exams from English into other languages. Each step is highlighted by examples (see also Hambleton, Sireci, & Robin,

1999). Prior to describing these steps, some background on the program and its scope is presented.

OVERVIEW OF MICROSOFT'S CERTIFIED PROFESSIONAL PROGRAM

Microsoft delivers more than 1 million exams per year to over 75 countries. Currently, 42 exams are available on a worldwide basis. In addition to English, each exam is adapted for local administration in as many as 13 languages. Currently, Microsoft offers certification exams in the following languages: English, Japanese, Korean, Simplified Chinese, German, Hungarian, Polish, French, Russian, Italian, Spanish, Brazilian Portuguese, and Czech.

Historically, personality and IQ tests have been adapted; now there's a shift to the international delivery of exams in other languages for professions such as information technology, medical, securities, and accounting. Even college admission tests such as the Scholastic Aptitude Test are now available in Spanish (e.g., see chap. 7, this volume).

CHARACTERISTICS OF A MICROSOFT CERTIFICATION EXAM

Microsoft certification exams are developed with the input of technical professionals in the industry and reflect how Microsoft products are used in organizations throughout the world. Microsoft certification exams typically comprise the following item types:

- Traditional multiple-choice (MCQ) items that measure basic knowledge and comprehension of Microsoft products and technologies.
- Scenario-based MCQ items that measure candidates' ability to analyze situations.
- Scenario-based multiple rating items that measure candidates' ability to analyze and synthesize information and then evaluate the quality of a given solution.
- Simulation items that measure candidates' ability to use a simulated version of the software product. These are true authentic assessments of the examinee's ability to actually use the software product to complete specified tasks.
- Point-and-click items that measure the candidates' ability to identify an area in a graphic. An example of one of these items might be that the examinee is asked to place the pointer

(mouse) on the part of the network diagram that corresponds to the server that is hosting the company's web site.
- Drag-n-drop items that measure the candidates' ability to organize information (text or graphics) by moving it from one screen and placing it on another. An example here might be that the examinee is asked to design a network. To do this, the examinee would drag three workstation icons onto a palette and then connect them to a server.

In addition to these item types, Microsoft uses complex case study scenarios and relies heavily on the use of graphics, tables, and other exhibits. For additional information on these formats and other aspects of their certification programs, see their web page at http://www.microsoft.com/learning/mcp/ and the excellent review paper describing emerging item formats by Zenisky and Sireci (2002).

ADAPTING ENGLISH-LANGUAGE TESTS FOR USE INTERNATIONALLY

The test adaptation process at Microsoft consists of four phases: development of the English exam, prelocalization, localization, and postlocalization.

The development of the English version of the exam follows the traditional exam development steps of conducting a job task analysis, item development, field testing of items, item analysis, forms assembly, and standard setting.

The prelocalization phase occurs concurrently with the latter stages of the development of the English exam. During prelocalization, translators review English beta exam items to anticipate problems that may arise from working with localized products.

The localization phase consists of the translation of exam content based on the final English exam files. Translators are provided with training and guidelines for completing the translations. Translators are instructed to translate the intent of the item instead of a word-for-word translation.

The final phase, postlocalization, involves an extensive technical review and the exam delivery. The technical review is performed by an SME in the native country. Reviewers are provided with an electronic version of the exam so that they may view it exactly as it is going to appear to the examinee. Reviewers provide feedback directly into the electronic-review version of this exam. Once the feedback has been verified, the exam is recompiled, published, and delivered worldwide. Examinees may take the exam in the language of their choice. The remainder of this chapter involves a detailed description of each of these phases and presents examples of the tools, forms, checklists, and so on, that are used.

DEVELOPMENT OF THE ENGLISH EXAM

The development of the English exam is pretty standard from job task analysis and building test specifications to field testing of exam items to the live release of the exam. What's unique is that because these exams may be adapted to other languages, attention is given up front to selection of content so that it generalizes across languages and cultures. An example of this would be that if a component of a software product was not available in the localized product (this could be a function or feature of the product) then it could not be a central part of the assessment. Also, the case studies are chosen with an eye to how it would perform in an adaptive form. Examples would include developing an application based on national laws, diseases that are more prevalent, sports, accounting principles, and the like. This process follows what's generally referred to in the literature as de-centering. In short, Microsoft tries to anticipate problems and develop examples that are relevant globally.

PRELOCALIZATION

Even though the item writers and test developers are sensitive to issues relative to the use of these exams in multiple languages, this is a rather informal process. The prelocalization step is an attempt to make this step more formal. This involves the recruitment of SMEs who can bring to the attention of the exam development team any differences in the product itself or the way that it is used in other countries. This phase is critical because the functionality of Microsoft software is not always consistent across languages due to constraints such as availability of specific hardware components. Items are also reviewed to determine if they meet a number of additional criteria, such as the ability to localize scenarios, server names, and graphics, to name a few. On average, the prelocalization process takes about 2 weeks.

All of the issues found during this phase are tracked using the Localization Resolution Form. Table 8.1 provides an example of a completed Localization Resolution Form. In the example, under the issue column, the person who completes the form has indicated that there were seven issues identified. The table also specifies the resource that identified the issue, how the issue will be resolved, and

TABLE 8.1
Localization Resolution Form (Excerpt Only)

Issue Number	*Issue*	*Resource*	*Resolution*	*Language*
1	Measurement of distance and/or quantities vary among countries.	Editing, International Quality Assurance Group (IQA)	Translators can use measures that would be most common to the culture.	All
2	Difficult to translate You.	Editing, IQA	Translators can use the form of you that would be most common to the culture.	Spanish
3	The scenario in one of the questions involves a health inspection. Do all countries have health inspections?	Localization Manager	Not all countries do have health inspections. An alternative scenario will have to be used.	This is true for many countries outside the United States.
4	Stacking technical terms/names is difficult to translate and intimidating toward a candidate.	IQA	Per an e-mail to the translation company, translators need to refer to the vendor kit as to how IQA suggests handling stacking.	All
5	Stacking adjectives makes localization difficult.	Item Writer, Editing	We are aware of this difficulty. Translators need to forward these to MS for resolution. Again our hope is that we can identify and resolve this in the prelocalization review.	All
6	Translators are unfamiliar with MS acronyms.	IQA	A list of acronyms will be handed off at the start of each project.	All
7	Provide code-wrapping info. Where can it be broken?	Program Manager, Item Writer	We are working on the best way to handle this. We will have a general guideline but be flexible.	All

which languages are most affected. In the example provided in Table 8.1, measurement units and quantities were identified as an issue (Issue 1) by the editing team and by the International Quality Assurance Group (IQA) at Microsoft. The resolution is that translators should use the measures that are most common to the culture so English units would need to adapted to metric for the European countries. The second issue identified involves the use of the term *you*. In languages such as Spanish, there is more than one word that can be used to say *you*. The resolution for the translator is that the form of *you* that is most common to the culture should be used.

LOCALIZATION

Once the prelocalization phase is complete, the actual translation of the content of the exam takes place. Table 8.2, the Item Review Form, contains a set of criteria for evaluating items. The criteria in this table are not applied to just the language versions of the exam, but also to the English exam. The use of this table provides a framework for the evaluation of items in multiple languages. The table is used as a tool because there is not an in-house resource to advise translators of when changes can be made. Table 8.2 provides an excerpt of a completed Item Review Form. This review form is organized around six sections. First are general comments around the item, then comments about the scenario, in cases where a scenario is used. The third and fourth sections pertain to item stem and answer choices. Section 5 includes specifications about diagrams and tables and Section 6 provides information about screen shots that may or may not be present.

For each of the comments and specifications, it is necessary for one or more resources to indicate that the item pool has met the specifications provided for the exam. As one can see from the excerpt provided, the item writer is responsible for ensuring that the item pool meets all of the criteria. The program manager, the lead on the exam development project, is responsible for things such as ensuring that the items map to the skill levels indicated in the exam objectives. An editor is more focused on the actual wording of the exam content. Many of the issues are also validated during the alpha or prefield-test phase of the exam development process. Finally, the translator is responsible for ensuring that the translated content meets all of the specifications provided. This process takes an average of 30–35 days.

Microsoft also provides the translator with many additional documents and tools during the localization phase. These include the list of

TABLE 8.2
Item Review Form (Excerpt Only)

Writer	PM	Editor	Alpha Pre-field-test review (PFR)	Specifications
Overall Items				
X			X	Have been tested for accuracy against the appropriate build of the product.
X	X			Map to skill level and intent of corresponding objectives.
X			X	Use accurate technical terms that match the formatting, punctuation, spacing, spelling, and capitalization in the product UI and documentation.
X		X	X	Include no acronyms, interface labels, terms, features, or functionality that are made up or borrowed from other products.
Scenarios (Where Appropriate)				
Writer	*PM*	*Editor*	*Alpha*	*Specifications*
X	X		X	Are based on real-world, on-the-job experience.
X			X	Are not found verbatim in instructional material or product documentation.
X		X		Present background information, current situations, and goals in chronological order.
X		X		Start and continue in present tense.
X		X		Use company names and people names from approved name lists.
Question Sentences				
Writer	*PM*	*Editor*	*Alpha*	*Specifications*
X		X	X	Avoid subjective words, such as best, most, and usually. Use objective criteria.

Writer	PM	Editor	Alpha	Specifications
X	X	X		Are complete and self-contained—so that examinees could answer in essay form without seeing the answer choices.

Answer Choices

Writer	PM	Editor	Alpha	Specifications
X			X	Include a correct answer that is unquestionably correct.
X			X	Include a sufficient number of distractors, all of which are unquestionably incorrect but are plausible to examinees who have insufficient technical expertise.
X		X		Are parallel (similar in construction and intent) with at least one other answer choice.

Diagrams

Writer	PM	Editor	Alpha	Specifications
X	X			Are based on current VisioNewArtTemplate.vsd template. (Writer retains source version of diagrams for handoff after alpha.)
X				Are saved as 16-color bitmaps. (Writer retains bitmap version of diagrams for handoff after alpha.)
X	X			Are displayed with their corresponding items in Word Normal view.

Screen Shots

Writer	PM	Editor	Alpha	Specifications
X	X			Are no larger than 595 pixels high by 410 pixels wide.
X				Are saved as 16-color bitmaps. (Writer retains bitmap version of screen shots for handoff after alpha.)
X	X			Are displayed with their corresponding items in World Normal View.

resolutions to issues raised during the prelocalization phase, the International Quality Assurance Localization Kit, Style Guides, and Product Glossaries. As you will note, although the examples provided are in the information technology domain, the concept of creating and providing these tools for the translator is not specific to the IT arena. These tools are available in English, as well as the native language.

The International Quality Assurance (IQA) Localization Kit is an extremely comprehensive document that is developed in Microsoft's International Division for product development. An example of the topics covered in the IQA Kit is provided in Table 8.3. The Kit consists

TABLE 8.3
IQA Localization Kit (Excerpt Only)

	German IQA Localization Kit	
	Contents	*Document*
1.	Country Names *The latest list of translated names of countries.*	Ge_Country_Names.xls
2.	Country Specs *Country standards for Germany, Austria, and Switzerland.*	"Country Specs.doc'
3.	Fictitious Names and Addresses *This list includes fictitious examples of Northwind Traders [Access], a few approved fictional names and addresses as well as the German, Austrian, and Swiss subsidiary addresses.*	Ge_Addresses_fictitious.xls
	See also the attached information regarding Fictitious IP addresses, which could be helpful during the localization of documentation.	"Ficticious IP addresses.doc"
4.	Graphical User Interface Elements: Core Terms *The bitmaps contained in the embedded zip file are intended as an overview of the most important GUI elements and terms.*	GUI.doc
5.	Legal Glossary and reference material *The 2 previous files have been combined into one reference file for all translations containing legal text, such as EULAs, copyright text, legal text in the software.*	Legal_References_EULA_glossary.ZIP

of a table of contents with a series of embedded documents. For example, if the translator wanted to know what fictitious names and addresses should be used in question scenarios, then he or she would click on the corresponding spreadsheet and would see a complete list of names and addresses for Germany, Austria, and Switzerland.

Because the IQA Localization Kit is designed for the localization of Microsoft software, it may not always cover all of the issues that may arise when adapting a computer-based exam. Therefore, it is also necessary to provide the translators with a style guide similar to the one provided in Table 8.4. For example, in this style guide, terms such as *buffer, caching,* and *host names* are defined.

The style guide shown in Table 8.4 is used in conjunction with the Product Glossary shown in Table 8.5. The Product Glossary is particularly useful because it indicates the precise wording that should be used in the native language for each of the terms used in the product. For example, the German translation for "File Opens" is listed exactly as it should be used.

Armed with all of the information as shown in Tables 8.3, 8.4, and 8.5, the translator translates the final item pool and then does a copy edit on the translated exam content. In addition to the item pool, the translator is responsible for comparing item exhibits against screens from the actual localized product. Translation experts are evaluated on their ability to meet translation accuracy criteria within the specified timeframes.

Microsoft uses various tools to expedite the translation process. A sample user interface would look something like the following set of screenshots shown in Fig. 8.1 to 8.5. Figure 8.1 enables the translator to select the language and exam number needed. In this example, the translator has selected an exam about architecture basics and will be translating it into French.

Figure 8.2 enables the translator to select the question and case study to be translated. In this exam, the translator has picked a multiple-choice item (1.CLEE.1.a) that is associated with all of the cases.

Once an item is selected, then the translator is ready to enter the translated content. Figure 8.3 provides an example of the interface that is used to enter the translated content.

Figure 8.4 illustrates the mechanism used by translators to make global changes to the exam across the entire item pool.

Figure 8.5 illustrates the ability to preview what the item will actually look like to the examinee in both English and the translated language. To view both simultaneously, the translator can either arrange the screens by moving them around or use the "arrange all" command under the Menu option, Window.

TABLE 8.4

Windows NT 4.0 Technical Terminology Style Guide (Excerpt)

Account policy: the Windows NT security policy that controls how passwords are used by user accounts.

broadcast messages A network message sent from a single computer that is distributed to all other devices on the same segment of the network as the sending computer.

buffer: a reserved portion of memory in which data is temporarily held before it is printed.

caching A method used by DNS name servers to improve performance. As DNS name servers process requests, they temporarily keep the information in local storage (cache) and use it to answer additional requests for the same information.

Catalogs: Information about each of the backup sets and their location stored on a set of tapes. Catalog information includes the number of tapes in a set of tapes as well as the date the tapes were created and the dates of each file in the catalog. catalogs are stored on the last tape in the set. Catalogs are created for each backup set.

discovery: the attempt by a computer's Net Logon service to locate a domain controller running Windows NT Server in the trusted domain when a computer running Windows NT Workstation or a member server running Windows NT Server starts up.

domain controllers: computers running Windows NT Server that share one directory database to store security and user account information for the entire domain.

full synchronization: The PDC sends a copy of the entire directory database to a BDC.

host name: a part of the DNS naming structure. A host name refers to a specific device connected to a TCP/IP internetwork. In a fully qualified domain name (FQDN), the host name is the leftmost part (the set of characters before the first period) of the name.

host: the main computer in a system of computers or terminals connected by communications links.

TABLE 8.5
Product Glossary (Excerpt Only)

English	*German*	*Type*	*Name*	*Product*
# File Opens	Dateien geðffnet	COM	NTLANUI.DL_	NT
# Opens%0	Öffnungen%0	TXT	NETMSG.DL_	NT
#10: S=Specify Additional SCSI Adapter (10029)	#10: Z=Specify Additional SCSI Adapter (10029)	TXT	USETUP.EX_	NT
#12: O=Overwrite (10065)	#12: U=Overwrite (10065)	TXT	USETUP.EX_	NT
#16: U=Continue Upgrade (10087)	#16: A=Continue Upgrade (10087)TXT	USETUP.EX_	NT	
#17: Y=Yes, I agree (10089)	#17: J=Yes, I agree (10089)	TXT	USETUP.EX_	NT
#Programs#*.exe;*.pif;*.com;*.bat;*.cmd#All files (*.*)#*.*#	#Programme#*.exe;*.pif;*.com;*.bat;*.cmd#Alle Dateien (*.*)#*.*#	TXT	SHELL32.DL_	NT
$* Symbol replaced by everything following macro name on command line.	$* Symbol für alles, was auf der Befehlszeile nach dem Makronamen folgt	TXT	AUTOCHK.EX_,AUTOCONV.EX_,ULIB.DL_	NT

POSTLOCALIZATION

After the exam items have been prepared for use in a second language, an exam review disk is created. The corporate-based localization manager sends the disk to a Microsoft representative in the native country for a technical review by a native speaker who is also fluent in English. The objective of the technical review is to verify that the exam content meets the specified psychometric (as discussed earlier in this chapter), technical, and cultural guidelines

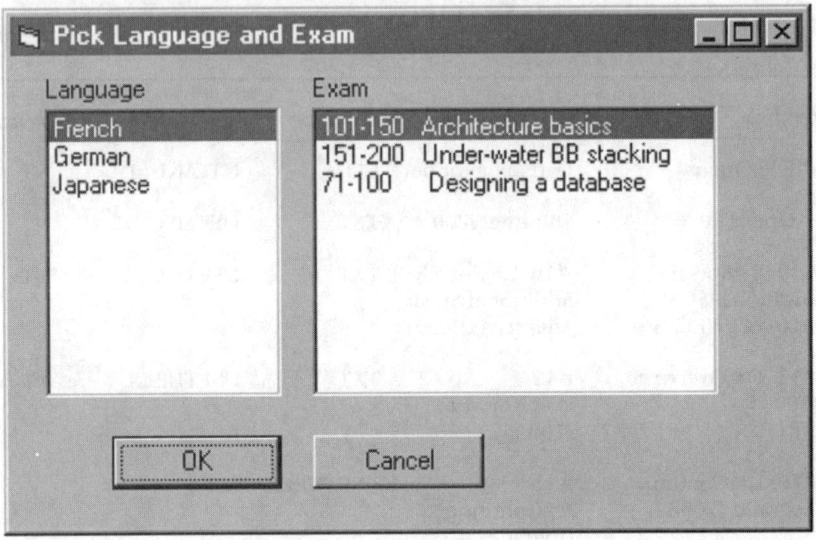

FIG. 8.1. Language selection screen shot.

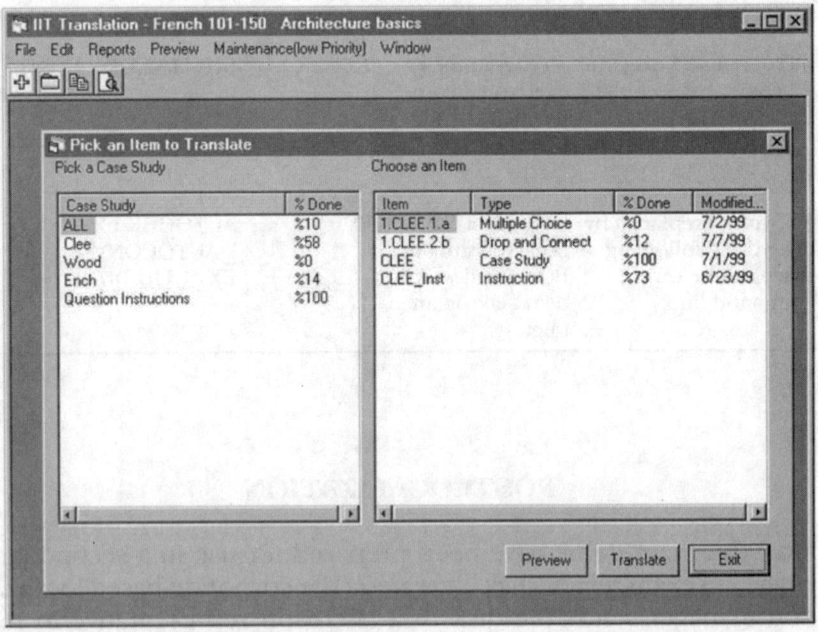

FIG. 8.2. Item selection screen shot.

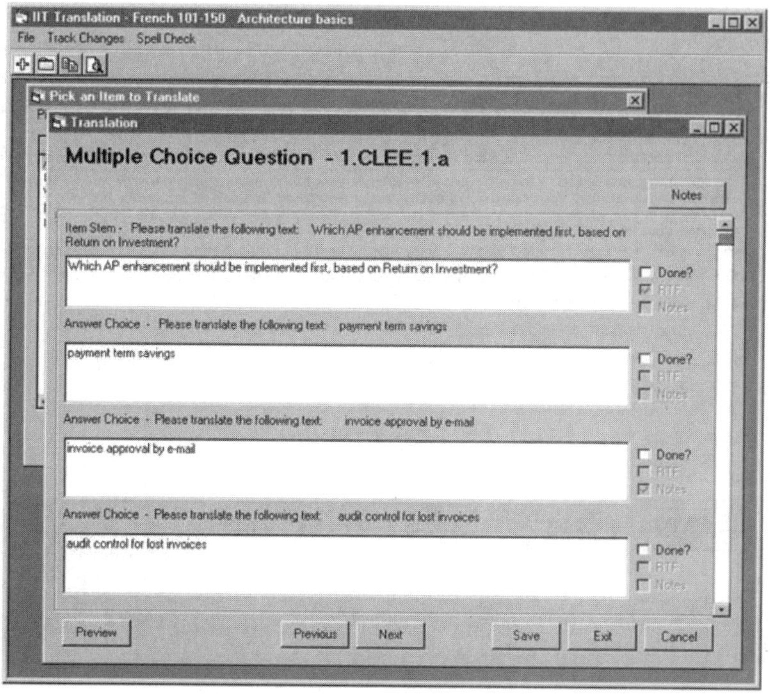

FIG. 8.3. Item translation screen shot.

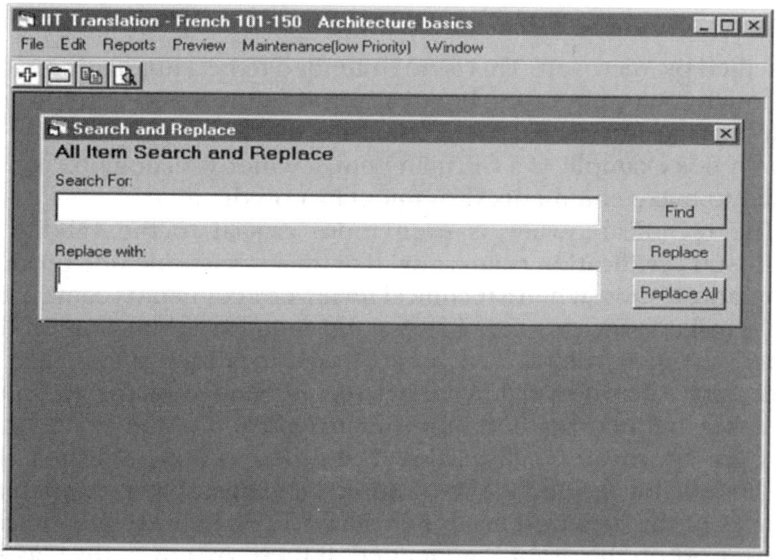

FIG. 8.4. Search-and-replace screen shot.

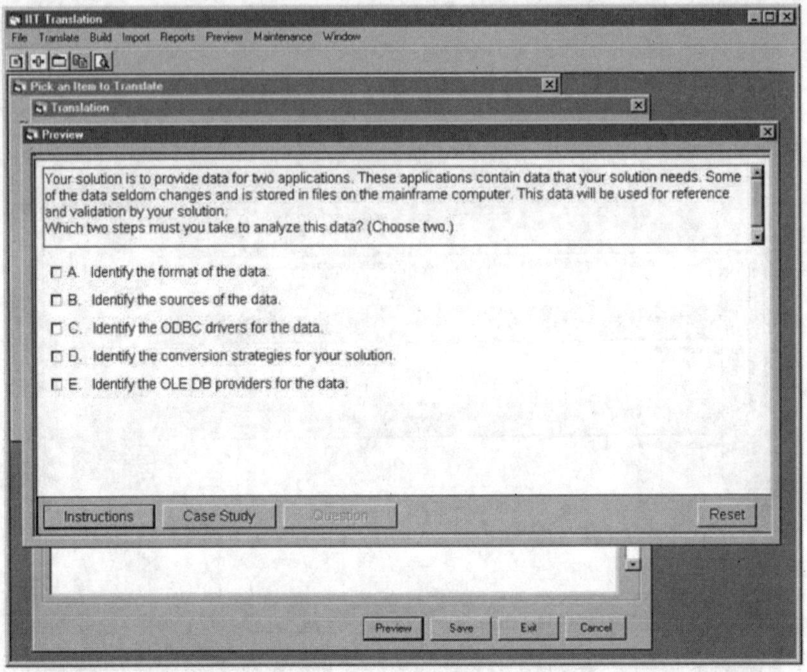

FIG. 8.5. Item preview screen shot.

specified by Microsoft. This is not intended to be a linguistic review, although in certain cases, linguistic arbitration is necessary. An example of the interface used to complete this task is provided in Fig. 8.6. In this example of a German item, a window/dialog box is provided to make comments (Kommentare) on the item.

The technical review is even more crucial to the validity of Microsoft certification exams now that these exams include product simulation items. When a technical reviewer's comments come back, the translator reviews the changes and requests arbitration on disputed changes from the corporate-based localization manager, as necessary. All appropriate changes recommended by the technical reviewer are incorporated into the final version of the exam, once they are approved by all parties. Then the exam is published and made available worldwide in multiple languages. Once enough instances of the localized exam items have been delivered, an in-service report on the exam is generated. If there are any items that are not performing, both a quantitative and a qualitative analysis are performed (for an example of the type of empirical analyses that

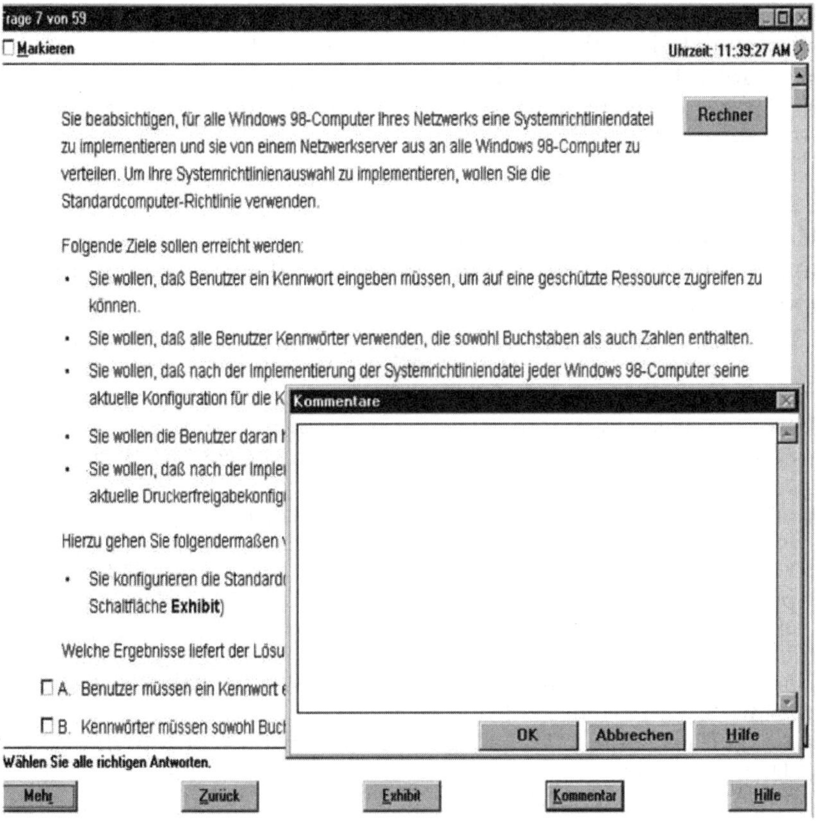

FIG. 8.6. Reviewer comment screen shot.

Microsoft has carried out, see, Robin, Sireci, & Hambleton, 2003). This data are gathered via exam comments within the exam, in addition to exam escalations sent to Microsoft in the form of e-mails, faxes, and letters. In addition, Microsoft conducts various differential item functioning studies (Muniz, Hambleton, & Xing, 2001; Robin et al., 2003; Sireci, Fitzgerald, & Xing, 1998) on their most popular exams to determine if an exam update is required.

Like anything at Microsoft, things are always changing at a rapid pace. Historically where we have relied on only one translator, now two or more may be used, as recommended by the ITC Test Adaptation Guidelines. As more emphasis is placed on empirical validation of the localization process, the question now becomes: Are the differences across languages due to specific content differences or more general differences? Or are differences due to problems in test translation or the training? It's important to continue to look for trends and to feed the results back into improving the entire process. We've found that adding additional tools and checkpoints up front in the process adds to the success in the final translation.

ACKNOWLEDGMENTS

Recognition and appreciation is given to Anne Mrie McSweeney and Angela Johnson, Microsoft Corporation, for their assistance in developing the processes described within this chapter.

REFERENCES

Hambleton, R. K. (1994). Guidelines for adapting educational and psychological tests: A progress report. *European Journal of Psychological Assessment, 10,* 229–244.

Hambleton, R. K., Sireci, S., & Robin, F. (1999). Adapting credentialing exams for use in multiple languages. *CLEAR Exam Review, 10*(2), 24–28.

McKillip, J., & Cox, C. (1998). Strengthening the criterion-related validity of professional certifications. *Evaluation and Program Planning, 21*(2), 191–197.

Mills, C. N., Potenza, M., Fremer, J. J., & Ward, W. C. (Eds.). (2002). *Computer-based testing: Building the foundation for future assessments.* Mahwah, NJ: Lawrence Erlbaum Associates.

Muniz, J., Hambleton, R. K., & Xing, D. (2001). Small sample studies to detect flaws in item translations. *International Journal of Testing, 1,* 115–135.

Robin, F., Sireci, S., & Hambleton, R. K. (2003). Evaluating the equivalence of different language versions of a credentialing exam. *International Journal of Testing, 3*(1), 1–20.

Sireci, S. G., Fitzgerald, C., & Xing, D. (1998, April). *Adapting credentialing examinations for international uses.* Paper presented at the meeting of the American Educational Research Association, San Diego.

Zenisky, A. L., & Sireci, S. G. (2002). Technological innovatins in large-scale assessment. *Applied Measurement in Education, 15*(4), 337–362.

9

Conversion of the Wechsler Adult Intelligence Scale Into Spanish: An Early Test Adaptation Effort of Considerable Consequence

Carlos Y. Maldonado
Putnam/Northern Westchester BOCES

Kurt F. Geisinger
The University of St. Thomas

In many instances psychological tests are translated or adapted from one language to another so that international uses such as educational comparisons may be made (see, e.g., Grisay, 2003; Hambleton, 2002). In other cases, such adaptations come about because the construct validity of one instrument or one psychological characteristic is well known in a single language and culture and it is hoped that research may be conducted in another language and culture using either the same instrument, or at least one that is as similar as possible to the original device. As countries such as the United States become increasingly diverse, however, psychological instruments of proven worth in languages other than English are needed to a greater extent, even within the borders of the country (Geisinger, 1992).

Frequently, when Spanish-language versions of well-regarded tests and assessments are not available, psychologists who need to administer psychological measures use what might be considered as informal approaches to make psychological assessments:

> Some of the ways in which we have observed the WAIS–R used include (a) administering the instrument in English and attempting to take language difficulties into account when interpreting the scores, (b) administering only the performance subtests, using either English or Spanish instructions, (c) using an interpreter, or (d) referring the testing to a Spanish-speaking colleague or assistant who can translate instructions and test items during the test administration. Adherence to any of these procedures is unsatisfactory and in some cases, unethical. (López & Romero, 1988, p. 264)

Though problems involving such informal use of tests can occur in many languages, they are perhaps most likely to occur in Spanish in the United States, especially in so-called "high-stakes" testing situations, given the large and growing size of this demographic group.

"Psychological tests are more likely to be administered in Spanish than any language other than English in the U.S.; 1990 U.S. census data indicate that 10% of the total population is Hispanic, with higher concentrations in Florida, New York, California, and Texas" (Demsky, Mittenberg, Quintar, Katell, & Golden, 1998, p. 115). Most of the test development efforts adapting English-language instruments into Spanish have been aimed at measures for use with children (López & Romero, 1988; McShane & Cook, 1985). In McShane and Cook's literature review on the use of Spanish translations of the Wechsler instruments, for example, approximately 70 such studies were located; only 2 involved the assessment of adults.

The *Escala de Inteligencia Wechsler para Adultos* (EIWA) is the Spanish-language adaptation of the Wechsler Adult Intelligence Scale (WAIS) published, like the other Wechsler intelligence instruments, by the Psychological Corporation. The EIWA scale was introduced in 1968 after an adaptation into Spanish of the English-language version (along with associated changes to assure cultural equivalence) and a complete restandardization in Puerto Rico. Many subtest items were modified, deleted, or added in an effort to make the test more psychometrically sound, and more appropriate and culturally relevant for the Puerto Rican and, it was hoped, other Latino populations. For the most part, the EIWA retained the fundamental subtest structure of the WAIS (Green, 1964). Some of the specific adaptations of the WAIS to construct the EIWA are noted later in this chapter; see Green and Martinez (1967) for a more complete description. The EIWA has achieved a wide level of use in clinical practice, but research on its effectiveness has been limited, especially until quite recently. A search through the computerized PsycINFO database from 1967 through July of 1998 revealed only 12 published and unpublished studies that dealt with Spanish versions of the WAIS. One of the studies (Conde López & Domeneca López, 1977) is not directly relevant to our study because it critiqued translations, currently used in Spain, of the original Wechsler–Bellevue and the WAIS but did not mention the EIWA. Since its introduction in 1968, only about 11 published studies have dealt with the EIWA in any manner.

When first introduced, the EIWA was the only psychometric instrument with seemingly adequate, published norms that could be used for the intellectual assessment of adult Hispanics and it remains one of the few measures for this purpose today. Because of this unrivaled position, the EIWA has become the foremost instrument used for the intellectual assessment of Hispanics in the United States, including Puerto Rico. It has been and continues to be widely used in making often high-stakes psychodiagnostic decisions.

Because Hispanics represent the most rapidly growing minority group in the United States (Eyde, 1992; Macias, 1977), one might have expected to find that the availability of the EIWA would have brought about much interest in the test and a reasonably large body of research exploring the reliability and validity of the instrument. Despite its frequent use, the EIWA was, until very recently, virtually ignored by researchers in comparison to research on the English-language Wechsler measures.

SCORE DIFFERENCES ACROSS LANGUAGES

Since shortly after its inception, Spanish-speaking psychologists noted informally that the EIWA frequently yielded inflated IQs for individuals when compared with scores from English-language measures, or when developed cognitive abilities were estimated from known levels of functioning. The informal way in which this observation has been communicated is in part responsible for the lack of adequate information about the possible basis for the differences. Only recently—and more than 20 years after the EIWA was first published—reports in journals have started to ameliorate this situation by disseminating information that bears relevance to using the EIWA (e.g., López & Romero, 1988).

At the present time, different opinions exist in the effort to account for the alleged differences in scores. On the one hand, higher scores on the EIWA might plausibly reflect the test's cultural sensitivity toward Hispanics and thereby do not represent inflated scores per se, but rather are more valid estimates of intelligence than those emerging from the WAIS. Such a belief follows from the thought that the WAIS is biased and unfair when administered to those for whom English is not their native language. From this standpoint, the higher score represents a "truer" estimate of the examinees' level of functioning. From this perspective, a clinician's opinion regarding the relationship between intelligence and functional level is valid only for the specific language and population from which the observations were derived. Preliminary construct validation of the EIWA, however, has largely replicated the nomological net of the WAIS for the EIWA, suggesting that this position is unlikely to be true (e.g., Gómez, Piedmont, & Fleming, 1992).

Alternatively, one can explain away differences between an estimated IQ derived from a known level of functioning and an obtained IQ on the grounds that they are measuring different psychological traits or attributes, at least to some extent. Proponents of this position believe that by translating almost all of the items and by altering many of them, the test has changed sufficiently from its original domain so that now it only overlaps rather than reproduces whatever attribute or attributes the WAIS measures. Once again, initial construct validation research would seem to reduce the likelihood of such a possibility.

Yet a third possibility for explaining the apparent disparity in scores is a position that rejects the validity claims of the EIWA at least in part and places the reason for the differences squarely on the test itself. Proponents of this position are the first to note that the EIWA was almost magically endowed with an assumed validity just because it was developed from the highly reputed WAIS. From this perspective, differences in scores are attributable not to population differences but rather to faulty norms, standardization, scaling of subtests, test items and related materials, the processes of construction/adaptation, and/or item analyses. A modification of this third approach would be that the test is valid correlationally, but needs to be equated in a more reasonable fashion to the WAIS on which it was based. Fortunately, some of these alternative explanations can be empirically verified.

ISSUES WITH THE EIWA STANDARDIZATION SAMPLE

What evidence exists that there might be problems inherent in the EIWA? Unfortunately, few published studies address the question directly. However, careful scrutiny of the EIWA manual and its technical report do uncover some surprising details. For example, one of the easiest factors to verify is whether there were any major discrepancies in the standardization sample as compared with the 1960 Census data of Puerto Rico. Like the WAIS, the EIWA used a stratified sampling procedure that controlled for six population characteristics: age, gender, geographic region, occupation, education, and urban–rural residence. Race (White–non-White) was controlled for in the WAIS and the WAIS–R (Wechsler Adult Intelligence Scale–Revised) but not in the EIWA. The standardization sample used for the EIWA came entirely from Puerto Rico.

Chi-square analyses comparing the 1960 Census data and the EIWA standardization group across all six factors were performed by López and Romero (1988) and as part of the present research study. Although the EIWA manual reports the distribution of these factors in percentages and across two or more factors at a time, it was possible, given the standardization sample size (N = 1,127; 604 women, 523 men), to reconstruct the tables in terms of frequencies and to isolate the six stratification factors.

The analyses suggest that the gender factor was adequately sampled from the population. But, although the EIWA manual (Wechsler, 1968) states that "*la muestra de estandarización representa la población de Puerto Rico muy adecuamente* [the standardization sample represents the Puerto Rican population very adequately]" (p. 8), this analysis demonstrated that age, region, occupation, and education showed marked differences ($p < .001$) from population parameters. The importance of this difference for the age factor is probably less than that for region, occupation, and education. Because an examinee's performance on the EIWA is compared with age-referenced norms, the importance of obtaining a standardization sample in which sampling approximates population age parameters is probably not too consequential. Including greater or lesser numbers in any age group rather affects the reliability of the norms within a given age range.

Differences in sampling by region of Puerto Rico, occupation, and education were also statistically significant, however, and should be regarded as potentially important. Overall, the data suggest that the towns located in the center of the island toward the north coast (Region III) were underrepresented. There are consequential differences across these regions of Puerto Rico regarding education and other socioeconomic status variables. Also, the occupational distribution showed a greater preponderance of laborers, housewives, students, and unemployed, while showing a very large deficit in those classified in the "other" Census occupational category. The impact of such differences is difficult to assess. More likely of significance, however, are educational differences that were caused by systematically including too few examinees who had below 8 years of education and including too many with 9 years or more, resulting in a standardization sample that had a higher than average level of education. One or two of these issues are noted briefly in the manual and subsequent reports, but the overall conclusion of those adapting the test was that the sampling was quite appropriate. In fact, the EIWA manual (Wechsler, 1968) mentions only the discrepancy found in educational level but then goes on to state that the error was in line with known population trends, that is, that the educational level of Puerto Ricans was increasing during the 1960s, since the 1960 Census data were collected.

A dissertation study by an EIWA research associate used the standardization data set (Herrans, 1969) to investigate the relationship between EIWA scores and several other variables, including gender, education, and zone of residency in Puerto Rico. She found that men performed better than females on all women and on the Verbal, Performance, and Full Scale scores of the tests, regardless of education or zone of residence. Herrans also found, as expected, that examinees from the urban zone scored higher than those from a rural zone, regardless of their gender or education. Finally, she found that the more educated an examinee, the higher his or her score was, regardless of gender or zone of residence. These findings are consistent with and underscore the importance of the previously mentioned conclusions regarding the possible inappropriateness of the norms due to sampling imperfections. López and Romero (1988) also reviewed these data and considered standardization matters of major significance in the interpretation of scores from the EIWA.

CONSTRUCT VALIDITY ISSUES

Gómez et al. (1992) performed a factor-analytic study of the EIWA. Their study subjected both the EIWA and the WAIS to principal component analysis in order to examine their comparability (using coefficients of congruence). Their results suggested that, despite the content differences between the two tests, "the EIWA, at least structurally, emerges as a psychometric reflection of the WAIS" (p. 320). This study does much to assure us that the basic intellectual dimensions captured by the EIWA are similar to those captured by the WAIS. However, it did not address the issues of comparability between the norms of each.

Martinez-Urrutia and Spielberger (1973) used the EIWA in their effort to measure the relationship between state and trait anxiety and intelligence. They administered the EIWA and the Spanish edition of Spielberger's State–Trait Anxiety Inventory (STAI) to 40 male psychiatric patients at the San Juan Veterans Administration Hospital. The prediction that measures of state and trait anxiety would be negatively related to performance on the EIWA was confirmed. Unfortunately, for our purposes, the authors made no mention of the distribution of EIWA scores in their study. However, one of the authors (A. Martinez-Urrutia, personal communication, January 26, 1984) disclosed that despite their examinee population being a psychiatric one, the mean Full Scale IQ on the EIWA was close to 120. Martinez-Urrutia could not explain this relatively high average. Though certainly not conclusive by any means, this observation corroborates the experience of clinicians who commonly obtain EIWA scores that are higher than expected.

ISSUES BEARING UPON THE TRANSLATION AND ADAPTATION OF THE INSTRUMENT

Herrans (1973) described some of the translation and cultural issues relating to the adaptation of the EIWA. Herrans reported that those involved in the adaptation employed the most universal Spanish language available and avoided regionalisms so that the EIWA could be more easily used in other Spanish-speaking countries as well as Puerto Rico. To help ensure this effort, after the manual was translated, it was sent to several linguists in three or four South American countries for their recommendations with regard to wording. In some places in the manual, for example, testers are instructed to use the corresponding words typical of their own country—a quite unusual procedure in a standardized test administration. Herrans also reported that many of the items were changed or eliminated because in the judgment of the Puerto Rican staff members, the original items were not valid for Puerto Ricans because they did not tap the experiential world found in Puerto Rico. "For instance item #18 in the Figure Completion Subtest of the WAIS, was eliminated because it does not snow in Puerto Rico" (p. 28). She admitted, however, that pretesting was limited to the test developers themselves, a few students at the University of Puerto Rico, and two small samples. Difficulty levels of items were set based upon these two small samples.

Another study (Melendez, 1994) focused on the ethical considerations of the EIWA. Melendez documented various serious testing issues with instrument that make score comparability with the WAIS difficult at best and possibly impossible. As he stated in comparing the WAIS and the EIWA:

> If the statistical and factorial aspects of these two tests are similar, the content, scoring, and consequences of taking one or the other test are dramatically different. One certainly would expect that a proper translation across cultural (as well as linguistic) domains would result in significant changes of the items of a test, especially those which are clearly cultural. But the changes found in the EIWA are so pervasive that they appear to exceed any reasonable cultural correction by altering not only the content of the tests, but their length, cut-off points, and scoring. All of these changes make the EIWA a more lenient test, even to the extent that some answers which are marked wrong in English are marked right in Spanish. There should be no "cultural" or any other reason for scoring incorrect answers as being correct. (p. 389)

Melendez (1994) noted that in some cases, the nature of questions on the WAIS required changes on the EIWA for purely cultural reasons. These include almost all of the Vocabulary, Information, and Comprehension questions. For example, one WAIS question asks the test taker to name four U.S. presidents since 1900. It was replaced by a question querying three languages that are spoken in the United States (with full credit given for naming just two). Overall, in English the Information subtest has 29 items on the WAIS, and the examiner stops testing after five consecutive errors, whereas the EIWA contains 32 Information items and the examiner continues until seven consecutive errors are made. Melendez documented that identically translated answers to given questions receive 1 point on the EIWA and no points on the WAIS. For example, if the English test taker can name only two of three requested types of blood vessels, he or she does not receive any credit; on the Spanish version, two such answers are worth 1 point.

Melendez (1994) also documented various scoring issues that confound comparability across the two measures. "If someone is able to repeat six digits forward and five digits backward in English, he or she will obtain a scaled score of 10" (p. 390). If, however, that same performance is accomplished in Spanish on the EIWA, a scaled score of 14 is generated. Clearly, the same behaviors should yield the same scaled score from the perspective of score meaningfulness. Melendez argued that this score inflation exists for all of the subtests and is based ultimately on the problem that the test was normed to have a mean of 100 on the Island of Puerto Rico, rather than to have been equated to the WAIS itself. He opined that the EIWA overestimates IQ, when compared to the WAIS, by 20 points in the lower and middle levels of the distribution and by about 12 points at the top, due presumably to a ceiling effect.

CONCURRENT VALIDATION STUDIES/COMPARISONS WITH ENGLISH-LANGUAGE WECHSLER TESTS

Surprisingly, only a few studies to date have attempted to investigate the concurrent validity of the EIWA by comparing it to other Wechsler instruments. Davis and Rodriguez (1979) investigated the validity of the EIWA with data independent of those collected from the original normative group. Their study was done at the Continued Treatment Unit of the Canal Zone Mental Health Center using a Panamanian, psychiatric inpatient population. Two research strategies were employed. For the first, samples ($N = 14$ each) of English- and Spanish-speaking examinees were matched by age, gender, education, and age at first admission and were administered either the EIWA or WAIS Vocabulary and Block Design subtests. The tests were administered by a bilingual examiner for the EIWA group and an English-speaking examiner for the WAIS group using the standard instructions. Full Scale, Performance, and Verbal scores were estimated from the available two subtest scores. Their results showed that patients tested with the EIWA scored 27 Full Scale points higher ($p < .005$, degrees of freedom not reported), 25 Verbal Scale points higher ($p < .01$, degrees of freedom not reported), and 40 Performance Scale points higher ($p < .05$, degrees of freedom not reported) than those tested with the WAIS.

The second research design employed in the same study by Davis and Rodriguez (1979) relied on a within-subject strategy. A single group ($N = 12$) of bilingual inpatients were chosen using essentially random procedures and were assigned to one of four administrations in which the testing order of the EIWA and WAIS Vocabulary and Block Design subtests were counterbalanced. The examinees were all tested by a bilingual examiner. English Verbal IQ and Performance IQ values were again estimated from the Vocabulary and Block Design measures. The results using this design were somewhat similar to their previous research. Scores on the EIWA were 19 Full Scale points higher than on the WAIS ($p < .05$, degrees of freedom not reported), 22 Performance Scale points higher ($p < .01$, degrees of freedom not reported), and 11 Verbal Scale points higher (n.s., degrees of freedom not reported). The authors concluded that the score equivalence of the EIWA and WAIS is questionable, although their low sample size and other factors were clearly a limitation.

Unfortunately, the preceding study was fraught with other serious methodological shortcomings that limit its external validity. For example, the examinees used were all Panamanians, whereas the EIWA had been adapted for and standardized on a Puerto Rican population; the examinees were all chronic, primarily schizophrenic (80%) inpatients; the test procedure involved only 2 out of 11 subtests; no objective measure of bilingualism was included; and the group sizes were small. Nevertheless, the study is an important one in that it marks the first independent, published attempt at validating the EIWA and comparing its scores to the WAIS.

The study by López and Romero (1988) provides one of the most comprehensive examinations of the structure of the EIWA. The stated objective of this study was to identify specific differences between the EIWA and the WAIS with respect to administration, content, scoring, and standardization sample characteristics. In pointing out differences, they used the WAIS as their baseline for comparison because the EIWA was derived directly from the WAIS. With respect to administration, López and Romero noted that there are only five subtests on the EIWA with identical administrative procedures as the WAIS. The rest differ in starting number and in the number of failures necessary before the subtest is discontinued. The contents of the two tests are such that they share more differences than similarities. Only the Digit Span and Object Assembly subtests were deemed identical in the two test versions. Major differences were found with respect to scoring differences as well. López and Romero plotted the conversion of raw scores to scale scores for the two identical subtests, Digit Span and Object Assembly. Their plots revealed a consistent elevation of the resulting EIWA scale score for any given raw score. Their study suggests that the mean performance of the Puerto Rican standardization sample for the EIWA was probably significantly lower than the mean performance of the United States (WAIS) sample. This finding was based on estimates of mean differences and standard deviations because the actual means and standard deviations for the subtests have not been published by the Psychological Corporation. Finally, López and Romero also noted that the standardization sample for the EIWA differed from the WAIS sample in regard to rural/urban status ($p < .001$), occupational level ($p < .001$), and educational background ($p < .001$). The authors discussed the implications of their findings for practitioners, with the most important being that use of the EIWA may result in an "inflated score" if the individual being tested is from a more educated background. López and Romero concluded by suggesting that future researchers needed to adopt the research strategy of Davis and Rodriguez (1979) and administer both tests to a normal adult population.

López and Taussig (1991) examined whether using the WAIS–R could lead to an underestimation of Spanish-speaking older adults' functioning and whether using the EIWA could lead to an overestimation of this group's functioning. They used 47 Spanish-speaking and 44 English-speaking examinees—some of whom were afflicted with Alzheimer's disease—and comparison groups with no known neurological disorders. All examinees were given four Wechsler subtests: Similarities, Vocabulary, Digit Span, and Block Design. The authors stated that these subtests were chosen because they provide measures sensitive to neurological impairment and because they are close equivalents. They claimed of the Digit Span and Block Design subtests, "the only difference between the two tests is the language in which the test is administered" (p. 450). In fact, although the Digit Span subtests are identical, Block Designs item numbers 8 and 9 on the WAIS–R and item numbers A, 1, and 10 on the EIWA are unique. López and Romero (1988) had previously identified Digit Span and Object Assembly as the only two subtests that are identical across the EIWA and the original WAIS.

The results of the López and Taussig (1991) study reinforced those of López and Romero (1988). They pointed out that the EIWA standardization norms convert raw scores to higher standardized values than do the WAIS–R norms. López and Taussig concluded that the EIWA, in some cases, overestimated functioning and in other cases reflected it accurately. They suggested that the EIWA be used with examinees who have limited education and are monolingual.

Demsky, Gass, and Golden (1997) looked at two short forms of the EIWA for purposes of yielding short-form validities and reliabilities. It is interesting to note that both studies using either the translated or short-form version involved no restandardizations; they merely reported on translations or abridged tests with informal modifications.

SUMMARY OF EIWA RESEARCH

Thus, the available literature on the EIWA has been shown to comprise a mere handful of empirical studies to date. It also has been demonstrated that the EIWA has not yet been subjected to validation at a level commensurate with its importance and clinical use. Instead, it has achieved acceptance inferred largely from the reputation of the WAIS, which has more than 1,300 published studies confirming both validity and reliability.

COMPARABILITY OF THE WAIS AND THE WAIS–R

The present research compared scores that individuals achieved on the EIWA and the WAIS–R. Because the EIWA was originally adapted from the WAIS, not the WAIS–R, some mention of the differences between the WAIS and the WAIS–R is needed. Several articles (Lippold & Claiborn, 1983; Urbina, Golden, & Ariel, 1982) have compared the WAIS and the WAIS–R. These articles, along with the WAIS–R manual, point to differences between WAIS and WAIS–R Full Scale scores on the order of about 8 IQ points. In each study, the WAIS scores were higher than the WAIS–R scores.

Changes that have been observed between WAIS and WAIS–R scores underscore the need to be aware of three specific issues. First, because all obtained scores are relative to a normative group, the reference population needs to be an appropriate one. Second, because populations change over time and test items may become dated, tests must be revised and renormed from time to time. Third, it is imperative that updated or revised tests be equated to their predecessors. When tests are equated, it enables decisions to be made on a stable yardstick. Without such equating, clinical decisions based on an IQ number will show variation with time and across different test versions.

Methodology and Procedures

The present study utilized a group of 50 Puerto Rican men and women who were between 17 and 59 years of age and who either were born in Puerto Rico or had biological parents who were both born there. Candidates exhibiting productive symptoms indicative of an active psychotic state were excluded. The educational and occupational backgrounds of the examinees were recorded but were not used as criteria for inclusion or exclusion from the study.

The main criterion for selection of examinees was in the area of language proficiency. In that the present analysis employed a within-subject design, it was essential that language differences be "equated" to the extent possible. Thus, in order to be included in the study each examinee had to score at the same level in English and Spanish proficiency as measured by the *Bilingual Syntax Measure II* (Burt, Dulay, Hernandez, & Taleporos, 1980).

If examinees differed greatly between their English- and Spanish-language proficiency, then any differences found in Full Scale IQs conceivably could be attributed to differences in language fluency of the examinees. Thus, the determination of relatively equal language proficiency of our examinees was critical. Without such an analysis, the framework from which to assess accurately any differences between the EIWA and the WAIS–R would have been flawed, because they may reflect, at least to some extent, language differences.

A dearth of tests exists to assess language dominance effectively. Oakland, DeLuna, and Morgan (1977), in reviewing 27 such measures, found that only 4 provided information on both validity and reliability. The lack of adequate investigation of these instruments warns us to use most of them with cautious skepticism.

Three important criteria guided our choice of a language proficiency test in this study. First, the test needed to be supported by research attesting to its reliability and validity; second, it had to have a range of measurement that included at least a high school–level language development; and last, to avoid a confounding with intelligence measures, it could not employ vocabulary as its major criterion from which to assess language proficiency (because vocabulary correlates so highly with intelligence). The test that appeared to be best suited to fulfill these requirements was the *Bilingual Syntax Measure II* (BSM–II).

Test Administration

All examinees in this experiment underwent essentially the same procedure. Those applicants who fulfilled the selection criteria, as described previously, were asked to sign an informed-consent form and were given a brief description of the study. The examinees were told that the purpose of the study was to gather data that would explore the comparability of the EIWA and the WAIS–R. Any individual who asked for a more detailed explanation of the hypotheses involved was told explicitly that such explanation would be provided after the tests were completed, along with an opportunity to withdraw their test protocol from the study if they so desired. None of the examinees withdrew their protocol after testing.

After this brief introduction, the examinees were given the BSM–II. Operationally, all examinees were initially assumed to be included in the study and hence were tested at that time with either the EIWA or the WAIS–R. Only one protocol was eventually excluded because the examinee's BSM–II measure showed a difference in language proficiency. All subjects included in this study scored in the same category of language proficiency in English and Spanish on the BSM–II.

Examinees were given both the EIWA and the WAIS–R in a counterbalanced sequence in order to control for order effect. To minimize possible practice effects, the administration of each intelligence test was separated by a time lag of between 1 and 2 weeks. All of the tests were individually administered and scored by a bilingual psychologist according to the standard instructions of each test.

Results

Fifty individuals were examined between 1984 and 1992. All subjects were recruited and obtained from community mental health and educational institutions throughout the greater Metropolitan New York area including Westchester County, a suburb just north of New York City. Of the 50 people tested, 31 were female and 19 male. Their ages ranged between 17 and 59, with a mean of 31.9 and a standard deviation of 8.77. Education ranged between 4 and 21 years, with a mean of 14.1 years and a standard deviation of 3.05. Table 9.1 shows the overall results obtained by the 50 examinees on the Verbal, Performance, and Full Scale scores on both the EIWA and the WAIS–R.

A Hotelling T^2 analysis was performed to test whether or not there were any differences across any of the 11 subtests. The Hotelling–Lawley Trace statistic was significant at greater than the .001 level (Wilks' l = 0.390, *df* [degrees of freedom] = 40). Because the Hotelling T^2 was significant, a series of 14 matched-pair *t* tests were performed across the 11 subtests and the three composite scores. The results of the *t* tests are shown in Table 9.2.

The results obtained in Table 9.2 show that there were clear, significant differences ($p < .001$, $df = 49$) between the WAIS–R and EIWA Full Scale, Verbal, and Performance IQs. Further analysis across each of the subtests showed that the differences were not the result of one or two flawed subtests. Instead, the results suggest that those differences are attributable to differences across all of the subtests ($p < .001$, $df = 49$).

A special analysis was performed on the Vocabulary subtest to provide an indication of the comparability of the WAIS–R and the EIWA.

TABLE 9.1

Descriptive Statistics of Examinees' Test Scores

	EIWA			*WAIS–R*		
	Verbal	*Performance*	*Full Scale*	*Verbal*	*Performance*	*Full Scale*
M	116.6	125.4	121.5	92.4	97.4	93.8
SD	10.52	9.63	9.23	11.85	12.37	11.44
Maximum	137	144	140	118	130	126
Minimum	88	106	97	69	75	73

TABLE 9.2
Matched Pair *t*-Test Results

IQ or Subtest	*WAIS–R Mean*	*WAIS–R SD*	*EIWA Mean*	*EIWA SD*	*Mean Difference*	*t*
Full Scale IQ	93.8	11.4	121.5	9.2	27.7	33.7*
Verbal IQ	92.4	11.9	116.6	10.5	24.2	26.3*
Performance IQ	97.4	12.7	125.4	9.6	28.0	25.2*
Information	8.6	2.4	13.1	2.6	4.5	16.1*
Digit Span	8.4	2.7	12.5	2.8	4.1	11.5*
Vocabulary	9.3	2.7	12.1	2.2	2.8	8.4*
Arithmetic	8.1	2.3	12.6	2.5	4.5	19.5*
Comprehension	9.0	2.6	14.1	2.7	5.1	15.8*
Similarities	9.0	2.8	13.5	1.6	4.5	14.5*
Picture Completion	9.0	2.7	14.1	1.9	5.1	15.7*
Picture Arrangement	9.5	3.0	13.7	2.1	4.2	10.7*
Block Design	9.0	2.4	13.6	2.0	4.6	18.6*
Object Assembly	9.3	2.6	14.8	2.4	5.5	18.6*
Digit Symbol	9.5	2.7	14.2	2.6	4.7	22.6*

*$p < .001$, $df = 49$

This subtest was subjected to separate analyses to see whether item presentation order agreed with the level of difficulty (as expected) that our examinees experienced. The WAIS–R correlation for the hierarchical ordering of items was +.934, suggesting a strong concordance between the way our examinees answered the items and their order on the test. In contrast, the EIWA's correlation was +.777, a statistically significant reduction ($F = 3.158$; $p < .001$) in the absolute value of the correlation. The Vocabulary subtest correlated .80 ($p < .001$; $df = 47$) with Full Scale IQ on the WAIS. The comparable correlation coefficient on the EIWA was .66 ($p < .001$; $df = 47$). The difference between the two correlation coefficients was not statistically significant. All of the subtest correlation coefficients with Full Scale IQs may be found in Table 9.3.

Discussion and Implications

This study has shown that there are significant differences in scores generated by the same bilingual population taking both the EIWA and the WAIS–R. The Full Scale IQs showed a mean difference of 27.7 points. Verbal and Performance IQs showed 24.2- and 28.0-point differences respectively. These differences were both highly statistically significant and clinically meaningful.

A 27.7-point difference—almost 2 standard deviations—between Full Scale scores on both tests is an interpretative nightmare for clinicians. Certainly, one can take the stance that both scores are correct—that the EIWA is giving a person's score relative to the 1967 standardization sample and the WAIS–R relative to its 1980 standard-

TABLE 9.3
Correlation Coefficients of Subtests and Full Scale IQs

Subtest	*WAIS–R Full Scale IQ*	*EIWA Full Scale IQ*	*df*
Vocabulary	.80	.66	47
Comprehension	.77	.78	47
Arithmetic	.72	.73	47
Similarities	.71	.64	47
Information	.71	.63	47
Digit Span	.68	.60	47
Picture Arrangement	.64	.66	47
Block Design	.62	.61	47
Object Assembly	.54	.61	47
Picture Completion	.52	.73	47
Digit Symbol	.48	.51	47

ization sample. This stance, however, is not useful for the practical purposes for which the tests are given. Note that such a difference would probably be lessened by about 8 Full Scale points had the WAIS rather than the WAIS–R been used in this analysis. The difference is nevertheless greater than a full standard deviation and is of considerable consequence.

Before having empirical evidence for the disparity in scores, some discussion had already been launched trying to explain the presumed differences. One notion suggested that the high scores on the EIWA might reflect the "cultural sensitivity" of the test. This idea implied that because the test was constructed in Puerto Rico, the item content, or at least the Verbal portion, would have greater relevance to the population. Following this idea, one might expect that Verbal IQs would reflect greater disparity in scores because these items are traditionally thought to be more culturally loaded.

The results obtained by this study, however, showed that Performance IQ differences were greater than Verbal IQ differences. Therefore, the explanation that the test's higher scores reflect cultural sensitivity was not supported by these results unless one is willing to support the notion that cultural differences may be reflected in the Performance subscales to a greater degree than in the Verbal ones. Of course, culture does affect both the Performance as well as the Verbal domains of intelligence, but differences in the contrary direction were nevertheless expected.

The second notion, that differences arise because the two tests are measuring essentially different psychological traits, also was not supported by this study, as there were no significant differences in the way that the subtests of the EIWA and the WAIS–R correlated with their respective Full Scale scores. Furthermore, the factor-analytic study of the structure of the EIWA (Gómez et al., 1992) corroborated that its structure was a strong reflection of the WAIS.

The most compelling evidence seems to suggest that there are continuing problems with the EIWA. It was already shown that the standardization sample differed from the census population parameters with respect to region, occupation, age, and education. However, the evidence presented herein suggests that the differences are more complex. To see whether or not difficulties existed at the subtest level, the Vocabulary subtest was scrutinized further.

It was found that the correlation between item difficulty and order of placement on the Vocabulary subtest was substantially lower on the EIWA than on the WAIS–R. Such a disparity lends credence to the anecdotal experience of clinicians who complain that they almost never reach a well-defined "testing of the limits" in the EIWA vocabulary subtest. Psychologists frequently report that the full subtest must be given because the subject repeatedly scores an intermittent word correct before the discontinuation criteria of seven wrong in a row is met (on the WAIS, five consecutive errors terminates the subtest administration). This manifestation not only adds to unreliability of the subtest, but also increases the frustration of the examinee, who must endure the humiliation of facing many more words for which he or she does not know the meaning.

There are many interesting observations that can be made with respect to the current study and the seminal work of Green and Martinez (1967), which produced the EIWA. Clearly, although the EIWA enjoys substantial use, it has serious problems. Those problems at least include uncertainties associated with the standardization of the instrument and its related issue of score interpretation. The issues raised by Melendez (1994) and by López and Romero (1988) perhaps best identify the reasons that the score inflation occurs: The same behaviors on the EIWA lead to a much higher score than they do on the WAIS. The rationale for this happening, quite simply, was that the average tested performance on the standardization sample of the EIWA was lower than was found on the WAIS. Such differences are presumably due to gross differences in educational background and social and economic status between mainland and Puerto Rico. Then, when the average performance on the EIWA was set to 100, the average score difference became essentially intrinsic to the test. The work of Melendez documents that scores on the EIWA simply do not mean the same thing as scores on the WAIS in terms of the cognitive skills that might be expected.

A restandardization of the EIWA is desperately needed. Green and Martinez (1967) noted that, "in the United States, restandardizing is needed each 12 to 18 years." Their comment was based on the extensive experience with the WAIS in the United States. They also emphasized that in a region like Puerto Rico, where population characteristics were changing rapidly, such restandardization was especially important.

Despite the clear-sighted forewarning given by Green and Martinez (1967), the EIWA has not undergone any revisions by the Psychological Corporation since the original test was published in 1968. Apart from the major issues of keeping a test psychometrically current, the published EIWA manual is plagued with annoying minor flaws that should have been corrected. A common one is that the manual was typed with words having aberrant spaces between them. For example, the first item of the Information subtest uses the Spanish word *pajaros* and it is printed "paj aros." The second item uses the word *pelota* but prints it "pel ota." The third item uses the word *yerba* and prints it "yer ba." And the fourth item uses the word *planta,* which is printed "pl ant a."

Test items are not the sole place where these errors occur. In just the first paragraph (five lines) of the instructions for the Information subtest, there are at least a dozen misspaced words. This type of error, wherein random spaces invade the integrity of words, is pervasive in the manual and is extremely annoying to any native Spanish speaker. Despite one's acquaintance with the language, such aberrant spacing within words is highly distracting and causes one to pause unnaturally while reading test items. Even accent marks in the manual seem to be penciled-in. Interestingly, the type-spacing errors were not evident in the sections of the final text submitted by Green and Martinez (1967), but only in the published manual. The effects of such internal distractions in the testing situation are not known for sure but could, unquestionably, hamper accurate assessment.

Such standards of quality are not the hallmark of the Psychological Corporation, as one can see by the stark contrast with the refinements found in the WAIS–R and WAIS–III (Wechsler Adult Intelligence Scale, 3rd ed.) manuals. However, the EIWA does not meet contemporary professional standards.

In comparison to the WAIS–R, many clinicians feel that the EIWA is "too easy" and yields "inflated" scores. Surprisingly, in 1967 Green and Martinez lamented that "the difficulty level of the test was set too high" (p. 10) and that correcting this would have required "one to two more years of efforts in the area of item development and testing" (p. 52). How can there be such an apparent disparity? Such opposing observations may be a result of poor standardization sampling or they may be a reflection of the rapid change in population characteristics. Over time, the original standardization sample no longer accurately represents the increasingly sophisticated population and underscores the urgent need for restandardization. The present study affirms the significant disparity between the EIWA and the WAIS–R and the inability of a test to keep up with population norms in a group that is rapidly shifting in education and other relevant parameters.

At this point in time, the EIWA holds a virtual monopoly in the intelligence testing of adult Hispanics in the United States. The increase in the Hispanic population and their service needs will sooner or later prompt an increased need for Spanish-language measures of developed abilities. It has been demonstrated by a convergence of recent studies that the norms for the EIWA are both flawed and dated and that the only solution is for the EIWA to undergo a readaptation and restandardization process. If such a reformulation is made, it is hoped that current standards for test adaptation will be followed (Geisinger, 1994; Hambleton, 1994).

This research showed that there are indeed major discrepancies between the two tests. The EIWA was shown to have problems ranging from test construction issues to issues of norms that would plague any test dependent on a normative population. At the test construction level, it was shown that there were difficulties in obtaining a standardization sample that matched the census population variables. It also was shown that the Vocabulary subtest in the EIWA differed widely from the WAIS–R in the accuracy with which the items were rank-ordered for difficulty. This finding and those of Melendez (1994) suggest that the EIWA's 1967–1968 test construction procedures may have been flawed, or even if perfect, are now quite dated and that the Hispanic population of the 1990s is markedly different from that of Puerto Rico in 1967. The EIWA remains a substantial first effort at producing a Spanish-language adaptation of the WAIS. Unfortunately, it has been virtually ignored by the testing community after its inception and never benefited from constant scrutiny or updates as has its English-language counterpart.

The present research suggests strongly that the EIWA has not aged gracefully and is thus in dire need of restandardization. Furthermore, given the results obtained in this study, the EIWA and WAIS–R are almost certainly not functionally equivalent. In the light of this study, continued use of this test by psychologists, without a severely modified interpretation of the scores, raises serious ethical questions.

ACKNOWLEDGMENTS

The present chapter is based on a dissertation conducted in the Psychology Department of Fordham University by the first author under the direction of the second author. The authors much appreciate a critical reading of the paper by Dr. Janet F. Carlson; any errors, of course, that remain are those of the authors.

REFERENCES

Burt, M. K., Dulay, H. C., Hernandez, E., & Taleporos, E. (1980). *Bilingual Syntax Measure II technical handbook.* New York: Psychological Corporation.

Conde López, V., & Domeneca López, B. (1977). Algunas reflexiones sobre las adaptaciones españolas de las Escalas de Wechsler para Adultos [Some reflections about the Spanish adaptation of the Wechsler Scale for Adults]. *Revista de Psicología General y Aplicada, 32,* 619–645.

Davis, T. M., & Rodriguez, V. L. (1979). Comparison of WAIS and EIWA scores in an institutionalized Latin American psychiatric population. *Journal of Consulting and Clinical Psychology, 47,* 181–182.

Demsky, Y. I., Gass, C. S., & Golden, C. J. (1997). Common short forms of the Spanish Wechsler Adult Intelligence Scale. *Perceptual & Motor Skills, 85,* 1121–1122.

Demsky, Y. I., Mittenberg, W., Quintar, B., Katell, A. D., & Golden, C. J. (1998). Bias in the use of standard American norms with Spanish translations of the Wechsler Memory Scale–Revised. *Assessment, 5,* 115–121.

Eyde, L. D. (1992). Introduction to the testing of Hispanics in industry and research. In K. F. Geisinger (Ed.), *Psychological testing of Hispanics* (pp. 167–172). Washington, DC: American Psychological Association.

Geisinger, K. F. (Ed.). (1992). *Psychological testing of Hispanics.* Washington, DC: American Psychological Association.

Geisinger, K. F. (1994). Cross-cultural normative assessment: Translation and adaptation issues influencing the normative interpretation of assessment instruments. *Psychological Assessment, 6,* 304–312.

Gómez, F. C., Piedmont, R. L., & Fleming, M. Z. (1992). Factor analysis of the Spanish version of the WAIS: The Escala de Inteligencia Wechsler para Adultos (EIWA). *Psychological Assessment, 4,* 317–321.

Green, R. F. (1964). Desarrollo y estandarización de una escala individual de inteligencia para adultos en español [Design and standardization of the individual intelligence scale for adults in Spanish]. *Revista Mexicana de Psicología, 1*(3), 231–244.

Green, R. F., & Martinez, J. (1967). *Standardization of a Spanish-language adult intelligence scale* (Final Report, Project No. 1963, Contract No. O. E. 3-10-128). Washington, DC: U.S. Department of Health, Education and Welfare.

Grisay, A. (2003). Translation procedures in OECD/PISA 2000 international assessment. *Language Testing, 20*(2), 225–240.

Hambleton, R. K. (1994). Guidelines for adapting educational and psychological tests: A progress report. *European Journal of Psychological Assessment, 10,* 229–244.

Hambleton, R. K. (2002). Adapting achievement tests into multiple languages for international assessments. In A. C. Porter & A. Gamoran (Eds.), *Methodological advances in cross-national surveys of educational achievement* (pp. 58–79). Washington, DC: National Academy Press.

Herrans, L. L. (1969). Sex differences in the Spanish WAIS scores. *Dissertation Abstracts International, 30,* 1432–1433.

Herrans, L. L. (1973). Cultural factors in the standardization of the Spanish WAIS or EIWA and the assessment of Spanish-speaking children. *School Psychologist, 28,* 27–34.

Lippold, S., & Claiborn, J. M. (1983). Comparison of the Wechsler Adult Intelligence Scale and the Wechsler Adult Intelligence Scale–Revised. *Journal of Consulting and Clinical Psychology, 51,* 315.

López, S. R., & Romero, A. (1988). Assessing the intellectual functioning of Spanish-speaking adults: Comparison of the EIWA and the WAIS. *Professional Psychology: Research and Practice, 19*(3), 263–270.

López, S. R., & Taussig, I. M. (1991). Cognitive-intellectual functioning of Spanish-speaking impaired and nonimpaired elderly: Implications for culturally sensitive assessment. *Psychological Assessment, 3,* 448–454.

Macias, R. F. (1977). Hispanics in 2000 A.D.—projecting the number. *Agenda,* 7(3), 16–20.

Martinez-Urrutia, A., & Spielberger, C. D. (1973). The relationship between state–trait anxiety and intelligence in Puerto Rican psychiatric patients. *Revista Interamericana de Psicologia, 7,* 199–214.

McShane, D., & Cook, V. J. (1985). Transcultural intelligence assessment: Performance by Hispanics on the Wechsler scales. In B. B. Wolman (Ed.), *Handbook of intelligence: Theories, measurements, and applications* (pp. 737–785). New York: Wiley.

Melendez, F. (1994). The Spanish version of the WAIS: Some ethical considerations. *Clinical Neuropsychologist, 8,* 388–393.

Oakland, T., DeLuna, C., & Morgan, C. (1977). Annotated bibliography of language dominance measures. In T. Oakland (Ed.), *Psychological and educational assessment of minority children.* New York: Brunner/Mazel.

Urbina, S. P., Golden, C. J., & Ariel, R. N. (1982). WAIS/WAIS–R: Initial comparisons. *Clinical Neuropsychology, 4,* 145–146.

Wechsler, D. (1968). *Manual para la Escala de Inteligencia Wechsler para Adultos* [Manual for the Wechsler Intelligence Scale for Adults]. New York: Psychological Corporation.

10

Developing Tests for Use in Multiple Languages and Cultures: A Plea for Simultaneous Development

Norbert K. Tanzer
Alliant International University

The globalization of the economic market, the increasing mobility of the world's workforce, and the emergence of complex multicultural societies such as the European Union have brought new challenges to educational and psychological testing that exceed the traditional scope of monocultural/monolingual assessment. The need for instruments that are valid in multicultural/multilingual assessment situations becomes progressively more important (Bartram & Coyne, 1998; Hu & Oakland, 1991; Oakland, 1997, 2004; Oakland & Hu, 1992).

It is now widely accepted that developing such multicultural/multilingual instruments or tests[1] involves more then a mere translation, that is, the rewriting of a text from one language into another. Even though a team of professional translators using a translation–back translation method (Brislin, 1980) may produce multilingual test versions that are linguistically equivalent, these versions do not necessarily share the same psychological meaning.

[1]In this chapter, we use the terms *test* and *instrument* as synonyms.

The correct translation of the item "*watched more television than usual*" will still be an inappropriate item when applied to Sahel dwellers who do not have electricity in their homes (Van Haaften & van de Vijver, 1996). This example clearly illustrates that multicultural/multilingual assessments require a balanced treatment of psychological, psychometric, linguistic, cross-cultural, and cultural considerations so as to ensure cross-lingual/cross-cultural validity of the construct ("construct equivalence"), the test designed to measure it ("instrument equivalence"), the test administration ("administration equivalence"), and the inferences drawn from the test scores (Bracken & Barona, 1991; Brislin, 1980, 1986; Geisinger, 1994; Greenfield, 1997; Hambleton, 1994; van de Vijver & Hambleton, 1996; van de Vijver & Leung, 1997a, 1997b; van de Vijver & Tanzer, 1997). Note that a significant part of the enculturation (or socialization) process is transmitted through language and, thus, persons with different mother tongues also have different cultural backgrounds. Therefore, assessments conducted with different language versions for testees with different mother tongues are almost always multicultural. Consequently, multilingual assessments are usually multicultural assessments (i.e., "multicultural/multilingual assessments"). Note also that different ethnic groups, even if they speak a common language (e.g., majority/minorities) still constitute different cultural groups. Hence, assessments in monolingual multiethnic societies are multicultural even if they are conducted with the same language version of a test (i.e., "multicultural/monolingual assessments").[2]

CONSTRUCT EQUIVALENCE

Whereas monocultural/monolingual tests can be developed by basing solely on mainstream theories of the construct(s) they intend to measure, developing valid instruments for multicultural and multilingual assessments requires the cross-cultural generalizability of the construct(s) across all intended cultures and languages. In their conceptualization of the psychological constructs, monocultural test developers tend to run the risk of ethnocentric bias that may threaten the cross-cultural validity of the instruments. For example, a growing body of literature has demonstrated that Western personality instruments do not capture indigenous Chinese personality aspects such as "face" and "harmony" (Cheung, 2004; Cheung et al., 1996; Yang & Bond, 1990; Zhang & Bond, 1998).

[2]Monocultural/multilingual assessment situations are rather rare.

INSTRUMENT AND ADMINISTRATION EQUIVALENCE

Above and beyond the cross-cultural/cross-lingual equivalence of the construct(s), test developers must also provide evidence for the cross-cultural/cross-lingual equivalence of their instruments (i.e., absence of "instrument bias") and their administration procedures (i.e., absence of "administration bias"). In order to facilitate this task, the International Test Commission (ITC) had prepared the *ITC Test Adaptation Guidelines,* a set of 22 guidelines on recommended practices for developing multicultural/multilingual tests, given in chapter 1 of this volume (see also Hambleton, 1994, 2002; van de Vijver & Hambleton, 1996). Emphasizing the multilingual and multicultural *context* of assessments, the Guidelines address various criteria for the *development* (Guidelines 3–12), *administration* (Guidelines 13–18), and *documentation* (Guideline 19) of multicultural/multilingual instruments as well as the *interpretation of the test scores* (Guidelines 20–22).

The ITC Test Adaptation Guidelines, in particular, emphasize the need to provide evidence for the cross-cultural validity of the construct (Guideline 2) and the test (Guidelines 1, 3–6, 10–11) across all intended populations and languages. They also stress the importance of specifying and justifying valid comparisons between results (e.g., test scores) obtained with different language versions or from different cultural groups (Guidelines 12, 14, 20–22). Furthermore, they also place emphasis on documenting (Guidelines 4, 17, 19) all changes that were necessary during the adaptation or development process including item contents or stimulus material (Guidelines 6, 14), response formats (Guidelines 5, 14), test instructions (Guidelines 4, 16), administration procedures (Guidelines 5, 15, 16, 18), and scoring rules (Guidelines 12, 20–21). Finally, they stress the importance of implementing appropriate statistical techniques and data collection designs for detecting possible sources of inequivalence and for studying the effectiveness of any countermeasures taken (Guidelines 7–11, 13). Last but not least, the qualification of test users for conducting multicultural/multilingual assessments (Guidelines 14, 18) is also highlighted.

SIMULTANEOUS VERSUS SUCCESSIVE DEVELOPMENT OF INSTRUMENTS FOR MULTICULTURAL AND MULTILINGUAL ASSESSMENT SITUATIONS

Although the rationale behind each guideline is commented upon and illustrated with empirical examples (van de Vijver & Hambleton,

1996), the ITC Test Adaptation Guidelines are normative rather than prescriptive. They do not provide strategies for obtaining valid multicultural/multilingual tests nor do they discuss the advantages and disadvantages of existing approaches.

In the *simultaneous test development approach*, a new instrument is developed for use in a number of predefined[3] cultural groups ("reference cultures") and/or languages ("reference languages"). It usually involves a "committee approach," that is, a multilingual task force from various cultural backgrounds and with complementary expertise in "mainstream" psychology (including knowledge of the construct and its measurement), psychometrics, test construction techniques as well as cultural (i.e., indigenous) psychology, cross-cultural psychology, and linguistics. The advantage of this approach is that it ensures maximum linguistic and cultural decentering in the definition of the construct and the test designed to measure it. Idiosyncracies specific to a particular language (e.g., local idioms) or culture (e.g., social norms) can be detected and removed during early stages of the test development. Therefore, the simultaneous approach is instrumental in developing valid multicultural/multilingual tests with equally good characteristics for each of the reference cultures. However, this involves more than just producing several language versions of an instrument and collecting data in arbitrarily chosen cultural groups ("safari studies").

In the *successive test development approach*, by far the most common practice, a test is developed and validated by one or several test developers from a particular monocultural/monolingual background for use within this monocultural/monolingual context ("source" language/culture). Very often, years after a test has become popular, it is then adapted by the original test developer(s) or by a new task force for use in other cultures and/or languages ("target" languages/cultures). Usually, the monocultural/monolingual developers of the source test would have formal training in mainstream psychology, psychometrics, and test construction but not in cultural or cross-cultural psychology. This lack of cultural and/or cross-cultural psychology can, unknowingly, lead to implementing ethnocentric bias or cultural specifics that restrict subsequent development of equally good versions in new target languages and/or cultures. This problem is further aggravated if the task force involved in the test adaptation does not have the full range of expertise as described in the simultaneous approach. Nevertheless, given the number of existing excellent

[3]For practical purposes, it may be necessary to restrict this to a limited number of "key cultures" or "key languages."

monocultural/monolingual tests, the successive approach will be frequently employed in the foreseeable future.

PITFALLS AND REMEDIES IN MULTICULTURAL/MULTILINGUAL TEST APPLICATIONS

Researchers engaged in the development of multicultural/multilingual tests will encounter problems and pitfalls that are absent in monolingual/ monocultural test applications. Using a number of examples from self-report inventories and nonverbal aptitude tests, we illustrate the broad range of these pitfalls, identify ITC Test Adaptation Guidelines that may apply to them, and suggest possible remedies. Further examples of pitfalls and possible remedies are provided in Greenfield (1997), van de Vijver and Leung (1997b), and van de Vijver and Tanzer (1997).

Pitfalls Caused by Single Items

Unlike construct and instrument/administration bias, "differential item functioning" (Sireci & Allalouf, 2003) or "item bias" is caused by distortions at the item level. A biased item has different psychological meanings across cultures. Although item bias can be produced by many sources, it is most frequently caused by (a) measurement artifacts such as poor item translation or ambiguities in the original item content, or by (b) genuine "cultural specifics" such as low familiarity/appropriateness of the item content in certain cultures (Guideline 6). As is illustrated in the following example, it is often difficult in multilingual *and* multicultural settings to decide which of these two possibilities could have triggered off the different interpretations and/or reactions of the subjects.

Ambiguous Item Content (Example 1). In the *State–Trait Anger Expression Inventory* (STAXI; Spielberger, 1988) three styles of anger expression are distinguished. Anger-out is the expression of anger toward other people or objects, Anger-in is the suppression of angry feelings, and Anger-control is the attempt to control the expression of anger. By and large, the postulated three-factor structure of anger expression was confirmed in several U.S. samples (Spielberger, 1988), a sample of Singaporean Chinese (Tanzer, Sim, & Spielberger, 1996) as well as in adaptations into German (Schwenkmezger, Hodapp, & Spielberger, 1992), Italian (Spielberger & Comunian, 1992), and Norwegian (Håseth, 1996). However, in some studies (e.g., Spielberger & Comunian, 1992; Tanzer, Sim, & Spielberger, 1996), the item "*I am secretly quite critical of others*" shifted from Anger-in to Anger-out.

Problem Identification. It is important to note (Guideline 13) that this item can be interpreted either as "*holding grudges and not talking about it to other people,*" which would be an Anger-in expression or as "*talking negatively behind someone's back,*" which conveys a covert Anger-out expression instead. In a cross-cultural panel study,[4] German-speaking and Italian-speaking college students in South Tyrol were given the STAXI in their native-language version. At the retest, they were asked how they would interpret the item. Although about half of the German-speaking students (53%, $n = 347$) chose the first alternative, only one third of the Italian-speaking college students (64%, $n = 241$) chose this alternative. Thus, given the ambiguity of the item content, even minor variations between different language versions can trigger off substantial shifts in the prevalence of the alternative interpretations (Guideline 7).

Even though the expression of and coping with anger are universal emotions, they are nevertheless governed by cultural factors (Mesquita & Frijda, 1992). For example, the concepts "need for harmony" and "giving face" prevalent in Chinese societies (e.g., Bond, 1990; Cheung et al., 1996; Gao, 1998) preclude open and direct confrontations that characterize U.S.-American ways of Anger-out expression. Thus, an indirect, nonconfrontational mode of anger expression as conveyed by the second interpretation would be preferred. In this case, the observed shifts would reflect genuine cultural differences in the way Anger-out is expressed (Guideline 3).

Controversial Anchor Items (Example 2). The *Job Stress Survey* (JSS; Spielberger & Reheiser, 1994) is a self-report inventory designed to measure the impact of job-related stress. It consists of 30 statements that describe job-related events identified as stressful by employees in various occupations ("job stressors"). Each job stressor is rated twice: One rating concerns the frequency in which it has occurred within the last 6 months ("frequency" ratings) and, the second, the amount or degree of stress evoked by a single occurrence of the stressful event ("severity" ratings). For the severity ratings, subjects are instructed to compare the amount of stress

[4]I would like to thank Bettina Unterholzner for collecting the data. Further information on the sample and design of the study can be found in Unterholzner (1997).

associated with each stressor to the amount of stress evoked by the stressor "*Assignment of disagreeable duties,*" selected as an *anchor with a preassigned value of medium severity*.

Problem Identification. While adapting the JSS, the appropriateness of the German translation of the anchor was studied by converting this stressor to a free rating item (Guidelines 8, 9, 13). Despite fairly average mean ratings, this item consistently received controversial ratings in a number of studies regardless of the response formats and instructions used (Hodapp, Tanzer, Maier, Pestemer, & Korunka, in press). Moreover, a high test–retest stability of this stressor found in a panel study (r_{tt} = .68; N = 156) indicated that the broad dispersion of the ratings (see Fig. 10.1) cannot simply be attributed to random effects. In another study that used this item as an anchor with a preassigned value of medium severity, a number of subjects did not comply with the instruction. They canceled the preassigned medium severity rating of the standard stressor, and

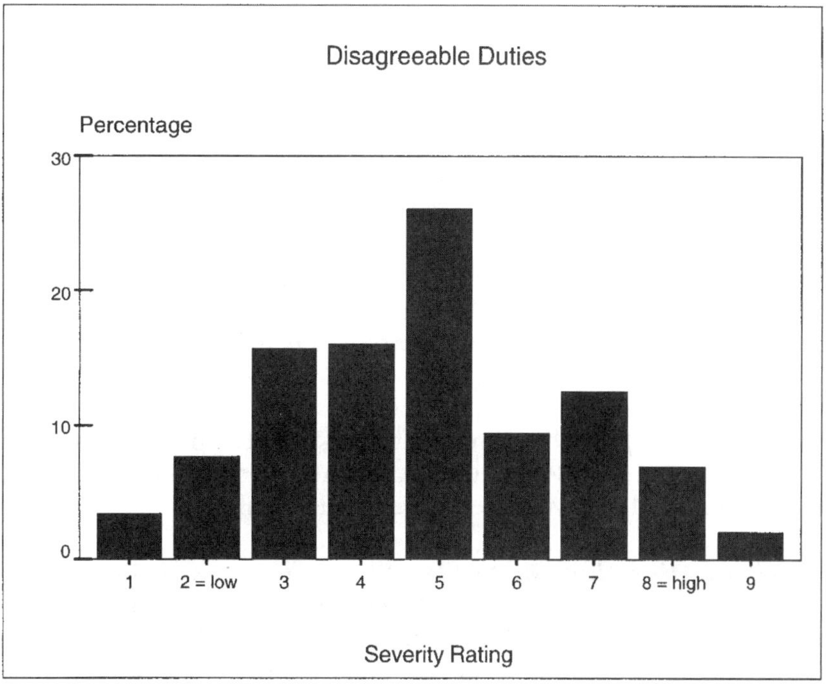

FIG. 10.1. Distribution of the severity ratings for the JSS-stressor "Assignment of disagreeable duties" on a 9-point scale.

marked a different rating category instead. In short, the results indicated that this item did not evoke the same amount of stress for all German-speaking respondents, a necessary requirement before it can be established as a valid anchor item.

Suggested Remedies. Collect "collateral information" (e.g., the testees' interpretation of the item content in the first example, and nonstandard ways of test administration in the second example) for testing multicultural/multilingual test validity (Guideline 14).

Pitfalls Caused by Culturally Incompatible Test Designs

A widespread opinion among mainstream psychologists is that the problems and pitfalls encountered in multicultural/multilingual test applications are mainly caused by using verbal material (e.g., in self-report inventories or verbal ability tests such as the Wechsler Intelligence Scale for Children/Wechsler Adult Intelligence Scale adaptations) too extensively. Consequently, employing "nonverbal" tests such as Raven's Standard Progressive Matrices Test (SPM) in ability assessment or "pictorial" tests in personality assessment would substantially reduce the problem of developing valid multicultural/multilingual instruments. The following examples demonstrate that this is not necessarily the case.

Cultural (In-)Compatibility of Pictorial Material (Example 3). A number of tests in personality and health psychology use stimuli consisting exclusively of pictorial material. Examples are the Rosenzweig Picture-Frustration Test (e.g., Rosenzweig, 1977), the Preschool Symptom Self-Report (Martini, Strayhorn, & Puig-Antich, 1990), and the Pictorial Evaluation of Test Reactions (Toubiana, 1994). As all the items contain elements specific to a certain culture (e.g., Western style of dressing, unisex hairstyles or clothes), time period, or ethnic group (e.g., White faces), a valid cross-cultural application would require the complete redrawing of all pictorial material (Guidelines 1, 3, 6). Consequently, an entirely new test would have to be assembled and validated for each new culture.

Writing Direction (Example 4). In a cross-cultural study (Piswanger, 1975; see also Fischer & Formann, 1982), the Viennese Matrices Test (VMT; Formann & Piswanger, 1979) was administered to Nigerian and Togolese Arabic-educated high school students, and their responses were compared to those of the Austrian calibration sample. The VMT is an inductive-reasoning test that uses matrices items similar to those of Raven's SPM. The most striking finding showed that identifying and applying rules from left to right as compared to top to bottom was more difficult for African-Arab than Austrian students.

Problem Identification. The mismatch between the direction of writing in the Arabic culture (i.e., right-to-left in Arabic as compared to left-to-right in Latin) and the Western way of designing matrices items with the missing element at the *bottom right* corner (see left side of Fig. 10.2) is a plausible (post hoc) explanation. To illustrate the cognitive interference that may be caused by culturally incompatible item designs, imagine the confusion of Arabs reading a Western three-picture advertisement for a washing machine. In their reading sequence from right to left, a woman (a) looks happy at a stack of clean laundry, (b) puts the laundry into the machine and switches on the machine, and (c) is then terrified by heaps of dirty laundry.

Suggested Remedy. The use of a culture-conform design of matrices items may overcome this problem (Guidelines 5, 14, 15). As illustrated in the right side of Fig. 10.2, a "mirrored" test version in which the matrix elements are arranged in such a way that the missing element is at the bottom left corner may eliminate this type of bias for Arab subjects.

Meaning of Distractors (Example 5). Another example of culturally incompatible item design is provided by Greenfield

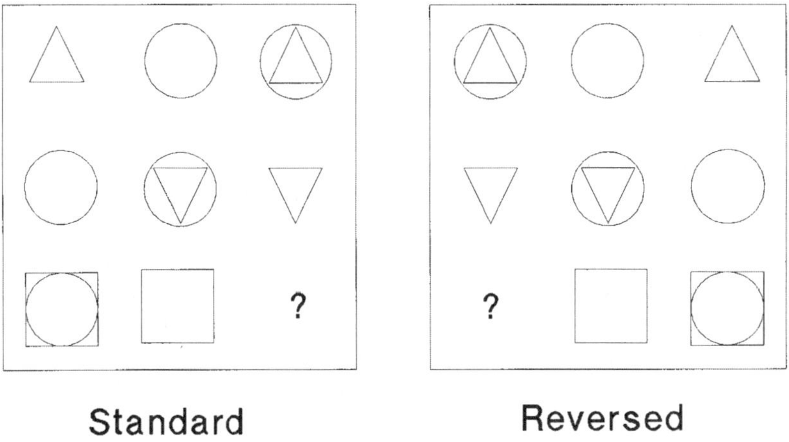

FIG. 10.2. A matrices test item (without multiple-choice distracters) in normal and "reversed" design.

(1997). The meaning of distractors in multiple-choice tests may be interpreted by subjects from different cultures differently (Guidelines 5, 14):

> In the multiple-choice format, the respondent is given a set of alternatives. All but one of them is functionally useless information. The problem is that participants in many cultures will assume that the communicator [the tester] is presenting an ensemble of information relevant to the goal of solving the problem .... The tester [and test developer] assumes the aim of the alternative answers is to eliminate incorrect possibilities, while selecting the correct alternative. The testee assumes the aim of alternative answers is to use the materials given by the experimenter [tester] to construct a solution to the problem. (pp. 1120–1121)

Suggested Remedy. As Greenfield (1997) pointed out, the problem carries its own solution: Do not use multiple-choice formats in multicultural/multilingual applications unless all testees are fully familiar with the concept of distractors. Instead, let the subjects *produce* (e.g., draw) rather than select the solution.[5]

Intratest Practice Effects (Example 6). Depending on their prior knowledge or previous experience with material similar to the test items (Guideline 6), subjects will benefit differently from intratest practice effects, especially at the beginning of a test (Guideline 14). The following illustration is drawn from cross-cultural studies of the Three-Dimensional Cube Comparison Test (3DC; Gittler, 1990), a cube comparison test measuring spatial ability. An example item is shown in Fig. 10.3. These cross-cultural studies (Broer, 1996; Tanzer, Gittler, & Ellis, 1995; Tanzer, Gittler, & Sim, 1994) indicated that students in countries with no formal education in descriptive geometry, as compared to their Austrian counterparts, gained more from working on the first few test items.

Suggested Remedy. Use a sufficient number of ***hidden warming-up items,*** that is, items presented like real test items at the beginning of the test but not to be used for scoring. In the monocultural source version of the 3DC (Gittler, 1990), the first test item is used as a hidden warming-up item, and the remaining 17 test items are used for scoring. However, the aforementioned cross-cultural studies indicated that more hidden warming-up items are needed to ensure valid score comparisons in multicultural contexts (Guidelines 20, 21). Note that this problem cannot be solved by simply presenting

[5]This would also eliminate the problem of guessing.

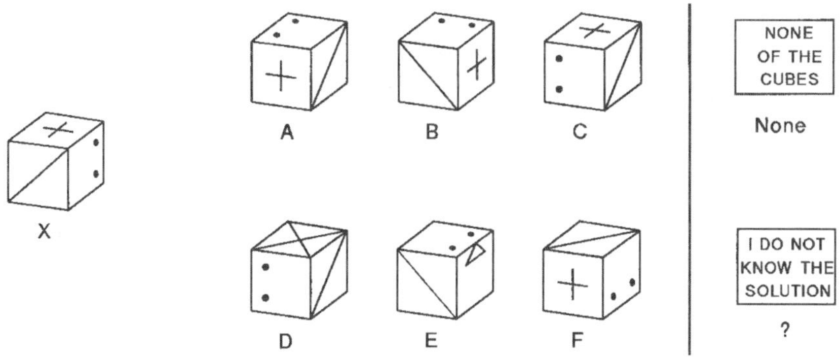

FIG. 10.3. Example item used in the 3DC instructions given in the Appendix.

more practice items with their solutions given because most subjects approach practice items differently from real test items. Within each culture, the necessary number of hidden warming-up items can be determined by randomly assigning subjects to the standard test version versus a test version with reversed item sequence, and then comparing the item difficulties between the two test versions (Guidelines 8, 9, 22).

Pitfalls Caused by Ethnocentric Test Instructions and Administration Procedures

Other sources of ethnocentric bias in nonverbal intelligence/aptitude tests may be hidden in test instructions and administration procedures. For example, the testees' preference points on the speed–accuracy trade-off curve may be influenced by culture-specific values of time and accuracy.

Enforcing Time Limits in Power Tests (Example 7). Although the VMT and the 3DC were designed as power (i.e., self-paced) tests, the test authors recommended a liberal time limit for economic test administration. In a cross-cultural study with these two tests (Broer, 1996; Tanzer, Ellis, Gittler, & Broer, 1996; Tanzer et al., 1995), the recommended time limits of 25 minutes for the VMT and 35 minutes for the 3DC were increased so as to give all subjects ample testing time (Guideline 13). Participants were university or college students from Austria (n = 244), Chile (n =173), and the United States, with one Anglo-American (n =196) and one Hispanic (n = 144) sample. As can be seen in Fig. 10.4, a substantial percentage of Chilean subjects ex-

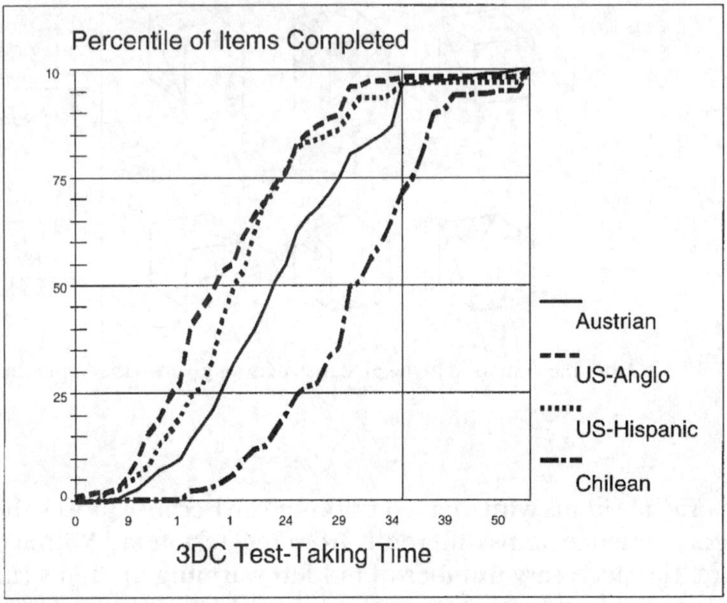

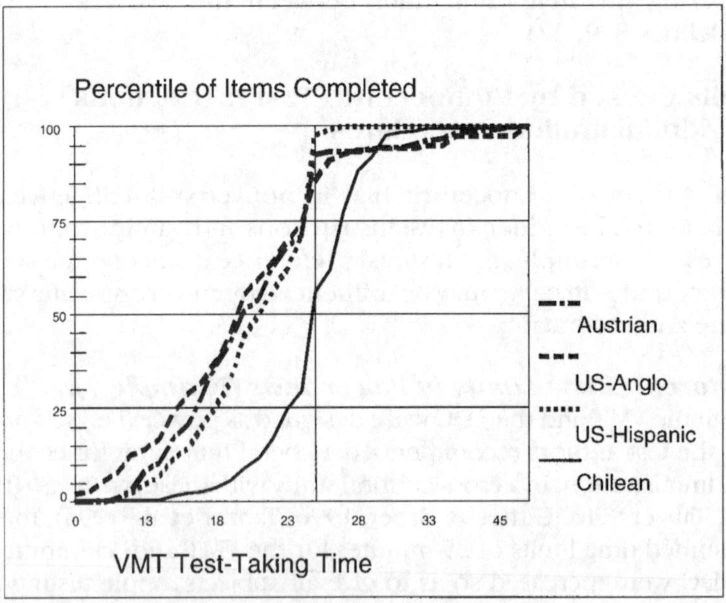

FIG. 10.4. Percentiles of subjects who completed the 3DC (Fig. 10.4a) and the VMT (Fig. 10.4b) plotted as a function of their test-taking time (in minutes) for the Austrian (n = 244), Chilean (n =173), U.S. Anglo-American (n =196), and U.S. Hispanic (n = 144) sample.

ceeded both recommended time limits. Whereas almost all of the Austrian and U.S. subjects completed the spatial ability test within 35 minutes, only 75% of the Chilean sample did so. The situation was even more pronounced for the matrices test: Almost all of the Austrian and U.S. subjects completed the VMT within 25 minutes whereas only half of the subjects in Chile completed all the test items within the recommended time limit. The average test scores obtained with unlimited testing time did not differ significantly. Hence, the cross-cultural differences obtained under standard instructions would have been significant and, thereby, incorrectly indicating that the groups differ in inductive reasoning skills (Guidelines 14, 22). As time limits in power tests can disadvantage certain cultural groups, we strongly recommend recording test-taking time to be used as "collateral information" (Guideline 20) in cross-cultural test applications of power tests.

Translatability of Test Instructions (Example 8). Instructions in monocultural/monolingual tests are often fine-tuned to their intended monocultural/monolingual application and, thus, tend to capitalize on linguistic idiosyncracies ("surfing on the language"). Brislin (1986) formulated a number of guidelines to enhance the translatability of verbal material that can also be applied to the formulation of test instructions (Guideline 4).

Documentation of Meta-Instructions (Example 9). Published test instructions are usually developed through a series of versions, and the "know-how" gained during this process (e.g., appropriate segmentation of information, key elements of the instruction, educational background required for comprehension, etc.) is implemented in the final version. However, this know-how is rarely documented and, thus, usually not available to the task force involved in subsequent adaptations of the test. We propose publishing this meta-information together with the final version of the instructions (Guideline 17). This could be done as a hypertext document (e.g., Conklin, 1987) as illustrated in the Appendix for the English 3DC instructions.

Multicultural/Multilingual Adaptation of a Concentration Test (Example 10). Each of the previous examples focused on only one pitfall. To highlight the number of problems one may encounter even for relatively simple tests, the following example provides a holistic picture of a multicultural/multilingual test adaptation.

The German Original. The *d2* (Brickenkamp & Zillmer, 1998) is a Bourdon-like letter cancellation test designed to measure short-term concentration. It was originally developed in Germany (Brickenkamp, 1962), and is still frequently used in German-speaking countries. Subjects have to scan 14 rows of *d*'s and *p*'s with dashes above and/or below the letters for embedded targets as fast as possible without making errors. The three types of targets are (a) *d*'s with two dashes above, (b) *d*'s with two dashes below, and (c) *d*'s with one dash above and one dash above. The original test material consists of a double-sided landscape test sheet with personal particulars, target characters, an example line, and a hand-scoring table on the front page (recto), and 14 test lines with scoring rubrics on the back page (verso). The *d2* is administered under speed conditions (i.e., timed) with about 4 minutes testing time, and all instructions are given orally.

Successive Development of a Decentered Test Version. A multicultural/multilingual team of psychologists (Tanzer, Ellis et al., 1997) set out to develop culturally and linguistically decentered test versions that should be valid under the following predefined conditions: (a) All testees must have at least 8 years of formal education, and (b) the majority of them may not have had previous experience with Bourdon-like cancellation tests; (c) the testing can be conducted in small to medium-size groups, and (d) the instructions are to be given in the native language of the testees; (e) testers either can be: (i) trained foreign psychologists with ample expertise in psychological assessment and in *d2* administration but with a strong foreign accent and relatively little knowledge of local circumstances, (ii) trained local psychologists with ample knowledge of local circumstances and experience in psychological assessment in general but not with the *d2* administration in particular, or (iii) senior undergraduates with varying expertise in psychological testing.

Based on both judgmental procedures (Guideline 7) and empirical evidence (Guideline 9) collected in a series of cross-cultural studies with samples of 150-250 college or university students, decentered versions were developed for Chinese, Croatian, English (used in U.S. Anglo-American and Hispanic samples), French (used in a Moroccan sample), German (used in Austrian samples), and several Spanish dialects (used in Argentinean, Chilean, and Spanish samples). Given the simplicity of the *d2*, it may seem that a correct translation of the test instructions would be sufficient. However, as illustrated next, a number of changes in the design of the test material, test instructions, and administration procedures were necessary in order to ensure cross-lingual and cross-cultural equivalence.

Design of the Test Sheet (Example 10a). The layout of the original test form was simplified by removing the table for hand scoring and all bio-data fields except a personal code from the instruction page (recto), and the scoring rubrics from the test page (verso). To ensure that testees will understand the instructions under all the aforementioned conditions, the core part of the instructions were given in written form on the instruction page. This also allowed us to remove the explanations "*d as in dog*" and "*p as in pig*" from the (oral) instructions given in the English edition[6] (Brickenkamp & Zillmer, 1998), which are more confusing than helpful in cultures that do not use the Latin alphabet (e.g., China). Finally, the three target characters were highlighted in a box and marked twice on the sample line.

Administration (Example 10b). To ensure reliable administration under the various field conditions mentioned previously, the time segmentation was changed from 20 seconds for each of the 14 lines to 2 minutes for each of the two blocks (Parts A and B) of 7 lines. In addition, a detailed list of guidelines was compiled for administering the decentered version in multicultural contexts (Guidelines 17, 8).

Instructions (Example 10c). As a number of testees used different ways to mark the targets (e.g., ticks, crosses, scribbles, and circles), the requested way ("*to mark with a single stroke*") was emphasized, justified ("in order to save time"), and illustrated twice in the sample line. Likewise, the different ways of correcting wrong markings (e.g., crossing-out, scribbling out, erasing with a rubber) were standardized to "*crossing out*" ("X-out" in the U.S. samples) and illustrated on a blackboard or a transparency. Special attention was also given to the translation of key phrases. In the English edition,[7] the three types of possible targets (i.e., all *d*'s with two dashes in total) were referred to as "Examples" (Brickenkamp & Zillmer, 1998). However, as the term *examples* did not convey the meaning of an exhaustive set, it was changed to "Targets." In addition, the ambiguous formulation "*to cross out*" was repeatedly used (e.g., "not supposed to cross out the other letters," "the letter *p* as in 'pig' should never be crossed out") in the oral instructions. The requested way of marking ("to cross out ... by making a single line through the

[6]"d (wie Dora)" and "p (wie Paula)" in the German edition.

[7]"Beispiele" in the German edition.

letter") was specified only once. As the term "*to cross out*" can be interpreted either as a specific way of marking (i.e., to "X-out") or as more general concept of deleting/canceling that includes other types of marking ("to strike out," "to blot out"), it was substituted by a more precise phrase ("*to mark with a single stroke*"). Finally, the phrase "*Stop*. Continue with B" given after the first 2 minutes caused some subjects to literally stop working and, thus, was changed to "*Time*. Continue with B."

Limitations of Successive Test Adaptations: A Plea for Simultaneous Development

In all examples presented, professional translations ("test applications"; van de Vijver & Leung, 1997a, 1997b) could not have provided valid multicultural/multilingual instruments. Even in the case of a relatively simple test such as the *d2* (Example 10), a number of substantial modifications were necessary ("test adaptation"). Adapting tests may involve modifying single items (Example 1), response formats (Examples 2 and 5), design of items (Example 4) and test sheets (Example 10a), scoring rules (Example 6), administration procedures (Examples 7 and 10b), and test instructions (Examples 8, 9, and 10c). In other cases (Example 3), it may be necessary to adapt the instrument to such an extent that, practically speaking, an entirely new instrument has been created ("test assembly").

In fact, despite the substantial efforts to achieve a culturally and linguistically decentered version of the *d2,* the following two serious problems that can be resolved only by a complete redesigning of the test (i.e., test assembly) remained.

Latin Target Characters (Example 11). The use of Latin characters (*d*'s and *p*'s) in the *d2* may disadvantage testees who do not use the Latin alphabet in their daily life. On the other hand, testees trained in memorizing and recognizing complex pictograms such as Mandarin characters may be able to screen the lines simultaneously for the three targets instead of scanning for *d*'s first and then checking the number of dashes. Note also that letter cancellation tests are classical examples of ethnocentric test constructions because there is virtually no need to rely on this sort of stimuli (Gittler & Tanzer, 1990/1998; Moosbrugger & Oehlschlägel, 1996).

Working Direction (Example 12). A number of subjects from Western samples did not comply with the instruction "*work linewise from left to right*" and worked in "serpentines" instead.

This phenomenon was also not eliminated by the additional instructions "*work as if you are reading a book*" (used in Western samples). Thus, it was probably not caused by misunderstanding of the instructions. It was more likely to be caused by right-handed subjects who, unlike left-handers, were handicapped by this working direction because their hand covers the rest of the characters. This problem becomes aggravated in a multicultural context because the instructed writing direction clearly disadvantages Arab subjects (see also Example 4).

The pitfalls illustrated in the previous examples will only have an impact on the cross-cultural validity of the measurement (i.e., the test) but not on the cross-cultural validity of the underlying construct. The following example illustrates that "transporting a test" (Greenfield, 1997) from a monocultural to a multicultural context can even affect the conceptualization of the underlying construct (Guideline 2).

Subcomponents of Academic Self-Concept (Example 13). Academic self-concept research consistently found Reading and Mathematics self-concepts to be uncorrelated, that is, "domain-specific." In most of these studies, academic self-concept was measured by the Self-Description-Questionnaire I (SDQ–I; Marsh, 1988), which uses scales consisting of cognitive and affective/motivational items to measure domain-specific academic self-concept. In a cross-cultural comparison of Australian and Singaporean Chinese students (Tanzer, 1995, 1998; Tanzer & Sim, 1991; Tanzer, Sim, & Marsh, 1992, 1997), substantial cross-cultural differences in the endorsement rates emerged for competence/task-easiness items but not for interest/eagerness items (see Fig.10.5). As the original English-language version of the SDQ–I was used in both countries ("multicultural/monolingual assessment"), translation problems are certainly not the cause for this phenomenon (Guidelines 7, 16).

Subsequent intracultural factor analyses in Australia (Marsh, Craven, & Debus, 1999), Austria, Italy, Singapore, and the United States (Tanzer, 1998) also supported the separation of cognitive (i.e., Competence/Task-Easiness) and affective/motivational (i.e., Interest/Eagerness) subcomponents of domain-specific academic self-concept. Thus, the integration of cross-cultural and intracultural (i.e., differential psychology) research helped to gain a deeper conceptual understanding of academic self-concept.

This example also illustrates the limitations of the successive test development approach: New intracultural and cross-cultural results regarding the conceptualization of the construct and its measure-

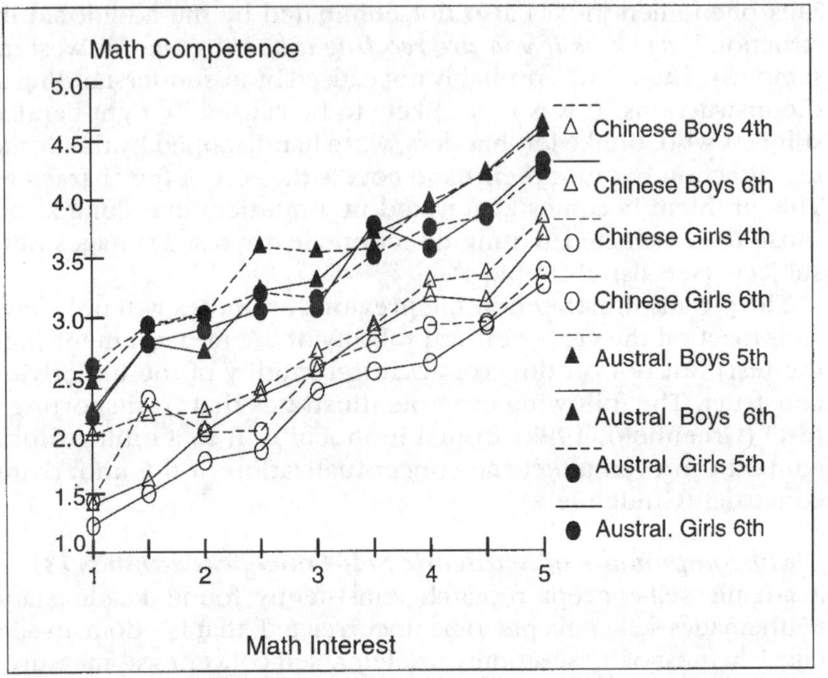

FIG. 10.5. Regression of math competence on math interest for each of the eight Age × Gender × Culture (Singaporean Chinese vs. Australian) subgroups.

ment can be integrated only into new lingual/cultural target versions but not in the source version. For example, the German SDQ–I adaptation (Tanzer, 1998) fully integrated the two-component concept of domain-specific academic self-concept whereas the original English version provides only short "post hoc" scales for this purpose. Moreover, the large body of theory and research conducted with the original instrument (e.g., the SDQ–I research on domain-specificity of academic self-concept; see Marsh, 1988; Marsh & Craven, 1997) may not hold completely for the reconceptualized construct.

Designing Tests for Use in Multiple Cultures and Languages

Given the limitations of successive test adaptation procedures, we recommend simultaneous development of new multicultural/multilingual tests. Unlike the successive approach, simultaneous test development allows the integration of results from cross-cultural and intracultural studies by reformulating the conceptualization of the construct and its measurement at a relatively early stage of the test development. With carefully selected reference languages/cultures, the simultaneous approach can also substantially reduce the risk of construct bias in multicultural assessment contexts (see Example 13) and allows a much larger degree of linguistic and cultural decentering than successive test adaptations (see Example 10).

Simultaneous Development of a Concentration Test (Example 14). Unlike the *d2,* the Progressive Test Series (PTS; Gittler & Tanzer, 1990/1998) was a priori designed for use in multicultural/multilingual settings. It consists of nine subtests with increasing cognitive complexity, ranging from subtests requiring only sensorimotor speed to subtests involving several components of fluid intelligence. Like a "Russian doll," the cognitive task required by each subtest forms part of the next subtest and, thus, yielding a quasi-simplex structure. This design also facilitates the test instructions because only the difference between two adjacent subtests needs to be explained.

To avoid ethnocentric bias in the test material, the items of the nine subtests consist of simple geometric elements (dots, circles, frames, bars, and gray-shaded areas) that should be familiar to educated persons in all cultures (Guideline 6). Likewise, the response alternatives ("0,1,2," "1,2,3," or "yes/no") displayed underneath each item can easily be translated into every language (Guideline 5). In addition, the "know-how" gained in the multicultural/multilingual *d2* adaptation (see Examples 10–12) was used for redesigning the PTS material (Guidelines 13, 14). As shown in Fig. 10.6, visual aids regarding the task and the marking/correcting of answers were used. To balance out handedness and writing direction in one's native language (Guidelines 1), testees have to work through the test in "serpentines" as illustrated in Fig. 10.7. Finally, to ensure that even testees with little education can understand the task required (Guidelines 4, 10), it can be instructed by a "naturalistic cover story." The paraphrased cover story for Subtest C (see also Fig. 10.6) is as follows:

Look at the frames [or "windows"]. They can be empty or filled up with one to three grey bars [or "bricks"]. For the first frame, you can count the number of grey bars. For the other frames, you must estimate them from the height of the grey-shaded area. The circles above each frame indicate how many bars must be in the frame. Your task is to decide [yes/no] for each frame if this is the case.

CONCLUSION

Developing tests for use in multiple cultures and languages requires the successful integration of a number of psychological, psycho-

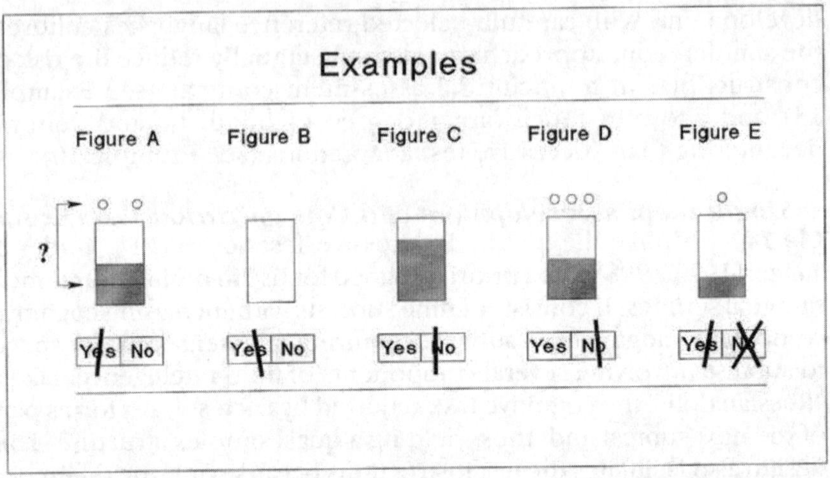

FIG. 10.6. Example line used in Subtest C of the Progressive Test Series (PTS).

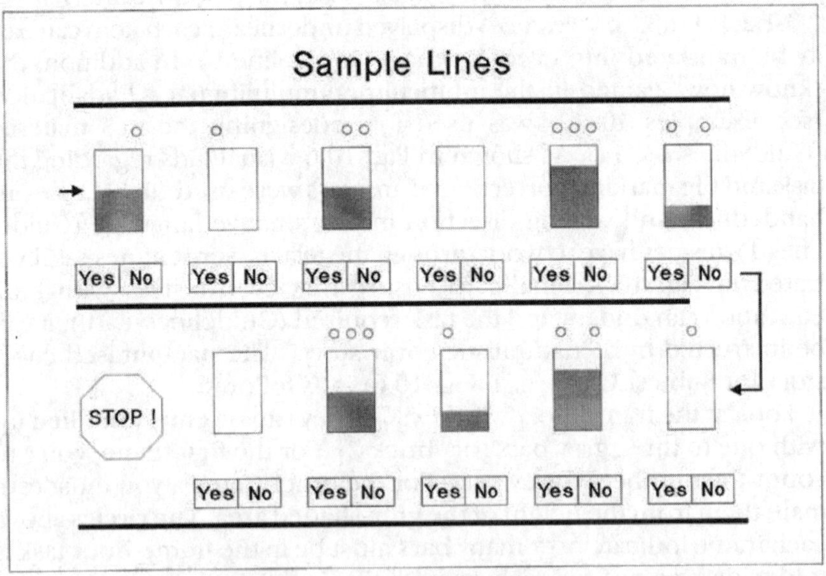

FIG. 10.7. Sample lines used in Subtest C of the PTS.

metric, cultural, cross-cultural, and linguistic considerations so as to guarantee the cross-cultural/cross-lingual validity of the underlying construct, the test designed to measure it, the test administration, and the inferences drawn from the test scores. Given the limitations of successive test adaptation procedures even in the case of relatively simple tests such as the *d2,* we recommend the simultaneous approach for developing multicultural/multilingual tests because it allows maximum linguistic/cultural decentering. However, this approach can warrant valid multicultural/multilingual assessments only if the following prerequisites are fulfilled:

1. Evidence for Construct Equivalence. A prerequisite for developing valid instruments for use in multiple languages and cultures is the generalizability of the underlying construct(s) across all reference cultures and languages (Guideline 2). In addition to evidence compiled from literature in cultural (indigeneous) and cross-cultural psychology, ethnology, and linguistics, both judgmental and empirical evidence should also be collected during the test development/adaptation process (Guidelines 7–9).
2. Taxonomy of Cross-cultural/Cross-lingual Equivalence. Another prerequisite is a taxonomy of cross-cultural/cross-lingual equivalence. This taxonomy has to specify under which conditions can certain types of results (e.g., factor loadings, test scores) obtained with different language versions or from different cultural groups be compared across languages and cultures (Guidelines 12, 20–22). A relatively comprehensive proposal for such a taxonomy was provided by van de Vijver and Leung (1997a, 1997b).
3. Classification of Multicultural/Multilingual Bias. A further requirement is a comprehensive classification of possible sources of construct and measurement bias (including method, administration, and item bias) in cross-cultural/cross-lingual test applications. This classification should specify which types of equivalence are likely to be affected by which forms of bias, and should be substantiated with a large body of empirical illustrations (Guidelines 13, 14). Together with classifications suggested by van de Vijver and Leung (1997a, 1997b) or van de Vijver and Tanzer (1997), the ITC Test Adaptation Guidelines with their rationales and empirical illustrations are a preliminary step toward this comprehensive classification.
4. Taxonomy of Remedies. The assembly of a "cookbook" that specifies recipes for all sources of bias arising in multicultural/multilingual assessments is probably a hopeless enterprise. Nevertheless, future progress in multicultural/multilingual testings needs a taxonomy of remedies (Guidelines 1, 13) that is based on a cross-classifica-

tion of different types of equivalence and different sources of bias. The classification of remedies suggested by van de Vijver and Tanzer (1997) is a first step in this direction but, in order to provide a more global picture, input from measurement theory and cultural psychology (Greenfield, 1997) must also be integrated.

5. Methodological Framework for Bias Detection and Evaluation of Remedies. Without a sound methodology for detecting sources of inequivalence, the aforementioned classification of bias and remedies cannot be transformed into practical applications (Guidelines 7–9, 11, 13). The required methodological framework has to specify which strategies are effective for detecting which sources of bias, and also to evaluate the effectiveness of countermeasures taken. This "strategies toolkit" should include judgmental procedures, psychometric techniques (implemented in easily available and user-friendly software), as well as experimental designs (e.g., Gittler & Tanzer, 1998). It should also include guidelines on the *collection of collateral information* (e.g., recording working time in self-paced tests or using "thinking-aloud" techniques) because they give a deeper insight into possible cultural specifics of cognitive and motivational processes (Guideline 22).

6. Documentation Archives. The accessibility of a large and well-maintained *archive providing full-text documents on the development and application of multicultural/multilingual tests* (Guidelines 4–6, 10–11, 17–19, 22) will help to continuously update the aforementioned classification of bias and taxonomy of remedies, and to evaluate their usefulness on the basis of new evidence. If this archive is well maintained, test developers will also be able to consult the taxonomy of remedies for identifying effective countermeasures (Guideline 13). The recent paper by Hambleton, Li, and Sireci (2003) in which these researchers catalog many of the common errors found in the test adaptation literature is one initial step toward the proposed archive.

7. Complementary Expertise of Test Developers. Multicultural/multilingual tests developers need to have not only multilingual competence and expertise in "mainstream" psychology (including knowledge of the construct and its measurement), psychometrics, and test construction techniques but also competence in linguistics and cross-cultural and cultural (i.e., indigenous) psychology, as well as be knowledgeable about cultural specifics (e.g., taboo topics; Goodwin & Lee, 1994) in all intended reference cultures. Obviously, no single person can combine all these different fields of expertise. Therefore, the focus must be on establishing procedural competence regarding the set-up and successful manage-

ment of a multicultural/multilingual task force with experts from complementary disciplines.

8. Qualification of Test Users. In addition to expertise in the administration, scoring, and interpretation of a particular test, test users need to have general competence in conducting assessments in a multicultural/multilingual context (Guidelines 14,15, 18). This includes cultural sensitivity and intercultural communication competence (Asante & Gudykunst, 1989; Cohen, 1987; Landis & Bhagat, 1996; Schneller, 1989) as well as multicultural counseling (McFadden, 1993; Paniagua, 1994; Ponterotto, Casas, Suzuki, & Alexander, 1995; Wehrly, 1995).

All these requirements, obviously, exceed the capabilities of individual test developers and test users. Thus, *the development and institutionalization of qualification programs for test developers and test users*[8] covering these requirements should be a major issue for professional and scientific organizations interested in educational and psychological testing.

REFERENCES

Asante, M. K., & Gudykunst, W. B. (Eds.). (1989). *Handbook of international and intercultural communication.* London: Sage.

Bartram, D., & Coyne, I. (1998). *The ITC/EFPA survey on testing and test use in countries world-wide. Narrative report* (Research Report). Hull, England: University of Hull, Psychology Department.

Bond, M. H. (1990). *Beyond the Chinese face. Insights from psychology.* Hong Kong: Oxford University Press.

Bracken, B. A., & Barona, A. (1991). State of the art procedures for translating, validating and using psychoeducational tests in cross-cultural assessment. *School Psychology International, 12,* 119–132.

Brickenkamp, R. (1962). *Aufmerksamkeits-Belastungstest (Test d2)* [The d2 test of attention] (1st ed.). Goettingen, Germany: Hogrefe.

Brickenkamp, R., & Zillmer, E. (1998). *d2. Test of attention.* Seattle: Hogrefe & Huber.

Brislin, R. W. (1980). Translation and content analysis of oral and written material. In H. C. Triandis & J. W. Berry (Eds.), *Handbook of cross-cultural psychology* (Vol. 1, pp. 389–444). Boston: Allyn & Bacon.

---

[8]Criteria for multicultural/multilingual test use had been integrated in a number of codes on test users qualification. A joint committee from the American Psychological Association (APA), American Educational Research Education (AERA), and the National Council on Measurement in Education (NCME) had revised their standards on test users qualifications and also responsible test use of educational and psychological tests. Likewise, the International Test Commission (ITC) had prepared guidelines for test user standards, and the European Association of Psychological Assessment (EAPA) has developed guidelines for the assessment process.

Brislin, R. W. (1986). The wording and translation of research instruments. In W. J. Lonner & J. W. Berry (Eds.), *Field methods in cross-cultural research* (pp. 137–164). Newbury Park, CA: Sage.

Broer, T. (1996). *Rasch-homogene Leistungstests (3DW, WMT) im Kulturvergleich Chile-Österreich. Erstellung einer spanischen Version einer Testbatterie und deren interkulturelle Validierung in Chile* [Cross-cultural comparison of the Rasch-calibrated tests 3DC and VMT between Chile-Austria and the development of a Spanish version of the test battery]. Unpublished master's thesis, University of Vienna, Austria.

Cheung, F. M. (2004). Use of western and indigenously-developed personality tests in Asia. *Applied Psychology: An International Review, 53*(2), 173–191.

Cheung, F. M., Leung, K., Fan, R. M., Song, W. Z., Zhang, J. X., & Chang, J. P. (1996). Development of the Chinese Personality Assessment Inventory. *Journal of Cross-Cultural Psychology, 27,* 181–199.

Cohen, R. (1987). International communication: An intercultural approach. *Cooperation and Conflict, 22,* 63–80.

Conklin, J. (1987). Hypertext: An introduction and survey. *IEEE Computer, 20,* 17–41.

Fischer, G. H., & Formann, A. K. (1982). Some applications of logistic latent trait models with linear constraints on the parameters. *Applied Psychological Measurement, 6,* 397–416.

Formann, A. K., & Piswanger, K. (1979). *Wiener Matrizen-Test. Ein Rasch-skalierter sprachfreier Intelligenztest* [The Viennese Matrices Test. A Rasch-calibrated nonverbal intelligence test]. Weinheim, Germany: Beltz Test.

Gao, G. (1998). "Don't take my word for it."—Understanding Chinese speaking practices. *International Journal of Intercultural Relations, 22,* 163–186.

Geisinger, K. F. (1994). Cross-cultural normative assessment: Translation and adaptation issues influencing the normative interpretation of assessment instruments. *Psychological Assessment, 6,* 304–312.

Gittler, G. (1990). *3DW. Dreidimensionaler Würfeltest. Ein Rasch-skalierter Test zur Messung des räumlichen Vorstellungsvermögens. Theoretische Grundlagen und Manual* [The Three-Dimensional Cube Test, 3DC. A Rasch-calibrated spatial ability test. Theoretical background and test manual]. Weinheim, Germany: Beltz Test.

Gittler, G., & Tanzer, N. K. (1990/1998). *The Progressive Test Series (PTS).* Unpublished test, University of Vienna and University of Graz, Austria.

Gittler, G., & Tanzer, N. K. (1998, August). *Establishing cross-cultural equivalence of item complexity using the linear logistic test model (LLTM).* Paper presented at the 24th International Congress of Applied Psychology, San Francisco.

Goodwin, R., & Lee, I. (1994). Taboo topics among Chinese and English friends. A cross-cultural comparison. *Journal of Cross-Cultural Psychology, 25,* 325–338.

Greenfield, P. M. (1997). You can't take it with you. Why ability tests don't cross cultures. *American Psychologist, 52,* 1115–1124.

Hambleton, R. K. (1994). Guidelines for adapting educational and psychological tests: A progress report. *European Journal of Psychological Assessment (Bulletin of the International Test Commission), 10,* 229–244.

Hambleton, R. K. (2002). Adapting achievement tests into multiple languages for international assessments. In A. C. Porter & A. Gamoran (Eds.), *Method-*

ological advances in cross-national surveys of educational achievement (pp. 58–79). Washington, DC: National Academy Press.

Hambleton, R. K., Li, S., & Sireci, S. (2003). *Pitfalls and obstacles in the test adaptation process: A meta-analysis* (Center for Educational Assessment Research Report No. 489). Amherst, MA: University of Massachusetts, School of Education.

Håseth, K. J. (1996). The Norwegian adaptation of the State–Trait Anger Expression Inventory. In C. D. Spielberger & I. Sarason (Eds.), *Stress and emotion* (Vol. 16, pp. 83–106). Washington: Taylor & Francis.

Hodapp, V., Tanzer, N. K., Maier, E. R., & Pestemer, I. A., & Korunka, C. (in press). The German adaptation of the Job Stress Survey: A multi-study validation in different occupational settings. In C. D. Spielberger & I. G. Sarason (Eds.), *Stress and emotion* (Vol. 17). Washington, DC: Taylor & Francis.

Hu, S., & Oakland, T. (1991). Global and regional perspectives on testing children and youth: An empirical study. *International Journal of Psychology, 26,* 329–244.

Landis, D., & Bhagat, R. S. (Eds.). (1996). *Handbook of intercultural training* (2nd ed.). London: Sage.

Marsh, H. W. (1988). *Self-Description-Questionnaire I. SDQ–I manual and research monograph.* San Antonio, TX: Psychological Corporation.

Marsh, H. W., & Craven, R. (1997). Academic self-concept: Beyond the dustbowl. In G. Phye (Ed.), *Handbook of classroom assessment: Learning, achievement, and adjustment* (pp. 131–198). Orlando, FL: Academic Press.

Marsh, H. W., Craven, R., & Debus, R. (1999). Separation of competency and affect components of multiple dimensions of academic self-concept: A developmental perspective. *Merril–Palmer Quarterly, 45,* 567–601.

Martini, D. R., Strayhorn, J. M., & Puig-Antich, J. (1990). A symptom self-report measure for preschool children. *Journal of the American Academy of Child and Adolescent Psychiatry, 29,* 594–600.

McFadden, J. (Eds.). (1993). *Transcultural counseling: Bilateral and international perspectives.* Alexandria, VA: American Counseling Association.

Mesquita, B., & Frijda, N. H. (1992). Cultural variations in emotions: A review. *Psychological Bulletin, 112,* 179–204.

Moosbrugger, H., & Oehlschlägel, J. (1996). *FAIR. Frankfurter Aufmerksamkeitstest* [Frankfurt attention test]. Bern, Switzerland: Huber.

Oakland, T. (1997). Test use among school psychologists: Past, current, and emerging practices. *European Journal of Psychological Assessment, 13, 2–9.*

Oakland, T. (2004). Use of educational and psychological tests internationally. *Applied Psychology: An International Review, 53*(2), 157–172.

Oakland, T., & Hu, S. (1992). The top 10 tests used with children and youth worldwide. *Bulletin of the International Test Commission, 19,* 99–120.

Paniagua, F. A. (1994). *Assessing and treating culturally diverse clients: A practical guide.* Thousand Oaks, CA: Sage.

Piswanger, K. (1975). *Interkulturelle Vergleiche mit dem Matrizentest von Formann* [Cross-cultural comparisons with Formann's Matrices Test]. Unpublished doctoral dissertation, University of Vienna, Vienna, Austria.

Ponterotto, J. G., Casas, J. M., Suzuki, L. A., & Alexander, C. M. (Eds.). (1995). *Handbook of multicultural counseling.* Thousand Oaks, CA: Sage.

Rosenzweig, S. (1977). *Manual for the children's form of the Rosenzweig Picture-Frustration (P-F) Study.* St. Louis, MO: Rana House.

Schneller, R. (1989). Intercultural and intrapersonal processes and factors of misunderstanding: Implications for multicultural training. *International Journal of Intercultural Relations, 13,* 465–484.

Schwenkmezger, P., Hodapp, V., & Spielberger, C. D. (1992). *Das State-Trait-Ärgerausdrucks-Inventar STAXI* [The German adaptation of the State-Trait Anger Expressions Inventory]. Bern, Switzerland: Huber.

Sireci, S. G., & Allalouf, A. (2003). Appraising item equivalence across multiple languages and cultures. *Language Testing, 20*(2), 148–166.

Spielberger, C. D. (1988). *State–Trait Anger Expression Inventory research edition. Professional manual.* Odessa, FL: Psychological Assessment Resources.

Spielberger, C. D., & Comunian, A. L. (1992). *STAXI. State–Trait Anger Expression Inventory. Versione e adattamento italiano a curi di Anna Laura Comunian. Manuale* [Test manual of the Italian version of the State–Trait Anger Expression Inventory]: Firenze, Italy: Organizzazioni Speziali.

Spielberger, C. D., & Reheiser, E. C. (1994). Job stress in university, corporate, and military personnel. *International Journal of Stress Management, 1,* 19–31.

Tanzer, N. K. (1995). Cross-cultural validity of Likert-type scales: Perfect matching factor structures and still biased? *European Journal of Psychological Assessment, 11,* 194–201.

Tanzer, N. K. (1998). *Assessment of domain specificity in school-related Likert-type inventories: Conceptual issues, psychometric approaches, and cross-cultural evidence.* Unpublished habilitation monograph. Graz, Austria: University of Graz.

Tanzer, N. K., Ellis, B. B., Gittler, G., & Broer, T. (1996, August). *The use of collateral information in establishing the cross-cultural validity of tests.* Paper presented at the 26th International Congress of Psychology, Montreal, Canada.

Tanzer, N. K., Ellis, B. B., Zhang, H.-C., Sim, C. Q. E., Broer, T., & Gittler, G. (1997, July). *Cross-cultural decentering of test instructions in a letter-cancellation test: A field test of the ITC Guidelines for Test Adapations.* Paper presented at the 5th European Congress of Psychology, Dublin, Ireland.

Tanzer, N. K., Gittler, G. & Ellis, B. B. (1995). Cross-cultural validation of item complexity in a LLTM-calibrated spatial ability test. *European Journal of Psychological Assessment, 11,* 170–183.

Tanzer, N. K., Gittler, G., & Sim, C. Q. E. (1994). A cross-cultural comparison of a Rasch calibrated spatial ability test between Austrian and Singaporean adolescents. In A. Bouvy, F. J. R. van de Vijver, P. Boski, & P. Schmitz (Eds.), *Journeys into cross-cultural psychology* (pp. 96–110). Lisse, Netherlands: Swets.

Tanzer, N. K., & Sim, C. Q. E. (1991). *Self-concept and achievement attributions. A study of Singaporean primary school students* (Research Rep. No. 1991/5). Graz, Austria: University of Graz, Department of Psychology.

Tanzer, N. K., Sim, C. Q. E., & Marsh, H. W. (1992). Using personality and attitude inventories over cultures: Theoretical considerations and empirical findings. *Bulletin of the International Test Commission, 19,* 151–171.

Tanzer, N. K., Sim, C. Q. E.,& Marsh, H. W. (1997). *Where cross-cultural and differential psychology meet: Competence/task-easiness and interest/eager-*

ness as subcomponents of academic self-concept (Research Rep. No.1997/1). Graz, Austria: University of Graz, Department of Psychology.

Tanzer, N. K., Sim, C. Q. E., & Spielberger, C. D. (1996). Experience and expression of anger in a Chinese society. The case of Singapore. In C. D. Spielberger & I. Sarason (Eds.), *Stress and emotion* (Vol. 16, pp. 51–65). Washington, DC: Taylor & Francis.

Toubiana, Y. (1994). *Pictorial evaluation of test reactions (PETER)*. Petach-Tikva, Israel: PETER.

Unterholzner, B. (1997). *Validierung einer italienischen Form des Prüfungsstressinventars (PSI) von Tanzer* [Validation of an Italian adaptation of Tanzer's Examination Stress Inventory]. Unpublished master's thesis, University of Graz, Austria.

van de Vijver, F. J. R., & Hambleton, R. K. (1996). Translating tests: Some practical guidelines. *European Psychologist, 1,* 89–99.

van de Vijver, F. J. R., & Leung, K. (1997a). Methods and data analysis of comparative research. In J. W. Berry, Y. H. Poortinga, & J. Pandey (Eds.), *Handbook of cross-cultural psychology* (2nd ed., Vol. 1, pp. 257–300). Chicago: Allyn & Bacon.

van de Vijver, F. J. R., & Leung, K. (1997b). *Methods and data analysis for cross-cultural research.* Newbury Park, CA: Sage.

van de Vijver, F. J. R., & Tanzer, N. K. (1997). Bias and equivalence in cross-cultural assessment: An overview. *European Review of Applied Psychology, 4,* 263–279.

Van Haaften, E. H., & van de Vijver, F. J. R. (1996). Psychological consequences of environmental degradation. *Journal of Health Psychology, 1,* 411–429.

Wehrly, B. (1995). *Pathways to multicultural counseling competence: A developmental journey.* Pacific Grove, CA: Brooks/Cole.

Yang, K.-S., & Bond, M. H. (1990). Exploring implicit personality theories with indigenous or imported constructs: The Chinese case. *Journal of Personality and Social Psychology, 58,* 1087–1095.

Zhang, J. X., & Bond, M. H. (1998). Personality and filial piety among college students in two Chinese societies. The added value of indigenous constructs. *Journal of Cross-Cultural Psychology, 29,* 402–417.

APPENDIX

***Paraphrased 3DC Instructions in Hypertext Format*[9].** Look at the first example. [Each cube <shown>L_1 <has>L_2 six <different patterns>L_3 on its <sides>L_4]I_1, but {only three <sides>L_4 are <visible>L_5}K_1. On the <basis of>L_6 these <patterns>L_3, [<your task is to determine>L_7 if any of the cubes labeled A to F {<can be identical>L_8 to cube X}K_2]I_2, <displayed>L_1 on the <left-hand side>L_9. If {<none>L_{10} <can be identical>L_8 to cube X}K_2, choose <response alternative>L_{11} <"none">L_{10} indicating that "<none>L_{10} of the cubes <is identical>L_8 to cube X." When you <solve>L_{12} a problem, you

[9]The corresponding example item is shown in Fig. 10.3. See also Example 8.

<can imagine>L_{13} that cube X has been turned over either once or several times in any direction. Thus, {a <new pattern>L_3 that is <hidden>L_5 on cube X <may become visible>L_5}K_1. In this example, the <correct answer>L_{14} is D. Cube X has been turned over so that a <new pattern>L_3 is <visible>L_5. Keep in mind that a [<specific pattern>L_3 <may occur>L_2 only once on each cube]I_1. For each problem , there is [only one <correct solution>L_{14}]I_3, either one of the cubes labeled A to F or <"none">L_{10} (<solution>L_{14} not given).

Note. The parentheses indicate hypertext links from instructional elements (phrases or key information) to explanatory notes. Links with the same subscript refer to instructional elements that are related to each other (e.g., L_2) or should be distinguished (e.g., L_4 and L_9). For phrases, the hypertext links (denoted by arrowed brackets with subscripts L) refer to notes regarding their usage or the underlying linguistic concept. Square brackets with superscripts I indicate hypertext links for key elements of the instruction which are important for defining the problem space. Brackets with superscripts K highlight a geometrical fact that is useful for solving the items but may not be known by all testees.

Examples of Hyperttext Metainformation

I_1: Without the restriction that each cube shown has six different patterns, the 3DC items do not have a unique <correct solution>L_{14}.

K_1: Only in "one-turn" and "three-turn" rotations, a < new pattern>L_3 which was previously <hidden>L_5 will <become visible>L_5, and a previously <visible>L_5 one will become <hidden>L_5. For "two-turn" solutions, the three <visible>L_5 <patterns>L_3 will remain the same.

K_2: The existence of <hidden>L_5 <sides>L_4 on the target cube X and the <correct alternative>L_{14} preclude a definite decision whether the <correct alternative>L_{14} <displays>L_1 in fact the target cube X in a different perspective. This uncertainty requires the formulation <can be identical>L_8 in the instruction I_1 to ensure a unique <correct solution>L_{14}. See also L_8.

L_1: <shown> or <displayed> in the meaning of "drawn" in the example. Distinguish it from <visible>L_5 which refers to the <sides>L_4 of a cube.

L_2: <occur> in the meaning of "appear".

L_3: <pattern> refers to the complete picture drawn on a particular <side>L_4 of a cube.

L_4: In this context, <sides> refers to the cubes. Distinguish it from <left-hand side>L_9 which refers to a location at the example.

L_5: <visible> and its opposite <hidden> are used for "can (not) be seen." It is a joint characteristic of a particular <pattern>L_3 drawn on a cube and a particular perspective taken.

L_8: See I_1 and K_2 for the use of <can be> and <may> in combination with <identical>.

11

The Psychometrics of Adaptation: Evaluating Measurement Equivalence Across Languages and Cultures

Fritz Drasgow and Tahira M. Probst
University of Illinois at Urbana-Champaign

The North American Free Trade Agreement (NAFTA) and the integration of the European Union are just two signs of the growing internationalization of world markets. As one indicator of the pace of change, U.S. international trade exports grew from $382.7 billion in 1985 to $1.1 trillion in 1996 (Bach, 1998). In addition to countries forming economic alliances, it has become commonplace for large corporations based in different countries, such as Chrysler and Daimler-Benz, to merge for the purpose of integrating their business activities. As a result of this globalization of world markets, the need for understanding cultural differences among people of diverse backgrounds is becoming increasingly clear.

A landmark in cross-cultural research occurred in 1980 with the publication of Gerte Hofstede's book, *Culture's Consequences*, which documented several important dimensions along which cultures varied. By factor analyzing over 116,000 questionnaires from IBM employees in 40 different nations, Hofstede found that cultures differ in power distance, uncertainty avoidance, masculinity, and individualism. Power distance refers to the tendency to see large distances between higher and lower levels of the social hierarchy, uncertainty avoidance reflects the avoidance of situations where the outcome may be unclear, and masculinity refers to the proclivity of members of a culture to value activities that are traditionally viewed as more manly in their culture. By far the most closely examined dimension, however, is that of individualism-collectivism.

Triandis (1990, 1994, 1995) has documented some of the obvious and subtle differences in the way that people in individualistic and collectivistic cultures view the world. For example, in cultures that are individualistic, such as the United States, Canada, and much of Western Europe, individuals focus on the self. Individuals emphasize the needs and wants of the individual before those of the group. Individuals are assumed to be autonomous; behavior is determined largely by individual goals. As a result, in-groups have relatively little influence on individuals.

On the other hand, South and Central America, Asia, and many parts of the developing world are collectivistic. According to Triandis (1990), collectivists emphasize the views, needs, and goals of the in-group rather than those of the self. Here the individual's desires tend to be subordinated to the in-group. Behavior is largely determined by social norms and duties rather than individual desires. Moreover, in-group harmony is highly valued.

Although researchers in industrial-organizational psychology and human resources management realize that cultural differences cannot be ignored in multinational organizations, empirical research in these areas has progressed slowly due to numerous practical and theoretical difficulties. Gaining research access to international facilities in multinational organizations is often even more challenging than gaining access to American businesses. Once permission has been granted, the cost of conducting cross-cultural research can be prohibitively large. However, perhaps the greatest obstacle to overcome in the attempt to conduct methodologically sound cross-cultural research occurs at the instrument adaptation phase. Adapting an instrument from an original source language to a target language has been heralded as "probably the most complex type of event yet produced in the evolution of the cosmos" (Richards, 1953, p. 250). Although Richards's statement is surely an exaggeration, this chapter and this entire book is a testament to the challenges inherent in the translation and adaptation process.

There are several steps that researchers need to take to ensure the quality and measurement equivalence of their adapted instruments. These steps are crucial; without them, enormous quantities of researcher time, effort, and money can be spent for naught. The adaptation process begins with a complete questionnaire usually originally developed to be administered in a particular *source* language. When conducting cross-cultural research, it is often necessary to develop adaptations of the instrument into one or more *target* or *focal* languages. Ideally, two sets of bilingual translators would be hired. The translators from the first set independently translate the questionnaire from the source language into the *target* language, after which the first set of translators meet and resolve differences in their translations.

This agreed-upon translated document is then given to each translator from the second set. These translators independently *back-translate* the questionnaire from the target language to the source language. After the back-translators resolve their differences, the original questionnaire is then compared to the back-translated document. At the conclusion of this long and often cumbersome process, it is very reassuring when the back-translation is highly similar to the original questionnaire.

Often, however, there are discrepancies between the original and back-translated documents. For example, across several adaptation efforts, we have repeatedly encountered difficulties with the translation of American idiomatic expressions. Describing a job as "relaxed" may make sense to American employees. In Marathi, however, it is translated as "done easily". It is also easy to see that referring to coworkers as a "waste of time" in English might be mistakenly translated to indicate coworkers "waste time".

In addition to these idiomatic expressions, difficulties can also be encountered when translating relatively simple formal prose. English is a language of many synonyms. Often, scales are developed by asking the "same" question using multiple similar words or phrases. Because synonyms often develop linguistically because a concept is important in a particular culture (e.g., Eskimos have more than 100 words to describe snow), other cultures that do not stress the concept may only have one meaningful descriptor. As an example, in our research, the Stress in General (SIG) scale developed by Smith, Sademan, and McCrary (1992) asks respondents to indicate if their job is "hectic" or "frantic." However, in Marathi, "bothersome" is the closest translation possible. Therefore, in order to use the full SIG scale, we had to be content with "bothersome" and "extremely bothersome" as our translation of "hectic" and "frantic." When serious discrepancies between the source and focal language versions occur, the translation process must iterate until adequate convergence is achieved. Of course, yet another difficulty in the adaptation process is the determination of what constitutes "adequate convergence."

Although a high degree of similarity between the original and back-translated versions of the questionnaire is important, it still does not guarantee equivalence of the target and source versions of the questionnaire. For example, a garbled translation might be back-translated to something close to the original text if the back-translators can guess what the translators meant. A more subtle problem can be caused by the fact that bilinguals are different from monolinguals of either language (Landar, Ervin, & Horowitz, 1960). This point is of more than academic interest. When we examined the quality of a translation of a scale assessing job satisfaction using bilinguals (Hulin, Drasgow, & Komocar, 1982) we found very little evidence of nonequivalence across English and Spanish versions; just 3 of 72 items seemed to measure differently across languages. Later, we compared the same two forms of the job satisfaction scale using monolingual English speakers and monolingual Spanish speakers (Drasgow & Hulin, 1988) and found many differences across languages (about a third of the items of the scale).

In spite of carefully following the adaptation process described previously, there are at least three reasons that an analysis of the measurement characteristics of the items on a scale might reveal differences across languages. The first, and most obvious, reason is that the items were not translated correctly. For example, the difference between "farm" and "ranch" is subtle and choosing a word in the target language that exactly matches "farm" rather than "ranch" can be very difficult. Second, certain concepts that are familiar in one culture may be difficult or impossible for members of another culture to grasp. For example, "do your own thing" or "you only live once" place an emphasis on the self that is understood and even advocated in individualist cultures; however, such disregard for friends and family may be difficult to comprehend for people from a collectivistic culture. Finally, it is sometimes believed that people from different cultures use response scales differently. More specifically, people from some cultures tend to avoid using the extremes of a response scale (e.g., the response options 1 and 7 from a 7-point Likert-type response scale), whereas members of another culture may be much more inclined to make extreme ratings (Hui & Triandis, 1989; Triandis, 1972). For example, Marin, Gamba, and Marin (1992) found that Hispanics are more likely to use extreme responses and to agree with statements more than non-Hispanics. This may reflect in part cultural differences in societal norms of acquiescing.

These problems make it clear that comparing responses of people speaking different languages and embedded in different cultures is very difficult. How can researchers empirically determine whether items and scales administered to such diverse groups of people actually measure equivalently? The purpose of this chapter is to illustrate one approach to such an analysis. We use item response theory (IRT) to examine whether the relation between the probability of endorsing an item and the underlying latent trait that the scale measures is identical across groups.

ITEM RESPONSE THEORY

In this section, we provide a brief description of IRT. More extended presentations are provided by Baker (1992), Hambleton and Swaminathan (1985), and Hulin, Drasgow, and Parsons (1983).

Let $u_1, u_2, \ldots, u_n$ denote the n items on a scale. For simplicity, we only consider models for dichotomously scored responses; here $u_i = 1$ for an affirmative response to a positively phrased item (e.g., a response of "Yes" to an item asking "Is your work satisfying?") or a negative response to a negatively phrased item (e.g., a response of "No" to an item asking "Is your work boring?"). The dichotomous variable $u_i = 0$ for a negative response to a positively phrased item (e.g., a response of "No" to an item asking "Is your work fascinating?") or a positive response to a negatively phrased item (e.g., a response of "Yes" to an item asking "Is your work frustrating?"). Polytomous models, which allow responses to be scored into ordered categories (e.g., Samejima's [1969] graded response model) or nominal categories (e.g., Bock's [1972] nominal model) have become increasingly popular (the March 1995 issue of *Applied Psychological Measurement* was devoted to polytomous models), but are beyond the scope of this chapter.

Moreover, we only consider unidimensional item response models (but note that the December 1996 issue of *Applied Psychological Measurement* was devoted to multidimensional IRT models). For unidimensional models, the scalar θ is frequently used to denote the single latent trait assessed by the n items on the scale. The item response function (IRF), sometimes called the item characteristic curve, is fundamental to IRT. It gives the probability of a positive response (i.e., $u_i = 1$) to item i as a function of θ and is typically denoted by $P_i(\theta)$. In this chapter, we focus on the two-parameter logistic model, which uses the mathematical form

$$P_i(\theta) = \frac{1}{1 + \exp[-Da_i(\theta - b_i)]}.$$

In the preceding equation, D is a constant set equal to 1.702 for historical reasons (i.e., so that the logistic model IRFs closely match normal ogive IRFs) and $\exp[x] = e^x$, where e is the mathematical constant approximately equal to 2.718. In this equation, a_i and b_i are the item parameters, which are of central concern to us. The item discrimination parameter a_i indexes the steepness of the IRF; an IRF that rises steeply in an interval enables us to differentiate accurately between respondents with lower θs and respondents with somewhat higher θs. The item difficulty parameter b_i is a location parameter; when $\theta = b_i$ note that $P_i(\theta) = .5$ so that b_i is the point along the latent trait continuum where a respondent has a 50% chance of a positive response.

Figure 11.1 displays the IRF for a hypothetical item. At low levels of θ, the IRF indicates that respondents would have near zero probabilities of endorsing the item; respondents would have probabilities of responding positively that are close to one at high θ values. Note that the curve rises relatively steeply for intermediate levels of θ and therefore the hypothetical item would provide good discrimination between respondents with moderately low and moderately high θs.

The use of IRT to assess the equivalence of measurement for an item across two cultural groups proceeds along the following lines. First, reasonably large and representative samples from both cultures must be collected. Then item parameters are estimated separately for the groups. After linking θ metrics for the two groups (i.e., placing pa-

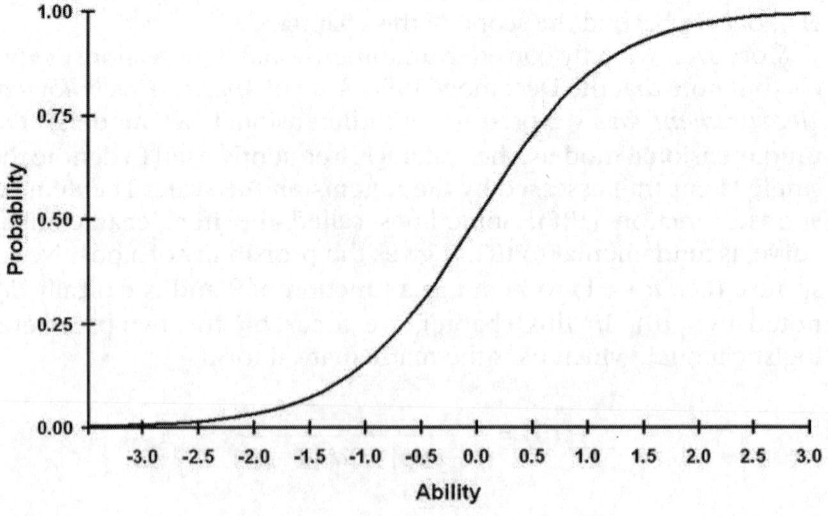

FIG. 11.1. Item characteristic curve for a hypothetical item.

rameter estimates on the same scale), we can compare whether the IRF for the first culture significantly differs from the IRF for the second culture. This evaluation is accomplished by a multivariate significance test comparing the estimates of a_i and b_i from the sample of respondents from the first culture to the estimated a_i and b_i from the second culture. In the following section, each of the steps in the analysis that we have used to examine the cross-cultural equivalence of adapted scales is described in more detail.

Steps in the Data Analysis

Dimensionality. For the most part, studies examining cross-cultural measurement equivalence with IRT have used unidimensional models (i.e., models in which θ appears as a scalar rather than as a vector). In the research described in this chapter we use the two-parameter logistic model, which is unidimensional, and so it is important to check the degree to which the data satisfy this assumption. There are many ways to examine dimensionality; seemingly, there are as many ways of assessing dimensionality as there are psychometricians. Hattie (1985) provided a thorough review of methods for examining dimensionality.

The method we typically use to examine dimensionality is straightforward: Tetrachoric correlations are computed for the dichotomously scored item responses and then the correlation matrix is analyzed by principal axes factor analysis. Provided that none of the items is too extreme (i.e., nearly all respondents answer negatively or nearly all respondents answer positively), a first eigenvalue that is large relative to the second eigenvalue provides good evidence of a dominant underlying factor. Further support for unidimensionality is provided if all items have large loadings on the first (unrotated) factor. Note that a perfectly unidimensional set of items is not required for practical applications of IRT; instead, Drasgow and Parsons (1983), Reckase (1979), and Junker and Stout (1994) have all shown that a single *dominant* factor is sufficient.

Item Parameter Estimation. Provided that the factor analysis shows a single dominant factor, we next estimate item parameters. Simulation studies (e.g., Drasgow, 1989; McLaughlin & Drasgow, 1987) have shown that Bock's (Bock & Aiken; 1981; Bock & Lieberman, 1970) marginal estimation should be used here. The BILOG (Mislevy & Bock, 1989) computer program offers two options for marginal estimation: maximum likelihood and Bayesian. With large samples, these two estimation methods provide similar results, but in small samples Bayesian estimates are more stable. We usually estimate item parameters both ways. With samples of relative modest sizes (200–300), we frequently find that one or more item parameters estimated by maximum likelihood are too extreme to be credible (e.g., an estimated discrimination parameter of 3.0). Such extreme estimates typically have very large standard errors; the most appropriate interpretation of a maximum likelihood discrimination parameter estimate of 3.0 with a standard error of 1.2 is that a larger sample is needed for maximum likelihood estimation. Given the difficulty of, say, returning to India to collect more data, we resort to Bayesian estimation. Bayesian estimates are generally less extreme (the parameter estimated as 3.0 by maximum likelihood might be estimated as 1.3) and have smaller standard errors (the maximum likelihood standard error of 1.2 might be .20 for Bayesian estimation).

Fit Plots. After estimating item parameters, it is important to examine the extent to which one's IRT model adequately describes the item responses. A number of methods are available for this purpose. We have found that *fit plots* are particularly useful. Roughly speaking, a fit plot compares the actual proportion of respondents endorsing an item in a given θ interval to the estimated proportion (i.e., to the IRF). The difficulty in constructing a fit plot is that we do not know each respondent's θ value; we only have an estimate. Moreover, for short scales, we expect relatively large discrepancies between an estimated θ and a respondent's actual θ.

Drasgow, Levine, Tsien, Williams, and Mead (1995) described a procedure that addresses this problem. Rather than assigning each respondent to a single θ category based on a fallible estimate, it proportionally distributes each respondent across multiple θ categories based on the posterior probability that the respondent's actual θ lies in that interval. The "pseudo-count" of the number of respondents endorsing the item in each interval is divided by the pseudo-count of the number of respondents falling in the interval to obtain the "empirical proportions" endorsing the items; these empirical proportions are then compared to the IRF. See Drasgow et al. for technical details of this procedure and papers by Stone (Stone, 2003; Stone & Hansen, 2000) for details of a related procedure.

Linking Metrics. The BILOG computer program makes the default assumption that the latent trait has the standard normal distribution in the population from which a sample was drawn. However, there is no a priori reason to believe that diverse populations have the same mean (i.e., zero) and standard deviation (i.e., one) for the latent trait. Without loss of generality, one population can be scaled to have mean zero and unit standard deviation, but the latent trait scale for a second population must be *linked* to the first population's metric.

Several methods for linking latent trait metrics have been suggested (Segall, 1983, provided a good review). Research (e.g., Segall, 1983) has shown that Stocking and Lord's (1983) test characteristic curve linking works well, and Baker, Al-Karni, and Al-Dosary (1991)'s EQUATE program can be used to perform this type of linking. Baker et al.'s program provides slope and intercept coefficients (A and B, respectively) of a linear transformation that links metrics. The linked coefficients are

$$\hat{a}^* = \frac{\hat{a}}{A} \text{ and } \hat{b}^* = A \times \hat{b} + B.$$

Note that the elements of the variance–covariance matrix of the estimated item parameters must also be appropriately transformed,

$$Var(\hat{a}^*) = \frac{Var(\hat{a})}{A^2}, Var\left(\hat{b}^*\right) = A^2 \times Var\left(\hat{b}\right),$$
$$\text{and } Cov\left(\hat{a}^*, \hat{b}^*\right) = Cov\left(\hat{a}, \hat{b}\right).$$

Linking is straightforward when no items exhibit differential functioning across cultures. However, some differential item functioning (DIF) can occur even with the best adaptations, and linking can be distorted when items with DIF are included in the analysis. Consequently, the following iterative process can be used. After an initial linking, DIF is tested for each item (procedures are described later). Then the items with significant DIF statistics are temporarily set aside, and metrics are relinked using only items with no DIF. After linking, DIF statistics *for all items* are recomputed. This process of linking on items with no DIF and recomputing DIF statistics for all items continues until the same set of items is indicated to have DIF on successive iterations. Simulation studies (e.g., Candell & Drasgow, 1988) have shown iterative linking to be effective.

Multiple-Group Differential Item Functioning Analyses. Lord (1980) and others have considered DIF from the perspective of comparing a *focal* group to a *reference* group. However, when data from several groups are available for analysis, performing significance tests for all the pairwise combinations seems analogous to the use of multiple t tests to compare group means rather than an overall analysis of variance that simultaneously tests the equality of the means of all groups. Kim, Cohen, and Park (1995) made an important contribution to the study of DIF when they introduced their multiple-group DIF analysis to address this problem. Their procedure is an extension of Lord's chi-square test for evaluating DIF across two groups (Lord, 1977, 1980). Specifically, the null hypothesis for testing for equality of parameters for item i across K groups is

$$H_0\colon \mathbf{C}\xi_i = \mathbf{0},$$

where $\mathbf{C}$ is a contrast matrix containing p rows of linearly independent contrast vectors, and

$$\xi = \left(a_{i1}, b_{i1}, \ldots a_{iK}, b_{iK}\right),'$$

is the vector of item parameters. The test statistic developed by Kim et al. is

$$Q_i = (Cv_i)'(C\Sigma_i C')^{-1}(Cv_i),$$

where $\mathbf{v}_i$ is a vector containing item parameter estimates

$$v_i = \left(\hat{a}_{i1}, \hat{b}_{i1}, \ldots, \hat{a}_{iK}, \hat{b}_{iK}\right),$$

and p is the rank of $\mathbf{C}$, which is usually $2(K-1)$. The asymptotic distribution of Q_i is chi-square with p degrees of freedom (Kim et al., 1995).

Differential Test Functioning Analyses. Although it is extremely useful to assess the extent of differential functioning at the item level, in most applications researchers use a total scale score rather than individual items. Therefore, DIF, per se, may not matter in many situations. Instead, *differential test functioning* (DTF) is the issue of principal concern: Do respondents with equal θs, but sampled from different cultures and perhaps answering in different languages, have equal expected overall scale scores?

Raju, van der Linden, and Fleer (1995) introduced a method for testing DTF that allows compensatory item effects such that DIF operating in one direction can be canceled by DIF on another item functioning in the opposite direction. The virtue of Raju et al.'s method in the context of translating scales for use in cross-cultural research is that items exhibiting DIF need not necessarily be removed from the scale. Instead, items must be deleted only when the overall DTF index is large and statistically significant. From the perspective of the DTF analysis, traditional DIF procedures may unnecessarily remove valuable items; when overall DTF is not evident, there is no reason to delete items.

The DFITDUA program developed by Raju et al. (1995) can be used to assess DTF across pairs of samples; Raju (personal communication, April 2000) is currently developing a multiple-group extension of the DTF analysis. It produces a chi-square statistic that is used to assess the significance of DTF between two groups. When the DTF index is statistically significant, the DFITDUA program identifies and removes items with the largest contribution to the chi-square.

Fleer (1993) found that the DTF index was overly sensitive for large sample sizes. Therefore, to adjust for this sensitivity, Raju et al. (1995) recommend deleting items that result in a significant chi-square only when the overall DTF index was greater than .006.

Summary. The analytic procedure described above seems to provide a useful means for assessing the measurement equivalence of scales adapted for use across multiple languages and cultures. It checks the dimensionality assumption of IRT and examines the fit of the estimated model. Then recently introduced methods for comparing item parameter estimates across several groups and overall DTF are utilized. To provide an illustration of this procedure, we now describe an examination of the measurement equivalence of four scales that were originally developed in the United States and then translated into Spanish for use in Mexico, Polish for use in Poland, and Marathi for use in India.

METHOD

Samples

As part of a larger study examining the cross-cultural effectiveness of human resource practices, a survey was administered to 939 employees of a multinational publishing and printing company. Surveys were administered to employees in plants located in the United States (n = 239), Mexico (n = 253), India (n = 201), and Poland (n = 246). The vast majority of respondents were monolinguals. Respondents were sampled from manufacturing, administrative, and management levels within the organizational hierarchy.

Respondents were informed that their responses were completely confidential and that their participation was entirely voluntary. In addition, they were notified that corporate headquarters and upper-level management within each local plant had given permission for the survey to be completed during work hours.

Measures

The questionnaire assessed background and demographic characteristics of the respondents. Also included in the survey were scales assessing empowering leader behaviors, opportunity for continuous improvement, organizational withdrawal, and organizational commitment.

Of particular interest to this chapter are the scales used to measure the various facets of job satisfaction and general job stress. Nine-item versions of the Satisfaction With Coworkers, Satisfaction With Supervision, and Satisfaction With the Work Itself subscales from the *Job Descriptive Index* (JDI; Smith, Kendall, & Hulin, 1969), as revised by Roznowski (1989), were used. Respondents used a 3-point (yes, ?, no) response scale to indicate the extent to which each of several adjectives or phrases described their job. Smith, Sademan, and McCrary's (1992) Stress in General (SIG) scale assessees global occupational stress using a response format identical to that of the JDI. Table 11.1 contains the scales and the respective items in their entirety.

Analyses

Recoding of Variables. Responses to the JDI scales were recoded into dichotomous scores as required by the IRT model used in the present study. Agreement with positively keyed items or disagreement with negatively keyed items was scored as 1, agreement with negatively keyed items or disagreement with positively worded items was coded as 0, and question-mark responses were coded 0 due to empirical findings that such responses are more strongly associated with job dissatisfaction than with job satisfaction (Hanisch, 1992; Smith et al., 1969). Positive and negative responses to the SIG scales were coded analogously: Responses indicating more stress were coded 1 and responses indicating less stress were coded 0. However, question mark responses were coded 1. Finally, all scale response vectors with more than one missing item were dropped from further analyses.

TABLE 11.1

Coworker, Supervisor, and Work Satisfaction Items From the Job Descriptive Index and the Stress in General Scale

	United States				*Poland*				*Mexico*				*India*			
	p	r_b	a	b	p	r_b	a	b	p	r_b	a	b	p	r_b	a	b
Coworker Satisfaction																
Boring	.840	.624	.922	–1.448	.854	.878	.241	–1.350	.923	.694	.907	–2.112	.796	.646	.948	–1.212
Slow	.690	.773	1.179	–.638	.758	.643	.890	–1.102	.774	.788	1.161	–.951	.773	.929	1.366	–.937
Loyal	.426	.636	1.084	.287	.536	.679	1.118	–.101	.557	.678	1.219	–.128	.617	.661	.969	–.409
Responsible	.706	.739	1.134	–.702	.686	.728	1.087	–.647	.812	.967	1.396	–1.046	.759	.819	1.156	–.927
Waste of time	.651	.752	1.170	–.498	.808	.794	1.108	–1.214	.484	.258	.593	.118	.630	.426	.729	–.545
Lazy	.634	.792	1.287	–.420	.741	.828	1.189	–.887	.759	.752	1.121	–.916	.790	1.005	1.465	–1.000
Unpleasant	.758	.648	.962	–.976	.845	.809	1.132	–1.422	.844	.786	1.058	–1.348	.693	.784	1.135	–.650
Intelligent	.664	.686	1.017	–.563	.683	.811	1.264	–.605	.747	.662	.971	–.898	.716	.336	1.031	–.774
Work well together	.664	.686	1.024	–.567	.716	.782	1.178	–.759	.780	.855	1.241	–.963	.819	.761	1.066	–1.241

(continued on next page)

TABLE 11.1 (continued)

	United States				Poland				Mexico				India			
	p	r_b	*a*	*b*	*p*	r_b	*a*	*b*	*p*	r_b	*a*	*b*	*p*	r_b	*a*	*b*
Supervisor Satisfaction																
Hard to please	.515	.770	1.198	–.027	.379	.539	.865	.525	.648	.726	1.171	–.446	.286	.304	.689	.958
Impolite	.690	.782	1.178	–.660	.780	.881	1.308	–1.302	.855	.992	1.413	–1.289	.534	.793	1.356	–.140
Praises good work	.414	.638	.969	.338	.610	.577	.821	–.431	.728	.514	.806	–.930	.609	.727	1.122	–.358
Tactful	.450	.479	.729	.231	.599	.748	1.080	–.317	.636	.519	.817	–.505	.441	.061	.508	.239
Annoying	.573	.816	1.289	–.222	.640	.873	1.351	–.484	.800	.915	1.257	–1.052	.537	.800	1.377	–.136
Bad	.715	.875	1.426	–.713	.751	.890	1.320	–.936	.861	.900	1.292	–1.311	.637	.771	1.291	–.491
Interferes with my work	.745	.775	1.176	–.882	.785	.803	1.141	–1.109	.588	.291	.592	–.372	.525	.775	1.233	–.107
Gives confusing directions	.603	.668	.965	–.365	.662	.863	1.294	–.552	.714	.761	1.164	–.676	.576	.772	1.202	–.268
Knows how to supervise	.477	.813	1.294	.100	.580	.934	1.575	–.247	.750	.754	1.168	–.851	.551	.656	.944	–.187

Work Satisfaction																
Fascinating	.303	.759	1.288	.721	.203	.762	1.226	1.079	.604	.569	.915	–.353	.553	.511	.832	–.234
Satisfying	.601	.865	1.343	–.340	.543	.709	1.119	–.167	.783	.789	1.209	–.989	.822	.952	1.401	–1.183
Boring	.657	.729	.999	–.597	.648	.784	1.328	–.512	.849	.667	.982	–1.437	.777	.713	1.001	–1.152
Creative	.422	.773	1.151	.294	.244	.660	1.032	.941	.744	.600	.954	–.879	.559	.599	.942	–.262
Challenging	.686	.719	.996	–.721	.823	.413	.758	–1.564	.550	.311	.649	–.209	.697	.808	1.176	–.720
Gives sense of accomplish-ment	.644	.924	1.518	–.478	.404	.737	1.134	.319	.838	.814	1.219	–1.235	.731	.932	1.441	–.767
A source of pleasure	.343	.786	1.315	.570	.245	.733	1.179	.912	.500	.552	.999	.026	.620	.485	.789	–.506
Dull	.665	.846	1.233	–.586	.438	.642	.985	.221	.500	.589	1.000	.002	.620	.485	.789	–.506
Interesting	.628	.966	1.678	–.409	.534	.841	1.412	–.118	.846	.862	1.252	–1.271	.680	.730	1.058	–.723

(continued on next page)

TABLE 11.1 (continued)

	United States				Poland				Mexico				India			
	p	r_b	*a*	*b*	*p*	r_b	*a*	*b*	*p*	r_b	*a*	*b*	*p*	r_b	*a*	*b*
Stress in General																
Hectic	.612	.682	.975	–.432	.409	.527	.910	.282	.576	.452	.850	–.306	.589	.644	1.022	–.364
Tense	.565	.850	1.371	–.218	.641	.533	.894	–.566	.282	.696	1.131	.742	.481	.794	1.216	.032
Frantic	.278	.821	1.367	.788	.298	.460	.869	.701	.070	.534	.895	2.091	.350	.829	1.294	.507
Pressured	.648	.774	1.186	–.523	.813	.018	.530	–1.841	.372	.753	1.358	.381	.508	.841	1.313	–.051
Hassled	.333	.727	1.092	.616	.495	.572	.955	–.036	.080	.586	.917	2.000	.406	.882	1.409	.287
Relaxed	.638	.767	1.164	–.494	.840	.230	.680	–1.1661	.344	.628	1.138	.531	.520	.256	.574	–.154
Many things stressful	.612	.811	1.256	–.394	.583	.682	1.179	–.308	.448	.510	.858	.169	.500	.860	1.346	–.024
Nerve–wracking	.381	.845	1.390	.400	.473	.656	1.141	–.051	.162	.739	1.089	1.292	.307	.809	1.238	.649
More stressful than I'd like	.475	.744	1.075	.095	.378	.643	1.109	.327	.284	.304	.660	.979	.369	.778	1.048	.455

Test of Unidimensionality. In order to test the appropriateness of the unidimensionality assumption for the four scales, iterative principal factor analyses were conducted in each country as described previously. Factors with eigenvalues greater than 1.0 were extracted. Single-factor extractions and/or large loadings on the first principal axis factor (PAF) suggest that a scale measures a single dominant construct, thus providing support for the assumption of unidimensionality.

Item Parameter Estimates. BILOG (Mislevy & Bock, 1989) was used to estimate the item parameters of the two-parameter logistic model for each scale in each of the four samples. Upper limits of 100 EM cycles and 10 Newton–Raphson cycles were set, 30 quadrature points were used rather than the default number, and a convergence criterion of 0.001 was specified. A normal prior distribution, N(0, 1), for the item difficulty parameters was specified. In addition, a log normal prior distribution, N(0, .2), was set for the item discrimination parameters.

Iterative Linking of Metrics. Baker et al.'s (1991) EQUATE program was used to link the metrics of each focal group (Mexico, Poland, and India) to the reference group (the United States) by the Stocking–Lord (1983) method. Moreover, the iterative procedure described by Candell and Drasgow (1988) and Leung and Drasgow (1986) was used in the linking process. Here, an initial set of linking coefficients was produced to transform the parameter estimates from each of the focal groups to the reference group metric. Kim et al.'s (1995) multigroup DIF analysis was performed and items that were found to exhibit DIF were removed from the item pool and the Stocking–Lord linking method was reapplied using only the unbiased items; after relinking, all of the items were again checked for DIF . This process iterated until the same set of DIF items was detected in two consecutive trials.

The DTF analysis was performed after the item parameters estimates for the three focal groups had been linked to the reference group by the iterative process described previously. Here each of the three focal groups (Mexico, Poland, India) was compared to the reference group (United States) to determine whether there was any evidence of overall differential scale functioning for the each of the four scales.

RESULTS

Classical test theory statistics (i.e., proportion "correct" and item-total biserial correlations) for the stress in general scale and the coworker, supervisor, and work satisfaction scales are found in Table 11.1.

Dimensionality

Factor analyses conducted in each sample for each scale indicated that the scales were sufficiently unidimensional to proceed with the IRT analyses. PAF analysis results are shown in Table 11.2.

Coworker Satisfaction. Factor analysis of the nine-item Coworker Satisfaction scale resulted in the extraction of a single factor in each sample. This factor accounted for over one third of the variance in each sample. Item loadings were fairly high in the United States, ranging from .47 ("boring") to .68 ("lazy"). In Mexico, loadings ranged from .43 ("boring") to .75 ("responsible"). In India, loadings ranged from .36 ("waste of time") to .83 ("lazy"). Finally, in Poland, loadings were also high ranging from .51 ("slow") to .67 ("intelligent").

Supervisor Satisfaction. Factor analysis of the nine-item Supervisor Satisfaction scale also resulted in the extraction of a single factor in each sample, which accounted for over one third of the variance in each sample. Item loadings were fairly high, ranging from .41 ("tactful") to .73 ("bad") in the United States, .25 ("interferes with my work") to .71 ("knows how to supervise") in Mexico, .08 ("tactful") to .78 ("annoying") in India, and .46 ("hard to please") to .80 ("knows how to supervise") in Poland.

Work Satisfaction. Factor analysis of the nine-item Work Satisfaction scale led to the extraction of a single factor in each of the four samples. The variance accounted for by this factor ranged from 25.5% in Mexico to 38.7% in the United States. Overall, items loadings were fairly high in each sample. They ranged from .16 ("boring") to .80 ("interesting") in the United States. In Mexico, loadings ranged from .14 ("dull") to .77 ("interesting"). In India, loadings ranged from .31 ("dull") to .76 ("satisfying"). Finally, in Poland, loadings ranged from .06 ("boring") to .72 ("interesting"). It is interesting to note the convergence in factor loadings across the samples: In each country "boring" and "dull" had consistently low loading items, whereas "interesting" invariably had a high loading on the general factor.

General Job Stress. PAF analysis of the nine-item Stress in General scale also resulted in a single factor being extracted in each sample. Variance accounted for ranged from 25.7% in Mexico to 45% in India. Factor loadings were large in each of the samples. In the United States, loadings ranged from .56 ("hectic") to .79 ("tense"). In

TABLE 11.2

Principal Axis Factor Analysis Results for Coworker, Supervisor, and Work Satisfaction, and Stress in General Scales by Country

	United States		*Poland*		*Mexico*		*India*	
	# factors	*% variance*	*# factors*	*% variance*	*# factors*	*% variance*	*# factors*	*% variance*
Scale								
Coworker	1	35.9	1	37.9	1	35.2	1	37.9
Supervisor	1	40.0	1	42.8	1	33.8	1	37.6
Work	1	38.7	1	29.4	1	25.5	1	33.0
Job Stress	1	42.8	1	26.3	1	25.7	1	45.0

Mexico, loadings ranged from .28 ("hectic") to .61 ("nerve-wracking"). In India, the range went from .19 ("relaxed") to .77 ("tense"). Finally, in Poland, loadings varied from .13 ("relaxed") to .63 ("nerve-wracking"). Again, there was a fair degree of consistency across samples with respect to high and low loading items.

Item Parameter Estimates

The dichotomously scored item responses from the 939 workers described earlier were input into BILOG. The two-parameter logistic model was estimated for each scale using data from each country; the resulting parameter estimates are presented in Table 11.1 and discussed below.

Coworker Satisfaction. Initial (i.e., prior to equating) BILOG calibration of the coworker satisfaction items in each of the four countries suggested that the items were generally "easy" (i.e., frequently positively endorsed) with all but 2 of the 36 estimates having negative b_i estimates. Thus, individuals with satisfaction levels approximately ½ to 1 standard deviation (*SD*) below the average had a 50% probability of positively endorsing many of the items (i.e., indicating satisfaction). The mean b_i estimate in the United States was –.614 (*SD* = .461) and ranged from –1.448 ("boring") to .287 ("loyal"). In Mexico, the mean difficulty estimate was –.916 (*SD* = .645); estimates ranged from –2.112 ("boring") to .118 ("waste of time"). In India, the mean b_i estimate was –.855 (*SD* = .286); parameter estimates ranged from –1.241 ("work well together") to –.409 ("loyal"). Finally, in Poland, the mean was –.899 (*SD* = .422); parameter estimates ranged from –1.422 ("unpleasant") to –.101 ("loyal").

In addition, the items appeared to discriminate very well. The mean discrimination estimate for the coworker items in the United States was 1.086 (*SD* = .117) and ranged from .922 ("boring") to 1.287 ("lazy"). In Mexico, the mean a_i estimate was 1.074 (*SD* = .233); estimates ranged from .593 ("waste of time" to 1.396 ("responsible"). In India, the mean discrimination was 1.096 (*SD* = .222); estimates ranged from .729 ("waste of time") to 1.465 ("lazy"). Lastly, in Poland, the mean a_i estimate was 1.134 (*SD* = .109) and ranged from .890 ("slow") to 1.264 ("intelligent"). These means indicate that the items discriminate well.

Supervisor Satisfaction. Supervisor satisfaction items were also generally "easy," although the range of b_i estimates was greater than for the coworker satisfaction items. Mean item difficulty in the United States was –.244 (SD = .439); estimates ranged from –.882 ("interferes with my work") to .338 ("praises good work"). The mean b_i estimate in Poland was –.509 (SD = .500). Parameter estimates ranged from –1.302 ("impolite") to .525 ("hard to please"). In Mexico, the mean item difficulty was –.826 (SD = .351); estimates ranged from –1.311 ("bad") to –.372 ("interferes with my work"). Finally, in India the mean b_i estimate was –.054 (SD = .429). Parameter estimates ranged from –.491 ("bad") to .958 ("hard to please").

Inspection of the a_i estimates reveals that the supervisor satisfaction items discriminate well with only a few exceptions. In the United States, the mean discrimination estimate was 1.136 (SD = .213). Estimates ranged from .729 ("tactful") to 1.426 ("bad"). In Poland, the mean a_i estimate was 1.195 (SD = .243). Estimates ranged from .821 ("praises good work") to 1.575 ("knows how to supervise"). Mean item discrimination in Mexico was 1.075 (SD = .272); estimates ranged from .592 ("interferes with my work") to 1.413 ("impolite"). Finally, the mean a_i estimate in India was 1.080 (SD = .306). Estimates ranged from .508 ("tactful") to 1.377 ("annoying").

Work Satisfaction. Inspection of the item difficulty parameter estimates reveals that there is a wide range of item difficulties for the work satisfaction scale, particularly in the United States and Poland. In India and Mexico, item difficulty estimates tended to range on the "easy" end of the spectrum. Mean item difficulty in the United States was –.172 (SD = .547); estimates ranged from –.721 ("challenging") to .721 ("fascinating"). In Poland, the mean b_i estimate was .123 (SD = .840) and estimates ranged from –1.564 ("challenging") to 1.079 ("fascinating"). In Mexico, the mean b_i estimate was –.705 (SD = .576) with estimates ranging from –1.437 ("boring") to .026 ("a source of pleasure"). Finally, in India, the mean item difficulty was –.697, with item parameter estimates ranging from –1.183 ("satisfying") to –.234 ("fascinating").

The work satisfaction items appear to discriminate well in each of the four samples as well. Mean item discrimination in the United States was 1.280 (SD = .223), with estimates ranging from .996 ("challenging") to 1.678 ("interesting"). In Poland, the mean a_i estimate was 1.130 (SD = .194); item parameter estimates ranged from .758 ("challenging") to 1.328 ("boring"). The mean discrimination estimate in Mexico was 1.020 (SD = .189), with item estimates ranging from .649 ("challenging") to 1.252 ("interesting"). Finally, in India, the mean slope estimate was 1.113 (SD = .248); estimates ranged from .832 ("fascinating") to 1.441 ("gives sense of accomplishment").

General Job Stress. The BILOG calibration of the 9-item stress in general scale showed a good spread of item difficulty. The mean difficulty in the United States was –.018 (*SD* = .509) with item parameter estimates ranging from –.523 ("pressured") to .788 ("frantic"). In Poland, the mean item difficulty was –.339 (*SD* = .881). Item difficulties ranged from –1.841 ("pressured") to .701 ("frantic"). The mean b_i estimate in Mexico was .876 (*SD* = .807) with estimates ranging from –.306.("hectic") to 2.091 ("frantic"). Finally, in India, the mean was .149 (*SD* = .341) and difficulty estimates ranged from –.364 ("hectic") to .649 ("nerve-wracking").

Item discrimination estimates were generally quite good. The mean a_i estimate in the United States was 1.208 (*SD* = .148) with estimates ranging from .975 ("hectic") to 1.390 ("nerve-wracking"). In Poland, the mean estimate was .919 (*SD* = .214). Estimates ranged from .530 ("pressured") to 1.179 ("many things stressful"). In Mexico, the mean a_i estimate was .988 (*SD* = .209) with estimates ranging from .660 ("more stressful than I'd like") to 1.358 ("pressured"). Finally, the mean estimate in India was 1.162 (*SD* = .256). Estimates ranged from .574 ("relaxed") to 1.409 ("hassled").

Linking Metrics and Multiple-Group DIF

Because the item parameter estimates described earlier are arbitrary with respect to origin and unit, the metrics of each focal group sample were linked to the reference group using the iterative linking procedure described previously. The United States was chosen as the reference group because the source language of each adapted instrument was English. However, it is important to note that any of the focal groups could equally have been chosen to be the reference group.

Linking converged in two iterations for each sample and each scale; the transformation constants in each iteration are found in Table 11.3. We use the Satisfaction With Coworkers scale to illustrate the iterative linking procedure. After the initial linking of focal groups to the reference group (e.g., A = .943 and B = .279 for Mexico), the multigroup DIF analysis was applied. One item ("waste of time") was found to exhibit DIF. Thus, this item was removed from the scale and linking coefficients were recomputed using the remaining eight items. The new linking coefficients (e.g., A = 1.037 and B = .446 for Mexico) were applied and DIF statistics were recomputed. "Waste of time" was once again found to exhibit DIF. Because no other items were found to exhibit DIF, the iterative linking procedure terminated.

Determining the critical chi-square value to use in classifying items as exhibiting/not exhibiting DIF is very important. The critical

TABLE 11.3
Linear Transformation Coefficients Linking Focal Groups to Reference Group for Each JDI and Job Stress Scale

	Iteration 1		*Iteration 2*	
	A	*B*	*A*	*B*
Coworker Satisfaction				
Mexico	.943	.279	1.037	.446
India	1.012	.272	1.081	.352
Poland	1.044	.334	1.059	.291
Supervisor Satisfaction				
Mexico	.941	.540	1.015	.727
India	.932	–.170	.907	–.094
Poland	1.039	.288	1.046	.297
Work Satisfaction				
Mexico	.808	.422	.841	.712
India	.905	.478	.902	.627
Poland	.851	–.305	.905	–.346
Job Stress				
Mexico	.779	–.687	.757	–.706
India	.971	–.172	1.062	–.167
Poland	.731	.176	.746	.232

value can depend on the number of focal groups, the number of parameters in the IRT model, the desired Type I alpha level, and the number of items in the scale. In the present study, there were three focal groups and two parameters; thus, the chi-square test statistic had 6 degrees of freedom. If we wished to maintain an overall alpha of .01 for testing DIF on each scale, applying the Bonferroni correction would produce a per item alpha of approximately .001 and a critical chi-square of 22.46. Interestingly, we found that many items had chi-square values near this value (see Table 11.4 for chi-square values for each item from iterations 1 and 2). Plots of IRFs for such items indicated relatively small differences, and so we decided to classify items with $\chi^2 \geq 50$ as exhibiting DIF (the IRFs for such items indicated relatively large differences). For each of the other three scales (Satisfaction With Supervision, Satisfaction With the Work Itself, and Stress in General), the linking procedure iterated only two times. In each case, the items identified as biased in iteration 1 were identical to the items found to be biased in the second iteration.

Relatively few items from the four scales were found to exhibit DIF. One item from the coworker satisfaction scale—"waste of time"—was found to be biased; it had $\chi^2_{(6)} = 78.90$. One item from the supervisor scale was identified as exhibiting DIF; "interferes with my work" had a $\chi^2_{(6)} = 93.23$. Two items on the work satisfaction scale exhibited DIF, "challenging" with a $\chi^2_{(6)} = 141.23$ and "dull" with a $\chi^2_{(6)} = 86.48$. Finally, two items from the Stress in General scale were found to be biased: "hectic", $\chi^2_{(6)} = 111.43$, and "relaxed", $\chi^2_{(6)} = 63.05$.

It is important to recall that multiple-group DIF analyses only determine that DIF exists between two or more of the groups studied. This analysis does not pinpoint where the differential functioning arises. In order to make that determination, traditional pairwise comparisons using Lord's chi-square would need to be conducted.

Differential Test Functioning Analyses

In order to assess differential functioning at the test level, pairwise comparisons were made between the United States sample as the reference group and each of the other three samples as focal groups. After a determination of the level of DTF was made, the DFITDUA program suggested items to remove in order to eliminate overall differential test functioning. An item was selected for removal if it contributed significantly to the overall DTF *and* if allowing the item to remain would have resulted in a DTF index of .006 or greater (Raju et al., 1995).

Satisfaction With Coworkers. Comparisons between the United States and Mexico revealed significant differential test functioning, DTF = .034, $\chi^2_{(252)} = 318.89$, $p < .01$. Four items were suggested for removal: "boring," "waste of time," "lazy," and "work well together." Eliminating these items resulted in a DTF index of .004 and a $\chi^2_{(252)} = 705.81$, $p < .001$. Interestingly, the chi-square became larger

TABLE 11.4
Multiple-Group DIF Chi-Square Statistics for Iterations 1 and 2

	Iteration 1 χ^2	*Iteration 2* χ^2
Coworker Satisfaction		
Boring	11.75	10.42
Slow	6.09	5.64
Loyal	6.46	5.46
Responsible	10.36	5.98
Waste of Time	63.50*	78.90**
Lazy	4.41	4.79
Unpleasant	16.78	17.92
Intelligent	3.18	2.56
Work Well Together	8.03	5.02
Supervisor Satisfaction		
Hard to Please	39.30	35.71
Impolite	10.88	13.45
Praises Good Work	34.10	30.51
Tactful	15.95	13.43
Annoying	3.20	1.27
Bad	0.65	1.90
Interferes with my Work	76.04*	93.23**
Gives Confusing Directions	6.95	9.85
Knows How to Supervise	12.39	7.48
Work Satisfaction		
Fascinating	25.98	10.59
Satisfying	3.99	7.94

TABLE 11.4 (continued)

	Iteration 1 χ^2	*Iteration 2* χ^2
Boring	7.40	10.33
Creative	31.02	12.41
Challenging	105.16*	141.23**
Gives Sense of Accomplishment	20.13	11.72
A Source of Pleasure	23.52	28.12
Dull	51.91*	86.48**
Interesting	16.53	13.84
Job Stress		
Hectic	51.53*	111.43**
Tense	4.16	2.57
Frantic	18.05	7.90
Pressured	16.91	22.58
Hassled	22.08	17.32
Relaxed	64.20*	63.05**
Many Things Stressful	28.84	23.68
Nerve-Wracking	1.12	3.64
More Stressful Than I'd Like	34.45	23.22

Note. Critical χ^2 (6 *df*)$_{(a = .001)}$ = 22.46.
*Item removed when estimating linking coefficients in Iteration 2.
**Item exhibits large significant Multiple-Group DIF after Iteration 2.

and is statistically significant; however, the DTF index is below .006 and according to Fleer (1993) no further items should be removed.

Comparisons between the United States and India displayed significant differential test functioning, DTF = .011, $\chi^2_{(200)}$ = 958.09, $p < .001$. One item was suggested for removal: "waste of time." Excluding this item resulted in a DTF index of .002, $\chi^2_{(200)}$ = 208.88, n.s..

Comparisons between the United States and Poland also revealed significant differential test functioning, DTF = .015, $c^2_{(245)} = 462.16$, $p < .001$. One item was suggested for removal: "waste of time." Eliminating this item resulted in a DTF index of .000, so no additional items were removed.

Satisfaction With Supervision. Comparisons between the United States and Mexico revealed significant differential test functioning, DTF = .085, $\chi^2_{(252)} = 1635.39$, $p < .001$. One item was suggested for removal: "interferes with my work." Omitting this item resulted in a DTF index of .000.

Comparisons between the United States and India showed significant differential test functioning, DTF = .055, $\chi^2_{(200)} = 609.07$, $p < .001$. One item was suggested for removal: "interferes with my work." Deleting this item resulted in a DTF index of .009, but with $\chi^2_{(200)} = 200.11$, n.s, so no further items were deleted.

Comparisons between the United States and Poland indicated little differential test functioning, DTF = .002, so no items were suggested for removal.

Satisfaction With the Work Itself. Comparisons between the United States and Mexico indicated large differences, DTF = .466, $\chi^2_{(252)} = 1568.25$, $p < .001$. Two items were suggested for removal: "challenging" and "dull." Deleting these two items eliminated the differences (the DTF index was .004).

Comparisons between the United States and India also exhibited substantial differences, DTF = .164, $\chi^2_{(200)} = 518.94$, $p < .001$. Two items were suggested for removal: "challenging" and "dull." Omitting these items resulted in a nonsignificant DTF index, $\chi^2_{(200)} = 208.23$, n.s.

Comparisons between the United States and Poland revealed no significant differential test functioning, $\chi^2_{(245)} = 272.86$, n.s.

Stress in General. Comparisons between the United States and Mexico demonstrated significant differential test functioning, DTF = .012, $\chi^2_{(252)} = 560.61$, $p < .001$. One item was suggested for removal: "many things stressful." Eliminating this item resulted in a DTF index of .006, $\chi^2_{(252)} = 266.15$, n.s. Comparisons between the United States and India revealed no significant differential test functioning, $\chi^2_{(200)} = 225.63$, n.s. Finally, comparisons between the United States and Poland resulted in significant differential test functioning, DTF = .074, $\chi^2_{(245)} = 448.23$, $p < .001$. Two items were suggested for removal: "hectic" and "pressured." When these items were excluded from the analysis, the DTF index was not significant, $\chi^2_{(245)} = 253.64$.

Consistency Between Multigroup DIF and DTF Analyses

Before discussing these results and their implications for scale translation, it is interesting to consider the rather substantial consistency between the two differential functioning analyses. Of particular note, the multigroup DIF and DTF analyses pinpointed the same Satisfaction With Supervision item ("interferes with my work") and Satisfaction With the Work Itself items ("challenging" and "dull") as biased. In addition, work satisfaction item "waste of time" exhibited DIF in both the multigroup DIF and DTF analyses. The only difference between the two analyses was that three additional items were suggested for removal when comparing the United States sample to the Mexican sample. Finally, results for the Stress in General scale were generally consistent across the two DIF methods. "Hectic" and "relaxed" were identified as DIF items in the multigroup DIF analysis; "hectic" was found to contribute to the DTF between the United States and Poland and "relaxed" was found to contribute to the DTF between the United States and India. However, the DTF analysis also suggested two additional items for removal when comparing the United States to Mexico and the United States to Poland.

DISCUSSION

In this chapter we have described an approach to empirically examining the equivalence of adapted scales to their original versions. It should be noted that alternatives are available for each step of this analytic procedure: There are multiple methods for studying dimensionality, estimating IRT item parameters and checking the fit of the estimated model, linking metrics, and quantifying the magnitude of DIF. The methods in our analysis were selected because they were found to work well in simulation studies (e.g., marginal estimation, iterative linking) or because they test a hypothesis of particular interest to us (e.g., Kim et al.'s [1995] multiple-group DIF, Raju et al.'s [1995] DTF). Note, however, that other methods might work as well or better than the methods used here. Moreover, no simulation research has compared the relative effectiveness of the combinations of analyses required for examining test and scale adaptations; a massive simulation study might factorial cross several methods for evaluating dimensionality, several methods for estimating item parameters, multiple methods for checking the fit of the estimated model, alternatives for linking, and methods for assessing DIF.

Factor analysis provides an alternative methodology for studying adaptations. Ordinarily, factor analysis models assume that the manifest variables are linearly related to the latent constructs and the manifest variables follow a multivariate normal distribution. These assumptions are drastically violated with dichotomously scored items and so factor analysis would not be expected to provide meaningful results. However, an item with seven—or even five—response categories can provide a good approximation to a normal distribution under some circumstances (i.e., when the middle categories are most often endorsed and relatively few people endorse extreme categories; see Drasgow & Dorans, 1982). In such cases, Sŏrbom's (1974) mean and covariance structure (MACS) analysis may provide a good alternative to IRT methods.

Both the IRT approach used here and the MACS analysis are useful to researchers in that they determine the fidelity of an adaptation by identifying the items that measure equivalently across cultures and the items that fail to provide such measurement. Provided that not too many items exhibit DIF, we can compare, say, Satisfaction With the Work Itself across cultures using only non-DIF items. However, as more and more cultures are compared simultaneously, it appears likely that the number of non-DIF items will become too small for meaningful comparisons. In such a case, how can researchers make valid comparisons of the level of work satisfaction across cultures?

We propose the use of test equating procedures (see Kolen & Brennan, 1995) to statistically link observed score metrics. In this analysis, a researcher might use Raju et al.'s (1995) DTF analysis to identify the subset of items that provide equivalent measurement for each target culture with the source culture. These items could be considered to be "common items" in the test-equating argot; the respondents in the two cultures would be considered as "nonequivalent groups" and the data would be viewed as obtained from the "common-item, nonequivalent groups" sampling design (see pp. 18–21 in Kolen & Brennan, 1995). Hence, any of the equating procedures appropriate for this design could be used to rescale scores for the translated version of a scale to the source language metric. After such an equating, it would be possible to directly compare, say, work satisfaction scores and conclude that employees in one culture are more satisfied than employees in another culture. Of course, the extent to which the samples from the source and target cultures are representative of the larger cultural populations would be a key issue, but test equating might provide a means for computing scores that are directly comparable.

ACKNOWLEDGMENTS

The research described here was supported by the University of Illinois Center for Human Resources management. We thank Chris Robert, Joe Martocchio, and John Lawler for their help. Tahira Probst is now at Washington State University.

REFERENCES

Bach, C. L. (1998, July). U.S. international transactions. *Survey of Current Business*, pp. 47–57.

Baker, F. B. (1992). *Item response theory: Parameter estimation techniques.* New York: Marcel Dekker.

Baker, F. B., Al-Karni, A., & Al-Dosary, I. M. (1991). EQUATE: A computer program for the test characteristic curve method of IRT equating. *Applied Psychological Measurement, 15,* 78.

Bock, R. D. (1972). Estimating item parameters and latent ability when responses are scored in two or more nominal categories. *Psychometrika, 37,* 29–51.

Bock, R. D., & Aitkin, M. (1981). Marginal maximum likelihood estimation of item parameters: Application of an EM algorithm. *Psychometrika, 46,* 443–459.

Bock, R. D. & Lieberman, M. (1970). Fitting a response model for *n* dichotomously scored items. *Psychometrika, 35,* 179–197.

Candell, G. L., & Drasgow, F. (1988). An iterative procedure for linking metrics and assessing item bias in item response theory. *Applied Psychological Measurement, 12,* 253–260.

Drasgow, F. (1989). An evaluation of marginal maximum likelihood estimation for the two-parameter logistic model. *Applied Psychological Measurement, 13,* 77–90.

Drasgow, F., & Dorans, N. J. (1982). Robustness of estimators of the squared multiple correlation and squared cross-validity coefficient to violations of multivariate normality. *Applied Psychological Measurement, 6,* 185–200.

Drasgow, F., & Hulin, C. L. (1988). Cross-cultural measurement. *Interamerican Journal of Psychology, 21,* 1–24.

Drasgow, F., Levine, M. V., Tsien, S., Williams, B., & Mead, A. D. (1995). Fitting polytomous item response theory models to multiple-choice tests. *Applied Psychological Measurement, 19,* 143–165.

Drasgow, F., & Parsons, C. K. (1983). Application of unidimensional item response theory models to multidimensional data. *Applied Psychological Measurement, 7,* 189–199.

Fleer, P. F. (1993). A Monte Carlo assessment of a new measure of item and test bias. (Doctoral dissertation, Illinois Institute of Technology, 1993). *Dissertation Abstracts International, 54-04,* 2266B.

Hambleton, R. K., & Swaminathan, H. (1985). *Item response theory: Principles and applications.* Boston: Kluwer-Nijhoff.

Hanisch, K.A. (1992). The Job Descriptive Index revisited: Questions about the question mark. *Journal of Applied Psychology, 77,* 377–382.

Hattie, J. A. (1985). Methodology review: Assessing unidimensionality of tests and items. *Applied Psychological Measurement, 9,* 139–164.

Hofstede, G. (1980). *Culture's consequences.* Beverly Hills: Sage.

Hui, C. H., & Triandis, H. C. (1989). Effects of culture and response format on extreme response style. *Journal of Cross-Cultural Psychology, 20,* 296–309.

Hulin, C. L., Drasgow, F., & Komocar, J. (1982). Application of item response theory to analysis of attitude scale translation. *Journal of Applied Psychology, 67,* 818–825.

Hulin, C. L., Drasgow, F., & Parsons, C. K. (1983). *Item response theory: Application to psychological measurement.* Homewood: Dow Jones–Irwin.

Junker, B., & Stout, W. F. (1994). Robustness of ability estimation when multiple traits are present with one trait dominant. In D. Laveault, B. Zumbo, M. Gessaroli, & M. Boss (Eds.), *Modern theories of measurement: Problems and issues* (pp. 31–61). Ottawa, Canada: Edumetrics Research Group, University of Ottawa.

Kim, S.-H., Cohen, A. S., & Park, T.-H. (1995). Detection of differential item functioning in multiple groups. *Journal of Educational Measurement, 32,* 261–276.

Kolen, M. J., & Brennan, R. L. (1995). *Test equating: Methods and practices.* New York: Springer.

Landar, H. J., Ervin, S. M., & Horowitz, A. E. (1960). Navaho color categories. *Language, 36,* 368–382.

Leung, K., & Drasgow, F. (1986). Relation between self-esteem and delinquent behavior in three ethnic groups: An application of item response theory. *Journal of Cross-Cultural Psychology, 17,* 151–167.

Lord, F. M. (1977). A study of item bias, using item characteristic curve theory. In Y. H. Poortinga (Ed.), *Basic problems in cross-cultural psychology* (pp. 19–29). Amsterdam, Netherlands: Swets & Zeitlinger.

Lord, F. M. (1980). *Applications of item response theory to practical testing problems.* Hillsdale, NJ: Lawrence Erlbaum Associates.

Marin, G., Gamba, R. J., & Marin, G. V. (1992). Extreme response style and acquiescence among Hispanics. *Journal of Cross-Cultural Psychology, 23,* 498–509.

McLaughlin, M. E., & Drasgow, F. (1987). Lord's chi-squared test of item bias with estimated and known person parameters. *Applied Psychological Measurement, 11,* 161–173.

Mislevy, R. J., & Bock, R. D. (1989). *PC-BILOG 3.* Mooresville: Scientific Software.

Raju, N. S., van der Linden, W. J., & Fleer, P. F. (1995). IRT-based internal measures of differential functioning of items and tests. *Applied Psychological Measurement, 19,* 353–368.

Reckase, M. D. (1979). Unifactor latent trait models applied to multifactor tests: Results and implications. *Journal of Educational Statistics, 4,* 207–230.

Richards, I. (1953). Toward a theory of translation: Studies in Chinese thought. *American Anthropological Association, 55* (Memoir 75). Chicago: University of Chicago Press.

Roznowski, M. (1989). An examination of the measurement properties of the Job Descriptive Index with experimental items. *Journal of Applied Psychology, 74,* 805–814.

Samejima, F. (1969). Estimation of latent ability using a response pattern of graded scores. *Psychometrika Monograph Supplement,* No. 17.

Segall, D. O. (1983). *Assessment and comparison of techniques for transforming parameters to a common metric in item response theory.* Doctoral dissertation, University of Illinois at Urbana-Champaign.

Smith, P. C., Kendall, L., & Hulin, C. L. (1969). *The measurement of satisfaction in work and retirement.* Chicago: Rand McNally.

Smith, P. C., Sademan, B., & McCrary, L. (1992, May). *Development and validation of the Stress in General (SIG) scale.* Paper presented at the meeting of the Society for Industrial and Organizational Psychology, Montreal, Canada.

Sðrbom, D. (1974). A general method for studying differences in factor means and factor structure between groups. *Psychometrika, 27,* 229–239.

Stocking, M. L., & Lord, F. M. (1983). Developing a common metric in item response theory. *Applied Psychological Measurement, 7,* 201–210.

Stone, C. A. (2003). Empirical power and type I error rates for an IRT fit statistic that considers the precision of ability estimates. *Educational and Psychological Measurement, 63*(4), 566–583.

Stone, C. A., & Hansen, M. A. (2000). The effect of errors in estimating ability on goodness-of-fit tests for IRT models. *Educational and Psychological Measurement, 60*(6), 974–991.

Triandis, H. C. (1972). *The analysis of subjective culture.* New York: Wiley.

Triandis, H. C. (1990). Cross-cultural studies of individualism and collectivism. In J. Berman (Ed.), *Nebraska Symposium on Motivation, 1989* (pp. 41–133). Lincoln: University of Nebraska Press.

Triandis, H. C. (1994). *Culture and social behavior.* New York: McGraw-Hill.

Triandis, H. C. (1995). *Individualism and collectivism.* Boulder: Westview Press.

12

Constructing, Adapting, and Validating Admissions Tests in Multiple Languages: The Israeli Case

Michal Beller
Educational Testing Service

Naomi Gafni and Pnina Hanani
The National Institute for Testing and Evaluation

The variety of goals for which translated tests are used affects the translation process and the role played by each of the languages involved. For each use a separate discussion of the considerations regarding the appropriateness of the translated versions is needed. A familiar use of test translation is applying an already well-established standard scale, such as IQ tests or personality questionnaires, for research and practical purposes. Such tests (e.g., Kaufman Assessment Battery for Children [K-ABC]) are used mainly for development of local norms required for making individual decisions, as well as cross-national comparisons for research purposes. In this case the translation process involves only the necessary minimal test adaptation (Poortinga, 1995).

International assessments of education (e.g., Trends in International Mathematics and Science Study [TIMMS]) are examples of cross-national research in which no particular language or content is considered to be dominant. Rather, all participating countries determine the contents of the assessment together, thereby assuring maximal common ground. The agreed-upon version is translated into all relevant languages (see, Grisay, 2003, for one excellent example). In this case the main purpose of the assessment is cross-national, although in some cases (e.g., Canada) comparisons have been carried out within the country between various subgroups.

Another goal of test translation is to establish a fair and valid selection procedure for candidates from various language groups who are applying to institutions of higher learning within a specific country and language of instruction. This is typical of countries that serve as targets for large-scale immigration (e.g., United States, Canada, Australia, Israel). In this case, the translation process may seriously affect the validity and fairness of individual high-stakes decisions. Using scores from admissions tests that are administered to all groups in the source language results in confounding of the measured construct and the level of familiarity with the source language. Therefore, there is a need to find ways to reduce the confounding of the two variables, for example, by translating admissions tests into the various languages of the applicants, and measuring mastery of the local language separately.

The goals of translation must be dealt with in the context of the target populations. The status of the target population for translation varies: In some cases, a country may have more than one official language (e.g., Switzerland, Canada, Israel), and, therefore, tests are routinely translated. Even in such cases, countries differ in that some provide their different language groups with a full educational system in their own language (e.g., Switzerland), whereas others provide only a semiseparate educational system (e.g., Canada and Israel). In Israel, for example, Arabic is a second official language, and the Arabic-speaking population has its own K–12 separate educational system (with the exception of some subjects that are taught in Hebrew). The lingua franca of higher education, on the other hand, is Hebrew and Hebrew alone; and there is one system for both populations.

Additional target populations for test translations are immigrants from different countries. Immigrants from a particular country should not be treated automatically as if they were a homogeneous group. They differ in their familiarity with their mother tongue and with the new local language, and in their acquaintance with the local culture and educational system (depending on their age at the time of immigration, the length of time they have spent in the new country, and their level of immersion in the culture of the new country). Therefore, translating a test into a specific language does not assure a valid comparison even among individuals within a given language group. The varied degrees of familiarity of each population with both the source and the target language influence the way in which the test is translated. In some cases, it might be advisable to translate only specific terms in the test rather than translating the test fully. For example, veteran Russian immigrants to Israel (who have already studied in Israel for several years) may prefer to take the admissions exam for higher education in Hebrew with a glossary containing specific terms translated into Russian, rather than in their natural language.

This chapter is focused on some of the major problems involved in test translation from the perspective of test usage and score interpretation. In particular, it deals with the extent to which the source language version needs to be translated, adapted or changed; the definition of criteria for evaluating the quality of the translation; and approaches to calibrating scores on different language versions. Methods for dealing with these issues are discussed and demonstrated using the various language versions of the Psychometric Entrance Test (PET). PET is a scholastic aptitude test constructed and administered by the National Institute for Testing and Evaluation (NITE). It is used, in conjunction with a matriculation certificate, by all Israeli universities and by other major institutions of higher learning for making admissions decisions. The matriculation certificate is based on both school assessment and external nationwide achievement tests[1]. PET measures various cognitive and scholastic abilities, in an attempt to estimate future success in academic studies. It consists of three multiple-choice subtests: Verbal Reasoning (V), Quantitative Reasoning (Q), and English as a second language (E). No correction for guessing is used for scoring the test and examinees are encouraged to guess when they do not know the correct answer. For a detailed description of PET, see Beller (1994).

In establishing admissions policy for the universities in Israel, policymakers and psychometricians have been faced with the problem of finding the best methods for predicting the academic success of non-Hebrew-speaking applicants (along with Hebrew speakers)

---

[1]For students of foreign origin, the school-based component is either missing or, more often, cannot be compared to the Israeli matriculation scores. Therefore, these candidates are rank-ordered on the basis of their PET score alone. In some universities, admissions decisions are based on a composite score composed of the PET score and the mean score achieved in preparatory courses that are required of non-Hebrew-speaking candidates before they are admitted to the university.

in institutions of higher education (where the language of instruction is Hebrew). In other words, the goal is to rank *all* different-language-speaking examiness on *a* common scale, that best predicts *a* common criterion, within the *same* cultural context. It was decided to administer PET in the language with which the applicant is most familiar, because it was believed that this procedure provides each applicant with the opportunity to perform optimally. PET is currently translated into the languages spoken by the majority of non-Hebrew-speaking university applicants: Arabic, Russian, French, Spanish, and English[2]. The translation process is an ongoing endeavor: Four, two, two, one, and one new forms are annually translated into Arabic, Russian, English, French, and Spanish, respectively (out of 10–18 new forms in Hebrew).

To familiarize examinees with PET, and to ensure that all persons fully understand the requirements of each type of task involved in the test, NITE publishes an information booklet that includes previously administered tests as well as explanations. This booklet is also translated into the five languages mentioned earlier. This procedure is particularly important, because the various language groups differ in terms of their previous experience with multiple-choice tests. Of the 66,731 examinees to whom PET was administered in 1998, for example, approximately 27% chose to take PET in one of these languages (15% in Arabic, 10% in Russian, and 2% in the other foreign languages). Examinees who take PET in a foreign language are required by some institutions to take an additional Hebrew Proficiency Test (HP), which is scored separately. The non-Hebrew versions of PET are essentially translations of Hebrew test versions administered to Hebrew-speaking examinees; They thus have a similar structure. The English subtest of PET is identical for all language versions. The Quantitative Reasoning subtest is translated from Hebrew. The rationale behind this is that, in general, translated math items are directly comparable to the source. The Verbal Reasoning subtest is translated only in part. Most of the items are selected from the pool of Hebrew items, but others are specially constructed for the various language versions (e.g., the Word and Expression items).

[2]The English version is actually a combined English and Hebrew version in which all of the questions are presented both in English and in Hebrew. It is offered to applicants whose native language is English, as well as to applicants who are not proficient in any of the languages mentioned above. A short dictionary appears at the bottom of each page, which contains a translation of selected key words into the languages most required by these examinees, according to their native language. Currently, these languages are: French, Spanish, German, Hungarian, Rumanian, Italian, Russian, and Amharic.

In the following sections, we discuss both procedural and substantive issues involved in the translation of PET. Special attention is devoted to the translation of the Verbal Reasoning subtest.

THE TRANSLATION PROCESS

Selecting a Test Form for Translation: Considerations

The tests in the five languages (Arabic, Russian, French, Spanish, and English) are translated from previously administered Hebrew test forms. This ensures that the items selected for translation are all high-quality items in psychometric terms. The following considerations are taken into account in selecting the Hebrew versions to be translated:

1. *Quality of calibration:* To reduce potential calibration problems, we try to identify a form previously taken by Hebrew-speaking examinees who are relatively similar in distribution of ability to the "other language" examinees (target group).
2. *Reliability:* It has been found that the reliability of the total score on the translated versions is almost as high as that of the original Hebrew version (see Table 12.1). In the past, the reliability of the Verbal Reasoning subtest for the Arabic-speaking population was lower than the reliability of the other translated subtests (see Table 12.1 for current values). This was caused mainly because this subtest was extremely difficult for Arabic-speaking examinees. To increase the reliability of the Verbal Reasoning subtest for this population, an easier test was constructed by selecting the easier half of the items from a Hebrew form (to be used later for calibration) and supplementing it with easy items from the item bank.
3. *Preservation of frequency of technical terms in reading comprehension texts:* Reading comprehension texts with an abundance of technical terms (scientific terms, legal language, or psychological jargon) are avoided when selecting texts for translation, because in many cases these terms are self-explanatory in one language but not in another. In addition, the frequency with which such terms are used is often different in different cultural and linguistic contexts; some terms might exist in one language but not in others. A text abounding with "foreign"[3] words will not be translated into Arabic, because Arabic-speaking examinees generally do not encounter such words in elementary school and high school.

[3]In this context, "foreign" refers to words from languages other than Hebrew that are, nonetheless, used by the Hebrew-speaking population (e.g., "technologia").

TABLE 12.1
Median Reliability Coefficients (KR-20) of PET Subtests and of the Composite Total Score for Each Language Version Administered During 1990–1997

Language	*V*	*Q*	*E*	*PET*
Hebrew (65)	0.90	0.90	0.94	0.96
Arabic (23)	0.84	0.86	0.82	0.93
Russian (18)	0.86	0.88	0.92	0.94
French (9)	0.82	0.87	0.90	0.93
Spanish (9)	0.82	0.87	0.93	0.94
English (15)	0.90	0.90	0.96	0.96

Note. The number of test forms appears in parentheses.

4. *Cultural context:* The cultural context of the test must be familiar to all examinees. A reading comprehension text that includes local cultural connotations will not be selected for translation.

5. *Sensitivity reviews:* The tests undergo item sensitivity reviews to avoid choosing items that might be provocative or offensive in their translated version. For instance, an item including the word "uprising" (INTIFADA) in Arabic would not be used because of the political sensitivity of this word. Texts that deal with politics, religion, sex, and so on, would also not be chosen.

The Stages in the Translation Process

The translation process meets the International Test Commission Test Adaptation Guidelines (Hambleton, 1994; see also chap. 1, this volume). There are four stages in the translation process:

1. *Initial translation:* A qualified and experienced translator, who is proficient and knowledgeable in both languages and cultures, especially in the target language, translates the original Hebrew version of the test into the target language. Problems arising during the translation process are discussed with the psychometrician in charge of the entire translation process. Following a recommendation by Hambleton (personal communication, 1997), two

independent Russian translations are being carried out instead of only one. Experience so far with this more costly procedure indicates that it improves the quality of the review that occurs in the next stage. The cost-effectiveness of this additional procedure is in the process of being evaluated.

2. *Independent reviews:* The translated versions undergo critical reviewing by several bilingual reviewers, some with a solid background in mathematics and logic, and others who are highly competent in verbal reasoning. Both American and British reviewers read the English version, and reviewers from various Spanish-speaking countries read the Spanish version. The reviewers are required to first critique the translated version without looking at the original Hebrew, and only afterward to compare the translated version with the original Hebrew version. They are then required to pay special attention to the accuracy of the translation as well as to the clarity of the sentences, the difficulty level of the words, and the fluency of the text. Each reviewer solves the test items, checking that no changes have resulted in the item's inner logic, that each item still has one, and only one, correct answer, and that the distractors are adequate in terms of their attractiveness. The psychometrician and the translator discuss the reviewers' comments and suggestions, and revisions are made accordingly.

3. *Back-translation:* A bilingual expert, who has not previously seen the original Hebrew version, orally translates the translated version back into Hebrew. This stage is carried out orally mainly because it allows for immediate interaction and discussion between the back-translator and the psychometrician. The back-translation is simultaneously compared with the original Hebrew version, and translated items are revised where necessary.

4. *Final check before initial administration:* The revised version of the translation is given to a native speaker of the target language who has seen neither the original Hebrew version nor the previous versions of the translation. He or she is requested to solve the questions without looking at the original Hebrew, and to ascertain that there is one, and only one, correct answer to each question. The psychometrician evaluates the answers, searching for wrong answers that may derive from translation inaccuracies.

Specific Problems in Translating the Verbal Reasoning Subtest

The Verbal Reasoning sections are the most problematic to translate because words and concepts in one language do not always have the same meanings, connotations, familiarity, or level of difficulty when translated into another language. Idioms and expressions are a typical source of difficulty, as they very often cannot be translated at all. Languages differ in the richness of their semantic fields. For example, Hebrew has a wide range of words relating to agriculture. In English you pick grapes, you pick olives, and so on, but in Hebrew there is a different verb for picking grapes, for picking olives, and the like. Similarly, there are different words in Hebrew for washing the floor, washing dishes, and washing clothes. English speakers use the same verb ***wash*** for all of these activities. English and Hebrew have only one word for camel. In Arabic there are a vast number of words, denoting the different types of camels according to their characteristics.

Translating into Arabic poses enormous problems. On the one hand, written Arabic is the same for all Arabs in all Arab countries. But spoken Arabic, which is very different from written Arabic, varies from country to country, and even from area to area in the same country. A "coat" in written Arabic is "MIATAF" and in spoken Arabic it is "KABBUT." A "hat" in written Arabic is "QUBBA" and in spoken Arabic it is "TAQIUA." In the Arabic translation, an effort is made to avoid words in spoken Arabic, and to use the written words instead, even though they are more difficult. Arabic-speaking examinees that read Arabic literature might encounter these words, but others might be unfamiliar with them.

The following sections discuss specific translation problems, ranging from item types that cannot be translated at all to those that can be translated directly or that require only slight adaptation.

Letter Exchange Items. These items are based on a morphological feature of Semitic languages not shared by Indo-European languages, namely, the fact that most of the vocabulary in Hebrew—all verbs and most nouns and adjectives—can be characterized as a combination of Root + Pattern. The Letter Exchange items are composed of four sentences. In each sentence, one word is altered by changing its root letters into a standard template (the letters **p.t.l**). In three of the four sentences, the standard template stands for the same three letters. In the remaining sentence, the template replaces another root. The examinees have to identify this sentence.

Because Arabic is a Semitic language, this item type can be used; however, the items cannot be translated and must be written in Arabic. New items of this type are pretested before they are used for scoring purposes. This item type cannot be included in any other language version.

Words and Expressions. Word and expression items cannot be translated from Hebrew, and are written directly in the target language. In the Arabic-language test version, it was found necessary and cost-effective to pretest these items before using them for scoring purposes.

Analogies. This item type is the most difficult to translate, as it involves meanings and connotations of single words and the relationships between pairs of words. There are few words that have a precisely equivalent meaning, connotation, and level of difficulty in another language. In translating analogies, the relationship between the two words in each pair must be retained as accurately as possible, while at the same time keeping in mind the difficulty level of the vocabulary. The original analogy is often designed to test command of Hebrew vocabulary in addition to analytical ability. In such cases, the translated item is often easier.

Sentence Completion. These items entail understanding of the logical and semantic relationships within a complex sentence. Sentence completion items are difficult to translate. In order to produce a natural sounding, smoothly flowing sentence in the target language, it is often necessary to change the structure of the sentence, and this affects the way the missing words are inserted into the translated sentence. Furthermore, the translator has to ensure that all four distractors produce sentences that are grammatically and syntactically correct, so that choosing the correct answer will depend solely on internal logic and not on structural and grammatical "hints." In addition, it is necessary to preserve, as much as possible, the level of the language (everyday, formal, literary, etc.), the complexity of the missing words, the number of blanks, and so forth.

Problems arise, for instance, in Arabic, where every noun has a grammatical gender that is not necessarily the same as its Hebrew counterpart. Arabic also has two plural forms: the plural for more than two items (plural) and the plural for two items (dual), with the verb conjugated accordingly. Moreover, sentences in Arabic usually begin with a verb, unlike Hebrew sentences, which usually begin with a noun. All of these problems call for many alterations in the item's structure and complicate the task of translating the sentence completion items.

When the structure of the sentence in the target language changes, the sentence might contain only three blanks instead of the four blanks in the original Hebrew version. There is no a priori reason not to use such items, but if in the calibration analysis the item is found to be considerably easier than its Hebrew counterpart, it will later be removed from the anchor for calibration.

Logic. Logic items must be translated very carefully and accurately. The translator must try to preserve all of the logical elements of the Hebrew item while adhering to the same structure as existed in the original item. Attention must be paid to whether the context is real or imaginary, and names and measurement units (kilometers vs. miles, etc.) must be adjusted, so that the terms used will be equally familiar to all examinees.

In an attempt to preserve the precise structure of the original logic items in the translated version (e.g., preserving negatives, double negatives, conjunctions such as "only," "also," etc.), it is sometimes necessary to change the structure so that the syntax of the target language will be correct. For example, the syntax of the Hebrew structure *"all p's are not q"* is ambiguous in English. Thus, a statement in Hebrew such as *All birds of prey are not green* (meaning that there is not even one bird of prey that is green) cannot be directly translated into English. In order to preserve the exact Hebrew meaning, the structure of the English sentence has to be changed as follows: *No birds of prey are green.* A similar difficulty arises when this sentence has to be translated into French. In French, "all" cannot be followed by a negative. Therefore, the translation has to be: *Aucun oiseau predat n'est vert.*

Another example is: *There are no Japanese-made cars that are not both large and fast.* In Arabic, words that mean "only" and "also" are usually placed at the end of a sentence, and it is not always clear what they are referring to. Therefore, in translating the aforementioned sentence into Arabic, some information has to be added: "... *which are not large and fast at the same time.*"

Reading Comprehension. In the translation of a text, the emphasis is on the following: translating accuracy; preserving the fluency, richness, and style of the language using concepts that are familiar in the target language; and being consistent in the use of the terms appearing in the text.

One of the criticisms of cross-cultural testing is that a translated text cannot convey the same meaning and preserve the same level of difficulty as the original text. Therefore, at NITE, a special team was established for the purpose of finding texts for Arabic speakers, the largest group of non-Hebrew-speaking examinees. The texts are written in Arabic, and adapted to NITE's test requirements. One of the questions that will have to be answered is whether scores that are obtained from a test that uses comprehension texts written originally in Arabic are comparable to scores derived from test versions that use texts originally written in Hebrew.

SCORING THE LANGUAGE VERSIONS

Each subtest is scored separately, using a number-right scoring-rule formula, and is standardized on a scale that, for the original norm group (Hebrew-speaking examinees in 1984), had a mean of 100 and a standard deviation of 20. The total PET score is a weighted sum of the scores on the three subtests (2V, 2Q, and E), with a mean of 500 and a standard deviation of 100. For a more detailed description of PET, see Beller (1994).

The same parameters are applied for scoring the English and the Quantitative subtests in all language versions (assuming that translation does not alter the meaning of the quantitative questions). A calibration procedure similar to the one described by Angoff and Modu (1973) is used in scoring the Verbal Reasoning subtest. An anchor is established between the Hebrew version and each of the other language versions. This is done by selecting items that have similar psychometric indices and a similar order of difficulty (using delta-plot techniques) for the two groups of examinees. Once an anchor is established, linear equating methods (Tucker or Levin) are applied.

Table 12.2 presents the means and standard deviations for the various language versions of PET and its subtests for the academic year 1997/1998. The French-, Spanish-, and English-speaking groups are very small; therefore, these results cannot be generalized beyond this specific context. The Arabic- and Russian-speaking groups are large and stable enough across the years to be representative of the two largest minority groups applying to institutions of higher education in Israel. Consequently, most of the following analysis and discussion is based on the Hebrew, Arabic, and Russian versions. As mentioned earlier, the Arabic-speaking population in Israel has a separate educational system, whose language of instruction is Arabic. In general, this educational system is less developed than the Hebrew educational system. The disparity between the Hebrew- and the Arabic-speaking populations is already evident in the early grades, as has been found in several national assessments of the educational system. The somewhat higher level of performance of Arabic-speaking examinees in mathematics, relative to verbal achievement, is also evident at an early age.

It is interesting to note that the greatest difference in performance between the Arabic- and the Russian-speaking groups and the Hebrew group is on the nontranslated English subtest.

TABLE 12.2
Means and Standard Deviations for the Various Language Versions of PET and Its Subtests in 1997/1998

		Total Score		*Verbal Reasoning*		*Quantitative Reasoning*		*English*	
Language	*N*	*M*	*SD*	*M*	*SD*	*M*	*SD*	*M*	*SD*
Hebrew	48,897	554	101	108	20	111	19	111	23
Arabic	9,949	431	85	86	16	92	19	82	16
Russian	6,366	512	101	92	18	106	18	95	22
French	511	521	84	99	16	104	19	112	17
Spanish	363	480	82	90	14	96	17	108	22
English	645	552	106	100	21	107	21	131	23

QUALITY OF THE TRANSLATED VERSIONS

In addition to the meticulous process of translation described earlier, the following quantitative criteria are also used to assess the quality of the translated versions: differential effect of guessing, item analysis, differential item functioning (DIF), reliability, construct equivalence, validity, and bias in prediction of criterion scores. These criteria are affected by translation as well as various other inseparable cultural group-distribution factors. Special attention is given to Russian, which is spoken by the largest immigrant population to Israel (15% of the overall Israeli population).

Differential Effect of Guessing

A study conducted by Gafni and Melamed (1994) investigated the following phenomenon: Despite being instructed to guess when they did not know the correct answer, only 75% to 93% of the examinees (depending on the specific subtests) responded to all the items on PET. It was postulated that different language groups might manifest different guessing behaviors. For example, it was expected that the English-speaking group would be more familiar with multiple-choice tests and would, therefore, be more likely to follow the test instructions closely. On the other hand, the Russian-speaking group, being less acquainted with this type of test, might be less inclined to guess. It was also hypothesized that the degree of familiarity of the general public with multiple-choice testing might have an effect.

The results suggested that people with differing cultural backgrounds differ in their tendency to guess. A language-group effect and a familiarity effect were found. In 1984, Russian-, Arabic-, and French-speaking examinees tended to omit more items than Hebrew-, English-, and Spanish-speaking examinees; in 1987 (after 4 years of PET administration), Russian-speaking examinees tended to omit more items than all other groups. The proportion of omitted items has dropped significantly for all groups, as the test has become more familiar and test preparation more prevalent. The 1994 study recommended that the importance of test instruction be emphasized, in particular among members of groups with a greater tendency to avoid guessing.

Item Analysis and DIF

The quality of each translated item is examined (in terms of its level of difficulty and degree of discrimination). In addition, the DIF of each translated item is examined, comparing Hebrew- and non-Hebrew-speaking examinees (DIF refers to the simple observation that an item displays different statistical properties for different groups, after controlling for differences in the abilities of the groups). If the statistical properties of certain translated items are poor, those items are reviewed, and possible (post hoc) reasons for their failure are raised. A decision is made regarding each item whether to include the item in the scoring of the translated version, and if so, whether to include it in the anchor used for calibration.

Gafni and Canaan-Yehoshafat (1993) examined DIF on the Verbal Reasoning subtests of three Russian forms of PET using a delta-plot technique proposed by Angoff (1972). The greatest DIF was found for analogies, and the smallest DIF for the logic and sentence completion items. These results are similar to those found by Angoff and Cook (1988) for English- and Spanish-speaking examinees taking the Scholastic Assessment Test (SAT), with the exception of the logic items, which are not included in the SAT verbal sections. The reading comprehension items showed relatively greater DIF than in the Angoff and Cook study.

Allalouf, Hambleton, and Sireci (1999) and Sireci and Allalouf (2003) reported results of their investigation of the relationship of

DIF (using the Mantel–Haenszel method) to item type and hypothesized sources of DIF. They analyzed three forms of the Hebrew and Russian versions of PET. The results reflect the extent of the problems involved in translating the different verbal item types, as described in the previous section. It was found that 42 out of 125 items (34%) functioned differentially across languages. The analogies were the most problematic, with 65% of them exhibiting DIF. On most of these items, the Russian-speaking examinees performed better than the Hebrew-speaking examinees. A large proportion (45%) of the sentence completion items also exhibited DIF, but in this case, neither group performed better than the other did. A panel of translators was asked to speculate on possible causes of DIF for each item. The main causes suggested were changes in word difficulty, changes in format, differences in cultural relevance, and changes in content.

Reliability

The internal reliability of each subtest, as well as that of the total score, is routinely estimated for each language version. Table 12.1 presents the median internal consistency coefficients (KR-20) for the three subtests and for the total score of the various language versions of PET. These reliabilities are relatively high, both for the Hebrew version and for the other language versions. The somewhat lower reliabilities in the foreign-language versions may be explained by translation-related problems. However, internal reliability is not determined solely by the quality of the test items and the quality of the translation, but also by the true variance within the group of examinees. From experience gained at NITE, it appears that in many cases the quality of the translation is confounded with differences in performance. When two groups differ in ability, this in and of itself might create differences in reliability, comparability, and item DIF. When items are too difficult for a certain group, the reliability of the test for that group is relatively low. For example, the median reliability for the Verbal Reasoning subtest of the first five Arabic forms, constructed between 1984 and 1989, was 0.68 (Beller & Gafni, 1995). To raise reliability, a Verbal Reasoning test, which included much easier items, was specially constructed for the Arab version. The median reliability obtained for 23 forms constructed in this way increased to 0.84. Although the reliability of this new subtest is higher, it probably introduces a larger equating error than that of the previous subtest.

As important as these results are, reliability is only a necessary, not a sufficient, condition for test development. It is the validity of various translated versions that provides the most important justification for using the scores obtained on them.

Construct Equivalence

To ensure that the translated versions of PET are measuring the same construct as the original Hebrew version, Allalouf, Bastari, Hambleton, and Sireci (1997) used exploratory factor analysis, multidimensional scaling, and confirmatory factor analysis to evaluate the structural equivalence of the Verbal Reasoning subtest in two Hebrew and Russian versions. Specifically, they analyzed four of the five content areas: analogies, logic, reading comprehension, and sentence completion. A total of 41 items were included in the analysis. In the analyses performed on the two versions, the structure of PET was found to be similar across the two language versions for the subset of items.

Validity

The validity of the selection procedure is routinely tested by examining the predictive validity of PET against the criterion of grade point average (GPA) at the end of the first year of university studies and at the completion of undergraduate studies. In this chapter, the focus is on a comparison of the results obtained for Hebrew- and Russian-speaking examinees. Results of validity studies and test bias regarding the Arabic version of PET can be found in Beller, Gafni, and Hanani (1999).

Predictive Validity of the Russian Versus the Hebrew Versions

The predictive validity of the translated Russian version is less affected by factors such as the large differences in ability between the Arabic- and Hebrew-speaking groups. Therefore, research regarding the Russian translation is discussed more extensively than research on the Arabic version.

In a study conducted recently by Gafni and Bronner (1998), the predictive validity of the PET score was calculated for the Russian-speaking group and compared with that of the Hebrew-speaking group. The predictors in this study were PET, its three subtests (V, Q, and E), and the admissions score (Adm). The Adm in this study was based on equal weights of PET and an achievement score obtained either in high school (Bagrut) or in a preparatory program for applicants who did not study in an Israeli high school[4]. This study included an additional predictor—the score on a Hebrew Proficiency test (HP)[5] administered to all non-Hebrew-speaking examinees. Validity coefficients for the various predictors for students who began their university studies between 1992 and 1996 were computed for two criteria: first-year GPA (FGPA) and third-year GPA (TGPA). The analyses were conducted for each department within each cohort, provided that it included at least five students from each language group. Results are reported across 463 departments that met the aforementioned condition for FGPA, and 83 departments that met this condition for TGPA. Table 12.3 presents the number of students, the mean, and the standard deviation of the various predictors and criteria.

TABLE 12.3

Means and Standard Deviations (in Parentheses) of the Predictor and Criterion Scores (Hebrew and Russian) for FGPA and TGPA

Language	*PET*	*V*	*Q*	*E*	*Adm*	*HP*	*FGPA*	*TGPA*
FGPA								
Hebrew	600	118	117	118	101	–	80	–
N = 55,434	(60)	(13)	(13)	(16)	(6.8)		(8.8)	
Russian	561	111	116	100	99	93	73	–
N = 7,313	(52)	(12)	(12)	(16)	(6.2)	(16)	(11.9)	
TGPA[a]								
Hebrew	590	116	116	116	101	–	82	84
N = 6,612	(57)	(12)	(13)	(15)	(6.2)		(6.7)	(6.9)
Russian	540	108	112	96	98	87	76	81
N = 1,011	(54)	(13)	(12)	(16)	(6.1)	(14.4)	(8.4)	(8.3)

[a]The samples for TGPA are much smaller than those for FGPA. This is partially due to attrition, but is mainly due to the fact that most students had not yet completed their third year of study at the time the study was conducted.

---

[4]The achievement score was not available separately.

[5]The HP comprises multiple-choice items (67%) and an essay (33%). It is scored separately with a mean of 100 and standard deviation of 20.

The largest difference between the two groups was found for E, with Hebrew-speaking examinees exhibiting better performance; no difference was found for Q. The difference for V was somewhere between the two. A slight difference in favor of the Hebrew-speaking examinees was found for Adm, implying a reverse pattern of differences on the achievement score (which is not calibrated) compared with PET. The difference on the FGPA criterion was similar to that on PET. It is interesting to note that the difference on TGPA decreased compared with that on FGPA.

The validity coefficients for the two language groups are presented in Table 12.4, averaged across all departments. The observed correlations (in parenthesis) are corrected for range restriction. The average validity coefficients of both the Adm and

TABLE 12.4

Predictive Validities (Correlations Corrected for Range Restriction) of PET, Admissions Score (Adm), and the Hebrew Proficiency Test (HP) for GPA at the End of the Freshman Year (FGPA) and Senior Year (TGPA) for Russian- and Hebrew-Speaking Examinees (Raw Correlations Appear in Parentheses)

Language	*PET*	*V*	*Q*	*E*	*Adm*	*HP*
FGPA						
Hebrew	.39	.32	.36	.24	.48	
	(.26)	(.21)	(.26)	(.12)	(.37)	
Russian	.35	.26	.30	.29	*	*
	(.27)	(.16)	(.21)	(.24)	(.38)	(.23)
TGPA						
Hebrew	.44	.36	.37	.29	.54	
	(.20)	(.16)	(.17)	(.12)	(.28)	
Russian	.45	.35	.38	.35	*	*
	(.26)	(.17)	(.19)	(.22)	(.33)	(.20)

Note. The corrected correlations are estimates based on a similar set of data where the population variances were provided for the non-restricted sample. In cases where * is denoted, the variances of the unrestricted populations were not available.

PET for the FGPA group were similar for both the Russian and Hebrew groups across all fields of study. However, the pattern of validity coefficients for PET subtests was different for the two language groups. Whereas Q had the highest validity for the Hebrew-speaking group, the most valid test for Russian-speaking examinees was E. V had the lowest validity for the Russian-speaking group, and this may indicate that V does not measure exactly the same construct in both languages, either due to the translation and adaptation of the test, or because of the specific test content, which was originally chosen for the Hebrew-speaking group. Apparently, numerous factors determine the validity of a test within a group, and the quality of the translation is only one of them.

The relatively high validity of E for the Russian-speaking group might be attributed to moderating variables not investigated in this study. For example, those students who immigrated to Israel from a large city with a good educational system might have had a better opportunity to learn English than immigrants who came from some remote town without a well-developed, modern educational system. It is also possible that some of the Russian-speaking examinees immigrated to Israel several years before taking PET and had the opportunity to study within the Israeli educational system. This could be reflected both in their English score and in their criterion score.

Test Bias

NITE has conducted research to detect whether there is test bias for the Russian-speaking examinees (Gafni & Bronner, 1998). The term *bias* refers to systematic errors in the predictive validity or construct validity associated with an examinee's group membership. The methods that follow from the definitions given in Darlington (1971) and the discussion by Linn (1984) were used to detect bias in the various predictors. Results regarding single predictors should be viewed with caution, due to the effect of excluding a predictor from a regression equation on which there are preexisting group differences (Linn & Werts, 1971).

Bias in Testing Russian-Speaking Examinees

The first sample consisted of 55,434 Hebrew-speaking examinees and 7,313 Russian-speaking examinees who began their studies in one of the years 1992–1996, and whose PET scores and FGPA scores were available. Six Israeli universities were included, for a total of 463 departments. The Adm was available for only a subsample consisting of 26,875 Hebrew speakers and 3,478 Russian speakers. For this predictor, the analysis was conducted on only 259 departments (Gafni & Bronner, 1998). Table 12.5 presents the number of significant cases of bias detected across all departments, with PET and the Adm as predictors. Hardly any clear bias was found for PET as a single predictor: In 3% of the 463 cases, there was a clear indication of bias against the Russian-speaking examinees, and in 2% of the cases, the bias was in their favor. Similar results were found for V and Q (the translated subtests), with a tendency to overpredict FGPA for the Russian-speaking group. A reverse tendency was found on the English subtest. For the admissions score, in about 10% of the 259 departments a clear indication of bias was detected, mostly in favor of the Russian-speaking examinees.

TABLE 12.5

Relative Frequency (%) of Significant Cases of Test Bias for Russian-Speaking Examinees, With FGPA and TGPA as the Criteria

Predictor	*Bias Against Russian Speakers*	*Bias Favoring Russian Speakers*
FGPA		
PET	3.0	2.0
V	0.5	1.5
Q	1.0	7.0
E	1.5	0.0
Adm	1.0	9.0
TGPA		
PET	8.0	5.5
V	2.7	5.5
Q	2.7	5.5
E	11.0	0.0
Adm	2.7	0.0

The aforementioned results do not provide any clear-cut answers as to the possible prediction bias resulting from translation: On the one hand, E, which is not translated at all, exhibited bias against the Russian-speaking examinees, but on the other hand, Q, which is also relatively unaffected by translation, exhibited bias in favor of this group. The Verbal Reasoning subtest, which is most affected by translation, produced results that do not indicate evident translation problems. It may be concluded that, if the translation process succeeds in more or less preserving the same difficulty level of the two language versions, and if the meaning of what is measured is as similar as possible, then no bias should be expected as a result of the translation per se.

One of the main criticisms of conventional bias studies is that they often overpredict the criterion scores of minority groups. The reason for this is that the transition to a college in which the student body is predominantly the majority population is initially more demanding for the minority students than for the majority students. Therefore, one might expect the overprediction to disappear in the third year of college. To test this assumption, a subsample consisting of 6,612 Hebrew-speaking examinees and 1,011 Russian-speaking examinees whose scores on PET and TGPA were available was examined. A total of 83 departments were included in this study. The Adm was available for only a subsample consisting of 2,687 Hebrew speakers and 338 Russian speakers. For this predictor, the analysis was available for only 37 departments. Table 12.5 presents the number of departments in which clear bias was detected against and in favor of Russian-speaking examinees. In general, when TGPA served as the criterion, a pattern similar to FGPA emerged, with a slight decrease in the tendency of the predictors to be biased in favor of the Russian-speaking group, as expected.

CONCLUSIONS

The issue of test translation should be approached while keeping in mind various dimensions, such as the goal of the translation, the target population, and the type and content of the test. A test can be translated for research purposes, where mainly group differences are of interest, and it can be used for individual high-stakes decision-making purposes, such as admissions to universities. The requirements for quality translation are higher in the latter than in the former.

The translation process of PET, a test used for admissions to higher education in Israel, from Hebrew to Arabic, Russian, French, Spanish, and English was described in detail, exemplifying inherent translation problems (in particular for the verbal sections). The quality of the translations was checked by applying various qualitative and quantitative methods, thus highlighting different aspects of the translatability of the various language versions. Several steps were taken to ensure the quality of the translation: (a) investing substantial effort in the qualitative check of the translations, in some cases using two independent translators; (b) examining response patterns and differential tendency of examinees to guess on multiple-choice items; (c) examining item analysis and DIF; (d) checking reliability and its relation to the groups' ability level; (e) investigating predictive validity for two criteria (first- and third-year GPA); and (f) analyzing predictive test bias for the various subgroups.

The extensive set of analyses presented in this chapter regarding PET and its translated versions provides a great deal of information regarding the complexity of the issue of comparability and equivalence of translated admissions tests. It is argued that when assessing the quality of translated tests in a context of individual high-stakes decisions, a broader view of test fairness and equivalence of versions should be adopted. An examination of predictive validity and test bias should be carried out in addition to the more common DIF-like analyses. The issue of validity and that of test bias are both necessary to establish the overall justification for using the translated test results for admissions (high-stakes) purposes. In the context of admissions tests, the criterion against which the test is validated is not of less importance than the test itself.

The results presented about PET demonstrate that when a proper translation process is applied, it can produce a set of translated tests that are construct-equivalent, reliable, and relatively valid and fair. However, even when all steps are taken to ensure the quality of translation and the comparability of scores, it is still not possible to assure that the original and translated versions are indeed fully equivalent. Yet the alternative of testing non-Hebrew speakers in Hebrew would seem to constitute a much less fair solution. Moreover, parameters related to cost-effectiveness and overall expected utility gains should be considered as well (e.g., weighing the costs associated with further improving the current process).

ACKNOWLEDGMENTS

We wish to thank Maya Bar-Hillel, Gershon Ben-Shakhar, Ruth Fortus, Chava Kassel and Jerry Levinson for their insightful comments, and Shmuel Bronner for his assistance in the data analysis.

REFERENCES

Allalouf, A., Bastari, B., Hambleton, R. K., & Sireci, S. G. (1997). *Comparing the dimensionality of a test administered in two languages* (Laboratory of Psychometric and Evaluative Research Rep. No. 319). Amherst, University of Massachusetts, School of Education.

Allalouf, A., Hambleton, R. K., & Sireci, S. G. (1999). Identifying the causes of DIF in translated verbal items. *Journal of Educational Measurement, 36*(3), 185–198.

Angoff, W. H. (1972, August). *A technique for the investigation of cultural differences.* Paper presented at the meeting of the American Psychological Association, Honolulu. (ERIC Document Reproduction Service No. ED 069686)

Angoff, W. H., & Cook, L. L. (1988). *Equating the scores of the Prueba de Aptitud Academica and the Scholastic Aptitude Test* (College Board Rep. No. 88-2). New York: College Entrance Examination Board.

Angoff , W. H., & Modu, C. C. (1973). *Equating the scales of the Prueba de Aptitud Academica and the Scholastic Aptitude Test* (Research Rep. No. 3). New York: College Entrance Examination Board.

Beller, M. (1994). Psychometric and social issues in admissions to Israeli universities. *Educational Measurement: Issues and Practice, 13*(2), 12–20.

Beller, M., & Gafni, N. (1995). Translated scholastic aptitude tests. In G. Ben-Shakhar & A. Lieblich (Eds.), *Studies in psychology* (pp. 202–219). Jerusalem: The Hebrew University, The Magnes Press.

Beller, M., Gafni, N., & Hanani, P. (1999, June). *Constructing, adapting, and validating admissions tests in multiple languages.* An invited paper presented at the International Conference on Adapting Tests for Use in Multiple Languages and Cultures, Georgetown University, Washington, DC.

Darlington, R. B. (1971). Another look at "cultural fairness." *Journal of Educational Measurement, 8,* 71–82.

Gafni, N., & Bronner, S. (1998, April). *An examination of criterion-related bias for Hebrew- and Russian-speaking examinees in Israel.* Paper presented at the meeting of the American Educational Research Association, San Diego.

Gafni, N., & Canaan-Yehoshafat, Z. (1993). *An examination of deferential item functioning for Hebrew and Russian-speaking examinees in Israel.* Paper presented at the 24th Annual Conference of the Israeli Psychological Association, Ramat-Gan.

Gafni, N., & Melamed, E. (1994). Differential tendencies to guess as a function of gender and lingual-cultural reference group. *Studies in Educational Evaluation, 20,* 309–319.

Grisay, A. (2003). Translation procedures in OECD/PISA 2000 international assessment. *Language Testing, 20*(2), 225–240.

Hambleton, R. K. (1994). Guidelines for adapting educational and psychological tests: A progress report. *European Journal of Psychological Assessment, 10,* 224–229.

Linn, R. L. (1984). Selection bias: Multiple meanings. *Journal of Educational Measurement, 21,* 33–47.

Linn, R. L., & Werts, C. E. (1971). Considerations for studies of test bias. *Journal of Educational Measurement, 8*(1), 1–4.

Poortinga, Y. H. (1995). Cultural bias in assessment: Historical and thematic issues. *European Journal of Psychological Assessment, 11*(3), 140–146.

Sireci, S. G., & Allalouf, A. (2003). Appraising item equivalence across multiple languages and cultures. *Language Testing, 20*(2), 148–166.

13

Cross-Cultural Adaptation of Educational and Psychological Testing

Peter F. Merenda
University of Rhode Island

The field of educational and psychological testing and assessment has been fraught with many faulty practices that have resulted in many serious consequences. Unfortunately, psychologists and allied professionals, in general, have failed to recognize the seriousness of the problems created by the misuse of tests and testing. Notable among one of the foremost errors that has been committed is the application and interpretation of assessment instruments indiscriminately to testees for whom language barriers and other cultural factors invalidate the testing process. Most pronounced perhaps has been the misuse of instruments transculturally in the misinterpretation of scores resulting from the application of assessments that are not appropriate to the receiving (target) culture.

During the past nearly 50 years that have transpired since these faulty practices were first initiated on a large scale worldwide, many psychometricians, cross-cultural and international psychologists, as well as textbook authors have written extensively on the pitfalls to avoid and the proper methods of culturally adapting measurement instruments (see, e.g., Behling & Law, 2000; Hambleton & de Jong, 2003; van de Vijver & Leung, 1997). Among these have been, to name only a few more, Berry (1997), Brislin, Lonner, and Thorndike (1973),

Cronbach and Drenth (1972), Geissinger (1994), Olmedo (1979), Poortinga (1995), and Sperber, Develles, and Boehlecke (1994).

Other problems that are not often discussed in the issues related to the transfer of assessment instruments across cultures are the rather naive assumptions in the receiving culture that: (a) instruments that are reliable, valid, and suitable in one culture will be quite readily adaptable to other different cultures; and (b) ignoring the fact that these same instruments may likely not be psychometrically sound in the originating culture as they are assumed to be (Merenda, 1994). The latter statement (b) applies to some of the most highly respected and widely adapted/transferred instruments across cultures (Merenda, 1990a).

In this chapter, a brief history—mainly throughout the early years of the 20th century—of test adaptations for the purpose of overcoming language barriers in both the United States and abroad is presented. The major portion of the chapter presents experiences and problems encountered by the author in nearly 40 years of constructing educational and psychological assessment instruments in the United States, and conducting extensive research in adapting them to foreign cultures. An outline of proper procedures in adapting instruments is also presented (also, see, Hambleton & Patsula, 1999; van de Vijver & Leung, 1997).

CROSS-CULTURAL ADAPTATION IN EDUCATIONAL AND PSYCHOLOGICAL TESTING

One of the most ineffective and dangerous practices in the field of educational testing and psychological assessment during the last half century, which continues to the present day, is the improper transporting of measurement instruments from one culture to another culture or subculture (Merenda, 1993). The faulty practice involves borrowing a test from one culture and adopting it in another. Note that the emphasis is on adopting not adapting it in another culture. Typically this involves only literal translation more often than not, merely forward rather than both forward and backward translation, and as is clear from other chapters in this volume, empirical verification is needed too. Though test translation may be followed by attempts at renorming, one more common practice is simply to interpret test scores based on the original norms. Adapting the items to the receiving culture, restandardizing the administration and scoring procedures, and confirmation of the structure of the constructs being measured are rarely given the consideration required in adapting a test for use in a different language, according to sound psychometric principles (American Educational Research Association, American Psychological Association., National Council on the Measurement of Education, 1999).

BRIEF HISTORY OF THE CULTURAL ADAPTATION OF TESTS

Early attempts to construct assessment instruments to overcome lack of proficiency in the language of the culture/subculture and/or the biasing effects of other factors that influence performance can be traced to the beginning of the 20th century. One of the major efforts in the United States was made during World War I with the Army Beta. This test was developed by psychologists assigned to The Corps of Sanitary Engineers, a special army unit commanded by Major R. M. Yerkes, who directed the test development process.

The Army Beta test was designed to evaluate recruits who were either illiterate or understood only foreign languages. It consisted mainly of pictures and diagrams that required very little or no knowledge of the English language, and included performance subtests such as mazes, block designs, and geometric constructions. The Beta was used extensively by the Army in 1917–1918, along with the verbal Army Alpha test.

Historically the Army Alpha and Beta were group-administered operationally in the United States on a large scale. Earlier, as early as 1904, form board performance tests that required no knowledge of the English language had been developed and used on a much smaller scale. Of special historical significance, perhaps due to the fame of its originator and user, was the form board developed by R. S. Woodworth. In 1904, he administered this test at the World's Fair in St. Louis to young children who did not speak English. Later, in a study of racial differences, he used and published the results with the form board and other performance tests (Woodworth, 1910).

Prior to the entrance of the United States in World War I (1917–1918), H. A. Knox (1914) realized the limitations and danger in testing immigrants at Ellis Island for possible mental defects with instruments developed in the English language in the United States. He set out to develop tests that required no English-language responses. The principal form board test that Knox developed was the Casuist Form Board. It was a more complex version of the more well-known Sequin Form Board and consisted mainly of wooden circles and partitioned circles. Also developed by Knox was a form board in which the testee was required to reproduce a pattern tapped out on a set of cubes. During the same decade (1910–1919) a number of similar developments took place. Healy and Fernald (1911) tested children at the Chicago Juvenile Psychopathic Institute who either spoke only a foreign language or had handicaps that prevented them from responding to the regular tests that were available at the time. Among the nonverbal tests that they used was a version of the Ebbinghaus Picture Completion Test.

In 1911, Rudolph Pintner and Donald Paterson were also beginning to develop their well-known and widely used Scale of Performance Tests. This scale, which was the first test developed for clinical use, was published and made available for operational use a few years later (Pintner & Paterson, 1917). It consisted of 15 tests of which 8 were nonverbal. Among the performance tests in the battery was the Sequin jig saw puzzles, a picture completion test, and an imitation test.

During the second decade of the 20th century, Stanley Porteus was developing his famous maze tests, which were first published in the middle of the decade (Porteus, 1915). At the beginning of the next decade Kohs (1920) developed the Kohs Block Design Test, which has endured to this day as part of a number of performance scales and intelligence tests developed in the United States and "borrowed" by other cultures. The development of nonverbal tests was followed by the Goodenough (1926) "Draw-a-Man" test for measuring intelligence of children, ages 3–13 years. The children were asked to "make a picture of a man; make the best picture you can." Scoring was in terms of how many important parts of a man, such as eyes, fingers, nose, mouth, and so on, were included in a child's drawing. No importance was attached to artistic quality of the drawing. Norms based on 4,000 children led to the derivation of mental age (MA) and intelligence quotient (IQ). In later years, it was further developed as a measure for diagnosing psychopathology in abnormal children.

DEVELOPMENTS OUTSIDE THE UNITED STATES

The first major effort outside the United States to develop an instrument that was not culturally biased, and in which written or oral language was held to a minimum, or even eliminated, is the universally administered Raven Progressive Matrices (Raven, 1938). Today, as it was used in Great Britain 50 years ago, the Progressive Matrices continues to be one of the most popular nonverbal assessment tools being administered throughout the world where large-scale assessment programs exist.

On the European Continent, a unique nonverbal test was being developed in Italy, during World War II. The Bedini Test of Distributed Attention was designed to measure a person's ability to focus attention on a task that must be performed very quickly, and then to shift that attention to a reverse task (Migliorino, 1947). The Bedini Test is useful in diagnosing possible brain damage or damage to the nervous system. The color coding of dots and lines is the key factor in test performance. The primary deterrents to successful performance are mostly physical (impaired vision and color-blindness). The Bedini test has been recently researched in the United States for the purpose of developing a standardized and validated instrument for use in the North American culture (Merenda & DiLeonardo, 1992).

Another Italian nonverbal test (Test "G"; Calvi, 1970) is used for assessing a person's conceptual reasoning ability. This test produces a single-factor measure of general intelligence that may be interpreted as a Total IQ or Spearman's "g," which is still available for operational use from Organizzazione Speciali. Calvi's Test "G" was designed for use in Italy where dominoes are well known and game sets are quite common in households within the country. The underlying concepts are deemed to be universally adaptable to any culture. Although a verbal set of instructions accompanies the test, it can be given in pantomime.

The test consists of series of faces of dominoes, each of which represents some inferred logical sequence. The testee is required to choose from among options in multiple-choice format, the correct face that completes the sequence. The accompanying manual and technical publications are readily translatable in the language of the receiving culture but it would still be necessary for the receiving culture to reestablish the psychometric properties of the test.

The items in the Calvi test are spiraled; that is, they are presented to the testee in increasing order of difficulty. Two very easy items are presented early in the sequence of items, which become increasingly more complex, and hence more difficult.

TESTING DEVELOPMENTS IN THE UNITED STATES DURING WORLD WAR II

During World War I the army psychologists developed two separate tests for recruits: (a) Army Alpha, a verbal quantitative test for classifying English-speaking, literate volunteers and drafters; (b) Army Beta for illiterate and/or foreign-speaking men. In World War II, no attempt was made on a large scale to accommodate soldiers and sailors who were handicapped by lack of language proficiency. Each of the military services, Navy, Army, and Army Airforce—later to become the U.S. Airforce after the war ended—had its own servicewide testing programs. The Navy developed a classification test battery for enlisted personnel. The battery consisted of a General Classification Test (GCT), Arithmetic Test (ARITH), Clerical Test (CLER), and Mechanical Test (MECH). The Army Airforce developed a battery of special aptitude and psychomotor tests for selecting trainees for three aircrew assignments: pilot, bombadier, and navigator. The Army developed the Army General Classification Test (AGCT), which yielded an overall standard score based on a scale with mean (M) = 100 and standard deviation (SD) = 20. The subtests of the AGCT measured reading, vocabulary, arithmetic computation, arithmetic reasoning, and spatial relations. Beside its use for classifying army recruits into occupational specialties, selecting those who earned a score of at least 1 standard deviation above the mean (120+), for officer training. But no attempt was made during the course of the war to develop an updated and modernized version of the Army Beta of World War I. The Army never explained publically why no test parallel to the Beta was developed during World War II. Data gathered and analyzed by the Social Science Research Council and published under its sponsorship clearly demonstrate the need for such a test. The AGCT categorized personnel into five levels on the basis of total score. The lowest categories (IV and V) were populated mainly by Blacks and Hispanics (Stouffer et al., 1950).

However, after the war, the Personnel Research Division of the U.S. Army Adjudant's Office in Washington, DC, signed a contract with the Educational Research Corporation in Cambridge, Massachusetts, to develop several alternate forms of a nonverbal test to replace the obsolete Army Beta. The president of ERC, a private reseach facility, was Phillip Rulon, Professor of Measurement and Statistics at the Harvard Graduate School of Education. Many of Dr. Rulon's students worked with him in fulfilling the provisions of the contract. In 1952 (Rulon, 1953) the Semantic Test of Intelligence (STI) was delivered to the Army. This nonverbal instrument was designed to assess a person's conceptual reasoning ability. In the test's administration, the testee is taught by pantomime the meaning of certain of related universal symbols, both concrete and abstract. Its construction was based on the principle of "culture saturated" as opposed to "culture fair." A combination of figures in plane geometry, for example, squares, circles, diamonds, and triangles, are related to black silhouettes of animals or to a human female in action or at rest, for example, jumping or supine stance. Published for use in the U.S. Army, the test has never been published in a civilian edition, as was the Army General Classification Test. Rulon had intended that the Army would release one of the forms to him for publication by the

Educational Research Corporation after he retired from Harvard University in 1967. But unfortunately he died in the spring of 1968 before he and his associates could publish a civilian edition.

DEVELOPMENTS AFTER THE END OF WORLD WAR II

Educational and psychological assessment instruments (tests, scales, and inventories) in the cognitive and affective domains began to be used on a wide scale shortly after the end of World War II. The instruments were developed mainly in the United States, Great Britain, and France, where widespread use of educational and psychological assessment expanded most rapidly. In the 1950s and 1960s, the growth of psychology as an academic discipline accelerated in the United States and professional practice was introduced and expanded, stimulating great interest in assessment. In undeveloped countries, due to the expertise and financial expense required for the development of assessment instruments, psychologists and other professionals in those countries began "borrowing" and transporting assessment instruments developed and standardized in an outside culture. Unfortunately, the primary and often the only procedure of such transfer from one culture to another was simple language translation. To a great extent the faulty practices continue to this day. In many cases, little or no attention is given to cultural differences that must be considered in the modification or replacement of items, nor to restandardization, renorming, and the equivalence of scores and protocols.

To clarify the previous statement, perhaps the point should be made that the faulty practices occur in the less developed or developing countries; in Europe, principally the nations in the Mediterranean regions. The countries north of the Alps, and the Scandanavian countries are essentially well informed and practice sound psychometric principles. And The Netherlands is producing a great number of well-trained psychometricians who are practicing on a worldwide scale. As one example, I checked three issues of *Psychometrika* (December 1998 to September 1999) and found that of 25 published articles, 13 were written by psychometricians from The Netherlands.

In the United States, diversity in cultural and ethnic populations also greatly increased in the 1950s and 1960s. Following the enactment of the first affirmative action laws in 1964, test publishers sought to have educational and psychological assessment instruments previously published in English translated into the language of minorities. This was especially true for Hispanic populations, particularly Chicano, Puerto Rican, and Cuban-speaking schoolchildren. There are, however, many psychometric problems with these Spanish and other foreign-language editions, because most of them are simple literal translations, not culturally adapted in compliance with sound psychometric procedures.

To confirm that this faulty and misleading practice continues in the United States among the leading test publishers, one merely has to study the current catalogs advertising for sale foreign-language versions of the English-language tests. With few exceptions, the foreign-language versions are primarily, or merely, literally translated replicas of the original instruments.

PROCEDURES FOR ADAPTING INSTRUMENTS

Appropriate procedures for adapting instruments across cultures are briefly outlined in this chapter and fully described and explained in other chapters of this book and in other publications (e.g., van de Vijver & Leung, 1997). These extensive and lengthy procedures account for the great costs in terms of money, time, and effort of proper adaptation. It is not unusual for the procedures, in order to be effective, to require several years of concentrated effort. These efforts should be assumed jointly by professionals in both the originating and receiving nations. The procedures are as follows:

1. An initial step is to seriously consider instruments, techniques, or devices that would be amenable to adaptation. This consideration should involve an objective and dispassionate evaluation of the soundness of the psychometric properties of the measures in the originating culture. A pitfall to avoid is to assume soundness simply on the basis of their popularity and wide-use.
2. Before proceeding to the translation step, thoroughly review the items and response formats from the standpoint of emic (culture-specific) or etic (universal) approaches.
3. In the translation step, provide for both forward (direct) translation and backward translation. Care must be taken to ensure that the translators are expert in both languages and work independently of each other in the two stages. Furthermore, it must be recognized that dialects and variations in language uses may substantially influence the correctness of the translation, in terms of both connotation and denotation. This is especially true for Hispanics, for example, Spanish for Puerto Rican/Cuban versus Mexican-Chicano; Portuguese versus South American Portuguese, or French versus Canadian French.

4. Carefully study each item with regard to adaptability to the receiving culture. Invariably, some items will be found clearly not to be directly transferable. These may be modified, amended, or discarded and replaced before proceeding to the development of an experimental form for use in the first pilot study.

5. Conduct a pilot study in which the experimental form will be administered according to cultural mores, practices, habits, and so on, to appropriate and sufficient stratified samples drawn from populations to which the measures are to be applied.

6. In analyzing the data yielded by the first administration of the experimental form, an early step to take, if applicable and warranted, is to study the structure and pattern (factor or component) of the instrument and compare it to that of the original (see, Gierl, 2000, for one example). (At this point the experimenters may decide that it is necessary to repeat some of the earlier steps before proceeding further.)

7. If the decision is that it is permissible to continue with steps toward developing the adapted form, the next step is to perform the necessary statistical analyses required for establishing the psychometric properties of the culturally adapted instrument. At this point, as a minimum, what should be calculated are the internal consistency coefficients of items, reliability coefficients of scores, and the norms.

8. A last step in the development of the experimental form would be to conduct some construct and criterion-related validity studies consistent with the purposes for which the instrument is intended to be used in the receiving culture. Positive validity research results would provide potential users and new publishers/distributors in the receiving cultures with realistic confidence that a new fully developed, culturally adapted instrument is likely ready for operational use.

The set of eight steps are very much in line with the International Test Commission Test Adaptation Guidelines introduced in chapter 1 of this volume (and expanded on by Hambleton & Patsula, 1999).

EXAMPLES OF PROCEDURES USED IN THE DEVELOPMENT OF ADAPTED INSTRUMENTS EXPERIENCED BY THE AUTHOR OVER A 28-YEAR PERIOD (1967–1995)

The instruments that have been culturally adapted were used primarily in one or more of three major cross-cultural research projects. These were: (a) Identification of Talent in Developing Countries, 1967–1977; (b) Identification of Young Children with Learning Problems, 1975–1995; and (c) Public Perception of International Leaders, 1964–1990. Each of the instruments was carefully translated from English to the language of the country in which the research was conducted.

A brief description of these instruments follows:

Activity Vector Analysis (AVA). An adjective checklist developed by Walter V. Clarke, AVA became operational in 1948, primarily for use in business and industry in the United States (Clarke, 1956). In the earlier forms, which were those used in the cross-cultural research studies, AVA consisted of 81 behaviorally descriptive adjectives that yield scores on four scales and three four-factor profiles designed to measure, respectively, a person's perception of the basic self, the social self, and a composite self. Its development was based on the underlying self theory of Lecky (1945) and the emotions theory of W. M. Marston (1928; Marston, W. M., King, & Marston, E. H., 1931).

Measurement of Skill (MOS). A battery of eight tests developed by Walter V. Clarke and his associates, the MOS was designed to assist personnel workers in the proper selection, classification, and assignment of employees. The instruments are short tests (5 to 7-minute time limits) that were developed to maximize validity per minute of testing. In this series of practical performance-cognitive tests, the skills that are measured are: (a) Vocabulary, (b) Numbers, (c) Shape, (d) Speed and Accuracy, (e) Orientation, (f) Thinking, (g) Memory, and (h) Finger Dexterity (Clarke, 1960).

Rhode Island Pupil Identification Scale (RIPIS). The RIPIS is a teacher rating scale designed to identify children in normal classrooms (K–2) who are experiencing difficulty in school progress for a variety of reasons. The scale consists of two parts. The 22 items of Part I are based on pupil classroom behaviors that can be observed or perceived by the teacher. The 19 items in Part II are based on academic performance records that the teacher has on file in each child's portfolio. There are five factors yielded by Part I in the original U.S. RIPIS: Body Perception, Sensory-Motor Coordination, Attention, Self-Concept, and Memory for Events. They account for 67.5% of the total variance. Four Part II factors—Memory for Reproduction of Symbols, Directional or Positional Constancy, Spatial and Sequential Arrangements, and Memory for Symbols for Cognitive Operations—account for 68% of the total variance (Novack, Bonaventura, & Merenda, 1972/1979).

Flanagan's Project Talent Inventories. Three of Flanagan's inventories were used in the cross-cultural research. They were: (a)

Interest Inventory, (b) Student Activities Inventory, and (c) Student Information Blank. The Interest Inventory consists of 205 items dealing with 122 occupations and activities in which students express interest on a 5-point rating scale. The Activities Inventory consists of 150 items to which the students respond on a 5-point rating scale to the statement, "Regarding the things I do and the way I do them, the statement describes me," from very well to not very well. The Student Information Blank consists of 394 carefully selected questions regarding the background, plans, and aspirations of high school students. It is divided into seven parts. Part I (k = 115) inquires about activities the students have participated in so far. Part II (k = 45) consists of questions referring to family and home. Parts III and IV (k = 35) refer to the nature of work performed by the student's parents or head of household, and other activities involving all members of the family. Part V (k = 42) refers to the health status of students. Part VI (k = 75) relates to the student's plans for the future. Part VII (k = 10) deals with future plans for matriculating at a university (Flanagan et al., 1964; Merenda & Migliorino, 1974).

Care was taken in each instance to ensure that the translations were appropriate for the language spoken by the population to which the instruments were adapted. For example: (a) the AVA adjectives were translated for different Spanish-speaking populations. Accordingly, three Spanish forms were developed: Castilian Spanish for use in Spain, Puerto Rican/Cuban Spanish for use in the Eastern United States, and Chicano Spanish for use in the Southwestern United States and Mexico. A similar process was employed in developing French forms. A Parisian French form was adapted for use in France, a French-Canadian form for use in Canada, and a modified French form for use in Senegal. Two Portuguese forms were developed, one for Portugal and the second for Brazil. The RIPIS has been translated in many different languages: Farsi (Iran), Mandarin Chinese (Taiwan), Polish (Poland), Danish (Denmark), Creole-French (Haiti), and Italian (Italy and Sicily). The Flanagan inventories were only translated in formal (Tuscan) Italian. Although those instruments were used in a major research project conducted in Sicily, and only formal Italian is the language employed in all schools throughout Italy, it was unnecessary to resort to the Sicilian language.

Despite the great care that was exercised in the translation phase of the adaptation process, many problems arose, some more serious than others. The most serious and costly one was one that occurred in the adaptation of the RIPIS in Italy. The Italian version of the RIPIS was first researched by D'Amico and his associates (D'Amico, Merenda, &

Sparacino, 1982). In the original U.S. RIPIS, the third factor, Attention, in Part I, is composed of three items: (#9, "Difficulty in sitting still"; #10, "Difficulty in standing still"; and #11, "Has short attention span"). Principal component analysis with varimax rotation revealed that most of the factors/components overlapped with the U.S. structure of the scale. However, a strange result was also revealed for Attention factor. Items 9, 10, and 11 failed to join the cluster, but two other items (#15, "Cries"; #16, "Fails to take reprimands well") loaded heavily in the cluster. In the U.S. RIPIS, Items 15 and 16 occur in the Self-Concept factor (.73 and .61) respectively (Novack, Bonaventura, & Merenda, 1972/1979). This serious discrepancy led to a replication of the study with a new sample of 1,571 schoolchildren in Grades K–2 in four schools in Palermo, Sicily. A fault was discovered in the translation from English to Italian for Items 9, 10, and 15. The sense of Items 9 and 10 was to measure that pupils may have difficulty in remaining standing or sitting once they have assumed that position whereas the translation, agreed upon by the four perfectly bilingual translators (2 forward, 2 backward) directed the teachers' response to the act of standing or sitting still. Item 15 was made more explicit by adding the word, *frequently*. Clarification of the intended meaning of the items was successful in bringing Items 9 and 10 together (.91 and .93, respectively, but further research was required in order to produce a fully adapted instrument). This was finally achieved in 1995, 20 years after the initial research was conducted in Italy!

A third sample (N = 1,311) was drawn in Palermo in four schools in Grades K–2. The Italian RIPIS is now a fully adapted modified version of the U.S. RIPIS (Sprini, Cardica, & Gangemi, 1992). In 1995, it became operational in Italy, and is distributed by the major Italian publisher, Organizzazioni Speciali,, in Florence.

In developing foreign-language forms of the AVA, it was necessary to replace adjectives with other grammatical structure, for example, adverbs, gerunds, and so on. It was not that a literal translation of an adjective did not exist, but rather that the translated often had very different meanings in the receiving target language. For example, in French, *gregarious* became "aime de vivre en groupe"—loves to live in a group (idiomatic). In Italian, *appealing* became "pieno di fascino"—full of charm. In Portuguese, *self-conscious* became "consciente de mim mesmo"—conscious of one's self. Much of the research with adjectives on the AVA was begun in 1957 in the United States and in 1967 was begun to be conducted in the many foreign countries in which the adjective checklist was being adapted for research purposes.

In addition to ensure both proper translation and the cultural content of items, an effective procedure to follow in the cultural adaptation of assessment instruments is to alter the administration of procedures to better ones if they are amenable in the target culture and are confirmed by developmental research data. Such an incident is reported in Merenda, Maio, Guadagnoli, and Yu-Wen (1984). The original scale (Novack, Bonaventura, & Merenda, 1972/1979) and all of the foreign forms except the Chinese form had classroom teachers base their ratings at the end of each month on their perceptions of each pupil's behavior in addition to documents of classroom performance in each of their respective portfolios. In planning the development of the Chinese form, Emily Miao convinced me that in Taiwan it would be possible and more appropriate to have each classroom teacher initiate and actually observe and record the pupil's response to the relevant items at the end of each month rather than depend on perceptual recall. This is what was done and proved to be successful in developing the operational Chinese form of the RIPIS. Such items were, for example, "Has difficulty catching a ball"; "Has difficulty jumping rope"; "Has difficulty remembering what is shown."

In the cultural adaptation process of adapting the several instruments in English to the language and culture of many different countries for inclusion in cross-cultural research projects between 1967 and 1995, unexpected and unpredictable incidents occurred. Regardless of the careful steps taken, as previously discussed, they did not always prevent problems that required correction from occuring. Project Talent for Sicily, which was initiated in 1967, in my first Fulbright year at the Laboratory of Applied Psychology, University of Palermo, was devoted to developing a test battery to identify the latent talents of Sicilian youth.

In the talent identification phase of the Project, the principal data were gathered on a battery of translated instruments, which included the Skill With Vocabulary (MOS-1) Test. This test presents to the testee a brief dictionary definition of a word plus the first letter of the word followed by a number of blank spaces equal to the number of letters required to complete the word. One of these items in the original U.S. form reads: "Money, especially ready money; currency or equivalent, paid promptly after purchasing." The correct response in English is cash. In the scoring key for the Italian form, it was indicated by "c," an eight-letter word beginning with *c*. The Italian equivalent to *cash* is *contanti*, and was expected to be as well known to high school students in Italy as *cash* is to junior high and high school students in the United States (Merenda, Clarke, & Jacobsen, 1965; Merenda, Hall, Clarke, & Pascale, 1962; Merenda, Jacobsen, & Clarke, 1966).

The tests in the MOS Battery were all spiral tests. When the item analysis on MOS-1 was performed with the Italian data, this particular item revealed a high difficulty level; that is, the *p* value of the item was low, contrasted to the high *p* value that was known to exist for U.S. samples. Subsequent review of the individual responses revealed that as many of the Italian students wrote *cambiale* as wrote the correct response in the scoring key. It was merely a coincidence that *cambiale* is an eight-letter word beginning with *c*. Although the word does not fit the dictionary definition, it was recognized immediately that cambiale had to be considered a correct response. Hence, with two correct responses to the item in the Italian form, the *p* value was increased to match that in the U.S. form. In the Italian culture in the 1960s, before credit cards were introduced in Italy, using cambiale was a way of life, especially among working-class people. They are analogous to scrip money and were used as cash if the person did not have the cash on hand to pay for the purchase. In Italy in those days, a person could go to the bank, just so long as he or she was gainfully employed and had no history of defaulting on payments to the bank, and be issued cambiale in the amount of the purchase. Hence, cambiale were equivalent to cash. Cambiale have now been mostly replaced by bank credit cards as well as American Express, MasterCard, and VISA. So if the Italian MOS-1 were to be used today, the scoring key would necessarily indicate that there is only one correct response, contanti.

In the initial attempts to develop an adapted Persian (Farsi) version of the RIPIS, during the data-processing step of performing factor analysis of the teachers ratings of children in Iran, the computer suddenly stopped. Upon investigation, it was discovered that item 25, "Turns in papers which show many erasures," was faulty. It simply was inappropriate for the sample that provided the data for the pilot study. At the point of generating the correlation matrix, no correlation coefficients could be calculated between this item and all the remaining items because it possessed zero variance. The responses of all the teachers to this item were "Never," which was assigned a scaled score of 1 point. Hence, the ratings for the item yielded a mean of 1 and a standard deviation of 0. In analyzing the cause of this unusual result with my Iranian collaborator, it was determined that in the particular schools in Iran from which the samples were drawn (Grades K–2), pencils with erasers were not used. Instead paint brushes were used in teaching these very young children to begin learning the Farsi language. However, not all schools in Iran followed the same method of teaching writing as these schools did. It was simply an unforeseen coincidence; the sample was an intended stratified one, representative of young schoolchildren drawn from state schools ranging from a socioeconomically deprived district to a private school in an upper-class district (Merenda, 1990b).

The problems that were experienced by the adaptive test development researchers were quickly understood by them and corrective action was taken. They are described here to illustrate what can and does happen even when all the necessary steps are taken to properly adapt instruments to a new culture. When translation is the only step taken in transporting instruments from one culture to another—no matter how accurately and effectively it is accomplished—incidents such as these do occur and go undetected. In order to properly adapt tests, substantial psychometric data must be gathered, analyzed, and explained.

ANOTHER REAL-LIFE EXPERIENCE

Before proceeding to the most serious and regretable occurences caused by faulty practices in transferring assessment instruments from one culture to another simply through translation, often faulty as well, the following incident is described: In the early 1970s, I served on an advisory board of the Scuola per i super-dotati (School for the super-gifted) in Petralia Sopranna, Sicily. The other members of the board were Scarvia Anderson, Samuel Messick, Miriam Goldberg, Margaret Mead, and her doctoral student, Josephine Danna. The school had been founded by the local priest of this Sicilian mountain town, Rev. Calogero LaPlaca. Through his untiring efforts, Father LaPlaca was able to obtain sufficient external funding to provide not only free education, but also room and board for the gifted children, and to annually expand the school's facilities. In identifying and selecting potential gifted students for each future class, Father LaPlaca would spend a good part of each year visiting schools throughout the island, and ask each principal to allow him to talk to the one student who in the principal's judgment was considered to be the very best. Father LaPlaca would then talk to the student, and if the student was interested in attending the "Scuola," he would then talk with the parents to convince them to allow their child to leave their own home town or city to become a student in the school for the gifted.

As it was my custom to spend my summers in Sicily working on my own research project at the University of Palermo, Father LaPlaca always looked forward to spending a few hours or days in consultation with me. One summer, during our first meeting that year, he immediately separated me from my wife and placed me in another car on our way to lunch, with another priest. It so happened that Father LaPlaca was deeply disturbed and wanted me to consult with the priest on what he had just reported to Father LaPlaca. The priest, who had taken a course at the University of Rome on the administration, scoring, and interpretation of the new Italian form of the Wechsler Intelligence Scale for Children, had recently tested all of the currently enrolled students at the school. With the exception of one "super-gifted" student who attained a total IQ of 108, all the other children fell in the borderline-dull/normal ranges (70s to 90s). Needless to say, I spent most of the automobile drive to the restaurant explaining to the two priests the fallacy of testing Italian children with a test developed, standardized, and normed in the United States, and simply translated into the Italian language. What had been translated were not only the items but the scoring procedures and how to determine scale scores, IQs, and qualitative description of intelligence ranges according to U.S. norms. Hence, the results were about what I would have expected and predicted!

MOST SERIOUS AND REGRETTABLE OCCURRENCES

The problems previously cited as examples of what were experienced over a long period of cross-cultural research in adapting test instruments were serious, but not devastating. Although they delayed the progress toward successful adaptation, and the developmental costs in terms of time, money, and effort were substantially increased, the problems were eventually resolved. However, other problems for which there was no immediate remedy caused the researchers much more than delay. These underlying causes were: (a) simply translating an instrument from the original language to another, and (b) assuming that the original instrument was psychometrically sound and/or sound psychometric properties would transfer from the originating to the receiving culture. The consequences were devastating to all who were involved in these incidents. Let me explain.

In early 1982, Leandro Almeida, Assistant in the Department of Psychology and Educational Sciences at the University of Porto, Portugal, was a doctoral student at the University of Louvain, Belgium. His major professor and dissertation supervisor was George Meuris, author of the *Meuris Differential Reasoning Test Battery*. Almeida, who later was to become a leading psychologist in Portugal and author of an adapted Portuguese version (Almeida, 1988), came to the

United States seeking consultation in psychological testing and psychometrics. He selected three of us to consult: Robert Rosenthal (Harvard), Robert Sternberg (Yale), and Peter Merenda (University of Rhode Island). He arrived first in Cambridge but learned that Rosenthal was on sabbatical leave and not available. He then sought me out in Providence before traveling to New Haven to consult with Sternberg. Thus began a long professional relationship that continues to this day.

In 1984, I took early retirement from the University of Rhode Island. The main reason why I retired early was to accept short-term appointments at universities abroad to teach psychometrics to psychology faculty members who were required to conduct substantive research in order to retain their positions and/or be advanced in rank. From 1984 to 1993, my principal assignments were in Portugal at the Universities of Lisbon, Porto, and Minho. During that period, as in other Mediterranean countries, for example, Italy and Greece, universities awarded only one degree—the Baccalaureate degree. Institutes or departments of psychology were staffed by either a single professor, or very few professors. The major responsibilities for teaching students rested with "Assistants" who primarily possessed the Baccalaureate in Psychology. In Portugal, there were two levels of Assistant, A and B (now comparable to assistant professor and associate professor). It was the approved research that was required in order to advance from Level A to Level B. Unsuccessful Assistants were dismissed from the university faculty and were destined to become high school teachers, at best. Therefore, acceptable research projects that could be completed and successfully defended assumed the highest priority to be accomplished by a Level A Assistant.

My short-term courses of instruction mainly involved teaching multivariate statistics, research methodology, factor analysis, psychometric methods, and computer-processing courses similar to those I had taught in the United States. In addition to teaching formal courses while I was in Portugal, I met regularly with the Assistants to review with them their research proposals and to advise them. On many of these occasions, I had strong reservations about the projects they were undertaking. It was the practice of the Assistants to select an assessment instrument in an area in psychology in which she or he was interested in conducting research and simply translate it into Portuguese. The sampling procedures in the research and the statistical methods employed in analyzing the data based on instruments that had been translated (mainly from English to Portuguese) were generally proper and accurate. However, in some cases, after months of hard work and personal expense, disaster occurred. When I returned to Portugal the following year or later, I would often find several Assistants who were anxiously awaiting my return. The problem underlying the anxiety was that the output of the analysis of data made little or no sense, neither to the researchers nor to their supervisors. More often than not, there were problems related to confirmation of the factor structure, the translated Portuguese version of an instrument, or often the lack of meaningful structure.

Two examples of such experiences, which were disappointing and frustrating to me and distressful to the researcher, are discussed:

1. An Assistant in Psychology at a university in Portugal, who was pursuing a Ph.D. degree at a university in France, had completed a substantial portion of her doctoral research. She had written a number of chapters in her dissertation, but was having considerable difficulty in explaining the voluminous data that she had processed while in France as a full-time doctoral student. With these ambiguous data she had waited anxiously for me to arrive to take up my teaching and advising duties in her faculty. To my disappointment and to her chagrin, it did not take long to discover the basis of the problem. The assessment instruments, which were evaluated by exploratory factor analysis methods, were faulty because they had not been properly and fully culturally adapted. Singular matrices were involved in the analyses so that negative, latent roots (eigenvalues) were extracted. In order for a correlation matrix to be legitimately factor analyzed, it must possess the property of being "gramian." A gramian matrix is one that is symmetrical and whose eigenvalues are all positive and near or at zero as a minimum. Such matrices are called "positive semi-definite" or "positive definite." All other matrices are known as singular matrices and should not be factored by any method of factor analysis. If a singular matrix is subjected to factor analysis, negative eigenvalues will be yielded and the results will not satisfy the basic equation for factor analysis (Merenda, 1997; Tatsuoka, 1971). Therefore, the factor analysis outputs revealed absolutely no structure for the instruments. The factor loadings for most items were in the .20s or less and many were near zero. These results made it impossible for me to advise her how the instruments could be modified and scored for renorming.

2. This case involved an Assistant who had previously been a student of mine, when I had previously helped her complete a major research project successfully, which had helped earn her a promotion in rank. She was again enrolled in one of my classes, had just completed another research project, and was vying for another

promotion. In the data-processing phase of her research, she was able to explain much of the data that had been analyzed, but was puzzled by the findings of a questionnaire from a culture outside of Portugal, which were basic to the main hypotheses of the study. These data were related to responses she had gathered by surveying mothers of schoolchildren, door-to-door. In modifying her questionnaire for adaptation to the Portuguese culture, she had followed my previous instructions to properly translate the items, and to change the item response format from dichotomous scoring to interval scaling of ratings on either 5-point or 7-point intervals. Unfortunately, the results were uninterpretable. I suspected that the intercorrelation matrices were not appropriate for factor analysis because they failed to possess the required properties. They, as in Example 1, were not nonsingular Gramian matrices (Merenda, 1997; Tatsuoka, 1971). Upon inspection of the computer output listings of the eigenvalues, they all produced some negative eigenvalues. What had caused the intercorrelation matrices to be distorted? The answer lay in the inspection of the 5-point and 7-point item response scale distributions. Some were disjointed; others were incomplete or severely and excessively skewed with obvious floor or ceiling effects. Either the items in the questionnaire were not culturally adapted, or possibly the original questionnaire was not psychometrically sound. There was no alternative for the researcher but to sacrifice 2 years of intensive research in endeavoring to adapt the questionnaire and to start all over again!

REFERENCES

Almeida, L. S. (1988). *Oraciocinio differencial dos jovens* [A reasoning differential test for juveniles]. Porto, Portugal: Instituto Nacional de Investigacas Cientifica.

American Educational Research Association, American Psychological Association, and National Council of Measurement in Education. (1999). *Standards for educational and psychological testing.* Washington, DC: American Educational Research Association.

Behling, O., & Law, K. S. (2000). *Translating questionnaires and other research instruments: Problems and solutions.* Thousand Oaks, CA: Sage.

Berry, J. W. (1997). Immigration, acculturation, and adaptation. *Applied Psychology: An International Review, 40,* 5–68.

Brislin, R. W., Lonner, W. J., & Thorndike, R. M. (1973). *Cross-cultural research methods.* New York: Wiley.

Calvi, G. (1970). *II Test G.* Firenze, Italy: Organizzazioni Speciali.

Clarke, W. V. (1956). The construction of an industrial selection personality test. *Journal of Psychology, 41,* 379–394.

Clarke, W. V. (1960). *Examiner's manual for the measurement of skill: A battery of practical placement tests.* Providence, RI: Walter V. Clarke Associates, Inc.

Cronbach, L. J., & Drenth, P. J. D. (Eds.). (1972). *Mental test and cultural adaptations.* The Hague, Netherlands: Mouton.

D'Amico, G., Merenda, P., & Sparacino, R. R. (1982). *Rhode Island Pupil Identification Scale (R.I.P.I.S.): Primo adattamento Italiano.* Palermo, Sicily: Stass.

Flanagan, J. C., Davis, F. B., Dailey, J. T., Shaycroft, M. F., Orr, D. B., Goldberg, I., & Neyman, C. A. (1964). *The American high school student* (Cooperative Research Project No. 635). Pittsburgh: Project Talent Office, University of Pittsburgh.

Geisinger, K. F. (1994). Cross-cultural normative assessment, translation and adaptation issues influencing the normative interpretation of assessment instruments. *Psychological Bulletin, 106,* 304–312.

Gierl, M. J. (2000). Construct equivalence on translated achievement tests. *Canadian Journal of Education, 25*(4), 280–296.

Goodenough, F. L. (1926). *Measurement of intelligence by drawings.* Yonkers, NY: World Book.

Hambleton, R. K., & de Jong, J. (Eds.). (2003). Advances in translating and adapting educational and psychological tests [special issue]. *Language Testing, 20*(2), 127–240.

Hambleton, R. K., & Patsula, L. (1999). Increasing the validity of adapted tests: Myths to be avoided and guidelines for improving test adaptation practices. *Journal of Applied Testing Technology, 1,* 1–13.

Healy, W., & Fernald, G. M. (1911). Tests for practical mental classification. *Psychological Monographs, 13* (Whole No. 54).

Knox, H. A. (1914). A scale based on the work at Ellis Island. *Journal of the American Medical Association, 62,* 741–747.

Kohs, S. C. (1920). The block-design tests. *Journal of Experimental Psychology, 3,* 357–376.

Lecky, P. (1945). *Self-consistency: A theory of personality.* New York: Island Press.

Marston, W. M. (1928). *Emotions of normal people.* New York: Harcourt.

Marston, W. M., King, C. D., & Marston, E. H. (1931). *Integrative psychology.* New York: Harcourt.

Merenda, P. F. (1990a). Present and future issues in psychological testing in the United States. *Evaluacion Psicologia/Psychological Assessment, 6,* 3–31.

Merenda, P. F. (1990b). The Rhode Island Pupil Identification Scale (RIPIS) in cross-cultural perspective. In L. L. Adler (Ed.), *Cross-cultural research at issue*. New York: Academic Press.

Merenda, P. F. (1993). Cross-cultural current and future issues in psychological testing. *International Journal of Group Tensions, 23,* 115–132.

Merenda, P. F. (1994). Cross-cultural testing: borrowing from one culture and applying it to another. In L. L. Adler & E. P. Gielen (Eds.), *Cross-cultural topics in psychology*. Westport, CT: Praeger

Merenda, P. F. (1997). A guide to the proper use of factor analysis in the conduct and reporting of research: Pitfalls to avoid. *Measurement and Evaluation in Counseling and Development, 30,* 156–164.

Merenda, P. F., Clarke, W. V., & Jacobsen, G. (1965). Relative predictive validities of the MOS and DAT batteries for junior high school students. *Psychological Reports, 16,* 151–154.

Merenda, P. F., & DiLeonardo, C. (1992). The American adaptation of the Bedini Test of Distributive Attention. In A. L. Comunian & U. P. Gielen (Eds.), *Advancing psychology and its applications: International perspectives*. Milan, Italy: Franco Angeli.

Merenda, P. F., Hall, C. E., Clarke, W. V., & Pascale, A. (1962). Relative predictive effeciency of the DAT and a short battery of tests. *Psychological Reports, 11,* 71–81.

Merenda, P. F., Jacobsen, G., & Clarke, W. V. (1966). Cross-validities of the MOS and DAT batteries. *Psychological Reports, 19,* 341–342.

Merenda, P. F., Maio, E., Guadagnoli, E., & Yu-Wen, H. (1984). *The Chinese form of the Rhode Island Pupil Identification Scale: Standardization and validation.* Providence, RI: AVA Publications.

Merenda, P. F., & Migliorino, G. (1974). Student information blank: Comparison between Sicilian and American responses. *Annali della facolta di Economia e Commercio, Dell' Universita' "di Palermo, 28,* 385–403.

Migliorino, G. (1947). Ricerca sulla strattura psicologica del reattivo di Bedini. *Rivista di Psicologia, 43,* 154–171.

Novack, H. S., Bonaventura, E., & Merenda, P. F. (1979). *Manual to accompany Rhode Island Pupil Identification Scale: A behavior observation identification scale: A behavior observation scale for the early detection of children with learning problems.* Providence, RI, Author. (Origianl work published 1972)

Olmedo, E. L. (1979). Acculturation: A psychometric perspective. *American Psychologist, 34,* 1061–1070.

Pintner, R., & Paterson, D. G. (1917). *A scale of performance tests.* New York: Appleton.

Poortinga, Y. (1995). Use of tests across cultures. In T. Oakland & R. K. Hambleton (Eds.), *International perspectives on academic assessment* (pp. 187–206). Boston: Kluwer.

Porteus, S. D. (1915). Mental tests for the feeble-minded: A new series. *Journal of Psycho-Asthenics, 19,* 200–213.

Raven, J. C. (1938). *Progressive matrices: A perceptual test of intelligence.* London: Lewis.

Rulon, P. J. (1953). *A semantic test of intelligence. Proceedings of 1952 Invitational Conference on Testing Problems.* Princeton, NJ: Educational Testing Service.

Sperber, A. D., Develles, R. F., & Boehlecke, B. (1994). Cross-cultural translation. *Journal of Cross-Cultural Psychology, 25,* 501–524.

Sprini, G., Cardica, M., & Gangemi, A. (1992). *The Italian form of the RIPIS scale: A format modifying proposal.* Palermo, Sicily, Italy: University of Palermo.

Stouffer, S. A., Guttman, L., Suchman, E. A., Lazarsfeld, P. F., Star, S. A., & Clausen, J. A. (1950). *Measurement and prediction.* Princeton, NJ: Educational Testing Service.

Tatsuoka, M. M. (1971). *Multivariate analysis: A technique for educational and psychological research.* New York: Wiley.

van de Vijver, F., & Leung, K. (1997). *Methods and data analysis for cross-cultural research.* Thousand Oaks, CA: Sage.

Woodworth, R. S. (1910). Race differences in mental tests. *Science N. S., 31,* 171–176.

14

Cross-Cultural Assessment of Emotional States and Personality Traits

Charles D. Spielberger, Manolete S. Moscoso, and Thomas M. Brunner
University of South Florida

In the introductory chapter to this volume, Hambleton reviews a wide range of general issues pertaining to the cross-cultural adaptation of measures of achievement, aptitude and personality. Important sources of error encountered in adapting tests are described, and guidelines for reducing error and enhancing test validity are offered (Hambleton, 1994; Hambleton & Patsula, 1999; van de Vijver & Hambleton, 1996). Three broad categories of issues and problems encountered in test adaptation are considered in detail in these publications: (a) cultural and language differences, (b) technical and methodological problems, and (c) factors that influence the interpretation of test results. Practical guidelines recently developed by the International Test Commission (ITC) for translating and adapting educational and psychological tests are also reported and discussed.

The ITC Test Adaptation Guidelines provide excellent recommendations of methods and procedures for the cross-cultural adaptation of educational and psychological tests. Following these guidelines is essential in adapting measures of achievement and aptitude to facilitate comparison of the relative performance of students from different languages and cultures. Whereas the ITC Test Adaptation

Guidelines are applicable to adapting all types of psychological tests, personality traits and emotional states are quite different from aptitudes and abilities (Anastasi, 1988). Emotional states and the behaviors that comprise personality traits are more subjective and less clearly defined than aptitudes, abilities, and achievement. Moreover, as Anastasi observed: "Even more than ability tests, personality tests can be expected to show large subcultural as well as cultural differences" (p. 532).

Differences in the interpretation of test instructions also contribute to problems in the cross-cultural adaptation of measures of emotions and personality. For example, Marsella and Leong (1995) observed that persons from non-Western cultures may be uncomfortable in giving true-or-false responses to the items of the Minnesota Multiphasic Personality Inventory (MMPI) because persons from collectivist cultures typically place greater emphasis on situational factors that influence their feelings and behavior. To illustrate this point, Marsella and Leong (1995) quoted a Filipino respondent to the MMPI who clearly expressed this concern: "Sir, sometimes true and sometimes false. I cannot tell you true or false all the time" (p. 208). Understanding such differences in the reactions to test instructions of respondents from different cultures requires knowledge of the special conditions and circumstances that are characteristic of a particular culture (Anastasi, 1988).

Construct equivalence is an essential requirement in the cross-cultural adaptation of all types of tests, and "care must be taken to choose situations, vocabulary, and expressions that will adapt easily across language groups and cultures" (Hambleton, see chap. 1, this volume). In adapting measures of personality and emotions, special attention must also be given to the state–trait distinction (Anastasi, 1988; Cattell & Scheier, 1960; Cohen, Swerdlik, & Smith, 1992, Lonner, 1990; Spielberger, 1966b), and to item intensity-specificity (Anastasi, 1988; Spielberger, Gorsuch, & Lushene, 1970). In assessing individual differences in personality traits, the relative frequency of occurrence of emotional states must also be evaluated (Spielberger, 1983, 1988).

The nonequivalence of constructs in different languages and cultures is perhaps the most serious source of error in adapting measures of personality and emotion, as was noted by Hambleton in the first chapter of this volume. Cross-cultural equivalence is especially difficult to obtain with measures of personality because there is, as yet, relatively little agreement in regard to the criteria for defining the fundamental personality dimensions (Cohen et al., 1992; Cronbach, 1990; Hall & Lindzey, 1970). For example, there is only limited coherence between measures of the clinical syndromes on which MMPI scale scores are based and the personality dimensions assessed by the MMPI. Recognition of this shortcoming has stimulated the development of the MMPI–2 Content Scales for assessing anxiety, fear, depression, anger, and other personality-related variables (Butcher, Graham, Williams, & Ben-Porath, 1989).

During the past 20 years, the so-called "big five" dimensions of personality have received substantial acceptance as fundamental personality constructs (e.g., Digman, 1990; Goldberg, 1981; John, 1990). However, Neuroticism, one of the big five personality dimensions assessed by the widely used NEO Personality Inventory (NEO PI–R: Costa & McCrae, 1992) and also by the Eysenck Personality Questionnaire (EPQ: Eysenck & Eysenck, 1975), is a highly complex heterogeneous construct composed of a number of more fundamental dimensions. This complexity was reflected in the identification of Anxiety, Anger-Hostility, and Depression, three of the six major *facets* of Neuroticism that are assessed by the NEO PI subscales (Costa & McCrae, 1992). These facets may be considered as major dimensions of the neuroticism syndrome.

This chapter focuses on relatively unique problems that are encountered in the cross-cultural adaptation of measures of emotion and personality. We first examine emotion and personality as psychological constructs. We then consider the cross-cultural equivalence of concepts of emotion and personality in an evolutionary context, and how cultural differences influence the meaning of words that are used to describe these constructs. The critical need to take the state–trait distinction into account in adapting measures of emotional states and personality traits is then analyzed, and culture-specific examples of the adaptation of anxiety measures from English into other languages are discussed. The effects of language and culture in adapting measures of the experience, expression, and control of anger in different Spanish-speaking cultures are also examined.

MEASURING PERSONALITY TRAITS AND EMOTIONAL STATES

According to Hall and Lindzey (1970), "no substantive definition of personality can be applied with any generality" (p. 9). Definitions of personality vary from comprehensive accounts of behavior in all of its complex details to specific descriptions of individual personality traits (Anastasi, 1988; Guthrie & Lonner, 1986). Anastasi emphasized the importance of defining personality in terms of meaningful trait concepts that describe categories into which behavior must be classified if it is to be accurately measured. Consistent with Anastasi's emphasis on fundamental traits, Cohen et al. (1992) defined personality as "an individual's unique constellation of psychological states and traits" (p.401). Anxiety, anger, and curiosity are examples of meaningful states and traits that are uniquely related to personality (Spielberger, Reheiser, & Sydeman, 1995).

The cross-cultural equivalence of anxiety and anger as emotional states and personality traits is facilitated by the fact that these fundamental emotions appear to be universal products of evolution. In his classic book, *Expressions of Emotions in Man and Animals,* Darwin (1872/1965) concluded, and others have confirmed (Ekman, 1973; Izard, 1977; Tomkins, 1962), that fear and rage are intense emotions that can be identified by facial expressions, not only in humans, but also in many animal species. Consistent with these research findings, Dimberg (1994, 1998) observed that distinctive facial reactions are manifested after very brief exposure to fear and anger-related relevant stimuli, such as snakes and angry faces, indicating that the perception of threatening stimuli can instantaneously evoke specific emotions.

Plutchik (1984) has proposed a "psychoevolutionary" theory that defines emotions as complex states that can be inferred from subjective reports, physiological changes, and various forms of behavior, which can best be understood in an evolutionary context. In endorsing a Darwinian ethological perspective, Plutchik (1984) pointed out the adaptive role of emotions in motivating what Cannon (1963) described as behavioral fight-or-flight reactions to environmental emergencies that increased the organism's chances for survival. However, as was noted by Plutchik, description of the feelings associated with these behavioral reactions will depend on a person's experience with a particular language.

The words used in different languages to describe emotional states and personality traits generally have a wide range of connotations (Rogler, 1999; Wierzbicka, 1994). Even within a particular language, the same word may have a variety of meanings in different subcultures (Anastasi, 1988). Therefore, differences between and within cultures, in the meaning of the words used to describe emotional states and personality traits, are especially problematic in the cross-cultural adaptation of measures of these constructs (Rogler, 1999). The following are examples of subcultural differences in the meaning of Spanish words (Cabrera, 1998):

- In Carribbean countries *guagua* means bus, but this same word refers to a baby or child in Chile, Colombia, and Peru.

- *Verraco* is a pig in Cuba, but has the connotation in Colombia of a person who is tough.
- In Cuba, *bicho* refers to an insect, but describes a penis in Puerto Rico.
- In Spain, the verb *coger* has the innocuous meaning to take or to seize, but means having sex in Mexico and Venezuela.

These examples clearly indicate that the successful adaptation of self-report measures of emotional states and personality traits requires the careful selection of key words (or idioms) that have essentially the same meaning in both the original (source) and second (target) languages. However, ensuring accurate representation of the psychological concepts that are assessed is often difficult because languages differ in the connotations of words used to describe the feelings and cognitions associated with different emotional states and personality traits. Moreover, as noted by Wierzbicka (1994) "the set of emotion terms available in any given language is unique and reflects a culture's unique perspective on people's ways of feeling" (p. 135).

Self-report measures of anxiety and other emotions cannot be simply translated and back-translated, but must be *adapted* for cross-cultural research. The process of 'back-translation' is traditionally used to facilitate adapting educational and psychological tests from one language into another language (Brislin, 1970, 1986). In the back-translation of test items, from the target language into the original language, the literal translation of words is emphasized. However, the back-translation of an original scale item is often less adequate than constructing a new item based on an equivalent cross-cultural conceptual definition of the emotional state or personality dimension that is being measured (Spielberger & Díaz-Guerrero, 1983). This is especially true in adapting idiomatic expressions.

LeCompte and Oner (1976) maintained that translating of key words and idiomatic expressions is especially difficult, and may require frequent consultations with language experts. From the standpoint of the literalness or exactness of the translation, they recommended that items be grouped into three categories: (a) items with key words whose translations closely fit the meaning of the word in the source language, (b) items with key words for which it is difficult to find corresponding items in the target language, and (c) items with a linguistic form that cannot be translated from the source language to the target language without changing the grammatical construction. A number of cycles of translation and back-translation may be required before an adequate adaptation can be developed for the latter type of item (Spielberger & Sharma, 1976).

In adaptating measures of emotional states and personality traits, the key word for an item in the source language may have several different translations that are equally acceptable in the target language. Different key words in two or more items in the source language may also be represented by a single word in the target language. Where the literal translation of a test item is not possible, it is important to retain the essential meaning of the original item by selecting a synonym of the key word that reflects its basic meaning in the target language.

When adapting idiomatic expressions, special care must be taken to translate the *feeling* connotation of the idiom, rather than translating the literal meaning of the individual words (Guthrie & Lonner, 1986). Identifying comparable idiomatic expressions in the language into which a scale is being translated is preferable to the literal translation of the original idiom. Consequently, in translating and adapting idioms, the cross-cultural equivalence of the theoretical concepts that are being measured is essential. Given the difficulties that are likely to be encountered in translating key words and idiomatic expressions, a substantially larger pool of items than will be eventually needed should be constructed in order to capture the full meaning of the construct that is being measured. Statistical procedures can then be used to determine which items have the best internal consistency as measures of the specified construct.

Measuring State and Trait Anxiety

Though contemporary interest in anxiety phenomena has historical roots in the philosophical and theological views of Pascal and Kierkegaard (May, 1977), it was Freud (1924, 1936) who first attempted to explicate the meaning of anxiety within the context of psychological theory. He regarded anxiety as "something felt," an unpleasant affective state or condition. According to Freud (1924), this state, as observed in patients with anxiety-neurosis, was characterized by all that is covered by the word *nervousness,* which includes apprehension or anxious expectation, and efferent discharge phenomena.

Anxiety is distinguishable from other unpleasant affective (emotional) states such as anger, grief, or sorrow, by its unique combination of phenomenological and physiological qualities. These give to anxiety a special "character of unpleasure" that, although difficult to describe, seems "to possess a particular note of its own" (Freud, 1936, p. 69). The subjective, phenomenological qualities of anxiety—the feelings of apprehensive expectation or dread—were emphasized by Freud, especially in his later formulations, whereas the physiological-behavioral (efferent) discharge phenomena, although considered an essential part of an anxiety state and an important contributor to its unpleasantness, was of relatively little theoretical interest to him. Freud was mainly concerned with identifying the sources of stimulation that evoked anxiety reactions, rather than analyzing the properties of such states. He hoped to discover, in the prior experience of his patients, "the historical element ... which binds the afferent and efferent elements of anxiety firmly together" (1936, p. 70).

Anxiety has been investigated in numerous studies in which participants who were presumed to differ in motivation or drive level (Spence, 1958) were selected on the basis of their extreme scores on questionnaires such as the Taylor (1953) Manifest Anxiety Scale (MAS), a self-report measure consisting of 50 MMPI items. The performance of high- and low-anxious subjects was then compared on a variety of tasks to test hypotheses derived from Hullian Learning Theory (Spence, 1958). The findings in these studies suggested that high MAS scores predicted performance on learning tasks, but only in situations involving some degree of stress (Spielberger, 1966a). Research on anxiety and learning has also shown that task difficulty, individual differences in intelligence, and factors that influence the relative strengths of correct and competing responses in a particular learning situation must be taken into account.

Cattell and Scheier (1958, 1961) pioneered the application of multivariate techniques to measuring the intensity of anxiety as an emotional state, and individual differences in anxiety proneness as a personality trait (Cattell, 1961, 1963). In investigations of the covariation, over time, of a number of different anxiety measures, relatively independent state and trait anxiety factors consistently emerged (Cattell, 1966). Physiological variables associated with activation (arousal) of the autonomic nervous system, which fluctuated over time and covaried over occasions of measurement (e.g., respiration rate and blood pressure), had strong loadings on the state anxiety factor, but only slight loadings on the trait anxiety factor.

Measures with strong loadings on Cattell's (1961) trait anxiety factor included self-reports of anxiety that were relatively stable over time. Scores on Cattell and Scheier's (1963) IPAT Anxiety Scale, a measure of trait anxiety, correlated .85 with the Taylor (1953) MAS. This finding provides strong evidence that the MAS measures anxiety proneness, or trait anxiety, rather than drive level, which is conceptually more closely related to the level of intensity of state anxiety at a particular time. The IPAT and the MAS appear to measure individual differences in anxiety as a personality trait, that is, the disposition to respond to situations perceived as stressful with more intense elevations in state anxiety, which contribute to higher drive level.

The concepts of state anxiety (S-Anxiety) and trait anxiety (T-Anxiety) refer to two related, yet logically quite different constructs (Spielberger & Krasner, 1988). S-Anxiety may be defined as a psychophysiological emotional state that consists of subjective feelings of tension, apprehension, nervousness and worry, and activation (arousal) of the autonomic nervous system (Spielberger, 1966b, 1972). Valid measures of S-Anxiety vary in intensity and fluctuate over time as a function of perceived threat. T-Anxiety has the characteristics of a class of constructs that Atkinson (1964) described as *motives*, and that Campbell (1963) called *acquired behavioral dispositions* (Spielberger & Díaz-Guerrero, 1983). The attributes of T-Anxiety include relatively stable differences between people in the tendency to perceive stressful situations as more or less dangerous or threatening, and in the disposition to respond to such situations with corresponding elevations in S-Anxiety. Measures of T-Anxiety assess the frequency that anxiety states have been experienced in the past, and the probability that S-Anxiety will be manifested in the future as a reaction to threatening stimuli (Spielberger, 1983; Spielberger & Krasner, 1988).

State–Trait Anxiety Theory posits that people who are high in T-Anxiety perceive social-evaluative situations as more threatening than do persons who are low in T-Anxiety (Spielberger, 1972, 1979). Consequently, persons high in T-Anxiety are more likely to experience intense elevations in S-Anxiety in such situations. The State–Trait Anxiety Inventory (STAI) was developed to provide reliable, relatively brief self-report scales for assessing state and trait anxiety in research and clinical practice (Spielberger et al., 1970). Freud's (1936) danger signal theory and Cattell's (1963, 1966) concepts of state and trait anxiety (Cattell & Scheier, 1958, 1961), as refined and elaborated by Spielberger (1966b, 1972, 1979), provided the conceptual framework that guided the test construction process.

Construction of the State–Trait Anxiety Inventory

The STAI S-Anxiety scale was constructed to measure variations in the intensity of anxiety as an emotional state. At low levels of S-Anxiety, a person feels calm and secure. Feelings of increased tension, apprehension, and nervousness are experienced as S-Anxiety increases, with extremes of fright and panic at the highest levels.

Thus, the concept of state anxiety implies an intensity dimension, and the concept of item-intensity specificity calls attention to the fact that items that measure the intensity of an emotional state will be more effective at some levels of intensity than at others (Spielberger et al., 1970).

Although the importance of item-intensity specificity was emphasized by Anastasi (1988), this concept has been largely ignored or, at best, only marginally recognized in the construction of measures of emotional states and personality traits. The importance of item-intensity specificity was implicitly recognized by Zuckerman (1960), who included items that described positive feelings to measure low levels of anxiety, in his Affect Adjective Check List (AACL). This concept explicitly guided the construction of the STAI (Form X) State Anxiety Scale, which included equal numbers of anxiety-present and anxiety-absent items to facilitate measuring of a wide range of intensity (Spielberger et al., 1970). The STAI anxiety-absent items, such as "I feel at ease," are more sensitive in assessing lower levels of S-Anxiety, whereas STAI anxiety-present items, with key words such as *tense* or *nervous,* are more effective in measuring high levels of intensity.

The initial goal in developing the STAI was to construct an inventory with a single set of items that could be used with appropriate instructions to assess both the intensity of state anxiety and individual differences in trait anxiety. In responding to the STAI S-Anxiety Scale, subjects were instructed to rate the intensity of their feelings of anxiety (e.g., "I feel nervous") "right now, at this moment" on the following 4-point scale: not at all; somewhat; moderately so; very much so. The instructions for the STAI T-Anxiety Scale required respondents to indicate how they "generally feel" by reporting how often they have experienced anxiety-related thoughts, feelings, and somatic symptoms on the following 4-point rating scale: almost never; sometimes; often; almost always (Spielberger, 1983).

In evaluating the stability and concurrent and construct validity of the preliminary STAI (Form A), the psycholinguistic connotations of the key words in several items interfered with their use as measures of both S-Anxiety and T-Anxiety. Altering the instructions could not overcome the strong state or trait implications of these key words (Spielberger et al., 1970). For example, "I feel upset" was found to be a highly sensitive measure of S-Anxiety, as reflected in significantly higher item scores under stressful conditions and lower scores under relaxed conditions. Moreover, when given with trait instructions, scores on this item were unstable over time, and correlations of these scores with other T-Anxiety items were relatively weak (Spielberger, 1985). In contrast, scores on the item, "I worry too much," correlated highly with other T-Anxiety items, but did not reliably increase under stressful experimental conditions, and failed to decrease under relaxed conditions, as was required for a valid measure of S-Anxiety (Spielberger et. al., 1970).

Given the difficulties encountered in measuring S-Anxiety and T-Anxiety with the same items, the test construction strategy for the STAI was modified, and separate sets of items were selected for measuring the intensity of S-Anxiety as an emotional state and individual differences in T-Anxiety as a personality trait. Twenty items with good concurrent validity as measures of T-Anxiety, as indicated by significant correlations with the MAS (Taylor, 1956), the IPAT Anxiety Scale (Cattell & Scheier, 1963) and the Welsh (1956) Anxiety Scale, were selected for the STAI (Form X) T-Anxiety Scale. The scores for these items were relatively stable over time (Spielberger et al., 1970).

The 20 items with the best construct validity as measures of S-Anxiety, as demonstrated by higher scores under stressful conditions and lower scores during relaxation, were selected for the STAI (Form X) S-Anxiety Scale (Spielberger et al., 1970). Only five items met the validity criteria for measuring both S-Anxiety and T-Anxiety, permitting them to be included in both scales. Thus, 30 of the 40 items comprising the STAI (Form X) S-Anxiety and T-Anxiety scales were sufficiently different in construct validity or stability to be regarded as unique measures of either state or trait anxiety.

On the basis of the insights gained from a decade of intensive research with the STAI (Form X), a major revision of this scale was undertaken (Spielberger, 1983). In the construction and standardization of the revised STAI (Form Y), more than 5,000 subjects were tested. The primary goal in revising the STAI was to develop "purer" measures of state and trait anxiety in order to provide a more valid basis for differentiating between anxiety and depression. Careful scrutiny of the content validity of the STAI (Form X) items with the best psychometric properties resulted in clearer conceptual definitions of the constructs of state and trait anxiety, which guided the construction of potential replacement items.

In constructing the STAI (Form Y), six items with content that seemed to be more closely related to depression than anxiety (e.g., "I feel blue," "I feel like crying") were replaced. Also replaced were ambiguous items with marginal psychometric properties for high school students, for example, "I feel anxious," which was interpreted by many of these students to mean "eager," as in "eager to please." Other replaced items contained idioms whose meaning had apparently shifted over the past decade, possibly as a consequence of expanded drug use by adolescents and young adults (e.g., "I feel high strung").

The selection of the final set of items for the revised STAI (Form Y) was based on factor analyses and item remainder correlations, resulting in the replacement of 30% of the original STAI (Form X) items. The item replacement procedures are described in detail in the revised STAI Test Manual (Spielberger, 1983). Factor analyses of the revised STAI (Form Y) items identified clear-cut state and trait anxiety factors (Spielberger, Vagg, Barker, Donham, & Westberry, 1980; Vagg, Spielberger, & O'Hearn, 1980), which were generally consistent with the results of previous factor analyses of Form X (Gaudry & Poole, 1975; Gaudry, Spielberger, & Vagg, 1975). However, the state and trait anxiety-absent and anxiety-present factors in the four-factor solutions for Form Y were more distinctive than the factors found in previous studies of Form X (Spielberger, 1983). The Form Y factors were also more differentiated, and had a better and more stable simple structure than the comparable factors in Form X. The psychometric properties of the revised STAI (Form Y) S-Anxiety and T-Anxiety scales were also improved (Spielberger, 1983).

Cross-Cultural Adaptations of the STAI

The STAI has been adapted in more than 50 languages and dialects, and used extensively in cross-cultural research (Spielberger, Sydeman, Owen, & Marsh, 1999). The internal consistency, stability, and concurrent and construct validity of the foreign-language adaptations of the STAI have also been demonstrated (Spielberger & Díaz-Guerrero, 1982), providing impressive evidence of the universality of anxiety as a meaningful psychological construct. The Chinese, Dutch, French, German, Hindi, Italian, Japanese, Portuguese, Russian and Spanish forms of the STAI have been carefully validated; most of these forms are also published commercially. The equivalence of the Russian and English S-Anxiety and T-Anxiety scales has been verified by the high correlations that were found for Russian-English bilingual subjects who responded to both forms of this measure (Hanin, 1986).

In generating translations and adaptations of the STAI S-Anxiety and T-Anxiety scales, the unique psycholinguistic properties of different languages have been utilized. In Spanish, for example, there are two forms of the verb "to be," *ser* and *estar*. *Ser* denotes a relatively stable or permanent characteristic of a person or situation, whereas *estar* has the connotation of a transitory state or temporary condition (Spielberger, Gonzalez-Reigosa, Martinez-Urrutia, L. Natalicio, & D. Natalicio, 1971). Similarly, the Hindi verbs, *raha hun* and the *rahta hun*, correspond, respectively, to the concepts of a transitory state and a relatively stable characteristic or personality trait (Spielberger, Sharma, & Singh, 1973).

The fact that the state–trait distinction is intrinsic to the Spanish and Hindi languages, as indicated by the psycholinguistic structure of these very different language systems, strongly supports the fundamental need to distinguish between emotional states and personality traits. Furthermore, as previously noted, the state–trait distinction is also clearly reflected in particular words that have the connotation of anxiety as a transitory state, such as feeling "upset," and by responses to items such as "I have disturbing thoughts," which imply a more persistent and enduring trait (Spielberger, 1983).

In addition to strong evidence of the state and trait connotations inherent in the linguistic structure of Spanish, Hindi, and other languages, and in the key words of many individual scale items, it is important to assess the full range of intensity that defines an emotional state or personality trait (Anastasi, 1988; Spielberger et. al., 1970; Spielberger & Sharma, 1976). Similar to the variations in physiological magnitude that are evaluated by measures such as heart rate and blood pressure, self-report scales for assessing emotional states and personality traits must be sensitive to variations in intensity. Therefore, in adapting measures of emotion and personality for cross-cultural assessment, identifying words in different languages that denote different levels of item-intensity specificity is an essential requirement.

The inclusion of approximately equal numbers of items in the STAI (Form Y) that describe the absence of anxiety not only enhances the sensitivity of this measure for assessing lower levels of this construct, but also makes possible the measurement of positive feelings such as happiness and self-confidence, which appear to be distinctive emotional states and personality traits. This methodological point was clearly recognized in constructing the STAI–JYZ, the Japanese adaptation of the STAI (Form Y). The STAI–JYZ contains equal numbers of state and trait anxiety-present and anxiety-absent items, and provides separate measures of the positive affective states and personality traits that are associated with anxiety.

It should also be noted that languages differ enormously in the size of their affective lexicons, and may also differ substantially in the number of words that designate either the presence or absence of an emotional state or its level of intensity (Wierzbicka, 1994). Moreover, as compared to English, languages such as Spanish contain a much larger pool of terms for describing various nuances of emotion and associated levels of item-intensity specificity (Spielberger et al.,1970). Furthermore, the intensity of an emotion can often be most clearly expressed by idioms. The process of adapting idiomatic phrases for use in Spanish adaptations of anger measures is discussed in the following section.

CROSS-CULTURAL ASSESSMENT OF THE EXPERIENCE, EXPRESSION, AND CONTROL OF ANGER

Over the last quarter century, interest in measuring the experience, expression, and control of anger has been stimulated by evidence that anger, hostility, and aggression were associated with hypertension and cardiovascular disease (Dembroski, MacDougall, Williams, & Haney, 1984; Williams, Barefoot, & Shekelle, 1985). Whereas definitions of anger-related constructs are often inconsistent and ambiguous, the experience and expression of anger are typically encompassed in definitions of hostility and aggression. Clearly, anger is the most fundamental of these overlapping constructs.

On the basis of a careful review of the research literature on anger, hostility and aggression, the following definitions of these constructs were proposed by Spielberger, Jacobs, Russell, and Crane, (1983):

> Anger usually refers to an emotional state that consists of feelings that vary in intensity, from mild irritation or annoyance to intense fury and rage. Although hostility involves angry feelings, this concept has the connotation of a complex set of attitudes that motivate aggressive behaviors directed toward destroying objects or injuring other people. The concept of aggression generally implies destructive or punitive behavior directed towards other persons or objects. (p. 160)

The physiological and behavioral manifestations of anger, hostility, and aggression have been investigated in numerous studies, but until recently, angry feelings have been largely ignored in psychological research. Consequently, psychometric measures of anger, hostility, and aggression generally do not distinguish between feeling angry and the expression of anger and hostility in aggressive behavior. Most measures of anger-related constructs also fail to take the state–trait distinction into account, and confound the experience and expression of anger with situational determinants of angry behavior. A coherent theoretical framework that recognizes the difference between anger, hostility, and aggression as psychological constructs, and that distinguishes between anger as an emotional state and individual differences in the experience, expression, and control of anger as personality traits, is essential for guiding the construction and cross-cultural adaptation of anger measures.

Measuring State and Trait Anger

The State–Trait Anger Expression Inventory (STAXI) was developed by Spielberger (1988, 1999) and his colleagues to measure the experience, expression, and control of anger (Spielberger et al., 1983; Spielberger et al., 1985; Spielberger, Krasner, & Solomon, 1988; Spielberger et al., 1995). There were four distinct stages in the construction and development of the six STAXI scales and five subscales. In the initial stage, the State–Trait Anger Scale (STAS) was constructed to assess the intensity of anger as an emotional state and individual differences in anger proneness as a personality trait (Spielberger et al., 1983). S-Anger was defined as "an emotional state marked by subjective feelings that vary in intensity from mild annoyance or irritation to intense fury or rage, which is generally accompanied by muscular tension and arousal of the autonomic nervous system" (Spielberger, 1988, p. 1). The STAS S-Anger Scale assesses the level of intensity of S-Anger at a particular time.

Trait anger refers to individual differences in the disposition to experience angry feelings (Spielberger et al., 1983). The STAS T-Anger Scale evaluates how frequently S-Anger is experienced. Research on the factor structure of the STAS T-Anger Scale has consistently identified two substantially correlated, but relatively independent factors: T-Angry Temperament and T-Angry Reaction (Forgays, Forgays, & Spielberger, 1997; Spielberger, 1988). The STAS T-Anger/Temp subscale assesses individual differences in the disposition to experience angry feelings without provocation. In contrast, the T-Anger/React subscale measures individual differences in the tendency to experience and express anger in situations that involve frustration, negative evaluations, or being treated unfairly (Spielberger, 1988).

Measuring the Expression and Control of Anger

In the second stage of the development of the STAXI, recognition of the importance of distinguishing between the experience and expression of anger stimulated the development of the Anger Expression (AX) Scale (Spielberger et al., 1985). The AX Scale assesses how often anger is suppressed (anger-in) or expressed in aggressive behavior (anger-out). The instructions for responding to the AX Scale differ markedly from the traditional trait instructions for the STAS T-Anger Scale. Rather than directing subjects to respond according to how they generally feel, they are instructed to report how often they react or behave in a particular manner when they feel "angry or furious" (e.g., "I say nasty things"; "I boil inside, but don't show it") by rating themselves on the same 4-point frequency scale that is used with the T-Anger Scale.

The AX Scale was originally designed to assess a unidimensional bipolar continuum of individual differences in how often anger was held in (suppressed), or expressed toward other persons or objects in the environment. However, factor analyses of the items constructed to measure this dimension consistently identified two orthogonal factors, which indicated that the AX items were tapping independent anger-in and anger-out dimensions (Spielberger et al., 1985). The correlations between the AX/In and AX/Out scales that were constructed to measure these underlying dimensions was essentially zero (Johnson, 1984; Pollans, 1983), providing further evidence that the STAXI AX/In and AX/Out scales assess two conceptually distinct and empirically independent constructs.

In the third stage of the development of the STAXI, the identification of anger control as an independent factor stimulated the construction of a scale to assess the control of angry feelings (Spielberger et al., 1988). The content of 3 of the 20 original AX Scale items (e.g., control my temper, keep my cool, calm down faster), which were included to assess intermediate levels of anger expression as an unidimensional bipolar scale, guided the generation of additional anger control items (Spielberger et al., 1985). Factor analyses of anger control items, along with the AX Scale anger-in and anger-out items, identified a strong anger control factor, that was relatively independent of the anger-in and anger-out factors. The anger control items with the strongest loading on the anger control factor, and essentially zero loadings on the anger-in and anger-out factors, were selected for the STAXI Anger Control (AX-Con) Scale to assess individual differences in how often a person endeavors to control the outward expression of angry feelings.

The fourth stage in the construction of the STAXI was stimulated by the research of psycholinguists, who identified English metaphors for anger, which called attention to the need to distinguish between two different mechanisms for controlling anger expression (Lakoff, 1987). The prototype of the anger metaphor was described as a hot liquid in a container, where blood was the hot liquid and the body was the container. The intensity of anger as an emotional state is considered analogous to the variations in the temperature of the hot liquid. The metaphor, *boiling inside,* has the connotation an intense level of suppressed anger; *blowing off steam* connotes the outward expression of angry feelings; *keeping the lid on* implies controlling intense anger by preventing the outward expression of aggressive behavior. Thus, Lakoff's anger metaphors suggested two quite different mechanisms for controlling anger: keeping angry feelings bottled up to prevent their expression, and reducing the intensity of suppressed anger by cooling down.

In the original STAXI scale, the content of all but one of the eight AX/Con items was related to controlling anger-out (e.g., "I Control my temper"). Therefore, a number of new items were constructed to assess the control of anger-in by reducing the intensity of suppressed anger (Spielberger et al. 1995; Sydeman, 1995). The content of these items described efforts to calm down, cool off, or relax when a person feels angry or furious. Factor analyses of the responses of large samples of male and female adults to the anger control items (Spielberger et al., 1995) identified two anger control factors for both genders: Anger/Control-In and Anger/Control-Out.

Construction of the Spanish Multicultural State–Trait Anger Expression Inventory

Spanish is spoken not only in Spain, but also in more than 20 countries in Central and South America and the Caribbean, and by more than 25 million native speakers of Spanish who reside in the United States. Although Spanish is the primary language in most of Latin America and for many Hispanic residents in the United States, the indigenous cultures of these persons often have profound effects on the Spanish they speak, and on the development of personality characteristics that influence their behavior. Therefore, it is important to recognize the exceptionally complex social and cultural diversity of Hispanic populations, and that language differences between these groups may outweigh the similarities. Consequently, in adapting English measures of emotion and personality for use in Spanish-speaking cultures, care must be taken to ensure that the key words and idiomatic expressions used for assessing anger-related concepts have essentially the same meaning in different Hispanic cultural groups.

The STAXI–2 was adapted to measure the experience, expression and control of anger in culturally diverse populations in Latin America, and in Spanish-speaking subcultures in the United States (Moscoso & Spielberger, 1999a). Toward achieving this goal, the Spanish Multicultural State–Trait Anger Expression Inventory (STAXI–SMC) was designed to measure essentially the same dimensions of anger that are assessed with the revised STAXI–2 (Spielberger, 1999). Scales and subscales were constructed to assess the following dimensions with the STAXI–SMC: (a) State Anger, with subscales for assessing Feeling Angry and Feel Like Expressing Anger; (b) Trait Anger, with subscales for measuring Angry Temperament and Angry Reaction; and (c) trait scales for measuring four dimensions of anger expression and control: anger-in, anger-out, and the control of anger-in and anger-out (Moscoso & Spielberger, 1999b).

Preliminary translations of the STAXI–2 items were constructed for the STAXI–SMC. These items were reviewed by 26 prominent Latin American psychologists, who were instructed to recommend modifications and corrections in conformance with linguistic descriptors of the experience, expression, and control of anger in their countries (Moscoso & Spielberger, 1999b). Based on the consensus of these experts, the STAXI–SMC items were revised, and the 56-item revised scale was administered to 257 participants (179 women, 78 men) at the 25th InterAmerican Congress of Psychology in San Juan Puerto Rico. The sample included respondents from Caribbean countries (48%), South America (32%), Central America (16%), and Spain (4%), who ranged in age from 20 to 78 years (median age = 36 years). All participants had completed training in psychology, or were currently enrolled in undergraduate or graduate psychology programs.

Factor analyses of responses to the 56 preliminary STAXI–SMC items confirmed the hypothesized structural properties of the inventory. The eight factors that were identified corresponded quite well with similar factors in the STAXI–2. These included two S-Anger factors, two T-Anger factors, and four anger expression and control factors (Moscoso & Spielberger, 1999a). In separate factor analyses of the S-Anger items, two distinctive factors were identified for both men and women: "Feeling Angry" and "Feel Like Expressing Anger." However, gender differences in the strength of the item loadings on these factors raised interesting questions in regard to how Latin American men and women may differ in the experience of anger. For women, the "Feeling Angry" factor accounted for 73% of the total variance, whereas this factor accounted for only 19% of the variance for males. In contrast, the "Feel Like Expressing Anger" factor accounted for 70% of the total variance of the men, but only 13% for women.

The factor analyses of the T-Anger STAXI–SMC items also identified separate Angry Temperment and Angry Reaction factors, providing strong evidence that the factor structure for this scale was similar to that of the STAXI–2. Factor analyses of the STAXI–SMC anger expression and control items identified the same four factors as in the STAXI–2. The items designed to assess anger-in and anger-out, and the control of anger-in and anger-out, had high loadings on the corresponding anger expression and control factors, which were similar for both sexes. The alpha coefficients for the STAXI–SMC State and Trait Anger scales and subscales, and the anger expression and anger control scales, were reasonably high, indicating that the internal consistency of these scales was satisfactory.

In summary, the results of the factor analyses of responses of the Latin American subjects to the STAXI–SMC items of the Latin American subjects identified eight factors that were quite similar to those found for the STAXI–2. Separate factor analyses of the S-Anger and T-Anger items confirmed the identification of two related but distinctive S-Anger factors: "Feeling Angry" and "Feel Like Expressing Anger," and two highly correlated but clearly different T-Anger factors, Angry Temperment and Angry Reaction. Factor analyses of the anger expression and control items also identified the same four factors that are found in the STAXI–2 (Spielberger et al., 1999). Thus, the multidimensional factor structure of the STAXI–SMC for the Latin American respondents was remarkably similar to the factor structure of the English STAXI–2.

DISCUSSION AND CONCLUSIONS

In adapting measures of emotional states and personality traits, the nonequivalence of psychological constructs in different cultures is a major source of error (see, e.g., Cheung, 2004). Cross-cultural equivalence is especially problematic in adapting personality measures because agreement is lacking in regard to the criteria for defining the fundamental dimensions of personality. Therefore, the cross-cultural equivalence of the concepts that define the dimensions that are being measured is essential. Special attention must be given to distinguishing between emotional states that vary in intensity, and individual differences in personality traits that are relatively stable over time. In constructing items to measure emotional states and personality traits, it is also essential to take item-intensity specificity into account so that the full range of intensity of an emotional state can be assessed.

The cross-cultural equivalence of anxiety and anger as psychological constructs is facilitated by the fact that these emotions appear to be universal products of evolution. Darwin observed that fear (anxiety) and rage (anger) are universal characteristics of both humans and animals. These emotions mediate and motivate fight-or-flight reactions that were recognized by Cannon as contributing to successful adaptation and survival. Both anxiety and anger vary in intensity as a function of how individuals react to stressful circumstances, and people differ in the intensity and frequency that they experience these fundamental emotions.

The words used in different languages to describe emotional states and personality traits are markedly influenced by cultural differences, which reflect the unique perspective of a particular culture in regard to the feelings associated with a particular emotion. In the cross-cultural adaptation of psychological tests, careful selection of words and/or idioms that have essentially the same meaning in both the source and target languages is required to ensure accurate representation of the psychological constructs that are being assessed. In adapting measures of emotional states and personality traits, it is also important to consider cultural differences in the meaning of words for persons who speak the same language. For example, *bicho* means an insect in Cuba, but refers to a penis in Puerto Rico.

Traditionally, the process of adapting educational and psychological tests has involved the back-translation of items from the target language to the source language. Although emphasizing the literal translation of each word, this approach gives relatively little consideration to the constructs that are being measured. Two major limitations of back-translation are the difficulty of finding words in the target language with meaning equivalent to key words in the source language, and translating idiomatic expressions. For idiomatic expressions, it is essential to adapt the feeling connotation of the idiom in the source language rather than translating the literal meaning of each word. It is also highly desirable to identify idioms with comparable meaning in the source and target languages.

The construction and selection of items for the STAI was guided by Freud's (1936) conception of anxiety as an unpleasant emotional state, and the constructs of state and trait anxiety identified by Cattell (1961; Cattell & Scheier, 1961). In constructing the STAI, the original intention was to use the same items with different instructions to measure state and trait anxiety. The items selected for the preliminary STAI had excellent concurrent and content validity as measures anxiety. However, several items that were relatively stable measures of individual differences in T-Anxiety lacked construct validity in assessing S-Anxiety because scores on these items were not higher under stressful conditions, nor lower after relaxation. Similarly, a few items with excellent construct validity as measures of S-Anxiety were unstable over time when given with trait instructions.

Given the difficulty of using the same items to assess S-Anxiety and T-Anxiety, the strategy for constructing the STAI was modified. The 20 items with the best construct validity as measures of S-Anxiety, as demonstrated by higher scores in stressful conditions and lower scores during relaxation, were selected for the STAI S-Anxiety Scale. The 20 items selected for the STAI T-Anxiety Scale were relatively stable over time. Each T-Anxiety item also had excellent concurrent validity, as was indicated by significant correlations with other widely used trait anxiety measures such as the MAS and IPAT Anxiety Scale.

Based on a decade of intensive research with the STAI, a major revision in this inventory was undertaken to distinguish between anxiety and depression. Items with content considered to be more closely related to depression than anxiety were replaced, along with items found to have marginal psychometric properties for less educated persons. The balance between items that assessed the presence or the absence of anxiety was also improved. Factor analyses of responses to the revised STAI (Form Y) items identified the following four factors: S-Anxiety Present; S-Anxiety Absent; T-Anxiety Present; T-Anxiety Absent.

The STAI has been successfully adapted in more than 50 languages and dialects. Cross-cultural adaptation of this measure was facilitated by the fact that the state–trait distinction appears to be intrinsic in the psycholinguistic structure of languages such as Spanish and Hindi, and is also clearly reflected in the key words of a number of items that have the connotation of anxiety as a transitory state, or that describe anxiety as a persistent and enduring personality trait. The inclusion of approximately equal numbers of anxiety-present and anxiety-absent items in the revised STAI (Form Y) contributed to the assessment of a wide range of intensity in the measurement of S-Anxiety and T-Anxiety. The application of procedures described in this chapter in the construction and development of a Japanese adaption of the STAI (Form Y) is described by Fukuhara.

In the cross-cultural adaptation of anger measures, it is essential to have equivalent conceptual definitions in the source and target languages that distinguish between the experience of anger as an emotional state, and individual differences in the expression and control of anger as personality traits. The construction and development of the Spanish Multicultural State–Trait Anger Expression Inventory guided by definitions of state and trait anger, and anger expression and anger control, as these constructs were conceptualized in the STAXI–2, the revised original English version of this measure. Factor analyses of the items constructed for the STAXI–SMC identified eight factors that were quite similar to the factor structure of the STAXI–2. Thus, statistical analyses of the responses to the STAXI–SMC items verified that the components of anger assessed with this inventory are similar to the anger components assessed with the STAXI–2. Research on the STAXI–2 and the STAXI–SMC clearly indicates that anger as a psychological construct can be meaningfully defined as an emotional state that varies in intensity, and as a complex personality trait with major components that can be measured empirically.

REFERENCES

Anastasi, A. (1988). *Psychological testing* (6th ed.). New York: Macmillan.

Atkinson, J. (1964). *An introduction to motivation.* Princeton, NJ: Van Nostrand-Reinhold.

Brislin, R. W. (1970). Back-translation for cross-cultural research. *Journal of Cross-Cultural Psychology, 1*(3), 185–216.

Brislin, R. W. (1986). The wording and translation of research instruments. In W. J. Lonner & J. W. Berry (Eds.), *Field methods in cross-cultural psychology* (pp. 137–164). Newbury Park, CA: Sage.

Butcher, J. N., Graham, J. R., Williams, C. L., & Ben-Porath, Y. S. (1989). *Development and use of the MMPI–2 Content Scales.* Minneapolis: University of Minnesota Press.

Cabrera, C. (1998, August). Tricky translations: When speaking Spanish, what's acceptable in some countries could get you in trouble in others. *The Tampa Tribune,* Baylife Section, pp. 1–2.

Campbell, D. T. (1963). Social attitudes and other acquired behavioral dispositions. In S. Koch (Ed.), *Psychology: A study of a science* (Vol. 6, pp. 94–172). New York: McGraw-Hill.

Cannon, W. (1963). *Bodily changes in pain, hunger, fear and rage.* New York, NY: Harper & Row.

Cattell, R. B. (1961). Theory of situational, instrument, second order, and refraction factors in personality structure research. *Psychological Bulletin, 58,* 160–174.

Cattell, R. B. (1963). Personality role, mood, and situation perception: An unifying theory of modulators. *Psychological Review, 70,* 1–18.

Cattell, R. B. (1966). Patterns of change: Measurements in relation to state-dimension, trait change, ability, and process concepts. In *Handbook of multivariate experimental psychology* (pp. 355–402). Chicago: Rand McNally.

Cattell, R. B., & Scheier, I. H. (1958). The nature of anxiety: A review of thirteen multivariate analyses comprising 814 variables. *Psychological Reports, 4,* 351.

Cattell, R. B., & Scheier, I. H. (1960). Stimuli related to stress, neuroticism, excitation, and anxiety response patterns. *Journal of Abnormal and Social Psychology, 60,* 195–204.

Cattell, R. B., & Scheier, I. H. (1961). *The meaning and measurement of neuroticism and anxiety.* New York: Ronald Press.

Cattell, R. B. & Scheier, I. H. (1963). *Handbook for the IPAT anxiety scale* (2nd ed.). Champaign, IL: Institute for Personality and Ability Testing.

Cheung, F. M. (2004). Use of western and indigenously-developed personality tests in Asia. *Applied Psychology: An International Review, 53*(2), 173–191.

Cohen, R. J., Swerdlik, M. E., & Smith, D. K. (1992). *Psychological testing and assessment: An introduction to tests and measurements* (2nd ed.). Columbus, OH: Mayfield.

Costa, P. T., & McCrae, R. R. (1992). Normal personality assessment in clinical practice: The NEO Personality Inventory. *Psychological Assessment, 4,* 5–13, 20–22.

Cronbach, L. J. (1990). *Essentials of psychological testing* (5th ed.). New York: Harper & Row.

Darwin, C. (1965). *Expression of emotions in man and animals.* Chicago: University of Chicago Press. (Original work published 1872)

Dembroski, T. M., MacDougall, J. M., Williams, R. B., & Haney, T. L. (1984). Components of type A, hostility, and anger-in: Relationship to angiographic findings. *Psychosomatic Medicine, 47,* 219–233.

Digman, J. M. (1990). Personality structure: Emergence of the five-factor model. *Annual Review of Psychology, 41,* 417–440.

Dimberg, U. (1994). Facial reactions: "Immediate" emotional reactions. *Psychophysiology, 31,* S40.

Dimberg, U. (1998). Fear of snakes and facial reactions: A case of rapid emotional responding. *Scandinavian Journal of Psychology, 39,* 75–80.

Ekman, P. (1973). Cross-cultural studies of facial expressions. In P. Ekman (Ed.), *Darwin and facial expression* (pp. 169–222). New York: Academic Press.

Eysenck, H. J., & Eysenck, S. B. G. (1975). *Manual of the Eysenck Personality Questionnaire.* San Diego: EdITS Publishers.

Forgays, D. G., Forgays, D. K., & Spielberger, C. D. (1997). Factor structure of the State-Trait Anger Expression Inventory for young adults. *Journal of Personality Assessment, 69,* 497–507.

Freud, S. (1924). *Collected papers* (Vol. 1). London: Hogarth.

Freud, S. (1936). *The problem of anxiety.* New York: Norton.

Gaudry, E., & Poole, C. (1975). A further validation of the state–trait distinction in anxiety research. *Australian Journal of Psychology, 27,* 119.

Gaudry, E., Spielberger, C. D., & Vagg, P. R. (1975). Validation of the state-trait distinction in anxiety research. *Multivariate Behavior Research, 10,* 331–341.

Goldberg, L. R. (1981). Language and individual differences: The search for universals in personality lexicons. In L. Wheeler (Ed.), *Review of personality and social psychology* (Vol. 2, pp. 141–165). Beverly Hills, CA: Sage.

Guthrie, G. M., & Lonner, W. J. (1986). Assessment of personality and psychopathology. In W. J. Lonner & J. W. Berry (Eds.), *Field methods in cross-cultural research* (Vol. 8, pp. 231–264). Beverly Hills, CA: Sage.

Hall, C. S., & Lindzey, G. (1970). *Theories of personality.* New York: Wiley.

Hambleton, R. K. (1994). Guidelines for adapting educational and psychological test: A progress report. *European Journal of Psychological Assessment, 10,* 229–244.

Hambleton, R. K., & Patsula, L. (1999). Increasing the validity of adapted tests: Myths to be avoided and guidelines for improving test adaptation practices. *Journal of Applied Testing Technology, 1,* 1–16.

Hanin, Y. L. (1986). State–trait anxiety research on sports in the USSR. In C. D. Spielberger & R. Díaz-Guerrero (Eds.), *Cross-cultural anxiety* (Vol. 3, pp. 45–64). Washington, DC: Hemisphere.

Izard, C. E. (1977). *Human emotion.* New York: Plenum.

John, O. P. (1990). The "big five" factor taxonomy: Dimensions of personality in the natural language and in questionnaires. In L. Pervin (Ed.), *Handbook of personality theory and research* (pp. 66–100). New York: Guilford.

Johnson, E. H. (1984). *Anger and anxiety as determinants of elevated blood pressure in adolescents.* Unpublished doctoral dissertation, University of South Florida, Tampa.

Lakoff, G. (1987). *Women, fire, and dangerous things: What categories reveal about the mind.* Chicago: University of Chicago Press.

LeCompte, W. A., & Oner, N. (1976). Development of the Turkish edition of the State–Trait Anxiety Inventory. In C. D. Spielberger & R. Díaz-Guerrero (Eds.), *Cross-cultural anxiety* (pp. 51–67). Washington, DC: Hemisphere.

Lonner, W. J. (1990). An overview of cross-cultural testing and assessment. In R. W. Brislin (Ed.), *Applied cross-cultural psychology* (Vol. 14, pp. 56–76). Beverly Hills, CA: Sage.

Marsella A. J., & Leong, F. T. (1995). Cross-cultural issues in personality and career assessment. *Journal of Career Assessment, 3*(2), 202–218.

May, R. (1977). *The meaning of anxiety* (Rev. ed.). New York: Norton.

Moscoso, M. S., & Spielberger, C. D. (1999a). Evaluación de la experiencia, expresión y control de la cólera en Latinoamerica [Assessing the experience, expression, and control of anger in Latin America]. *Revista Psicología Contemporánea, 6*(1), 4–13.

Moscoso, M. S., & Spielberger, C. D. (1999b). Measuring the experience, expression, and control of anger in Latin America: The Spanish multi-cultural State–Trait Anger Expression Inventory. *Interamerican Journal of Psychology, 33*(2), 29–48.

Plutchik, R. (1984). Emotions: A general psychoevolutionary theory. In K. R. Scherer & P. Eckman (Eds.), *Approaches to emotions* (pp. 197–219). Hillsdale, NJ: Lawrence Erlbaum Associates.

Pollans, C. H. (1983). *The psychometric properties and factor structures of the Anger Expression (AX) Scale.* Unpublished master's thesis, University of South Florida, Tampa.

Rogler, L. H. (1999). Methodological sources of cultural insensitivity in mental health research. *American Psychologist, 54*(6), 424–433.

Spence, K. W. (1958). A theory of emotionally based drive (D) and its relation to performance in simple learning situations. *American Psychologist, 13,* 131–141.

Spielberger, C. D. (1966a). The effects of anxiety on complex learning and academic achievement. In C. D. Spielberger (Ed.), *Anxiety and behavior* (pp. 361–398). New York: Academic Press.

Spielberger, C. D. (1966b). Theory and research on anxiety. In C. D. Spielberger (Ed.), *Anxiety and behavior* (pp. 3–20). New York: Academic Press.

Spielberger, C. D. (1972a). Anxiety as an emotional state. In C. D. Spielberger (Ed.), *Anxiety: Current trends in theory and research* (Vol. 2, pp. 23–49). New York: Academic Press.

Spielberger, C. D. (1979). *Understanding stress and anxiety.* London: Harper & Row.

Spielberger, C. D. (1983). *Manual for the State–Trait Anxiety Inventory* (Rev. ed.). Palo Alto, CA: Consulting Psychologists Press.

Spielberger, C. D. (1985). Assessment of trait and state anxiety: Conceptual and methodological issues. *Southern Psychologist, 2,* 6–16.

Spielberger, C. D. (1988). *State–Trait Anger Expression Inventory Manual.* Odessa, FL: Psychological Assessment Resources.

Spielberger, C. D. (1999). *State–Trait Anger Expression Inventory-2.* Odessa, FL: Psychological Assessment Resources.

Spielberger, C. D., & Díaz-Guerrero, R. (1983). Cross-cultural anxiety: An overview. In C. D. Spielberger & R. Díaz-Guerrero (Eds.), *Cross-cultural anxiety* (Vol. 2, pp. 3–11). New York: Hemisphere/McGraw-Hill International.

Spielberger, C. D., Gonzalez-Reigosa, F., Martinez-Urrutia, A., Natalicio, L., & Natalicio, D. (1971). Development of the Spanish edition of the State–Trait Anxiety Inventory. *Interamerican Journal of Psychology, 5,* 3–4.

Spielberger, C. D., Gorsuch, R. L., & Lushene, R. E. (1970). *STAI Manual for the State–Trait Anxiety Inventory.* Palo Alto, CA: Consulting Psychologists Press.

Spielberger, C. D., Jacobs, G. A., Russell, S. F., & Crane, R. S. (1983). Assessment of anger: The State-Trait Anger Scale. In J. N. Butcher & C. D. Spielberger (Eds.), *Advances in personality assessment* (Vol. 2, pp. 159–187). Hillsdale, NJ: Lawrence Erlbaum Associates.

Spielberger, C. D., Johnson, E. H., Russell, S. F., Crane, R. J., Jacobs, G. A., & Worden, T. J. (1985). The experience and expression of anger: construction and validation of an anger expression scale. In M. A. Chesney & R. H. Rosenman (Eds.), *Anger and hostility in cardiovascular and behavioral disorders* (pp. 5–30). New York: McGraw-Hill/Hemisphere.

Spielberger, C. D., & Krasner, S. S. (1988). The assessment of trait and state anxiety. In G. Burrows, R. Noyes, & M. Roth (Eds.), *Handbook of anxiety* (Vol. 2, pp. 31–51). Amsterdam: Elsevier Science.

Spielberger, C. D., Krasner, S. S., & Solomon, E. P. (1988). The experience, expression and control of anger. In M. P. Janisse (Ed.), *Health psychology: Individual differences and stress* (pp. 89–108). New York: Springer Verlag.

Spielberger, C. D., Reheiser, E. C., & Sydeman, S. J. (1995). Measuring the experience, expression, and control of anger. In H. Kassinove (Ed.), *Anger disorders: Definitions, diagnosis, and treatment* (pp. 49–67). Washington, DC: Taylor & Francis.

Spielberger, C. D., & Sharma, S. (1976). Cross-cultural measurement of anxiety. In C. D. Spielberger & R. Díaz-Guerrero (Eds.), *Cross-cultural research on anxiety* (pp. 13–25). Washington, DC: Hemisphere/Wiley.

Spielberger, C. D., & Sharma, S., & Singh, M. (1973). Development of the Hindi edition of the State–Trait Anxiety Inventory. *Indian Journal of Psychology, 48,* 11–20.

Spielberger, C. D., Sydeman, S. J., Owen, A. E., & Marsh, B. J. (1999). Measuring anxiety and anger with the State–Trait Inventory (STAI) and the State–Trait Anger Expression Inventory (STAXI). In M. E. Maruish (Ed.), *The use of psychological testing for treatment planning and outcomes assessment* (pp. 993–1021). Mahwah: Lawrence Erlbaum Associates.

Spielberger, C. D., Vagg, P. R., Barker, L. R., Donham, G. W., & Westberry, L. G. (1980). The factor structure of the State–Trait Anxiety Inventory. In I. G. Sarason & C. D. Spielberger (Eds.), *Stress and anxiety* (Vol. 7, pp. 95–109). Washington, DC: Hemisphere.

Sydeman, S. J. (1995). *The control of suppressed anger.* Unpublished master's thesis, University of South Florida, Tampa.

Taylor, J. A. (1953). A personality scale of manifest anxiety. *Journal of Abnormal and Social Psychology, 48,* 285.

Taylor, J. A. (1956). Drive theory and manifest anxiety. *Psychological Bulletin, 53,* 303–320.

Tomkins, S. S. (1962). *Affect, imagery, and consciousness. The positive affects.* New York: Springer-Verlag.

Vagg, P. R., Spielberger, C. D., & O'Hearn, T. P., Jr. (1980). Is the State–Trait Anxiety Inventory multidimensional? *Personality and Individual Differences, 1,* 207–214.

Van de Vijver, F., & Hambleton, R. K. (1996). Translating tests: Some practical guidelines. *European Psychologist, 1,* 89–99.

Welsh, G. S. (1956). Factor dimensions A and R. In G. S. Welsh & W. G. Dahlstrom (Eds.), *Basic readings on the MMPI in psychology and medicine* (pp. 264–281). Minneapolis: University of Minnesota Press.

Wierzbicka, A. (1994). Emotion, language, and cultural scripts. In S. E. Kitayama & H. R. M. Markus (Eds.), *Emotion and culture: Empirical studies of mutual influence* (pp. 133–195). Washington, DC: American Psychological Association.

Williams, R. B., Barefoot, J. C., & Shekelle, R. B. (1985). The health consequences of hostility. In M. A. Chesney & R. A. Rosenman (Eds.), *Anger and hostility in cardiovascular and behavioral disorders* (pp. 173–185). New York: Hemisphere/McGraw-Hill.

Zuckerman, M. (1960). The development of Affective Adjective Check List for the measurement of anxiety. *Journal of Consulting Psychology, 24,* 457–462.

Author Index

Subject Index